+ Michael

Thomas F Staley

NANCY HANKS

Pauline Chavez Bent

José A. Esquibel

Paul Kraemer

Margaret Espinosa McDonald

Betty W. Alvarez

[signature]

John [signature]

Josephine Gutierrez

Dr. Juan Romero

David H. Snow

Seeds of Struggle/Harvest of Faith

The Papers of the Archdiocese of Santa Fe Catholic Cuatro Centennial Conference

The History of the Catholic Church in New Mexico

edited by Thomas J. Steele, S.J., Paul Rhetts, and Barbe Awalt

LPD Press
Albuquerque
1998

FROM LPD PRESS

OUR SAINTS AMONG US:
400 YEARS OF NEW MEXICAN DEVOTIONAL ART
BY BARBE AWALT & PAUL RHETTS

THE REGIS SANTOS:
THIRTY YEARS OF COLLECTING 1966-1996
BY THOMAS J. STEELE, S.J., BARBE AWALT, & PAUL RHETTS

SANTOS: SACRED ART OF COLORADO
EDITED BY THOMAS J. STEELE, S.J.

FOLKED: THE DRAWINGS OF NICHOLAS HERRERA
EDITED BY BARBE AWALT & PAUL RHETTS

HISPANIC NEW MEXICAN POTTERY:
EVIDENCE OF CRAFT SPECIALIZATION 1790-1890
BY CHARLES M. CARRILLO

CHARLIE CARRILLO:
TRADITION & SOUL/TRADICIÓN Y ALMA
BY BARBE AWALT & PAUL RHETTS

TRADICIÓN REVISTA:
THE JOURNAL OF TRADITIONAL & CONTEMPORARY
SPANISH COLONIAL ART & CULTURE
BARBE AWALT & PAUL RHETTS, PUBLISHERS

LPD PRESS
2400 RIO GRANDE BLVD. NW #1213
ALBUQUERQUE, NEW MEXICO 87104-3222
505/344-9382   FAX 505/345-5129
EMAIL PAULLPD@AOL.COM

Cover illustration of Tecolote Church
courtesy Paul Rhetts and Barbe Awalt © 1997

Library of Congress Catalogue Card Number 98-66219

ISBN 1-890689-00-9 (cloth)
ISBN 1-890689-01-7 (paper)

Printed on 250-year acid-free paper
Printed in the United States of America

First Edition
10 9 8 7 6 5 4 3 2 1

Seeds of Struggle/Harvest of Faith

The Papers of the Archdiocese of Santa Fe Catholic Cuatro Centennial Conference

The History of the Catholic Church in New Mexico

edited by Thomas J. Steele, S.J., Paul Rhetts, and Barbe Awalt

CONTENTS

FOREWORD

When we heard of the symposium scheduled by the Archdiocese of Santa Fe to commemorate the four-hundredth Anniversary of both Spanish influence and Catholic faith in New Mexico, we began thinking of how wonderful it would be to capture these papers in some type of long-lasting document. Some of the greatest minds in Southwestern history were scheduled to look at various important segments of New Mexico's rich past.

The twenty-three presenters featured in this book had twenty to twenty-five minutes to give an overview of their topic during the symposium on September 8 and 9, 1997. The papers in this book go more in depth and have, in some cases, the benefit of charts, photos, and maps. The symposium was a true success, and thanks go to Marina Ochoa, Robert Torrez, Father Jerome Martínez y Alíre, and their volunteer committee.

We have approached this book differently from our previous publications because it is different. It doesn't contain color pictures of beautiful art but rather important historical information, the vast amount of which has never been in print before. Some of the authors are widely-published and some have never been before.

We are grateful to Father Thomas J. Steele, S.J., who meticulously edited each paper. It was a monumental job, one that we think he rather enjoyed because he had the opportunity to drink in the papers before anyone else. For someone so devoted to New Mexican religious-based history, it must have been a treat.

We thank all of the authors for working professionally with Father Steele and learning from his proposed edits. The papers that the authors submitted were important to them, and they all spent great amounts of time doing the research that went into their presentations.

We want to also thank Mary Ryland and Chancellor Father Richard Olona for seeing the value of this project as we did. The cooperation of the Catholic Cuarto Centennial Commission made this project possible. And of course, without the vision of Archbishop Michael Sheehan this important date might have gone without celebration by the Catholic Community. All these people and many more will insure that positive lasting memories will be made in 1998.

The ultimate goal of this publication was to place into the hands of libraries, schools, churches, historians, and individuals interested in the subject information that will help everyone appreciate what came before us all in New Mexico. For that reason it is a very important work, one that a large number of people made happen.

Barbe Awalt & Paul Rhetts
LPD Press

INTRODUCTION

Four Hundred Years of Catholicism in New Mexico
Michael J. Sheehan, Archbishop of Santa Fe

It is with joy in my heart and gratitude to our loving God that I address you, dear brothers and sisters of the Archdiocese of Santa Fe. Nineteen hundred ninety-eight marks the 400th anniversary of the establishment of the Catholic Church in New Mexico. In 1598 Don Juan de Oñate, leader of an expedition of Spanish colonists, including eight Franciscan friars, reached the east bank of the Rio Grande near its confluence with the Chama River, close to Española, and established its capital. The seeds of Catholicism were planted, took root and flourished. It is important for us to celebrate this historic moment and to reflect upon God's goodness to us and to our Church.

The history of the struggles and the accomplishments of the people who came to this remote corner of the Spanish Empire is fascinating. The threads that run through the fabric of 400 years is clearly a strong faith in God that has had such a powerful influence in the lives of the people.

Scriptual Background

In the 28th chapter of the Gospel of Matthew, the Risen Savior gives His disciples the great commission: "Go, make disciples of all nations, baptizing them in the name of the Father, and of the Son, and of the Holy Spirit." All those that are true followers of Jesus, not merely His admirers, have sought to obey that command. Thus it was with those who sought to bring the Gospel to the deserts, mountains and valleys of our beloved New Mexico 400 years ago.

In the 6th chapter of the Acts of the Apostles, there is a debate in the Sanhedrin about what should be done with the new Christian movement. Wise counsel was given when it was declared, "If this endeavor is of human origin, then it will destroy itself. But if it is of God, no one will be able to destroy it, it shall endure." This can be said of the faith first planted in New Mexico; if it had been based on human genius and merit, then we would not be celebrating its 400th anniversary - it would have failed. But since it is God who provides the seed and the harvest, the faith established here four centuries ago has not only endured, but flourished - even in the face of much struggle.

In the Beginning

It has often been said that the first Spanish explorers came to the New World for three things: glory, gold and God. This was true also in New Mexico. But if they came for all three, they only stayed for God and his service since they never found glory and gold. However, the Spanish explorers found a large population of native people, whom they believed deserved to hear the Gospel. New Mexico, then, was established as a colony first and foremost as a mission to the Indians.

This missionary effort was begun by the Sons of St. Francis of Assisi, known today simply as Franciscans, whose sandal-shod feet carried the Good News to the various tribes. Franciscan spirituality is therefore indelibly imprinted into the soul of New Mexico Catholicism. This is evident in the popular religiosity of the people even today, and in the names given to villages and objects of great natural beauty: the Royal Village of the Holy Faith of St. Francis of Assisi (the City of Santa

Fe); Holy Cross (the village of Santa Cruz); St. Claire (Santa
Clara Pueblo); the Blood of Christ (the Sangre de Cristo Mountains); etc.

If the Spaniards came to New Mexico thinking that they
were going to introduce the native peoples to the divine, they
were mistaken. For the Indian people here had for millennia
worshiped the Great Spirit as the sustainer of all life. His will
was made manifest to them in the cycles and mysteries of the
natural world, of which they were a part, not as masters, but
reverent caretakers. The stability and order in nature was to be
emulated in the daily life of the community. In all, their spirituality was a rich one, similar to the revelation given the people
of Israel. The Indians' "Old Testament" was waiting for fulfill-
ment in the Redeemer of all humankind. Their hearts thus
provided a receptive soil for the seeds of the Gospel.

First Struggles

An encounter between two vastly different people will
inevitably result in bringing out the best and worst in both.
This was true in New Mexico as the Spanish and Indians first
faced each other four centuries ago. The Spanish felt that they
had to make the Indians copies of themselves in order to make
them good Christians. Naturally, the Indians resented this, and
in their rejection of this "Europeanization," some rejected the
evangelization efforts as well. This resulted in a very sad chapter
in New Mexico's history, as the Pueblo Revolt of 1680 pitted
one group of God's children against another.

There was eventually a reconciliation in 1692. As the old
Spanish proverb says, No hay mal de que por bien no venga.
(There is no evil from which good cannot come). This was
true of the understanding reached between the two peoples
after they agreed to peacefully coexist. The Spanish returned
with a greater humility, still intent on preaching the Gospel,
but seeking to do so in a way that respectfully took into account all that was good and holy in the native beliefs. The
Indians, for their part, realized that they could not turn the
clock back and that much of what the Spanish brought was
beneficial, including the Catholic faith whose ritual and sym-
bolism was similar to their beliefs and practices.

It is clear to us today that there were many failings on the part of the Spanish, including the failings of the Franciscan friars. There were incidences of cruelty and mistreatment, lack of respect for the native autonomy, culture and religious values. There was bloodletting on both sides, Spanish and native people. For these failings we seek forgiveness and reconciliation.

Yet despite the failings, so much good has come to all people. Can you imagine the past 400 years without the cattle, horses and mules brought by the Spanish? What would it have been like these 400 years without the sheep and its wool to warm us on cold nights? The horses and the mules? Imagine a land without wheat and the horno in which to bake oven bread! Farm implements, codified laws, the idea of personal property, a written language. All these came with the settlers and enhanced the quality of life for all.

The eminent pueblo scholar and historian Professor Joe Sando has written of these positive accomplishments also. He notes that the Pueblo Indians have fared much better under the Spanish than the Indians on the East Coast of the United States. There are no Indian markets in Boston or New York! Their Indian culture was pretty well destroyed. Here in New Mexico, Indian culture still flourishes.

It is also clear that the Spanish benefitted from the Native American presence. Where would they or any of us be without beans, squash and corn and the tortillas made from the corn? And to live with the Native Americans in this enchanted and beautiful land with majestic snow-covered mountains, deep valleys, dark forests, trout-filled streams and incredible sunsets. We have all benefitted by the Indian's love for the land and care for the environment that God created for all. How powerful and meaningful are their dances, the sound of the drums and the tribal rituals. The Indian's respect for the Great Spirit and their hospitality at the celebration of their feast days is inspiring.

This isn't to say there was no mistreatment of the Indians. But we have to try to see the big picture and to appreciate that we all have sought to live together in peace for many years. But for us Christians, the greatest gift that the Spanish settlers

and friars brought was even better than livestock and bread. It
was our Catholic tradition, the Gospel message and Jesus in
the Eucharist. We can know many things about God from
natural religion. But at a certain point, God wanted us to know
through the teaching of His Son, Jesus our Savior, to love our
enemy, to treat all people regardless of ethnic background or
color, young and old, with respect. This is a legacy we cherish,
and a Church that guides us through this life to the eternal life
of heaven.

The Fruits of Reconciliation

What resulted from the first struggles was nothing less
than the birth of New Mexican culture and Catholicism that
can truly be called indigenous to this land. The reconciliation
between the Spanish and Indian people produced a faith capable of adapting to different circumstances, as well as being
inclusive of the many different peoples already present and
those that would follow. This can be called nothing less than
remarkable, for this understanding produced a stable, peaceful situation in New Mexico during the intervening centuries.

Reigning over this humble kingdom of the Lord is our
Blessed Mother who has always had a special place in the
hearts of the people of New Mexico. Whether under her title
as Queen of Peace conquering the divisions among her children, or as Our Lady of Guadalupe championing the poor and
forgotten, the Virgin Mary continues to intercede for her children.

The Catholicism New Mexico has produced is truly
unique. Its historic churches reflect an architecture truly born
of this land – monuments of adobe. The same can be said for
the lovely hand-carved bultos, santos and retablos, statues and
icons of our Lord and saints. The oraciones and alabados are
beautiful prayer forms that grace our public expression and
devotions. So, too, are the processions and passion plays a
result of this New Mexican spirituality. We are truly heirs of a
rich legacy of faith.

Just as remarkable, this faith has been sustained through
the years by the efforts and devotion of the laity. In this far

flung frontier, where priests were often scarce, the folk faith of the common people proved to be the backbone of Catholicism. To these forebears, we owe a great debt.

More Changes

In 1851, Jean Baptiste Lamy arrived in Santa Fe to head the newly established Vicariate Apostolic. When he arrived he found clergy and people who had kept the faith alive from those early beginnings. This flowering of faith was rewarded by the Vatican when Santa Fe was elevated to a diocese in 1853, and given its first bishop. The Frenchman Jean Baptiste Lamy and his European clergy effected many changes. They built up the institutional church and Lamy brought Jesuits and French priests to help in the on-going missionary endeavor in this vast land. He brought the Christian Brothers and the first women religious, the Sisters of Loretto from Nerinx, Kentucky, one of the first American communities of sisters dedicated to teaching, and the Sisters of Charity from Ohio to staff schools and hospitals. The basic structures of the Archdiocese of Santa Fe as we know them today were due in large part to the efforts of Archbishop Lamy and his co-workers.

The efforts of Archbishop Lamy and those that followed were much needed as New Mexico continued to grow with the influx of newcomers from all neighboring territories and states. Growth caused some tensions with those born here, but diversity added strength.

Today we have a wonderfully diverse faith community of many different languages, cultures and ways of life, truly "catholic" in its universal make up. It is not a melting pot of peoples, but rather a mosaic in which the unique beauty and contribution of each culture is not lost but rather enhances each other resulting in a more recognizable likeness of God's creative power.

Accomplishments of the Past

Building on their diversity, New Mexican Catholics have been able to accomplish much together and for which they can be proud.

- A Christian community older than the establishments at Jamestown or Plymouth Rock
- Spanish missions older by 150 years than the missions of California or Texas
- The oldest image of the Madonna in the New World (La Conquistadora, Our Lady of Peace in Santa Fe)
- The first native-born priest, Santiago Roybal ordained in 1732
- The first school system in the State of New Mexico
- The first hospitals in New Mexico
- A proud record of lay involvement in the spread and maintenance of the faith
- The mother diocese of all the other dioceses of the American Southwest

And, this list goes on and on!

Looking to the Future

The Cuarto Centennial is not just about looking back and celebrating past glories. It is a time for quiet thanksgiving to God who has prospered the work of our hands. It is a time to be comforted by knowing that a loving God, who has guided us safely this far, is not about to abandon us as we face the future. I believe that the best years of Catholicism in New Mexico are ahead of us, not behind us.

In 1998 we stand on the shoulders of countless ancestors in the faith who have handed down to us the priceless treasure of hope that the Kingdom of God is a reality beginning here on earth. Realizing that, we must become aware that succeeding generations of New Mexican Catholics will be standing on our shoulders. The kind of Church we bestow on them is already in our hands; it is in the process of becoming.

As Archbishop of Santa Fe, I invite all of our Catholic people to enter into the celebration of our 400th anniversary. In no other part of the United States can the Catholic Church claim such a long and wonderful history. God's blessings to us are indeed unique. Determine today to continue through your lived faith the good that was begun 400 years ago when the friars who accompanied the Spaniards lifted high the cross and planted the seeds of faith.

God has brought forth a great harvest through the years despite our struggles and challenges. May God continue to bless us with an abundance of spiritual fruits as we move toward the next millennium remembering seeds of struggle produce a harvest of faith!

Santa Barbara Church, Rodarte, New Mexico. Photograph by Barbe Awalt, 1997.

Transplanting "Deep, Living Roots": Franciscan Missionaries and the Colonization of New Mexico — the Fledgling Years, 1598-1616

Félix D. Almaráz, Jr.

The Franciscan presence in New Mexico, a highly visible component of Spanish colonization securely tied to the leadership of Juan de Oñate in 1598, evolved as a gradual leap-frog advancement of church and state into the northern wilderness. Significantly, the fraternity of the Spanish crown and the Catholic church, embodied in a compendium of diplomatic accords called El Patronato Real (The Royal Patronage), manifested itself in the New World as a pragmatic equation in which the state counseled its officials to promote ecclesiastical objectives while the venerable clergy obligingly supported the temporal aims of the government.[1] At the close of the sixteenth century in the hinterland of New Mexico, El Patronato Real developed into a unique system of checks and balances as reflected in human relationships that either advanced or retarded the progress of the colony. Although Governor Oñate exercised a combination of political, military, and judicial supremacy so as to administer the colony, the Franciscan missionaries who accompanied the expedition possessed the moral authority that justified all transit into unsettled territory. During the colony's fledgling decades, extending from 1598 to 1620, years of hardship, courage, privation, setback, renewal, and resolve, the friars' evangelization of the Pueblo natives repeatedly collided with the settlers' temporal initiatives and expectations. All the same, on the eve of the colony's departure into the far frontier, the Spanish pioneers of church and state looked to New Mexico with a curious mix of exuberant anticipation and timorous anxiety.

Seventeen years before, in rustic Nueva Vizcaya, then the northernmost boundary of colonial expansion, a religious lay brother stationed at Mission Santa Bárbara, Fray Agustín Rodríguez, wondered about the veracity of "tales of northern 'town' Indians," which, to him, seemed like a splendid opportunity to spread the Christian faith into "an entirely new region." To obtain permission for such an ambitious and perilous plan, Fray Agustín traveled to Mexico City to consult Franciscan superiors and secular authorities. Returning to Santa Bárbara in 1581, the friar and Capitán Francisco Sánchez Chamuscado organized an entrada, humble in comparison to previous and later expeditions, endowed with official sanction to investigate the possibility of introducing evangelization and trade in the upper Río Grande basin.[2] The June 1581 Rodríguez-Sánchez Chamuscado party included two additional missionaries, nine soldiers, nineteen native servants (two of whom were women), ninety horses, and a commissary of six hundred head of livestock (cattle, goats, hogs, and sheep). The expedition followed the banks of the Río Conchos to its juncture with the Río Grande (Junta de los Ríos), then veered north into the land of the Pueblos.[3] The explorers' confirmation of the existence of the Pueblo communities fulfilled the main purpose of the entrada, but it also inspired two of the missionaries to remain in the north country. For their dedication to the challenge of converting the natives, soon all three friars (Agustín Rodríguez, Francisco López, and Juan de Santa María) earned the crown of martyrdom in New Mexico.[4] With the conclusion of the expedition, reports of the untimely death of the two principal leaders (Rodríguez and Sánchez Chamuscado), instead of discouraging further exploration, actually stimulated public interest in similar ventures that ultimately culminated in the permanent occupation of New Mexico.[5]

A subsequent entrada in 1582, also originating in Nueva Vizcaya as a rescue operation, led by Fray Bernardino Beltrán and Antonio de Espejo, pursued the same river route into New Mexico and reinforced the Franciscan tradition in early exploration.[6] These two entradas created a flurry of applications from about a dozen serious bidders seeking the contractual license to colonize New Mexico. After prolonged negotiations with two applicants, including an award of contract and a prompt cancellation, and an emission of arrest warrants for two illegal expeditions, the government conferred the favor upon Don Juan de Oñate, scion of an affluent and socially prominent family in Zacatecas.[7] Regardless of Oñate's appointment as governor, extremely long delays occurred from the award of the contract in 1595 by Viceroy Luis de Velasco II near the end of his initial tour of duty, through its meticulous examination by the successor official, the Count of Monterrey, until the expedition's final authorization in 1598.

These awkward delays notwithstanding, the contract for the colonization of New Mexico reflected a spirit of social reform inherent in the New Laws of 1542-1543 and reiterated in the Recopilación de las Leyes de las Indias of 1573. The royal legislation prescribed that expeditions for the discovery and occupation of unsettled regions could only be conducted "under the guise of religious conquests." Although the crown paid the annual stipends for missionary personnel, church officials in Mexico City assigned the friars to the Oñate expedition. The original "Band of Franciscans" requested by Don Juan in 1596 included Rodrigo Durán as apostolic commissary (administrator), Cristóbal de Salazar (Oñate's cousin whom contemporaries described as an "eminent" scholar), Francisco de San Miguel, Diego Márquez, a gregarious individual who, ironically, represented the Holy Office of the Inquisition, and a missionary identified only as Fray Balthasar. Public announcement of the missionaries' appointment provoked an unpleasant jurisdictional dispute between the regular clergy and the bishop of Guadalajara, Monseñor Francisco Santos García de Ontiveros y Martínez, principally because of New Mexico's vague geographical boundaries and the possibility of striking a silver bonanza that would rival the prestige of Zacatecas. Asserting episcopal prerogatives, the prelate argued that New Mexico was located "within the confines of his bishopric" and that he possessed canonical authority to "exclude all friars pretending to administer the sacraments." Viceroy Monterrey dodged the controversy by seeking an "opinion" of theologians and of the Audiencia of Mexico, a combination judicial tribunal and advisory council.

Meanwhile, Bishop García de Ontiveros y Martínez, frail and ill, journeyed to Mexico City to present his case, hoping to garner support from influential bureaucrats in the Inquisition where previously he had served as a treasury official. Fortunately the dispute stopped short of creating an embarrassing scandal (temporal affairs superseding the "salvation of souls") when the bishop died on June 28, 1596, and his successor did not assume possession of the Diocese of Guadalajara until late in 1598. Hence, without episcopal opposition regarding prerogatives, New Mexico, even before its actual occupation by Oñate's settlers, emerged as an exclusive missionary domain of the Franciscan Order.[8]

As one controversy subsided, Viceroy Monterrey fomented a personal tempest by objecting to Fray Diego Márquez' dual appointment as missionary and surrogate of the Holy Office of the Inquisition. The viceroy perceived Márquez' presence on the expedition as a jurisdictional encroachment by the Inquisition. Without viceregal concurrence, which Monterrey refused to bestow, the Inquisition lacked authority in New Mexico. Accordingly, Fray Márquez, the jovial friar, withdrew from Oñate's plans.[9]

The Order of Friars Minor, founded by Francis of Assisi in 1209, enjoyed a few advantages in its apostolate among indigenous cultures in central Mexico because of its early arrival shortly after the Conquest. In response to a call for missionaries from Hernán Cortés, three Flemish-speaking friars volunteered for assignment to the Indies. Woefully unsuited for the task, notably because they could not communicate with conquistadores who sought spiritual guidance, one of the friars, Pedro de Gante (Peter of Ghent, a relative of Emperor Carlos V), eventually achieved remarkable success as a teacher of music at San José de los Naturales, an Indian school emphasizing the arts, crafts, trades, and catechetical instruction.[10] Gante's "apostolic ardor" to the contrary, without "a definite plan" or methodology for converting the natives, the scope of his meritorious work remained limited to the environs of Mexico City. The conversion of the natives, Cortés and others agreed, required a systematic approach.[11]

In mid-June of 1524, a second group of Franciscans, led by Martín de Valencia, arrived in Mexico. Known as "The Twelve Apostles," these new friars selected two zones for evangelization – the Valley of Mexico and the greater area of Puebla – both inhabited by extensive indigenous populations of cultural and political importance.[12] Accustomed to governance by constitutions and rules of their order, this second band of missionaries convened a chapter meeting in Mexico City a month after their arrival to create an administrative system to supervise their program of Christian evangelization. Dependent for supplies and personnel upon their home Province of San Gabriel de Estremadura in southwestern Spain, the friars in central Mexico promptly organized themselves into a subordinate Custodia del Santo Evangelio, or ecclesiastical Custody of the Holy Gospel, under the spiritual guidance of a father custos whom they elected for a three-year term.[13]

Exceptionally well prepared for an ultramarine apostolate, these early missionaries of the Holy Gospel Province, truly eminent scholars and accomplished preachers, profoundly influenced the direction of evangelization in Mexico during the sixteenth century.[14] For a more manageable administration of the sacraments, the friars subdivided each zone into two districts. In 1525, they established their first major convento, San Francisco el Grande, which served as headquarters for missionary work in adjacent areas north of Mexico City. Likewise, they founded another convento in Cuernavaca to superintend evangelization in the southern zone. Radiating outward from these conventos, the missionaries, often with minimal cultural data about the native tribes, ventured into the unknown terrain, motivated by a fervent desire to win converts for Christianity.[15] Gradually, as skilled artisans became available for work, the friars supervised the building of modest conventos, chapels, friaries (residences), and visitas (temporary stations served by the communities of friars in the vicinity). From these rustic beginnings evolved the construction of magnificent churches that dominated the landscape of central Mexico.[16] The first bishop of Mexico, Fray Juan de Zumárraga, encouraged the missionaries to use the printing press as a medium of evangelization. With "this instrument of enormous power," the friars printed "catechisms, grammars and dictionaries in various Indian dialects" as well as liturgical guides and "books of spirituality."[17] In addition, they recorded their impressions of the cultural terrain in journals for later consultation by newly arrived confreres. Deducing conclusions from their temporal experiences working among native converts and neophytes, the Franciscans (and later the Dominicans and Augustinians who entered the field in 1526 and 1533, respectively)[18] learned to differentiate the types of missions they conducted: occupation, penetration, and assimilation (enlace). A *mission of occupation* comprised an area where religious communities operated in close harmony and proximity. Conversely, a *mission of penetration* described a territory with relatively few Christian centers, all distantly situated in remote frontier regions too arduous to support in emergency situations. Early Franciscan missions in the Zacatecas-Durango corridor, and later in New Mexico, typified the penetration syndrome. Finally, a *mission of assimilation* signified a zone of evangelization where one congregation of converts served as a model town surrounded by a cluster of smaller communities of Christian faith, the composite of which reflected an integration of Old and New World values.[19]

From humble beginnings, by 1533 the mendicant orders gradually increased their membership ranks. Even so, compared to the potentially "abundant harvest" of converts to be gathered, the missionaries constituted "too few workers." Still, they persevered in their ministry. Every year, return trips to Spain or sudden vacancies by death produced gaps in personnel ranks which "fresh" recruits eagerly filled. By mid-century, the Spanish Franciscans, not without philosophical conflict, accepted religious candidates from the American-born criollo stratum of society, a phenomenon that considerably increased the number of missionaries for assignment to distant frontiers.[20]

Beginning in 1546 and gaining momentum by mid-century, the discovery of a "rich silver lode" in the greater Zacatecas region north of Mexico City stimulated dynamic migration into the central corridor inhabited by a multitude of belligerent clans loosely described as Los Chichimecas. Despite incessant warfare, Nueva Galicia, the nearest province within the corridor, developed rapidly as a result of the silver bonanza with a proliferation of "mining camps and little towns."[21] Among the prominent families that risked life and property to contribute to the founding of Zacatecas were the Oñates and the Ibarras.[22]

An almost constant search for silver deposits, combined with the related industries that mining fostered, pushed the systematical line of settlement beyond "the northern interior" of colonial Mexico. In the vanguard of migration trudged miners, missionaries, and soldiers. In 1562, as reward for frontier exploration and settlement, Francisco de Ibarra received the governorship of Nueva Vizcaya, a vast province that encompassed the "pioneer lands north and west of Zacatecas." One of Ibarra's trusted lieutenants, Rodrigo del Río, in 1567 colonized Santa Bárbara in an environment surrounded by "extensive mines" near the Conchos River. Initially thirty Spanish families settled in Santa Bárbara. Soon thereafter a sizeable complement of Tlascalan Indian families voluntarily augmented the town's population. Following the footsteps of the miners, in 1570 Franciscan missionaries established a convento in the verdant valley of San Bartolomé, twenty-five miles east of Santa Bárbara.[23] When Francisco de Ibarra surveyed the "fertile valley" from a distance he reportedly exclaimed that it was "the best thing I have seen in all of New Spain." The fertility of the small valley soon transformed San Bartolomé into the "bread-basket" of the immediate mining area.[24] On the eve of Juan de Oñate's departure from Zacatecas, approximately seven thousand residents lived in and around the mining town of Santa Bárbara.[25] Together with the Franciscan missions for the Conchos natives at San Bartolomé, Santa Bárbara and the adjacent mining camps beckoned as "the base of operations" for the temporal and spiritual colonization of New Mexico.[26]

Late in the summer of 1596, the vanguard of Oñate's entrada arrived at the southern outskirts of Santa Bárbara. Other complements sporadically joined the main party bivouacked below the Río Conchos. For sixteen long months a succession of frustrating delays, some politically inspired in Spain, kept the colony occupied with seemingly endless inventories and official wrangling. Each day of waiting diminished the level of consumable provisions which, under the watchful eye of a royal inspector, had to be replenished. Meanwhile, the indefinite stalemate prompted religious superiors of the Holy Gospel Province to recall most of the original band of Franciscans for reassignment elsewhere, leaving only the erudite Fray Cristóbal de Salazar and the septuagenarian Fray Francisco de San Miguel as the original friars with the Oñate expedition. For a final inspection, the governor led the caravan to a spacious grassy clearing near the Río San Gerónimo.

On December 22, 1597, the royal inspector, by now highly despised for his arrogant and officious manner, administered an oath to Governor Oñate, after which he conducted "a meticulous examination" of personnel and material. In the inventory Oñate fell short in two categories, personnel and provisions. To keep the entrada from disintegrating on two meager technicalities, Oñate secured loans to correct the deficiencies.

On January 26, 1598, Don Juan de Oñate confidently guided the colonists out of the San Gerónimo Valley.[27] Instead of following the route along the Río Conchos blazed seventeen years earlier by the Rodríguez- Sánchez Chamuscado entrada, the governor's journey broke a new road straight north to New Mexico "over dust and glare" that later added "more color and romance to the story."[28] With great difficulty, personal courage, and sheer engineering aptitude, the colonists, livestock, and carts traversed the swollen Río Conchos. The next day, following the celebration of a field Mass, the royal inspector, without any befitting ceremony whatsoever, gave to Oñate oral permission to advance into New Mexico.[29] Thirty miles north of the Conchos, Oñate halted the caravan at another river crossing to allow the colonists to rest while he dispatched his nephew, Sergeant Major Vicente de Zaldívar, with a mounted patrol to scout the terrain of the Chihuahuan desert for "a trail suitable for wagons" that showed "some promise of water." At the Río San Pedro, where the expedition waited for young Zaldívar's report, a new complement of missionary friars, escorted by playwright and captain Marcos de Farfán, arrived on March 3. Oñate hastily organized the soldiers into six columns to welcome the Franciscans with proper decorum. Fray Alonso Martínez, the commissary, led his confreres into the encampment.[30]

Strict observers of the rules of their Order, the Franciscans, attired in blue-gray habits with a cowl for warmth in inclement weather and tied with a white cincture, walked alongside packmules or carretas that transported their few personal belongings and essential church supplies (liturgical vestments, altar linen, sacred vessels, ornaments, altar wine, and prayer books). The Franciscan rules governing the vows of humility and poverty definitely prohibited the missionaries from riding horses except in a dire emergency, and the 1598 expedition failed to qualify as

a crisis. Fray Alonso Martínez introduced his humble band of
ordained priests – Juan Claros, Andrés Corchado, Alonso de Lugo,
Juan de Rosas, Francisco de Zamora – and lay brothers Juan de
San Buenaventura and Pedro de Vergara. Another Franciscan
lay brother, Juan de Dios, a gifted interpreter, joined the religious
contingent later. Together with veteran friars Cristóbal de Salazar
and Francisco de San Miguel, Fray Alonso Martínez led a community of ten Franciscans.[31]

Notwithstanding a pledge of support for the New Mexico
missions in the governor's royal contract, in which he promised
to contribute "all the necessary supplies" for the friars "and their
attendants for the entire journey; ... so that there may be no
obstacle to the conversion" of the Pueblo natives,[32] Fray Alonso's
community petitioned church and state authorities for clarification of their responsibilities in the remote wilderness. Apprehen-
sive that evangelization in an isolated frontier environment might
create tension and conflict among settlers, soldiers, and natives,
the friars asked that temporal officials be restrained "from inter-
fering in the establishment of mission churches and schools" and
be instructed to "assemble the Indians in towns" to facilitate the
conversion process. The friars also requested more personnel.
Although the jurisdictional question remained vague and unresolved, the Franciscans' petition eventually resulted in the de-
ployment of "other padres to New Mexico."[33]

On April 20, 1598, Governor Oñate and the vanguard, including the missionary contingent, approached the south bank
of the Río Grande below a mountain pass. After an arduous trek
across the desert Oñate ordered another halt to allow the rear
units of the expedition to rejoin the main caravan.[34] Ten days
later, in an elaborate ceremony that included "a very solemn"
concelebrated Mass of thanksgiving, during which "the learned"
father commissary delivered a "well thought out" sermon, and an
open-air drama written especially for the occasion by Capitán
Marcos de Farfán, the governor formally took possession of the
vast territory in the name of the Spanish sovereign.[35]

Guided by the custom of the Old Testament in which elders
proclaimed important messages three times before an assembly,
Don Juan de Oñate, surrounded by his officers, friars, and settler
families, in a loud voice reiterated the objectives of El Patronato

Real inherent in his commission for the occupation of New Mexico.

> I state that in the name of the most Christian king, Don Philip, our lord, sole defender and protector of holy mother church, and its true son, and for the crown of Castile and the kings of his glorious lineage who may reign there, for and on behalf of my … province [of Zacatecas] I take and seize tenancy and possession, real and actual, civil and natural, one, two, and three times, one, two, and three times, one, two, and three times, and all the times that by right I can and should, at this … Río del Norte, without excepting anything and without limitations, including the mountains, rivers, valleys, meadows, pastures, and waters.[36]

Next, to dispel any lingering doubts about the extent of his temporal authority, the governor declared the magnitude of its jurisdiction:

> In his name I also take possession of all the other lands, pueblos, cities, towns, castles, fortified and unfortified houses which are now established in the kingdoms and provinces of New Mexico, those neighboring and adjacent thereto, and those which may be established in the future, together with their mountains, rivers, fisheries, waters, pastures, valleys, meadows, springs, and ores of gold, silver, copper, mercury, tin, iron, precious stones, salt, morales, alum, and all the lodes of whatever sort, quality, or condition they may be, together with the native Indians in each and every one of the provinces, with civil and criminal jurisdiction, power of life and death, over high and low, from the leaves of the trees in the forests to the stones and sands of the river, and from the stones and sands of the river to the leaves [of the trees] in the forests.[37]

Oñate's dynamic style and colorful exploit stemmed from a heritage of religious idealism and patriotic zeal forged by his ancestors in combat "during the long centuries of the Reconquest." Regardless of how critics magnified "the discord and contradictions" between the Christian ideal of Oñate's soldiers and their personal conduct, their faith, observed François Chevalier, "had deep, living roots."[38] In the spring of 1598, the governor's pioneers of church and crown transplanted the "deep, living roots" of their faith on fertile soil along the Río Grande del Norte.

Finally, out of devotion to the solemnity of the Ascension of Christ, Oñate personally nailed a crucifix to a tree near the riverbank, to serve as a friendly symbol to later travelers of a safe crossing. Invoking the name of the Holy Trinity, the Blessed Mother, and St. Francis of Assisi, he knelt before the crucifix and prayed for the overall success of the colonial effort, one facet of which was the evangelization program.

> Cross, Holy Cross that thou art, divine gate of heaven, altar of the only and essential sacrifice of the body nd blood of the son of God, way of the saints and the attainment of His glory, open the doors of Heaven to these heathens, establish the church and altars where the body and blood of the son of God may be offered, open to us the way to security and peace for their preservation and ours, and give to our king, and to me in his royal name, peaceful possession of these kingdoms and provinces for His blessed glory. Amen.[39]

Compensating for the ceremony the royal inspector had denied to the expedition at Santa Bárbara, Oñate walked a short distance from the tree into an open field where, in full view of the congregation, "with his own hands" he raised aloft "the royal standard" and the escudo (coat-of-arms) of Philip II. Simultaneously, a bugler sounded a martial call as an order of decorous conduct, while a squad of harquebusiers fired their weapons in salute. Then the spectators in the assembly responded with "a great rejoicing."[40] After the missionaries had blessed the royal standard, Governor Oñate entrusted the banner to Ensign Francisco de Sosa Peñalosa.[41]

The colony remained at the riverside bivouac area for several days, allowing time for the father commissary to recuperate from an illness. On May 4, 1598, the governor ordered the various components of the expedition to cross the river to the east bank. Oñate's officers described the operation as El Paso del Río del Norte, an engineering feat that suggested a commemorative name for the historic passageway.[42]

Trudging upriver behind the vanguard, Oñate's pioneers slowly penetrated the heartland of New Mexico. As the Spaniards entered the pueblo of Santo Domingo, named by the friars in honor of St. Dominic, the expeditionary caravan proudly displayed its pageantry and bravado. The weary travelers rested in the heat of the day while the governor performed another ritual of Spanish sovereignty. Through native interpreters who accompanied the expedition, Don Juan summoned "a multitude of Indian chieftains and common people" from at least seven pueblos around Santo Domingo. On July 7, after attending a Mass in the pueblo plaza attended by all the personnel of the entrada, Oñate asked the chieftains to meet with him in "the great kiva." Accompanied by the royal notary and secretary Juan Pérez de Donís, Fray Alonso Martínez and several missionaries, Sergeant Major Zaldívar and "other captains and soldiers," Oñate climbed down into the kiva. Before this assembly, the governor informed the chieftains "that he had been sent by the most powerful king and ruler in the world," Philip II, monarch of Spain, "who desired especially to serve God our Lord and to bring about the salvation of their souls, but wished also to have them as his subjects and to protect and bring justice to them, as he was doing for other natives of the East and West Indies." Oñate further explained that he and the colonists had journeyed from "distant lands to theirs, at enormous expense and great effort." Since the conversion of the Pueblos was the principal reason for the expedition, he tried to convince the chieftains that "it was greatly to their advantage that, of their own free will and in their own names and in those of their [respective] pueblos ... [that] they render obedience and submission" to El Rey Felipe II and to "become his subjects and vassals, as had [done] the people of the kings of Mexico, Tezcuco [sic], Michoacán, Tlaxcala, Guatemala, and others." The native leaders, through the interpreters, not only engaged Oñate in a dialogue, but they also discussed the matter "sometimes among themselves and at other times with their people."

Finally, after hours of repetitious discussion, hesitantly and with trepidation, the chieftains "knelt and kissed the hand of the father commissary and rendered obedience to the governor." Oñate then directed the royal secretary, Pérez de Donís, to draft "a sworn statement of the ceremony," for his signature at Santo Domingo pueblo, "stamped with the great seal of his office" and certified by no fewer than three witnesses.[43] The ceremony at Santo Domingo became the standard ritual that Oñate would use at other pueblos in seeking obedience and vassalage to the Spanish sovereign.

Continuing their north-bound journey, Oñate's colonists and missionary pioneers maintained visual contact with the Río Grande on their left. Less than sixteen miles northeast of Santa Domingo, they encountered a formidable obstacle of steep "hairpin curves" which they overcame, again through physical stamina and engineering adroitness, to ascend to a higher elevation. Southbound travelers later referred to the descending slope as La Bajada.[44] For Oñate's pioneers who endured the exhausting climb, the experience was La Subida. Finally, the colonists arrived at their destination in the humid and temperate climate of northern New Mexico. To commemorate the feastday of St. John the Baptist and the governor's given name, on June 24 the Franciscans established their first mission at a pueblo they designated as San Juan Bautista.[45] The Spaniards then explored other pueblos east and west of the Río Grande, an assignment from which they derived an awareness of a Río Arriba district characterized by fertile highlands with ample timber and grazing fields and a Río Abajo zone discernable by its arid levelness below La Bajada. On July 11, Governor Oñate selected a site for the colonial capital of New Mexico. At a pueblo called Ohke, on the east bank of the Río Grande, he located his field headquarters, naming it San Juan de los Caballeros.[46] The designation of San Juan as the provincial capital (subsequently transferred to the pueblo of San Gabriel, on the left bank of the Río Chama, near its confluence with the Río Grande) signified the terminus of El Camino Real that connected New Mexico with Zacatecas and further south with Mexico City.

At the pueblo of San Juan Bautista, capital of the fledgling colony, the Spaniards celebrated the founding of a mission with proper ceremony, a ritual they repeated elsewhere, undoubtedly with less fanfare but certainly with high expectation and fervent zeal. Soldier artisans, with native helpers, began construction of the church on August 23, 1598. Two weeks later, assessing the rate of progress as adequate, Oñate and the friars scheduled a "dedicatory" observance on September 8.[47] The following day the governor assembled the native chieftains of the region as he had done two months earlier at Santo Domingo to obtain their act of obedience and vassalage to King Philip II. Apostolic Commissary Fray Alonso Martínez and seven of his brethren witnessed the ceremony along with Oñate's nephews, Juan and Vicente Zaldívar, and "all the other officers and captains in the army." The royal notary, Juan Pérez de Donís, transcribed the proceedings. With assistance of Juan del Casso Barahona, an "interpreter of the Mexican language," Fray Juan de Dios, and two interpreters of the pueblo dialects (Don Tomás and Don Juanillo), Governor Oñate shortened the formalities by explaining to the native leaders "the purpose of his coming and what it was right for them to do." After the requisite act of obedience, Oñate implored the chieftains to take the missionaries to their villages so that they might learn their dialects. In turn, he said, the friars would "teach them the law of God and the religion of Christ." In closing the ceremony, through the interpreters the governor repeatedly asked them three times to "look after the padres, treat them well, and support and obey them in every respect." Then he warned them, again in triple unison, that "if they failed to obey any of the padres or caused them the slightest harm," they and their pueblos and villages "would be put to the sword and destroyed by fire." As dual symbols of church and state, Alonso Martínez and Juan de Oñate assigned the missionaries to the pueblos.[48]

With modest support from Oñate's soldiers due to limited manpower, the father commissary assigned missionary priests to outlying pueblos, focusing attention on an oblong area in a north-south axis that roughly corresponded "to the immediate drainage" of the Río Grande from Taos to Isleta. Similarly, in an east-west parallel, the Franciscans established missions located "at right angles" from the river, with Pecos as the easternmost foundation and Zuñi as the western outpost.[49] In assigning religious personnel to the missionary field, Fray Alonso stretched his thin human resources. For example, Fray Juan de Rosas voluntarily took both the Tano area and the Keres pueblos of San Felipe, Santo Domingo, and Cochití. His confrere Andrés Corchado accepted responsibility for the remote pueblo of Zía, with circuit duties at Ácoma,

Zuñi, and the Hopi villages. Fray Alonso de Lugo traveled west into the isolated pueblo of Jémez. The elder Fray Francisco de San Miguel, with assistance of a lay brother, Fray Juan de Dios, went to the eastern pueblos of the Salinas area just east of the Manzano Mountains. The assignment of the pueblo of San Juan Bautista, in the highlands of the Río Grande, devolved upon the governor's cousin, Fray Cristóbal de Salazar, assisted by lay brothers Juan de San Buenaventura and Pedro de Vergara. Finally, like counterweights at opposite ends of the riverine corridor, Fray Juan Claros received the care of the Tiwa pueblos of the middle Río Grande in the semi-arid south, while Fray Francisco de Zamora journeyed upriver to the northern semi-humid villages of Picurís and Taos.[50] During Oñate's tenure as governor, Apostolic Commissary Fray Alonso Martínez directed the evangelization of the pueblos, first from Mission San Juan Bautista and later from Mission San Gabriel. However, after Oñate's departure from New Mexico, a successor apostolic commissary transferred the missionary headquarters to Santo Domingo Pueblo because of its central location.[51]

Meanwhile, in early October when the artisans had completed work on the church at San Juan Bautista, the settlers commemorated the "festive" event with a mock battle, signifying that a "crusading spirit" still prevailed late in the sixteenth century. Oñate's soldiers aligned themselves into opposing armies, with one side called Moros and the other group identified as Cristianos. In the mock engagement, the Christian warriors "fought on horseback with lances and shields," while the Moors conducted warfare "on foot and used muskets." The spectators cheered the prearranged victory of the Christian crusaders.[52]

Notwithstanding the euphoria associated with the founding of the New Mexico missions, the work of converting the natives, beset with language barriers and meager resources, advanced haltingly. In the spring of 1599, three friars (Martínez the commissary, Pedro de Vergara, and Cristóbal de Salazar) traveled to Mexico City on a recruiting trip. Of the trio only Fray Pedro returned to the northern New Mexico in 1600. Arriving "a day or two before Christmas," Vergara brought eight new missionaries, including a lay brother who was a physician, Fray Damián Escudero. Another friar, Alonso de la Oliva, arrived much earlier

in September, 1600. With the help of new personnel (Juan de
Escalona, commissary, Lope de Izquierdo, Luis Mairones, Gastón
de Peralta, and Francisco de Velasco), the pioneer friars increased
the number of missions among the pueblos.[53]

During the colony's fledgling years, Governor Oñate's continuous problems with disgruntled settlers, some of whom clamored for abandoning New Mexico, severely handicapped the friars' spiritual labor among the natives. As a general rule, the
Franciscans confronted setbacks with dedication and renewal.
Within a year of the initial foundations, the friars inaugurated a
school for the Pueblo Indians.[54]

Affiliated with the early years of mission education was the
work of Fray Cristóbal de Quiñones, who arrived in New Mexico
at the dawn of the seventeenth century. A gifted musician assigned to San Felipe mission, Fray Cristóbal typically attended to
multiple duties such as studying the dialect of the Queres and
supervising construction of a church, a friary, and an infirmary.
At a critical time when survival in New Mexico constituted a
grave temporal concern, Fray Cristóbal installed a small organ in
his mission chapel where he instructed the natives in basic musical skills. From among numerous natives he recruited the most
promising converts, all endowed with musical talent, to sing in
the mission choir. Another musician, Fray Bernardo de Marta,
arrived in New Mexico in 1610. Fray Bernardo taught Spaniards
and Pueblo converts to play the organ. This talented friar labored
for nearly three decades at Zía, using music as a method of conversion.[55] As he prepared for the occupation of New Mexico,
Governor Oñate had anticipated such methodology. In his requi-
sition to the king he asked that "some trumpets or church musical instruments" be included in the inventory of ecclesiastical
supplies.[56] Still another teaching technique the Franciscans used
in early New Mexico was churchyard drama. Oñate's soldiers
periodically performed the drama of Los Moros for the entertainment of the settlers, who already knew the historical significance
of the reenactment, as well as for the instruction of the mission
converts. As more friars arrived at the New Mexico missions
they introduced variations of popular churchyard dramas such
as Los Pastores and Los Matachines.[57]

The missionaries' success with music education and church-yard theater in the conversion of the Pueblo natives quickly faded against the evolving squabbles between Governor Oñate and a growing number of disgruntled colonists who, disappointed because they had not found instant riches, clamored for abandonment of the colony. The disagreement spilled over into the church arena shortly after the arrival of Fray Juan de Escalona as apostolic commissary in New Mexico. By remaining silent in the controversy but allowing some missionaries to answer an inter-

Music in evangelization of New Mexico. By José Cisneros (courtesy the author).

rogatory compiled by four disloyal captains, Escalona unwittingly sided with the malcontents, several of whom deserted the colony in 1601 during Oñate's untimely absence from the capital at San Gabriel. Relations between the clergy and the civil authorities in New Mexico became so "embittered" that some friars, "active critics" of Oñate's "arbitrary" governance of the colony, joined the deserters in their southward journey.[58] In the summer of 1601, the Franciscan missionary field tottered on the edge of collapse. Only three friars (Escalona, Velasco, and Vergara) remained at work in the missions.[59]

Upon arriving at a safe haven in Mexico City, the deserters vociferously denounced Oñate, describing him "in the blackest colors." Viceroy Monterrey consulted a cadre of "theologians and jurists" who advised him "to protect the settlers from Oñate's wrath." Ironically, the partial desertion of the colony revealed "the true nature" of Oñate's accomplishments in New Mexico which tilted in favor of the evangelization of the pueblos. Clearly, the absence of "fabled wealth" forced royal officials to accept the truth about New Mexico and to draft an alternate plan for "the permanent growth" of the colony as a missionary domain.[60]

Fortunately for New Mexico, the viceroy, the Count of Monterrey, dispatched replacement personnel for the distant missions. The viceregal government provided supplies and transportation for four friars in 1603 (led by Fray Francisco de Escobar, who within a year assumed the office of apostolic commissary) and two additional missionaries in 1605. Among the new arrivals, Fray Lázaro Ximénez, Fray Isidro Ordóñez, and Fray Alonso de San Juan, a lay brother, contributed to the stabilization of the missionary field. In the meantime, two friars died in the conduct of their ministry, Juan de Escalona, former commissary, at Mission San Gabriel in 1607, and Cristóbal de Quiñones, the musician, at Mission San Felipe in 1609. Just prior to the end of Juan de Oñate's governorship, Fray Alonso de Peinado, as successor commissary, arrived in New Mexico with a fresh contingent of missionaries who reinforced the process of evangelization at the pueblos.[61]

The administration of Juan de Oñate ended ignobly in 1610. Arriving in the province in the depth of winter, a successor governor, Pedro de Peralta, suppressed the earlier capital at San Gabriel de Chama and inaugurated the Royal Villa of Santa Fé, located thirty miles to the southeast. Besides complying with the Laws of the Indies regulating the founding of civil settlements at sites uninhabited by indigenous cultures, the transfer of the provincial capital signified the end of proprietary rule and the advent of royal authority. It also created a new terminus for El Camino Real.[62]

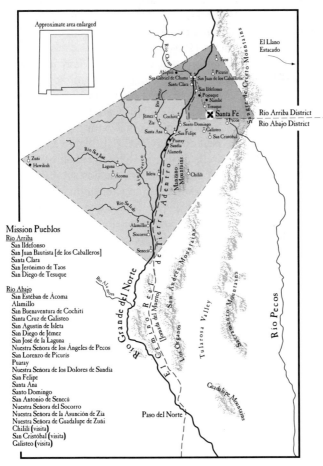

Mission Pueblos

Rio Arriba
San Ildefonso
San Juan Bautista [de los Caballeros]
Santa Clara
San Jerónimo de Taos
San Diego de Tesuque

Rio Abajo
San Esteban de Ácoma
Alamillo
San Buenaventura de Cochiti
Santa Cruz de Galisteo
San Agustin de Isleta
San Diego de Jémez
San José de la Laguna
Nuestra Señora de los Ángeles de Pecos
San Lorenzo de Picuris
Puaray
Nuestra Señora de los Dolores de Sandía
San Felipe
Santa Ana
Santo Domingo
San Antonio de Senecú
Nuestra Señora del Socorro
Nuestra Señora de la Asunción de Zia
Nuestra Señora de Guadalupe de Zuñi
Chilili (visita)
San Cristóbal (visita)
Galisteo (visita)

The Founding of New Mexico, 1598-1610

Coincidental with the founding of Santa Fé and the arrival of military reinforcements, ample supplies, and eight additional friars, the Franciscans selected the pueblo of Santo Domingo, recommended by its central location near the Río Grande, as missionary headquarters. Encouraged by recent changes in the governor's office yet cautiously watching for unexpected developments, the Franciscans reestablished abandoned missions and extended their spiritual activities farther into the arid wilderness. By 1616, following the ecclesiastical designation of New Mexico as the Custody of the Conversion of St. Paul, a semi-autonomous adjunct of the Franciscan Provincia del Santo Evangelio, the first father custos, Fray Estévan Perea, reviewed the laudable record of "eleven flourishing missions staffed by about twenty friars, who ministered to approximately ten thousand Christianized Indians."[63] Constant in their resolve to remain in New Mexico (with conventos or friaries at Santa Fé, Chililí, Galisteo, Isleta, Nambé, San Ildefonso, San Lázaro, Sandía, Santo Domingo, and Zía), the Franciscans astutely petitioned royal officials to provide temporal assistance for their missionary initiatives. Eventually the royal government's policy decision created the mission supply service, a caravan that plodded along El Camino Real from Mexico City to Santa Fé about every three years. In addition to escorting replacement personnel for the pueblo missions, the supply train, an aggregate of pack-mules and carretas, conveyed an assorted inventory of requisitions, the chief categories being consumable provisions, clothing, dry goods, hardware, kitchen wares, liturgical stores, essential medical needs, musical instruments, office necessities, sewing notions, and tools and equipment.[64] Viewed from the heights of Mexico City, the province of Nuevo México loomed as a Christian island, "a lost community beyond the immense, deserted, semi-arid plains of the north."[65]

Apart from the temporal aspect of the mission supply service that provided an economic foundation for the friars' work at the pueblos, the caravan offered an animated channel of information, mostly through the oral tradition, about life in New Mexico to residents of Durango, Zacatecas, and Mexico City. Similarly, in the north-bound journey, the arrieros (teamsters) transmitted lively descriptions of current events in the southern region to settlers, soldiers, and friars in New Mexico.[66]

With a steady arrival of religious personnel each triennium, the Franciscan missions in New Mexico slowly entered the golden period of development. In the subsequent period of evangelization, the missionaries not only continued their ministry among the natives of the Río Grande basin, but they extended their labor in the direction of Pecos, Picurís, Taos, the Jémez towns, and even the pueblo of Abó.[67] During the fledgling years of the Spaniards' presence in New Mexico, 1598-1616, the friars not only had furnished the justification for Oñate's occupation of the province, but by their adamantine commitment to the evangelization of the pueblo natives they saved the colony from abandonment. The "deep, living roots" the Spanish pioneers transplanted into New Mexico's harsh environment survived and flourished in the seventeenth century. Notwithstanding hardship, drought, and turbulence, by their steadfast devotion to the ministry of saving souls the Franciscans earned meritorious distinction as New Mexico pioneers along with soldiers, settlers, natives, and governors.

Notes

1. W. Eugene Shiels, *King and Church: The Rise and Fall of the Patronato Real* (Chicago: Loyola University Press, 1961), pp. 8-20.

2. Lansing B. Bloom, "The Chihuahua Highway," *New Mexico Historical Review* 12 (July 1937): 213. [Hereinafter cited as *NMHR*.]

3. Carroll L. Riley, *Río del Norte: People of the Upper Río Grande From Earliest Times to the Pueblo Revolt* (Salt Lake City: University of Utah Press, 1995), pp. 227-230.

4. Atanasio G. Saravia, *Los Misioneros Muertos en el Norte de Nueva España* (Mexico: Ediciones Botas, 1943), p. 27. The third friar, Juan de Santa María, volunteered to inform church and royal officials about the favorable possibilities of the northern missionary field. En route south, after crossing the Sandía Mountains, Fray Juan stopped "to rest under a tree" in the vicinity of a Tigua village. Hostile natives killed him and covered his remains (Paul J. Foik, *The Martyrs of the Southwest* [Austin: Texas Catholic Historical Society, 1929], pp. 4-5).

5. George P. Hammond, "Don Juan de Oñate and the Founding of New Mexico," *NMHR* 1 (January 1926): 49; Oakah L. Jones, Jr., *Nueva Vizcaya: Heartland of the Spanish Frontier* (Albuquerque: University of New Mexico Press, 1988), p. 66. [Hereinafter the Hammond essay will be cited as "The Founding of New Mexico."]

Comparing their work to the magnificent entrada of Captain General Francisco Vásquez de Coronado of an earlier generation, Hernán Gallegos, chronicler of the Rodríguez-Sánchez Chamuscado expedition, pithily assessed the achievements of his brothers-in-arms: "Only nine men dared to enter that land and accompished what five hundred men were unable to do" (Hernán Gallegos, "Relación y concudío de el viaje y subseso que Francisco Sánchez Chamuscado con ocho soldados sus compañeros hizo en el descubrimiento del Nuevo México en junio de 1581," quoted in J. Lloyd Mecham, "The Second Spanish Expedition to New Mexico: An Account of the Chamuscado-Rodríguez Entrada of 1581-1582," *NMHR* 1 [1926]: 291).

6.   Hammond, "The Founding of New Mexico," *NMHR* 1: 49.

7.   Marc Simmons, *The Last Conquistador: Juan de Oñate and the Settling of the Far Southwest* (Norman: University of Oklahoma Press, 1991), p. 58; Agapito Rey, "Missionary Aspects of the Founding of New Mexico," *NMHR* 23 (1948): 28.

8.   Hammond, "The Founding of New Mexico," *NMHR* 1 (July 1926): 294-295; José Bravo Ugarte, *Diócesis y Obispos de la Iglesia Mexicana (1519-1963)* (Mexico: Editorial Jus, 1965), pp. 51-52.

9.   Simmons, *The Last Conquistador*, p. 84; Hammond, "The Founding of New Mexico," *NMHR* 1: 295.

10.   Pedro Borges Morán, *El Envio de Misioneros a América durante la Época Española* (Salamanca: Universidad Pontificia, 1977), p. 218; Carlos Alvear Acevedo, *La Iglesia en la Historia de México* (Mexico: Editorial Jus, 1975), pp. 41-42.

11.   Lino Gómez Canedo, "Franciscans in the Americas: A Comprehensive View," in *Franciscan Presence in the Americas: Essays on the Activities of the Franciscan Friars in the Americas, 1492-1900,* ed. Francisco Morales (Potomac, Maryland: Academy of American Franciscan History, 1983), pp. 30, 43; Robert Ricard, *The Spiritual Conquest of Mexico: An Essay on the Apostolate and the Evangelizing Methods of the Mendicant Orders in New Spain, 1532-1572* (Berkeley: University of California Press, 1966), p. 20.

12.   León Lopetegui and Félix Zubillaga, *Historia de la Iglesia en América Española: Desde el Descubrimiento hasta comienzos del Siglo XIX* (Madrid: Biblioteca de Autores Cristianos, 1965), pp. 301-302.

13.   John L. Kessell, *Kiva, Cross, and Crown: The Pecos Indians and New Mexico, 1540-1840* (Washington, D.C.: National Park Service/ U.S. Department of the Interior, 1979), pp. 73-74.

However, because of the geographic distance and the urgency to expedite the conversion of the indigenous people, Franciscan superiors in Europe suspended the rule that subordinated the Cus-

tody of the Holy Gospel to the Province of San Gabriel de
Extremadura and placed the missionary friars in Mexico directly
under the supervision of the minister general of the Order in
Rome or his commissary in Spain. For purposes of accountability,
this arrangement remained in force until 1535 when religious
superiors elevated the Mexican custody to the full-fledged Province of the Holy Gospel. As the evangelization progressed in central Mexico, the Provincia del Santo Evangelio "founded other
custodies" that evolved into exemplary models of their mother-
province (Kieran McCarty, "Franciscans North from Mexico, 1527-
1580," in *Franciscan Presence in the Americas*, pp. 538-539).

14.   Francisco Morales, "Los Franciscanos en la Nueva España: La época
de oro, siglo XVI," in *Franciscan Presence in the Americas*, pp. 51-54.

15.   Lopetegui and Zubillaga, *La Iglesia en América Española*, pp. 301-302.

16.   Ricard, *Spiritual Conquest of Mexico*, pp. 162-163.

17.   Gómez Canedo, "Franciscans in the Americas," in *Franciscan Presence in the Americas*, p. 30.

18.   Ricard, *Spiritual Conquest of Mexico*, pp. 22-23, 39.

19.   José Gutiérrez Casillas, *Historia de la Iglesia en México* (Mexico: Editorial Porrúa, S.A., 1974), pp. 81-82.

20.   Ricard, *Spiritual Conquest of Mexico*, p. 23. The construction of
Franciscan conventos kept pace with the recruitment process. In
the fledgling period of 1524-1532, the friars reported an unas-
suming total of thirteen convents in operation. In the next period,
1532-1540, they opened sixteen additional conventual centers.
Then, in the decade before mid-century, the Franciscans inaugurated eighteen more convents, including San Miguel de los
Chichimecas which connoted expansion toward the north. These
forty-seven spiritual foundations formed a sturdy springboard that
enabled the Franciscans to hasten their evangelization (Morelos,
"Los Franciscanos en la Nueva España," in *Franciscan Presence in the
Americas*, p. 65).

21.   John Francis Bannon, *The Spanish Borderlands Frontier, 1513-1824*
(New York: Holt, Rinehart and Winston, 1970), p. 28.

22.   Simmons, *The Last Conquistador*, p. 29.

23.   Riley, *Río del Norte*, p. 226.

24.   McCarty, "Franciscans North from Mexico," in *Franciscan Presence in
the Americas*, p. 255.

25.   Riley, *Río del Norte*, p. 226.

26.   McCarty, "Franciscans North from Mexico," in *Franciscan Presence in
the Americas*, p. 255.

27.   Simmons, *The Last Conquistador*, pp. 70-90.

28. Maud Durlin Sullivan, "Old Roads and New Highways in the Southwest," *NMHR* 10 (April 1935): 145.

29. Simmons, *The Last Conquistador*, pp. 91-92.

30. Ibid.

31. Hammond, "The Founding of New Mexico," *NMHR* 1: 321-322; France V. Scholes and Lansing B. Bloom, "Friar Personnel and Mission Chronology, 1598-1629," *NMHR* 19 (1944): 320-321.

32. Contract of Don Juan de Oñate for the Discovery and Conquest of New Mexico, December 15, 1595, in *Don Juan de Oñate: Colonizer of New Mexico, 1595-1628*, ed. George P. Hammond and trans. Agapito Rey, 2 vols. (Albuquerque: University of New Mexico Press, 1953), 1: 46. [Hereinafter cited as Hammond and Rey, *Don Juan de Oñate.*]

33. Mecham, "Founding of New Mexico," *NMHR* 1: 296-297.

34. Félix D. Almaráz, Jr., "Spain's Cultural Legacy in Texas," in *The Texas Heritage*, ed. Ben Procter and Archie P. McDonald (Wheeling, Illinois: Harlan Davidson, Inc., 1998), pp. 2-3; W. H. Timmons, *El Paso: A Borderlands History* (El Paso: Texas Western Press, 1990), pp. 13-14.

35. Gaspar Pérez de Villagrá, *Historia de la Nueva México*, trans. and ed. Miguel Encinias, Alfredo Rodríguez, and Joseph P. Sánchez (Albuquerque: University of New Mexico Press, 1992), Canto 14, verses 310-314, pp. 130-131.

36. Act of Taking Possession of New Mexico, April 30, 1598, in Hammond and Rey, *Don Juan de Oñate*, 1: 334-335. The act of possession, called La Toma, occurred near the site of a future presidio of San Elizario (Timmons, *El Paso*, p. 14).

37. Act of Taking Possession of New Mexico, in Hammond and Rey, *Don Juan de Oñate*, 1: 335.

38. François Chevalier, *Land and Society in Colonial Mexico: The Great Hacienda*, trans. Alvin Eustis, ed. Lesley Byrd Simpson (Berkeley: University of California Press, 1963), p. 26.

39. Act of Taking Possession of New Mexico, in Hammond and Rey, *Don Juan de Oñate*, 1: 335.

40. Ibid., 336.

41. Record of the Marches of the Army, New Spain to New Mexico, 1596-1598, in Hammond and Rey, *Don Juan de Oñate*, 1: 315.

42. Timmons, *El Paso*, pp. 13-14.

43. Act of Obedience and Vassalage by the Indians of Santo Domingo, July 7, 1598, in Hammond and Rey, *Don Juan de Oñate*, 1: 337-341. St. Dominic (1170-1221) was a contemporary of Francis of Assisi (1181-1226). Franciscan missionaries in the Spanish Borderlands frequently honored Santo Domingo on the same level as San

Francisco, founder of their Order (John J. Delaney, *Dictionary of Saints* [Garden City, N.Y.: Doubleday & Company, Inc., 1980], pp. 181-182, 234-235).

44. T. M. Pearce (ed.), *New Mexico Place Names: A Geographical Dictionary* (Albuquerque: University of New Mexico Press, 1965), p. 80.

45. Simmons, *The Last Conquistador*, p. 106.

46. Hammond and Rey, "Introduction," in *Don Juan de Oñate*, 1: 14.

47. Mecham, "Founding of New Mexico," *NMHR* 1 (1926):296-297.

48. Act of Obedience and Vassalage by the Indians of San Juan Bautista, September 9, 1598, in Hammond and Rey, *Don Juan de Oñate*, 1: 342-344.

49. Henry W. Kelly, "Franciscan Missions of New Mexico, 1760-1766," *NMHR* 15 (October 1940): 360.

50. France V. Scholes and Lansing B. Bloom, "Friar Personnel and Mission Chronology, 1598-1629," *NMHR* 19 (October 1944): 327; Hammond and Rey, "Introduction," in *Don Juan de Oñate* 1: 17-18; Mecham, "Founding of New Mexico," *NMHR* 1: 321-322.

51. Scholes and Bloom, "Friar Personnel and Mission Chronology," *NMHR* 19: 327; Fray Angélico Chávez, *Origins of New Mexico Families in the Spanish Colonial Period* (Santa Fe: William Gannon, 1975), p. 3.

52. Mecham, "Founding of New Mexico," *NMHR* 1: 320-321.

53. Scholes and Bloom, "Friar Personnel and Mission Chronology," *NMHR* 19: 321-322. Fray Cristóbal de Salazar, Oñate's cousin, died en route to Mexico City. Fray Alonso Martínez received a letter of obedience relieving him of duty as apostolic commissary. Consequently, he reported to another assignment, leaving only Fray Pedro de Vergara as the veteran pioneer who guided the group north to New Mexico.

54. Paul A. F. Walter, "First Meeting of the New Mexico Educational Association," *NMHR* 2 (January 1927): 73.

55. Lota M. Spell, "Music Teaching in New Mexico in the Seventeenth Century: The Beginnings of Music Education in the United States," *NMHR* 2 (January 1927): 73.

56. Sister Joseph Marie [McCrosson, I.H.M.], "The Role of the Church and the Folk in the Development of the Early Drama in New Mexico" (Ph.D. diss., University of Pennsylvania, 1948), 66.

57. Ibid., 74-79.

58. France V. Scholes, "The First Decade of the Inquisition in New Mexico," *NMHR* 10 (July 1935): 195-196.

59. Scholes and Bloom, "Friar Personnel and Mission Chronology," *NMHR* 19: 323.

60. Mecham, "Founding of New Mexico," *NMHR* 2 (January 1927): 49-50.

61. Scholes and Bloom, "Friar Personnel and Mission Chronology," *NMHR* 19: 323-326, 331.

62. Kessell, *Kiva, Cross, and Crown,* pp. 93, 99.

63. Cyprian J. Lynch, "Introduction," in *Benavides' Memorial of 1630,* trans. Peter P. Forrestal (Washington, D.C.: Academy of American Franciscan History, 1954), p. xx; Scholes and Bloom, "Friar Personnel and Mission Chronology," *NMHR* 19: 335.

64. France V. Scholes, "The Supply Service of the New Mexico Missions in the Seventeenth Century," *NMHR* 5 (January 1930): 93-105.

65. Chevalier, *Land and Society in Colonial Mexico,* p. 4.

66. Marc Simmons, "Arriera: The Art of Mexican Muleteering," *Southwest Heritage* 7 (Spring 1977): 31-32.

67. Scholes and Bloom, "Friar Personnel and Mission Chronology," *NMHR* 20 (January 1945): 632.

Sacramental Records and the Preservation of New Mexico Family Genealogies from the Colonial Era to the Present

José Antonio Esquibel

As we come together to commemorate the history of the Catholic Church in New Mexico from 1598 to the present, it is easy to focus on the history of the clergy and the ecclesiastical institution. Let us be reminded that the very foundation of the Church in New Mexico is the people who for centuries sustained the Catholic faith, people who served as vessels of tradition and diligently cultivated the faith from one generation to the next. Who were these people? A great many are no longer remembered, their names and deeds having faded in the long passage of time. Yet the faith that was nurtured through the colonial, Mexican, and territorial eras of New Mexico's history endured through the transition of three governments. Although lost to memory, the names of countless numbers of Catholics of New Mexico can be found in the surviving record books of sacraments. These records are documentation of events that joined individuals to the church as members of the body of Christ and strengthened that bond over the course of each lifetime.

Sacraments are regarded as the visible signs of God's invisible presence, signs through which faith is manifested and in which the grace of God is received and Christ is present.[1] In 1547, the Council of Trent (1545-1563) set forth the sanctioned dogma of the sacraments, formally recognizing their number to be seven: baptism, penance (reconciliation), confirmation, holy orders, matrimony, and extreme unction (anointing of the sick).[2]

Twenty-six years earlier, beginning with the founding of New Spain in 1521, clergy, soldiers, and colonists serving the two majesties, God and king, firmly established Catholic communities as new settlements were established and populated from Mexico City northward. In the area of New Mexico, several courageous but failed attempts were made between 1540 and 1598 to bring the word of God and establish the Catholic faith among the Native American people.[3]

When don Juan de Oñate organized his expedition to New Mexico in 1595 clergy were present from the start. The large body of volunteer recruits – men, women and children – required not only social and military leadership but also religious and spiritual leadership as well as the administration of the sacraments. The expedition formed a Catholic community under the guidance of Franciscan missionaries who would minister to the soldiers and colonists as well as to the native people met with in New Mexico.

It certainly took strength garnered from faith to endure the tribulations suffered due to the continuous delays and shortages of provisions before the expedition began its arduous journey into the northern wilderness in August 1597.[4] Eight months later, in late April 1598, following a route recently blazed by a small company of Oñate's army, the large expedition reached the banks of the Rio Grande near present-day El Paso, Texas.[5] Fording the great river, each and every individual entered into the region formally christened "La Nueva México." The group of travelers successfully traversed a most desolate terrain to arrive at the gates of a new kingdom. This was a momentous occasion that gave rise to the celebration of a High Mass on April 30th, marking the humble beginnings of the continuous celebration of the sacraments in New Mexico; an occasion which we prepare to commemorate as we approach the four-hundredth anniversary of the event.

As Oñate's army proceeded northward, the Franciscans did not miss the opportunities to baptize the Indians that they encountered, solemnly believing God's grace was conferred to each newly baptized person. Oñate, accompanied by his soldiers, set out in advance of the main body of the expedition and determined that the Pueblo christened San Juan de los Caballeros would be the base of the colony. Shortly after the arrival of the entire expedition, Oñate's cousin Fray Cristóbal de Salazar and the other friars gave sermons in which the Spanish soldiers and settlers were reminded they were "Apostles of Jesus Christ" and were "rendering a very great service to God by helping win souls for heaven."[6] From the early beginnings of the church in New Mexico, the administration of the sacraments created the initial spiritual and social bonds between the Spanish and their Indian compadres, forming the very foundation of the Catholic community of New Mexico that still thrives today.

It was common during the colonial era to record the events of baptisms, marriages, and burials; a custom the Spaniards brought with them from Spain and established soon after the conquest of Mexico City in 1521. Unfortunately, the early records of sacraments that were kept in New Mexico have long been lost or destroyed. No books of baptisms, marriages, or burials for the period of 1598 to 1680 have survived to the present day, many having been lost in the Pueblo Indian Revolt of August 1680.[7]

With the return of the Spanish in December 1693 from exile at El Paso, Catholic communities were again re-established at the Pueblos and Spanish settlements. The formal documentation of sacraments, in particular baptism and marriage, continued to be the norm. The records of sacraments that have survived from the colonial era are now part of the archival collection of the Archdiocese of Santa Fe. We are fortunate to have such records for twenty-eight colonial churches, including twenty Pueblo missions and eight Spanish community parishes. The earliest preserved books of baptisms are from the Pueblos of Tesuque and Zia dating from 1694. A few certificates of marriage date from 1680, the earliest from Santo Domingo Pueblo before the revolt. The earliest burial records date from 1694 for Tesuque Pueblo.[8]

Many of the records of sacraments from 1694 to 1725 are incomplete. Some churches are missing marriage records but have baptismal records. Some have only baptismal or marriage records. However, there is considerable improvement in the extant records through the remainder of the eighteenth century with baptismal, marriage, and burial records existing for similar years for most colonial churches.

In the early 1600s, Santo Domingo Pueblo was chosen as the custodial headquarters of the Franciscan missionaries in New Mexico, and thus all archival records pertaining to church activities, including matrimonial investigations and the filled books of baptisms, marriages, and burials were stored at the convent. A brief description of this custodial archive given for 1776 identified matrimonial investigation records from as early as 1619, as well as volumes of baptismal records and many more unbound sheets of burial and baptismal records from various churches.[9] Unfortunately, when the Rio Grande flooded in 1886 an unknown number of records were probably washed away with the old church and convent.[10] Through the nineteenth and early twentieth centuries, the ecclesiastic archival records were neglected.

In 1933, Archbishop Gerken initiated the assemblage of the archdiocesan archives at Santa Fe. Dr. Lansing B. Bloom did some early work with these documents. Col. José D. Sena followed and began to classify many of the different records. The enormous task of cataloguing and filing the entire collection of archival records was undertaken by Fray Angélico Chávez with approval of Archbishop Byrne in 1954.[11] The most significant decision regarding these records was the granting of permission to allow the collection to be microfilmed. This action has allowed access to these valuable documents by the general public, in particular historical and genealogical researchers, and has ensured the surer preservation of the information found in the collection.

The records of sacraments that are a part of the archives of the Archdiocese of Santa Fe are a lasting testament to the signs of faith of our ancestors, a faith that for many people with family roots in colonial New Mexico has been passed on for as many as sixteen generations, and for which there is documentation in sacramental records for the last three hundred years. Sacraments are esteemed as "moments when the Church becomes the Church."[12] In this respect, the books of baptisms, marriages, and burials document the continuous creation of the Church in New Mexico, the steadfast formation of the church consisting of numerous individuals.

Hidden in the records of sacraments of New Mexico is an intricate network of relationships – familial, social, and spiritual. Family genealogies and lineages can be constructed from the entries found in the different record books. A study of *compadrazgo* relations can identify significant interrelationships among kinship groups that influenced the social and economic events of New Mexico communities. Furthermore, the spiritual bonds created through the sacraments of baptism, confirmation, and marriage served to strengthen the Catholic community and perpetuate close relations between community members.

The availability of the sacramental records of the Archives of the Archdiocese of Santa Fe, combined with the seminal work of Fray Angélico Chávez, has been instrumental in fostering an increased interest among many people with roots in New Mexico to research and document their family genealogy.[13] Numerous lineages from the colonial era to the present have been constructed using sacramental records as primary sources. Two lineages originating in seventeenth century New Mexico and converging in the early nineteenth century are presented here as an example (see the genealogical chart on the following page). The progenitor of these two lineages was an Apache woman named Ana Velásquez, also referred to as Ana de Velasco, who most likely received her Spanish name through baptism as an adult. She appears to be the same Ana de Velasco identified as "Yndia" who had served in the household of Governor don Diego López de Mendizábal for eleven months around 1660-61 at Santa Fe.[14] She then came to serve in the household of the prominent Domínguez de Mendoza family. A known son of Ana Velásquez was Captain José Domínguez de Mendoza, born circa 1666 in New Mexico and thought to be an illegitimate son of one of the Domínguez de Mendoza brothers,[15] but he may have received his surname through baptism if a member of the Domínguez de Mendoza family had stood as his godparent.

In a petition presented to Fray Nicolás Hurtado dated April 8, 1682, at El Real de San Lorenzo near El Paso del Norte, José Domínguez de Mendoza requested to enter into the state of matrimony according to the order of "Nuestra Santa Madre Yglesia, Our Holy Mother Church." He identified himself as a native of New Mexico and a son of Ana Velásquez and an unknown father. According to a marriage certificate, he was married on April 19, 1682, with Juana López, a daughter of Sargento Mayor Diego López Sambrano and María de Suaso, all natives of New Mexico,

originally residents of the Villa de Santa Fe.[16] From this union
there was born a son, Domingo Domínguez, and a daughter, María
Domínguez (see genealogical chart), prior to the death of Juana
López.[17]

A widower by 1692, José Domínguez de Mendoza, holding
the military rank of Alférez, participated in the efforts of don Diego de Vargas to restore New Mexico to the Spanish crown. In
this endeavor, he was reunited in October 1692 with his sister,
Juana Domínguez, who had been taken captive by the Pueblo
Indians during the revolt of 1680.[18] In May 1697, mention was
made of the "orphan children of José Domínguez, Domingo and
María." They were recipients of livestock in a distribution made at
Santa Fe by Governor Vargas.[19] Apparently, Domínguez was away
at this time; however, soon after this he entered into his second
marriage with Gerónima Varela de Losada Perea, by whom he
had at least one known child.[20] It is the lineage from this second
union that will provide the example of sacramental records used
to construct a genealogy from the late seventeenth century into
the mid-late nineteenth century beginning with the death record
of Gerónima Varela at Santa Fe:[21]

Geronima   en once dias del mes de Abril de mill
                setesientos, y veinte y siete a^s. murio
                Geronima barela Biuda de Joseph,
                Domingues se recibio todos los santos
                sacramentos, y esta su cuerpo en su capilla
                de Nuestra Señora, y p^a. q^e conste de gratis
                lo firme
                         Fr. Joseph Antt^o Guerrero (rubric)

This record, dated April 11, 1727, identifies Gerónima Varela as
the widow of José Domínguez. Before her death she received "all
the holy sacraments," most likely referring to the sacraments of
penance, extreme unction, and Eucharist. This record is characteristic of the majority of burial entries. Burial records customarily began with either the date of burial or the date of death, followed by the name of the deceased. If the individual was married, the name of the spouse was recorded. The burial record of
Gerónima Varela indicates her body was interred "en su capilla
de Nuestra Señora" ("in her chapel of Our Lady"), a testament to

**Two Lineages from Ana Velásquez
to María Viviana Martín, 1660-1827**

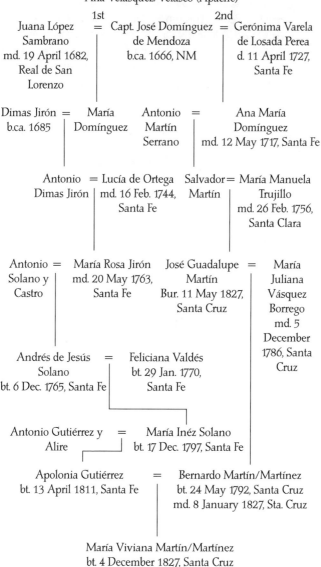

Ana Velásquez/Velasco (Apache)

	1st		2nd	

Juana López = Capt. José Domínguez = Gerónima Varela
Sambrano   de Mendoza   de Losada Perea
md. 19 April 1682,   b.ca. 1666, NM   d. 11 April 1727,
Real de San   Santa Fe
Lorenzo

Dimas Jirón = María   Antonio =   Ana María
b.ca. 1685 | Domínguez   Martín   Domínguez
                                  Serrano   md. 12 May 1717, Santa Fe

Antonio = Lucía de Ortega   Salvador = María Manuela
Dimas Jirón | md. 16 Feb. 1744,   Martín | Trujillo
                      Santa Fe   md. 26 Feb. 1756,
                                                            Santa Clara

Antonio = María Rosa Jirón   José Guadalupe =   María
Solano y | md. 20 May 1763,   Martín   Juliana
Castro   Santa Fe   Bur. 11 May 1827,   Vásquez
                                        Santa Cruz   Borrego
                                                               md. 5
                                                               December
Andrés de Jesús = Feliciana Valdés   1786, Santa
Solano   bt. 29 Jan. 1770,   Cruz
bt. 6 Dec. 1765, Santa Fe   Santa Fe

Antonio Gutiérrez y   =   María Inéz Solano
Alire   bt. 17 Dec. 1797, Santa Fe

Apolonia Gutiérrez   =   Bernardo Martín/Martínez
bt. 13 April 1811, Santa Fe   bt. 24 May 1792, Santa Cruz
                                        md. 8 January 1827, Sta. Cruz

María Viviana Martín/Martínez
bt. 4 December 1827, Santa Cruz

her devotion to Mary. During the colonial period, most people were buried in the local church or in a local chapel.

The one known daughter of José Domínguez and Gerónima Varela, Ana María Domínguez, was born circa 1698-99. She was first married to Pedro Antonio de Moya, a son of Mexico City natives Antonio de Moya Rivera y Moreno and Francisca Antonia Morales de Guijosa.[22] Pedro Antonio died at Taos in November 1716, and within the year Ana María entered into her second marriage at Santa Fe on May 12, 1717. The book of marriages for this period in Santa Fe no longer exists, but a certificate of this marriage was recorded as the concluding document in the prenuptial investigation records for Ana María and her second husband, Antonio de Jesús Martín Serrano, a native of Chimayó in the parish of Santa Cruz de la Cañada and a son of Cristóbal Martín Serrano and doña Antonia Moraga y Montaño.[23] The certificate reads:

> Zertifico yo Fray joseph Ant° Guerrero cura mi nisterio desta villa de Santa fe que leydos las tres amonestaciones y vista la zertificacion del p^e. p^l. Fray Juan Mingues cura ministro de la villa nueba de Santa Cruz y no habiendo resultado de unas, y otras (amonestaciones) case *in facie eclesie* ana Maria Domingues (viuda de Pedro de Moya) con Antt° de Jesus Martin el dia dose de mayo de mil setesientos y dies y siete años siendo testigos aberlos casar Diego Moraga y Juana de Moraga y p^a que conste lo firme
>
> Fray Joseph Ant° Guerrero (rubric)

This record refers to the three traditional banns of matrimony which were read to the congregation at church. Any person with information concerning any possible impediment to the proposed union would have the opportunity and obligation of sharing the information as part of the prenuptial investigation. Most importantly, it was necessary to identify if couples were related within the fourth degree of consanguinity. If so, then a dispensation from the Archbishop of Durango was required before New Mexico couples could be married according to the rites of the Roman Catholic Church. There were no impediments to the marriage of

Ana María Domínguez and Antonio de Jesús Martín. After the parish priests of Santa Fe and Santa Cruz collected information about the couple, they received the sacrament of marriage on May 12, 1717, in Santa Fe. The couple appears to have settled in the Chimayó area where many of their descendants resided for the next 120 years. A son of this couple, Salvador de Orta Martín, was married at the church of Santa Clara Pueblo on February 26, 1756, as this record documents:[24]

> Executadas las dilig[s]. que ordena el S[to] concilio, y no haviendo resultado en impedimiento casse i vele *in facie eclicie* a Salbador de Orta Martin vesino de la Cañada hijo de Antonio Martin y Ana Maria Domingues con D[a] Maria Manuela Truxillo Vecina de el Puesto de chama, hija de Pablo truxillo y Francisca marquez ambos Españoles fueron Padrinos D[n] Carlos Lopez, y M[a] Fran[ca] truxillo, y D[n] Carlos miraval: lo qual para q[e] conste lo firme en veinte y seis de Febrero año de mil setesientos sincuenta y seis
>
> Fray Mariano Rodríguez de la Torre (rubric)

The opening sentence of this record states that the pre-marital investigation (*diligencias*) had been executed according to the order of the "Santo Concilio," referring to the Holy Council of Trent. No impediment to the union of this couple was found and they were married and veiled ("casse i vele"), receiving the nuptial blessing in accordance with the rite of the Catholic sacrament of marriage. This particular marriage record is an exception to the majority of such records of this period because it provides the names of the parents of the couple. Most commonly the couple and the sponsors and witnesses were the only ones named in a marriage record. There was no standard form established at this time for recording the names of parents of married couples as part of the sacramental records of marriage. This type of information was collected during of the prenuptial investigation process, particularly in the petition of marriage written to the parish priest by the intended groom.

As long-time residents of Chimayó, Salvador de Orta Martín and doña María Manuela Trujillo raised nine known children

and were members of the parish church of Santa Cruz.[25]
Compadrazgo relations created close relationships with members
of the Gómez, Sánchez, Tafoya, and García de Noriega families,
as well as with several Martín and Trujillo relatives. One of the
sons of this couple was José Guadalupe Martín, born circa 1761
and married at the church of Santa Cruz on December 5, 1786, to
María Juliana Vásquez Borrego y Gurulé.[26] Six of the known
children of this couple were baptized at Santa Cruz Church, and
compadrazgo relations were formed with members of the González
and Sandoval families as well as with other Martín relatives. José
Guadalupe Martín lived to be about sixty-six years of age. He
died at Chimayó on May 10, 1827, and was buried the following
day at the church of Santa Cruz for the cost of "ocho pesos de la
tierra" (eight pesos of the land), most likely eight pesos worth of
goods.[27] His burial record indicates he received the sacraments of
penance, extreme unction, and the Eucharist before his death.
The record reads:

Jose Guadalupe	En esta Sta Ygl^a parroq^a. de la Cañada a los
Martin	once dias de el mes de Mayo de mil
Adulto	ochociento beinte y siete, di sepultura
	Ecca. En tob^a de ocho pesos de la tierra
	al Cadaber de José Guadalupe Martín q.
	murio en Chimallo el dia diez; resivio
	los sacramentos de la penitencia sagrado
	biatico y extrema uncion; fue casado con
	Juliana Borrego y p^a. q^e conste lo firme
	Manuel Rada (rubric)

This burial record begins by identifying the church and the day
of the burial. José Guadalupe was buried in the church of Santa
Cruz at the cost of eight pesos. Customary fees for the various
sacraments were set by the diocese. The cost was higher for people
identified as *españoles* as compared to the lower cost for mulattos
and Indians.[28]

The eldest son of José Guadalupe Martín and María Juliana
Vásquez Borrego was born May 20, 1792 at El Potrero, across the
streambed from Chimayó. Four days after his birth he was taken
by his parents and padrinos (godparents) to the church of Santa
Cruz to receive the sacrament of baptism and be welcomed as a

new member of the Catholic community. Christened as Bernardino Martín, but also known as Bernardo Martínez, he was part of the large generation of New Mexicans who were born citizens of Spain, married as citizens of the Mexican Republic, and died as citizens of the United States of America. His baptismal record is characteristic of the standard form which such records were written:[29]

Bernardino En la V^a de la Cañada en Veinte, y guarto
de mayo de nov^{ta} y dos: Yo Fr. Ramon
Gonz^z Mtro de dha V^a Bap^{te} solemnente
a Bernardino q^e nacío dia Veinte hijo
legitimo de Jose Guadalupe Martin, y
de Juliana Borrego: fueron Padrinos
Pedro Martin y Ygnacia Garcia V^s todos
del Potrero aguienes adverti el
Parentesco espiritual, y lo De mas de su
oblig^{on}, y lo firme
                Fr. Ramon Gonzalez (rubric)

This entry contains the typical information recorded in baptismal records. The date of baptism was written followed by the name of the presiding priest and the name of the infant who was solemnly baptized. If the age of the child was not provided, sometimes the day of birth was recorded. This did not occur consistently during the colonial period. After the parents were named, the names of the godparents were given. The words "parentesco espiritual" referred to the spiritual relationship in parallel to consanguinity or affinity which prevented marriage of godparent and godchild without a special dispensation. The godparents were also obliged to see that the child received religious guidance in the observance of the traditions of the Catholic faith. These relationships also placed the godparents in a special relationship with the parents of the child as *compadres*, co-parents.

At the age of twenty-nine, Bernardo was married to Santa Fe native Apolonia Gutiérrez, herself being a descendant of José Domínguez de Mendoza and his first wife Juana López Sambrano (see genealogical chart). Apolonia was baptized at Santa Fe on April 13, 1811, and was a daughter of Antonio Gutiérrez y Alire and María Inés Solano y Valdés. When she was a child, her

parents came to reside at El Potrero. According to her testimony
given as part of the prenuptial investigation, she had known
Bernardo since she was a child. At the age of 15, she was married
to him at the church of Santa Cruz on January 8, 1827. Bernardo
was among the first grantees of the Mora Land Grant in 1830,
and relocated his family to the Mora area. From late March 1848
until October 1848, he served in the U.S. Army as a member of
the Missouri Volunteers in New Mexico under the command of
Lt. Col. William Gilpin.[30]

Bernardo and Apolonia were the parents of two known children, both of whom received the sacrament of baptism at the
church of Santa Cruz. Their only daughter was born at El Potrero
on December 1, 1827, and baptized three days later. Her baptismal record provides an excellent example of a new standard in
recording the sacrament of baptism implemented just before the
beginning of Mexican Republic era in 1821. In contrast to earlier
baptismal entries, the names of paternal and maternal grandparents were recorded. This became a common, although not always consistent, practice for the next four to six decades. María
Viviana's baptismal record reads:[31]

> En este St[a] ygl[a] Parroq. de la Cañada a los cuatro dias
> de el mes de Dbre. de mil ochocientos veinte y siete
> yo el Presb[o]. Manuel de Jesus Rada Cura prop[o]. Vicco.
> y Juez Ecco. de dha villa Bautise solem[te] a una niña
> de tres dias de Nacida a la qe. le puso por nombre
> Maria Viviana es hija Lexitima de Bernardo Martin
> y de polonia Gutierres Lexitim[te] casados feligreses
> de esta parroquia: son Abuelos paternos Jose
> Guadalupe Martin y Maria Borrego: son Abuelos
> Maternos Ant[o] Gutierrez y M[a] Ynes Solano: todos
> del Potrero: fueron padrinos Mariano de Aguero y
> Dolores Sanches: a los qe. adberti el parentesco
> Espiritual y oblig[n] p[a]. con su hijada p[a]. qe. conste lo
> firme
>
> Man[l] Rada

An entry such as this is an exceptional genealogical record, documenting the names of three generations spanning almost seventy years.

María Viviana Martínez was co-founder of three distinct families of the Mora Valley: Bóne, Ébel, and Metzgar. She broke with social tradition in her relationship with men who had come to New Mexico over the Santa Fe Trail. One was of French-Canadian origin, and two were of German origin. Nonetheless, her children were raised in the Catholic faith that she had inherited from her ancestors. This faith continued to be observed and practiced by her descendants into the twentieth century. The names of her known descendants are recorded in sacramental records of various churches across northern New Mexico and southern Colorado.

The documentation of the lineage presented above provides one of countless examples of how sacramental records have preserved the genealogy of New Mexico families. In the past decade, there has been a dramatic increase of interest among people with roots in New Mexico to research their family genealogy. Often this work leads to the discovery of common ancestors shared by individuals who had no knowledge of their distant relationship. The diligent work of Fray Angélico Chávez and the dedication of the Archdiocese of Santa Fe to preserving and making available its archival documents to the public has been instrumental in nurturing this interest. Today, more people than before seek to uncover and restore the names of ancestors long forgotten. By documenting our family genealogy we identify our connection to ancestors and begin to develop an understanding of how the decisions they made in life have affected our own.

Although the surviving records of baptisms, confirmation, marriage, and burial are a valuable storehouse of genealogical information, they are also records of the transmission of the Catholic faith, evidence of the continuous building of the Church, generation by generation. As signs of faith, the sacraments sanctify the passage of life from birth to death. The sacraments are signs of the unity of the church, and they are keystones of the expression of the Catholic faith that has endured in New Mexico for four hundred years.

40 SEEDS OF STRUGGLE/HARVEST OF FAITH

Notes

1. Richard P. McBrien, *Catholicism* (Minneapolis: Winston Press, 1970), II:734-40.
2. Ibid., 744-45.
3. George P. Hammond and Agapito Rey, eds., *Narratives of the Coronado Expedition* (Albuquerque: University of New Mexico Press, 1940). George P. Hammond, ed., *The Rediscovery of New Mexico, 1580-1594: The Explorations of Chamuscado, Espejo, Castaño de Sosa, Morlete and Leyva de Bonilla, and Humaña* (Albuquerque: University of New Mexico Press, 1966).
4. George P. Hammond and Agapito Rey, eds., *Don Juan de Oñate: Colonizer of New Mexico, 1595-1628* (Albuquerque: University of New Mexico Press, 1956), I:314.
5. Ibid.
6. Ibid., II:729, 735.
7. Fray Angélico Chávez, O.F.M., *Archives of the Archdiocese of Santa Fe, 1678-1900* (St. Paul: North Central Publishing Company, 1957), 3.
8. Ibid.; Archives of the Archdiocese of Santa Fe (AASF), Roll #23, (Tesuque Pueblo, Baptisms 1694-1727).
9. Chávez, *Archives of the Archdiocese of Santa Fe*, 3; Eleanor B. Adams and Fray Angélico Chávez, eds. and trans., *The Missions of New Mexico, 1776: A description by Fray Francisco Atanasio Domínguez with Other Contemporary Documents* (Albuquerque: University of New Mexico Press, 1956), 234-237.
10. Chávez, *Archives of the Archdiocese of Santa Fe*, 4.
11. Ibid.
12. McBrien, *Catholicism*, 733.
13. The oldest group is the New Mexico Genealogical Society based in Albuquerque, and established around 1960. In the past decade, two other groups with a strong focus on New Mexico Hispano roots were formed and membership has grown considerably in subsequent years: The Genealogical Society of Hispanic America established in 1989 and based in Denver, with chapters in Pueblo, Trinidad, and Southern California; and The Hispanic Genealogical Research Center of New Mexico, formed in 1993 and based in Albuquerque.
14. Archivo General de la Nación, México, "Concurso de Peñalosa," Vol. I, Legajo 1, No. 2: 233.
15. Fray Angélico Chávez, *Origins of New Mexico Families: A Genealogy of the Spanish Colonial Period*, Revised Edition (Santa Fe: Museum of New Mexico Press, 1992), 27.
16. AASF Roll #59, Diligencias Matrimoniales (DM), 1682 (no. 5) Guadalupe del Paso.

17. Spanish Archives of New Mexico (SANM), Series I, no. 233; SANM, Series II, no. 65, frames 50-80, family no. 174.
18. John L. Kessell et al., eds., *By Force of Arms: The Journals of Don Diego de Vargas, 1691-1693* (Albuquerque: University of New Mexico Press, 1989), 525.
19. SANM II, no. 65, frames 50-80, family no. 174.
20. SANM I, no. 233; Fray Angélico Chávez, "New Mexico Roots. Ltd: A Demographic Perpesctive from Genealogical, Historical, and Geographical Data found in the Diligencias Matrimoniales, or Pre-Nuptial Investigations (1678-1869) of the Archives of the Archdiocese of Santa Fe," Santa Fe, 1982, Vol. 6: 1100, DM 1714, Oct. 1 (no. 4) Santa Fe.
21. AASF Roll #40, Santa Fe, Burials 1726-1834.
22. José Antonio Esquibel and John B. Colligan, "The Spanish Recolonization of New Mexico: An Account of the Families Recruited at Mexico City in 1693," unpublished manuscript.
23. AASF Roll #61, DM 1717, April 28 (no.2), Santa Fe.
24. AASF Roll #12, Santa Clara, Marriages 1728-1805.
25. Eight of the nine known children of Salvador de Orta Martín and María Manuela Trujillo were baptized (bt.) at the church of Santa Cruz: 1) José Guadalupe, born circa 1760-62; 2) Ygnacio, bt. November 8, 1761; 3) Lorenza, bt. July 18, 1764; 4) Antonia Josefa, bt. January 27, 1767; 5) María Damiana, bt. October 15, 1773; 6) María Andrea de Jesús, bt. December 3, 1775; 7) Salvador de Jesús, bt. July 2, 1776; 8) María Catalina Rafaela, bt. April 7, 1781; and 9) Paula Guadalupe, bt. March 10, 1783.
26. María Juliana Vásquez Borrgeo was baptized at the church of San Felipe Pueblo on December 25, 1772. She was a daughter of Diego Vásquez Borrego and Francisca Gurulé.
27. AASF Roll #39, Santa Cruz, Burials 1726-1859.
28. AASF Roll #51, Loose Documents, 1730, no. 4, Albuquerque; AASF Roll #52, Loose Documents, 1754, no. 3, Abiquiú, and 1760, no. 2, Isleta.
29. AASF Roll #13, Santa Cruz, Baptisms 1781-1794.
31. AASF Roll #6, Santa Cruz, Baptisms 1823-1832.

The Architectural Background of the New Mexico Missions

James E. Ivey

For almost sixty years, the architecture of the missions of New Mexico have been studied in isolation. George Kubler, who published his analysis of New Mexico mission architecture in 1940, emphasized the differences between the missions of New Mexico and those of Mexico in the previous century. Because he combined – homogenized – the physical evidence of the seventeenth, eighteenth, and nineteenth century churches to be found in the province, he obscured the distinctive set of characteristics peculiar to the developmental period in New Mexican mission church architecture in the seventeenth century. As a result, Kubler saw evidence for only the simplest of churches, requiring little craftsmanship.[1]

Kubler considered the New Mexico missions to be nothing more than the adaptation of the construction techniques of the local Puebloan architects to the needs of the Spanish conquerors. In his final summary of New Mexico churches in 1959, he dismissed the construction style as an architecture of "sun-dried clay," the result of "the resistance of the Indians to learning European techniques of construction." The only accomplishment of note was that "the friars succeeded in achieving Baroque light effects by introducing a transverse window, spanning the nave at the chancel, between the roof-levels of the nave and sanctuary."[2] Recent research, however, shows that although this harsh assessment might describe the churches of the nineteenth century at their lowest possible common denominator, it hardly applies to buildings constructed between 1598 and the Pueblo Rebellion of 1680.

Pre-Revolt church architecture was a dynamic endeavor, with clear phases of development. These fall into three general groups, which I have called "Temporary," "Interim," and "Permanent" churches. The first chapels and churches built in New Mexico were temporary structures; they were adapted pueblo rooms, or small flat-roofed structures built of stone or adobe, or buildings of *jacal*, with post walls covered with clay and roofed with thatch. These sorts of temporary buildings were used everywhere, from the valley of Mexico to the Yucatan and Florida peninsulas.

In most places, these temporary buildings were soon replaced with reasonably substantial stone buildings that would serve the needs of the mission community for some time. These churches were simplified versions of the generic back-country churches of northern Mexico along the Camino Real de Tierra Adentro. The Franciscans considered them interim buildings because they were not the standard, full-sized churches suitable as permanent, final buildings at the various missions. As the mission frontier moved northward, these interim mission church became fairly standard-ized. By the late sixteenth century, as the effort to establish a colony in New Mexico was begun, the standardized elements had be-come part of a "frontier" mission design, such as at Tlahuelilpan, built about 1560 near Tula in Hidalgo. Tlahuelilpan is a single-nave church, without transepts or side aisles. It is a relatively small building, perhaps twenty feet wide and eighty feet long.

This sort of church was usually covered with a simple wooden roof. Wooden roofs mean no additional stone cutting or gather-ing for vaults and massive buttresses; at the same time, a vaulted roof could be added later, when time or money permitted. The simplest version of the wooden roof is familiar in New Mexico as the flat, viga-supported, earth-covered roof. This basic roof was used in many places after the Spanish conquest of Mexico in 1520, especially on the mission frontier as it expanded from Mexico City.[3]

Not until about 1550 did the vaulted church became the goal at the more prosperous missions in significant towns near Mexico City; before this date, the principal buildings were not vaulted throughout, although some major buildings were con-structed with a vault over the sanctuary or sacristy. The most familiar of the early vaulted Franciscan missions is San Diego de Huejotzingo, Huejotzingo, Mexico (Figure 2, A).

"Interim" frontier church buildings were built sometimes of adobe bricks but more often of rough field-stone; shaped ashlar blocks were rare away from the areas where stone-cutting was a standard practice among the Indians. Walls tended to be thin if the building was intended to have a wooden roof and thicker if a vaulted roof was hoped for. If vaulting was eventually attempted, buttresses were usually added outside the original walls to help resist the new forces that the vaults imposed on the structure.[4]

Although some mission churches in principal towns were designed and built with vaulting as part of the original intent after 1550, in poorer or more peripheral areas, the missionaries could not afford the services of a mason, and the church roof remained a wooden structure for some time. In a few cases the original roofs still survive today, as is apparently the case at Tlahuelilpan, mentioned above, or the Templo de la Ermita, at Nombre de Dios, Durango, built by Franciscan missionaries about 1560 on the Camino Real heading north toward Santa Bárbara and, eventually, New Mexico.[5]

Most of the interior lighting for these churches came from several windows along one or both sides of the nave. The sanctuary was raised a few steps above the nave floor, and its roof was a few feet higher than the nave roof. This difference in roof line developed over time, with the sanctuary roof becoming higher towards the end of the sixteenth century. The sanctuary was separated from the nave either by an *arco toral*, an arch of cut stone constructed by a master mason, or by a support of massive wooden beams built by the Franciscans themselves. This arch supported the facing wall of the somewhat higher sanctuary roof. Some churches had one or two small windows in this facing wall. Kubler suggested that sometime in the last decades of the sixteenth century this practice led to the development of the transverse clerestory window, used at many churches in New Mexico.[6] The best surviving example is the church of San José de Gracia at Las Trampas, New Mexico.

This simple building style was brought to New Mexico as the first fairly substantial church to be used at the new missions of the province. The Franciscan fronier began expanding from

Figure 1. Temporary Mission Buildings

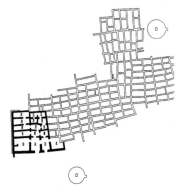

A. The convento and church in the pueblo rooms of Mound 7,
San Buenaventura de Las Humanas, ca. 1630.

B. The visita mission buildings at
San José de Giusewa, ca. 1598.

San Gabriel and its three visitas in 1609, when the colony changed
from proprietary, under Oñate, to royal. During the earlier years,
from 1598 to 1610, the New Mexico expedition was strongly
military, and the evangelical effort was far more tentative. The
churches built from 1598 to 1609 were temporary; they were
converted pueblo rooms or small, shed-like structures, little more
than shacks in which mass could be said (Figure 1, A and B).
With the changeover from a proprietary to a royal colony in
1609, however, the support for the Franciscan program increased
greatly.

When the major missionary effort began in New Mexico in
1610, the simple interim church of the frontier was put into use

Figure 2, A-F. Typical Mission Plans in Pre-Revolt New Mexico.

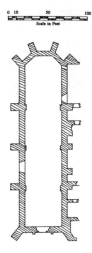

A. San Diego de Huejotzingo, ca. 1550.

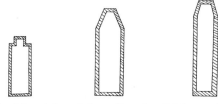

B. San Miguel de   C. Santa Cruz de   D. Nuestra Señora de
Analco, ca. 1610   Galisteo, ca. 1610   la Asunción de Zia,
                                           ca. 1612

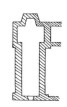

E. Nuestra Señora   F. Nuestra Señora
de los Ángeles de   del Socorro, ca.
Pecos, ca. 1617   1626

Figure 2, G-J Typical Mission Plans in Pre-Revolt New Mexico

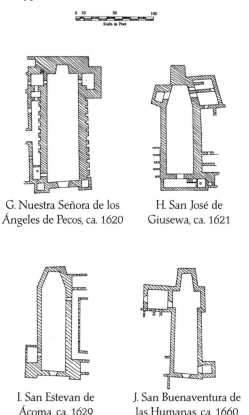

G. Nuestra Señora de los
Ángeles de Pecos, ca. 1620

H. San José de
Giusewa, ca. 1621

I. San Estevan de
Ácoma, ca. 1629

J. San Buenaventura de
las Humanas, ca. 1660

here as virtually everywhere else on the expanding frontier of New Spain when the Franciscans began construction of a church more lasting than the converted pueblo room or thatched jacal church that served for the first few years. From 1609 to 1620, the Franciscans built eleven new churches; those for which we have some description are typical "interim" missions (Figure 2, B-E). The pre-1620 churches about which we have some information in New Mexico were all relatively narrow, ranging from twenty to twenty-eight feet wide. They varied far more in length, between sixty-seven and one hundred fifteen feet. All had either polygonal or shouldered apses and flat, beam-supported roofs; there is no evidence for the use of transverse clerestory windows in these simple buildings.[7] With the addition of a few buttresses to help support the walls, a master mason could even roof some of these churches with stone vaults, as had been done with so many of the churches of Mexico that began with wooden roofs. Those built of adobe would retain a wooden roof, or they would have to be replaced.

Beginning in the 1620s, a powerful change in church design became apparent in New Mexico; churches at some of the important pueblos receiving new missionaries were built in an overwhelming style much larger than the typical "Interim" church (Figure 2, E and G). These permanent churches, best exemplified by Nuestra Señora de los Angeles at Pecos, embodied experiments with other building plans than the simple, single-nave church and other roofing designs than the basic flat viga-supported structure. The change can best be illustrated by comparing the plans of the two churches of Pecos at this time.

The smaller church was begun in 1617, and as can be seen is a typical member of the "temporary" group of buildings then serving as the mission churches of New Mexico. The larger church, begun about 1620 and completed about 1625, is the first of the New Mexico "Great Churches." Note that although the Pecos Great Church gives the impression of being cruciform, it is not; the apparent transepts are a side chapel for the Santo Niño on the upper side and the sacristy on the lower side.

The idea of the Great Church was clearly well-received; in 1621, the Franciscans began San José de Giusewa at the place now called Jemez Springs State Park, using the same Great Church approach (Figure 2, H).

San José at Jemez Springs has a sort of generic resemblance to Los Angeles at Pecos in that it is very large and has the appearance of being cruciform, while actually being a single-naved church. There, however, the resemblance ends; the two are quite dissimilar in their overall design philosophy (Figure 3).

In 1626 somewhat smaller churches of this general type were designed at both Quaraí and Socorro (see Figure 2, F, for a plan of Socorro). These two churches were rather small and plain when compared to the spectacular structures of Los Angeles and San

Figure 3. Cross-Section of San José de Giusewa, Jémez Springs, New Mexico, ca. 1621

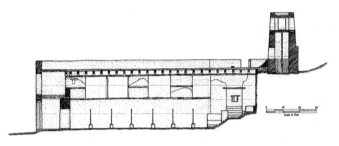

José, for they are more like the pre-1620 churches in their general dimensions; but these two buildings are the earliest known churches with a true cruciform plan in New Mexico. And Quaraí is the first for which we can demonstrate the certain existence of a transverse clerestory window. The available architectural evidence indicates that some form of simple transverse clerestory window was put into use by the 1590s in the general area of the Franciscan missionary province of Nueva Galicia, somewhere around Durango or Santa Barbara; the transverse window was not invented in New Mexico. Pecos, started six years earlier, probably had a similar window, to judge from its plan, and that would be the first use of this element of design in New Mexico.[8]

The complexity of plan and elevation, the "simulation," if you will, of transepts in the early 1620s, the use of true transepts and the transverse clerestory window by 1626, and the apparent introduction of intricate and highly decorated ceiling designs during this period such as a gabled wooden roof at Sandia all suggest that the driving inspiration behind this abrupt change in the typical design of mission churches in New Mexico was the arrival of the Baroque Counterreformation esthetics in the province about 1618 or 1619. Certainly this is the explanation given by George Kubler, who viewed the transverse clerestory window as a distinctly Baroque design element.[9]

It is surprising that the use of these elements in New Mexico in 1619 and the early 1620s predates the appearance of Baroque architecture in Mexico. The Franciscans of New Mexico were apparently at the cutting edge of this new way of thinking about buildings and their relationship to people. It seems reasonable to propose that the new friars arriving in New Mexico about 1620, several of whom were from Spain, had been inspired by the intellectual movement just beginning to sweep through Europe, and that some of these men decided to design their churches in a larger, more permanent and dramatic style, as at Los Angeles de Pecos, San José de Giusewa, San Estevan de Ácoma, or the unfinished San Buenaventura de Las Humanas, begun in 1660 (Figure 2, G, H, I, J). Meanwhile, the small interim church that had served in New Mexico for the last two or three decades continued to be used only in minor pueblos.

Since no master masons or master sculptors were available in the province, these churches had to be designed within the already existing building technology of the province. At the same time, however, they could be made to incorporate elements that broke away from the old Franciscan, late-medieval, apostolic simplicity and incorporate some of the new esthetic elements that were becoming popular in Spain, such as a greater complexity of plan in the form of transepts and dramatic lighting in the form of the transverse clerestory window or the large lateral clerestories at Giusewa.

Kubler was wrong in his assessment of the churches of New Mexico, at least those of the pre-Revolt period: rather than uninspired structures using only adaptations of local construction methods, they were instead part of the general pattern of church development everywhere on the northern frontier and indeed everywhere in the Catholic Church. It is surprising that this strong continuity of design has not been discussed in any study of the architectural history of the borderlands. Perhaps Kubler's masterful but minimizing evaluation of New Mexico churches left students with the conviction that there was nothing left to be said. Clearly, though, there is a great deal more waiting to be discovered in the architectural history of the missions of New Mexico.

Notes

1. George Kubler, *The Religious Architecture of New Mexico* (Albuquerque: University of New Mexico Press, 1972).

2. George Kubler and Martin Soria, *Art and Architecture in Spain and Portugal and their American Dominions, 1500 to 1800* (Baltimore: Penguin Books, 1959), p. 78.

3. Rafael López Guzmán *et al.*, *Arquitectura y Carpintería Mudéjar en Nueva España* (México: Azabache, 1992), p. 94, "El empleo de madera en las cubiertas estuvo, evidentemente, relacionado con la falta de recursos económicos." See also Miguel Toussaint, *Arte Colonial en México*, p. 64: "El empleo de los alfarjes fue general por una razón sencilla: era más fácil tender techos de madera donde ésta abundaba y los carpinteros eran hábiles, que no bóvedas, difíciles de construir y más costosas."

4. George Kubler, *Mexican Architecture of the Sixteenth Century* (New Haven: Yale University Press, 1948), pp. 267-68.

5. Unfortunately, these simple churches have been of little interest to architectural historians, and no plans for them are yet available.

6. Kubler, *Mexican Architecture*, pp. 273-74.

7. The plan of the church of Santa Cruz de Galisteo is based on measurements made during a site visit in 1991, while the plan of Nuestra Señora de la Asunción de Zia is derived from a plan made by George Kubler in the 1930s, the description of the church given by Fray Francisco Domínguez in 1776, translated in Domínguez, *The Missions of New Mexico, 1776*, Eleanor B. Adams and Fray Angélico Chávez, tr. and an. (Albuquerque: University of New Mexico Press, 1956), and the strong likelihood that the eighteenth century building is rebuilt from the partially destroyed pre-Revolt structure; see Domínguez, *Missions*, pp. 171-72 and note 2.

8. A late sixteenth-century transverse clerestory on a church has been described in Leon, Guanajuato, by Jorge Olvera; see *Southwestern Mission Research Center Newsletter*, v.20 n.66 (May, 1986), p. 8. Olvera described the building as a fortified chapel with a transverse clerestory window as "very similar to the religious architecture of New Mexico ... the southernmost example of the style of the missions of New Mexico" and possibly among the prototypes of the "New Mexican" style. Olvera's conclusions are supported by the research of Gloria Gifford, who reports finding a transverse-clerestoried church in Madera, Chihuahua, dating to the sixteenth or seventeenth century.

9. Domínguez, *Missions*, p. 139; Kubler, *Religious Architecture*, p. 59.

El Farol Indiano:
The Administration of Sacraments
to the Natives of New Spain, 1713

Joseph P. Sánchez

In his *Farol Indiano*[1], published in 1713, Father Manuel Pérez, an Augustinian priest, explained that his manual came about because there was a need to understand the relationship between Church doctrine and the native populations which missionaries served. He humbly disclaimed the ideas contained in the *Farol Indiano* were his own: "It is not my intention that this booklet be applauded for its brevity, or for its rhetoric, or for its fine wording, but for the substance it contains, since it is not mine but that of the learned and grave authors who are cited in the appropriate places; what is mine is any imperfection or misunderstanding in it."[2] Father Pérez's concerns were about misconceptions and misunderstandings that resulted between Christian doctrine and customs practiced by Indian peoples. He felt that there were moral issues implicit in doctrine which had been developed in earlier centuries and which ought not include Indians who were neither known nor considered by the early Church Fathers. Such Christian customs and privileges, he felt, had been applied "to the rest of the people [Spaniards] by moralists but did not concern Indians, according to the practice and experiences which I have had with all of them. And, to shed light on this, I propose a few comments for whoever wants to read them and practice them."[3] In the *Farol Indiano* Catholic doctrine and Indian culture come together in an attempt by missionaries to reconcile the two. The doctrinal conflict among churchmen permitted missionaries who were priests to minister only five of the seven sacraments to the natives of the New World. Holy Orders and Confirmation were excluded for they were reserved to the administration of bishops. Thus Baptism, Penance, Holy Communion, Matrimony, and Extreme Unction were the permissible sacraments to be administered by missionaries to natives.

In stressing his point that the natives were spiritually different from their European counterparts, Father Pérez was quick to state the feelings of many missionaries regarding their general views about the natives they encountered in New Spain. Of them he wrote with unsparing colonial bias: "They are people quite rustic, and yet these Indians are so intelligent that the ministers are daily forced to be ever vigilant in order to avoid trouble either from their rudeness or their cleverness."[4] The statement alone appeared to reflect Pérez's desire to rationalize the colonial thought behind the ministering of the sacraments to the natives of New Spain.

Pérez identified several issues regarding baptism to Indians. The test for an invalid baptism, wrote Pérez, depended on three principal factors: its substance, its ritual (especially the verbal formula recited), and the intention of the minister and the recipient. For example, Pérez wrote that in the area of substance or form, according to the Roman Ritual of Paul V, ministers must first ask whether the infant to be baptized belongs to that parish in order that the baptism be valid. Ministers, similarly, should belong to the parish where the baptism occurs. Although a properly performed baptism would be valid regardless of who performed it, especially if it were done in an emergency, "it is the minister" wrote Pérez, "who commits a mortal sin for having usurped the jurisdiction and rights of the appropriate resident minister." If, however, the bishop of a given bishopric were to grant permission to any priest to minister sacraments to anyone, Pérez surmised that he would resolve many problems in the administration of baptism. In such cases a priest need only present himself to the proper Church officials in any jurisdiction and acquire the proper licenses to practice within it. This went for priests who ministered to Spanish parishioners as well as for priests who ministered to mission Indians. But what if an Indian baptized another Indian? Pérez recounted the example of an Indian baptizing his own son. His response was that the Indian has no jurisdiction for ministering the Sacrament of Baptism to anyone.[5]

There was, however, another issue regarding substance related to Baptism: some Indians felt they should have more than two godparents. If more than two were to be present at a Baptism, only the woman holding the child to be baptized and the man who pours water on the child's head are to be considered the *compadres*.[6] Whoever becomes a godparent, explained Pérez, must declare his or her name and state whether they were married. If married, only the person representing the baptized child would be the rightful godparent. That is, if both godparents were married to someone else, their spouses could not be godparents in that same baptism. Married couples could be godparents at the same baptism only if both had been chosen to do so.

When baptized, abandoned children (*expuestos*) would be so identified in the baptismal register. If an illegitimate child were baptized, the register would mention the mother's name and declare the father's name unknown.[7] So that the onus of illegitimacy should not follow the child, it was declared that it was the mother who had sinned by having a child out of wedlock.[8] In the Church's view, there were no illegitimate children, only illegitimate parents. Pérez, however, demurring from giving the mother a social stigma by placing her name in the baptism book for the world to see, instead preferred simply to write the words *hijo de la iglesia*.[9]

This approach did have one major drawback. If the baptism books, which were read only by the priests, did not contain the name of the mother, how would a future priest attending to the grown child's matrimony know whether the child was not marrying a relative, like a first cousin on the mother's side of the family? Also other information could not be known unless the grown child revealed it to the priest. For example, Pérez explained that one of his *hijas de la iglesia* came to him to perform her marriage. He noticed that at her baptism she was listed as an *hija de la iglesia*. Upon further discussion with her, he learned that, subsequent to her baptism, her mother married her natural father. Therefore she was no longer illegitimate, much less an *hija de la iglesia*. As Pérez apparently knew her mother in a different circumstance, he would not have known she was the mother of the baptized

child because her name was not in the baptism book, nor would
he have known about the mother's marriage to the natural father
had the young women not told him. *"¿Cómo se supiera?* – How
could it be known?" he wrote.

Again Pérez raised the question about Indians baptizing Indians as a *bona fide* ritual. This time his point was that if the Indian
baptized another using the words of the Church, would not a
baptism have taken place? The situation, such as an emergency,
could have warranted the baptism, and so too could the circumstance of a child newly born when no priest was in the vicinity.
Trying to unravel the relativity of the situation in contrast to the
absoluteness of Church doctrine, Pérez wrote:

> It is difficult to judge whether the baptism is valid or
> not when it is necessary to baptize one in a home.
> Even *gente de razón* [Christians; literally, people with
> reason] are very ignorant on this point…as they may
> administer such a sacrament when so many circum-
> stances may require that it be done and salvation
> may depend on it. It is difficult [to decide]. In the
> second part of his remarks, folio 224, number 46,
> Father Fray Juan Baptista states that it should be
> taught in the Indian pueblos so that they may learn
> the form of Baptism for those necessary cases. [His
> proposal] creates a morally impossible circum-
> stance.[10]

In the first place, argued Pérez, if a baptism had theoretically taken
place, how could a baptism be undone so that a person could be
re-baptized? The Council of Trent of 1646 stated that re-baptism is
nothing more than a second baptism. Unless it can be demonstrated that the first baptism was invalid, then re-baptism would
be useless. On the other hand, "the second baptism performed by
a Catholic priest may validate the first" by assuring that it was
done correctly in the way mandated by the Church. Still, Pérez
demurred in admitting that Indians were capable of administering the sacrament of Baptism because they, unlike Spanish frontiersmen, did not have the intelligence to do it correctly. In all
likelihood, mistakes could be made by them, he argued.[11] He had
little confidence in them especially if they lived far from Mexico

City where Spanish was spoken a tad better than in the frontier areas. He felt that Indians farther away from Mexico City were less capable of performing a baptism correctly. "In the pronunciation of the ritual," he wrote, "it is difficult for them because they pronounce Latin badly; regarding Castillian, those Indians outside of Mexico wanting to speak the language make a thousand mistakes instead....[Thus] in their own languages, there can be no valid baptism, and I defended that thesis in public at the Royal University in 1703."[12]

As it would affect all other sacraments, Fr. Pérez explained the importance of language in the administration of the sacraments.

> No one denies that in the ritual of the Sacrament of Baptism things are expressed similarly in a Romance language as in Latin: [that being the case] it is certain that the ritual is substantially changed for any of the sacraments, [thus] the sacrament is not made. Thus, I suppose, the ritual for Baptism as for the other sacraments is owing to the rigorous pronunciation of the words and that these are pronounced without metaphysics or tenuity, but as Christ said them and the Church Councils have so ordered.[13]

Pérez went on to explain that a baptism performed in Nahuatl would be doubtful in terms of its validity. In his discussion, he examined the Nahuatl word for baptism *quastequia* (which was formed from three words which could mean "*echar agua en la cabeza* – pour water on the head").[14] Finally, he concluded that the words and the syntax that formed its meaning were inadequate because upon further analysis they instead meant "*mojar la cabeza* – wet the head."

On the importance of using the exact words of Jesus Christ, Pérez argued that the words for making the sign of the cross in Spanish beginning with "En el nombre del Padre..." are similar to the Latin "In nomine Patris." The words mean "In the name of the Father..." unlike the Nahuatl words "*ica itocátzin*" which mean "*Con el nombre* – With the name." That, by way of example, argued Pérez, would nullify the sacrament of Baptism, or any other sacrament. Even words like *itocatzin* would not work because it means "in the name of the name," or "in the power of the name."[15] To Pérez it was evident that the lack of precision in Nahuatl robbed the ritual of the verbal accuracy needed to confer the sacrament validly. Pérez went a step further. He recommended that baptisms made previously in Nahuatl were "conditional baptisms" and ought to be performed again because such baptisms were invalid. He stated unequivocally that ministers were obligated to perform the ritual again conditionally for those who had been baptized in Nahuatl. Doubt was enough to justify invalidating baptisms made in the Mexican language. "If the words do not explain, then the baptism is in doubt,"[16] wrote Pérez. Even if the intent was there, the words would lead the ritual astray, he concluded.

If baptism, a ritual in which one received a first name, at least appeared familiar to native peoples, the sacrament of Penance, in which one confessed his faults to a priest and received forgiveness from him even though he had not been present at the moment of the offense, must have been unthinkable and alien to the indigenous people of the New World. Father Pérez expressed doubts about the substance (*materia*) of Penance in regard to the Indians. "The sacrament of Penance is the only remedy following the offense,"[17] wrote Pérez on the importance of confession, that is, admitting fault and asking forgiveness. He did not, however, believe that Indians ever made a good confession, for many of them confessed to a priest but once a year as required and only at Easter time. "The substance of a good confession is the mortal sins or at least some venial ones,"[18] he stated. In his view, he felt that Indians spent too little time in church and too much time in taverns, "from which spring many thefts, homicides, acts of incest, and many other offenses."[19] Critical of their confessions, Pérez lamented with a colonial voice, "They come to confess themselves saying three or four sins, and all too often venial sins and no more. It is unbelievable that in the entire year these people who are given to viciousness only commit these few sins. I am not persuaded. Here enters my first doubt."[20]

Pérez doubted whether the confessor should ask Indians to express their sins. He felt, nevertheless, that unless they are asked, the sins would not be expressed and the penitent would lose an opportunity to "open his eyes to things which he ignores." On the other hand, he believed that forcing Indians to state the number of times a sin was committed would only result in a lie. What could the confessor expect if he pointed out to them the evil of their ways? Pérez concluded that the confessor would only place himself in a weakened position because, like an eighteenth century doctor who gave advice, it would prove difficult for the priest to monitor whether the penitent truly sought to correct his wayward path. Pérez's doubts were many.[21]

But there were other complications. Pérez stated that hearing a confession from a woman of a different culture presented yet another problem. For example, he wrote,

> One should not ask a girl questions the same as a single woman or a married woman. If a married woman tells me nothing *circa carnalia* [about sexual matters], then I only need ask her if she has offended her husband: if she denies it, I go on to the next question—has she or has she not done it. If she says she has not, then I cannot open her eyes, although she cannot deny that she does not know of others who have not done it. Prudence by the confessor, then, is the most certain rule.... I don't forget to ask them about missing Mass, cursing, accusing falsely, [and] hating, for there are few who do not succumb to these sins.[22]

Regarding the number of times a sin was committed, Pérez noted that Church authorities in Europe expected Spaniards to be able to quantify their sins at the beginning of the confession so that the priest would have a good idea regarding the gravity of the offense to God. If they did not know exactly, Spaniards would give a number followed by the words *"mas o menos."* But, interjected Pérez, that kind of thinking did not work with Indians for several reasons. First, they generally confessed once a year and could not possibly, much less customarily, give a number. Second, they did not understand the concept of *"mas o menos."* Usually, the natives thought six or eight times was a large number. In that sense, they had answered the question, albeit not to the satisfaction of the confessor. And, third, Pérez and his fellow missionaries did not believe that the natives were capable of giving a number, for they usually came up short for what the priest thought would be a norm for a year of sinning.[23] In an effort to jog the penitent's memory, the priest would usually say: "My child, in case you have forgotten something, try to confess yourself of all that you may have forgotten as if you have remembered it and ask God to help you remember it either now or the next time you go to confession."[24]

On another issue, European churchmen did not understand the situation in New Spain concerning the obligation for attending Mass during a holy day. They expected travelers who were within one league of a church to change their travel plans and go to Mass or at very least, try to get to a church. If they were more than a league, however, then they were excused. Pérez argued that such an expectation worked well for Spaniards who were strong and in good health and who could take the time and energy to travel a league out of their way to hear Mass. By contrast, since Indians could usually travel further than a European in one day, Pérez asked if the distance should not be greater for them? He pondered whether they should be excused from Mass on a holy day if being beyond a league from a church was no problem for them? "The Indians (especially those outside of Mexico City) are so robust that I have seen many of them travel twelve leagues in one day," wrote Pérez. His point was that Indians should not easily be excused from Mass because of the one-league rule. He gave the example of Indians in one pueblo who had waited for a priest to come and say Mass. The priest fell ill on the way and never got to the village. However, Pérez felt that the healthiest or most robust Indians among them could have gone to a nearby village to hear Mass or go and find another priest, but they did not do so because they were beyond a league from the next nearest church and were thereby excused.[25]

Pérez also noted what could constitute a sin in the mind of a native. For example, he thought they believed that it was a sin to punish their children, that it was no sin to eat meat on a day of abstinence, that it was a sin to dream (because priests asked if they believed in dreams), and that it was a sin to know someone else's sins.[26] Overall, Pérez suspected that the natives were so rustic that the concept of repentance was beyond them.

The sacrament of the Holy Eucharist presented a different issue to Pérez and others who had labored long in the mission field. Doubts about administering of Holy Eucharist to Indians seemed always to trouble the minds of the clergy: Should Holy Communion be administered to the natives? Pérez briefly traced the history behind this question:

> When this kingdom was recently discovered there was so much doubt regarding the rationality of the Indians that Pope Paul III had to issue a Papal Bull calling attention to the point that their (the natives') incapacity was widespread. Today, regardless of His Holiness's Papal Bull, it is recognized that not only are they rational, they possess much intelligence (especially those in the area of Mexico City and other large areas). I propose this note so that the title question for this chapter does not appear superfluous, for to receive Holy Communion requires not only capacity but devotion and reverence as well.[27]

But he had serious doubts about Indians who lived far away from Mexico City or other metropolitan centers. There are, he wrote, "Indians whose incapacities are so great that their rationality can be doubted; so distributing the Holy Communion to them weighs heavy on one's mind...they live in the mountains and hills, and when priests go to their pueblos they receive him with much repugnance."[28]

Fasting before going to Holy Communion was not a problem if the Eucharist was distributed before ten o'clock in the morning, as that was the usual time that Indians had breakfast in Mexico.[29]

"When a priest goes to say Mass, neither a metate nor a pot moves until every one has left the church,"[30] wrote Pérez, who knew well such experiences. Indians near Mexico City did prefer to receive Holy Communion in the morning because fasting was easier then. One Indian told Father Pérez, "Father, I would prefer that Communion with fasting take place in the morning."[31] But away from the Valley of Mexico and the metropolis, things were different. So rustic were the Indians in the frontier areas considered that solely educating them regarding the Holy Eucharist was not enough. Priests did not feel comfortable distributing Communion, but they did it anyway because they were mandated to do so whenever the Church calendar required it to "all who were qualified."[32] At times, when a Catholic Indian was near death, Holy Communion had to be given, regardless of how the priest felt about that person's readiness. The concept of transubstantiation was too difficult to explain, and missionaries were never certain if the Indians understood it. One solution, especially in areas outside of Mexico, was to delay giving Holy Communion to young people until they were twelve years old.[33]

The distribution of the Holy Eucharist at Mass followed a certain procedure. Pérez believed that the Indians were "quite timid, yet in the exterior they come with so much devotion to receive communion."[34] Following the recital of the act of contrition, the first thing a priest did was to assure with patience that the Indians lifted a towel to their chin so that if the Eucharist or a particle of it should fall, the towel would catch it.[35]

As with Baptism, the question came up whether a person receiving Communion outside of his parish or mission should be allowed to do so. Another priest had written a response to the issue:

> I cannot understand for my life how anyone receiving Holy Communion in one parish while living in the territory of another acquires parish status where he receives communion. Nor do I understand on what basis the practice prevails that a Spaniard lawfully receives communion in an Indian parish and is thereby considered a parishioner of the resident *cura de indios* [priest]. Yet no one speaks against that nor is it considered intolerable.[36]

The feeling among priests is that a person could only be a parishioner in the district in which he resides, as had been established in the Council of Trent. The point was still controversial, perhaps because of the requirement to tithe and pay tribute to support the churches. The same was true for the sacrament of Matrimony. The issue of parish jurisdictions was controversial when it came to the administration of the sacraments.

In regard to Matrimony, residency was a requirement in order to be considered a parishioner. The answer was easy when the bride and groom were from the same parish; otherwise permissions had to be granted when they were from different parishes. Marriage required that the couple be identified, their age given and their familial relationships documented. Turning to the woman, the priest asked her a series of questions regarding whether she was being forced to marry, was marrying under some threat, or had lost her virginity. If all the answers were negative, then the procedure continued quite easily. If any of the answers were in the affirmative, then the woman was asked to leave the room and the man was brought in and asked similar questions. Indeed, the situation was treated as a confession.[37] In search for the truth, the priest could deny matrimony to the couple based on their answers.

Perhaps jaded by his many years as a missionary, Pérez was very critical about what he felt was the norm in a wedding involving Indians. He wrote: "Ordinarily, the witnesses arrive drunk [especially in Mexico City] and the cause is that on the day of the wedding they are at the house of the bride and groom where there is a great quantity of pulque, and thus they leave the house for the church knowing neither where they are going nor for what reason they go."[38] Accordingly, wrote Pérez, if the witnesses are inebriated, then the marriage is invalid. So missionaries had to make an effort to educate the natives that the sacrament of matrimony had to occur in a legitimate, sober, and solemn way.

All records involving the persons to be married had to be reviewed by the priest. If a widow or a widower were to be married, then proof of death of the former spouse had to be shown. Witnesses were called in to attest that the spouse had died from natural causes, accident, or homicide. A copy of the burial record of the person had to be presented. And the priest needed to know if the widow or widower had remarried at any time since the death of their spouses.

Beyond the birth certificate and witnesses who could attest that the couple to be married were parishioners, had been baptized, were church-going Christians, tithed, were from a legitimate family, were pure (that is, had not engaged in pre-marital sex), and had made a good confession, all the priest asked was that on the wedding day the witnesses appear sober.

As the first sacrament, Baptism, opened the door to the Christian world, the last sacrament one could receive, Extreme Unction, shut the door on this earthly life. The Last Rites consisted of three sacraments: confession, the anointing of Extreme Unction, and Holy Communion received as Viaticum. The chapter on the Last Rites in Pérez's *Manual* is the shortest because, he said, there were so many manuals on the subject already. However, he did have some comments to make regarding a "few accidents which could befall" the administration of the sacrament of Extreme Unction.[39] The first thing a minister must do is explain to the Indian what the sacrament is about. Extreme Unction, warned Pérez, is only performed when there is "no hope for recovery"[40] from a fatal illness or accident.

One of the problems in knowing how close to death the infirm person was, according to Pérez, revolved around the kind of medical treatment he had received. Father Juan Bautista recommended that the time to administer the sacrament of Extreme Unction was when a doctor pronounced that there was no hope that the patient would live. But Pérez countered with an example that presented both stark reality and a dilemma for the missionary. Pérez complained that in most pueblos, the medic was usually "an old Indian woman...who without knowing what she does, brings in a root from a weed, the prickly leaf of a maguey, or some other similar medicinal items, that from my experience, if it does not kill the infirm, it certainly does not alleviate his illness."[41] How could one be assured that the old woman medic would know if the person were actually dying? His bias aside, the point Pérez made was that sometimes the person only appeared to be dying. Sometimes the person was unconscious, but revived. Still, Pérez recommended the ministering of Extreme Unction whenever the person was lucid so that the priest could explain the importance of the sacrament to the patient. Given that perspective, Pérez pronounced that "The danger of death...ought to be considered, based not only on the illness but on the circumstances"[42] that the priest is able to understand at that particular moment. On the other hand, if the priest judged that the patient would live, he could be wrong. So, said Pérez, unless the doubt was justified, it was best to administer the sacrament and hope for the best.

The issue of administering the sacraments to Indians presented theological and doctrinal issues to missionaries who sometimes had difficulty joining the dicta of the Church (which evolved in a purely European environment) and what they saw before them in the tribal villages of North and South America. Long before Catholicism had arrived in the New World, Indian cultures had successfully developed their own concepts of religion and spirituality. Often, Native Americans found Christian concepts quite alien and incomprehensible—just as Spanish missionaries did not understand the workings of the many Indian cultures they encountered. The contradistinctions witnessed by missionaries often made them reluctant to administer the sacraments, although they knew they had to at a certain point in the conversion process. Too often they blamed the many Indian cultures for the drawbacks, and they failed to understand that their own colonial biases did not permit them to see with clarity beyond the narrow limits of their own cultural insularity, albeit Father Manuel Pérez's *Farol Indiano* documents the perceptions and evaluations of eighteenth century missionaries in New Spain.

Notes

1. *Farol Indiano y Guia de Curas de Indios: Summa de los Cinco Sacramentos que administran los Ministros Evangelicos en esta America*...Por el P. Fr. Manuel Perez del Orden de N.P.S. Augustin...Dedicada al Santissimo Esposo de la Esposa, y Madre de Dios, y Patron de esta Nueva-España, Señor San Joseph...Mexico, 1713.
2. "Introduccion a el Intento de esta Obra," *Farol Indiano y Guia de Curas de Indios: Summa de los Cinco Sacramentos que administran los Ministros Evangelicos en esta America*....Por el P. Fr. Manuel Perez del Orden de N.P.S. Augustin...Dedicada al Santissimo Esposo de la Esposa, y Madre de Dios, y Patron de esta Nueva-España, Señor San Joseph...Mexico, 1713.
3. "Introduccion" *Farol Indiano*, 1713.
4. *Farol Indiano*, p.1.
5. Item 4, *Farol Indiano*, p. 2.
6. Item 4, *Farol Indiano*, p. 3.
7. Item 5, *Farol Indiano*, p. 4.
8. Item 5, *Farol Indiano*, p. 5.
9. Item 6, *Farol Indiano*, p. 5.
10. "De otros accidentes de el Bautismo," Capitulo II, *Farol Indiano*, p. 7.

11. *Ibid., Farol Indiano*, pp. 7-8.
12. *Ibid. Farol Indiano*, p. 8. Also see Robert Ricard, *La Conquista Espiritual de México* (México: Editorial Jus, 1947) Traducción de Angel María Garibay K. p. 146-7. Ricard discusses the same issue of indigenous languages and their relevancy in the administration of the sacraments. Indeed, he cites the work of Father Bernardino Sahagún, *Evangeliarium Epistolarium et Lectionarium aztecum.* Sahagún, who fluently spoke nahuatl, doubted that a precise translation of the Latin used in the sacraments could be made using indigenous vocabularies.
13. "No es verdadera, ni segura forma del Bautismo en Lengua Mexicana," *Farol Indiano*, Cap. III, pp. 8-9.
14. Pérez wrote: "La raçon es, que en este idioma ay verbos, y nombres metaphoricos, y compuestos unos con otros, uno de ellos es el verbo *Quastequi* que es el que usan para bautizar: componese de *Quastl* por la cabeza, *Atl* por el agua, y el verbo *Te quia* que significa echar, o difundir, conque todo el significa *Echar agua en la cabeza*....pero el verbo *Quastiquia* no es generico como los referidos, sino individual, que significa morjar la cabeza, y esto lo haze no ser suficiente, *Ibid., Farol Indiano*, Item 2, p. 9.
15. Ibid., *Farol Indiano*, p. 10.
16. Ibid., *Farol Indiano*, p. 12.
17. "Tratado II. Del Sacramento de la Penitencia," *Farol Indiano*, p. 15.
18. Ibid., *Farol Indiano*, p. 16.
19. Ibid., *Farol Indiano*, p. 16.
20. Ibid., *Farol Indiano*, p. 16.
21. Ibid., *Farol Indiano*, pp. 16-18.
22. "Resuelve la primera duda," *Farol Indiano*, Cap. II, p. 19.
23. Ibid., *Farol Indiano*, Cap. III, p. 25-26.
24. Ibid., *Farol Indiano*, p. 26.
25. Ibid., *Farol Indiano*, p. 29.
26. Ibid., *Farol Indiano*, p. 29.
27. "Tratado III del Sacramento de la Eucharistia," *Farol Indiano*, Tratado III, p. 94.
28. Ibid., *Farol Indiano*, p. 94.
29. Ibid. *Farol Indiano*, No. 2, p. 95.
30. Ibid, *Farol Indiano*, p. 95.
31. Ibid., *Farol Indiano*, p. 95.
32. Ibid., *Farol Indiano*, p. 96.
33. Ibid., *Farol Indiano*, p. 98.
34. Ibid., *Farol Indiano*, p. 98.
35. Ibid., *Farol Indiano*, p. 99.

36.   Ibid., *Farol Indiano*, No. 3, p. 100.
37.   Ibid., *Farol Indiano*, p. 130-31.
38.   Ibid., *Farol Indiano*, p. 135.
39.   "Tratado IV. Del Sacramento de la Extrema Uncion," *Farol Indiano*, IV, p. 117.
40.   Ibid., *Farol Indiano*, p. 117-18.
41.   Ibid., *Farol Indiano*, No. 3, p. 118.
42.   Ibid., *Farol Indiano*, No. 2, p. 118.

San Pedro Alcántara and the Barefoot Friars in New Mexico

Paul Kraemer

Throughout the Spanish colonial period, the religious life of New Mexico was promoted almost entirely by Franciscan missionaries. These missionaries were administered by the Holy Gospel Province and its subdivision for New Mexico, the Custody of the Conversion of San Pablo. In general, the friars assigned to New Mexico shared some degree of commonality in their training and philosophical background by their incorporation in the friaries of the Holy Gospel Province in New Spain before coming to New Mexico. Furthermore, throughout this period, the Holy Gospel Province, the largest and most important Franciscan province in New Spain, retained jurisdictional control over all church related activities in New Mexico. However, not all the friars that worked in New Mexico were incorporated into the Holy Gospel Province. For instance, in 1693, because of the extreme shortage of friars, eight priests from the Apostolic College of the *Propaganda Fide* at Querétaro were given temporary assignments to assist in the Vargas Reconquest.

The other major exceptions in both the seventeenth and eighteenth centuries were friars with origins in the austere Franciscan Descalzo – Barefoot – Order. These friars derived from a tradition of very strict observance of the Franciscan Rule that was developed under San Pedro Alcántara. The present paper reviews the story of San Pedro Alcántara and his Barefoot or Discalced Order and how their traditions came to New Mexico. In particular, it is of interest that these traditions and the presence of Barefoot Friars in New Mexico have been almost completely ignored by historians.

In the early 1500s, the Franciscans were grappling, as usual, with the problem of conflict between the practical and the ideal. Groups favoring strict observance of the Franciscan Rule were called Observants, while others favoring a more institutionalized order were called Conventuals. In Spain, the Observants became the only allowable type of Franciscan, and the Conventuals were almost but not quite suppressed; but the Observants were not strict enough to suit some reform groups, and these groups fought so hard for their independence that the Pope, apparently out of frustration, finally put them under the Conventual obedience. This paradox had far-reaching effects on the spiritual conquest of Mexico, for the Discalced Provinces, one of the most important of these reform groups that had arisen in 1496, came under the Conventual obedience during its early history. Pedro Alcántara joined the earliest of these Discalced Provinces, that of San Gabriel, in the year 1515. He was sixteen years old at the time.

These Discalced Franciscan Provinces, which used the word "Discalced" in their name, should be distinguished from the generic usage of the word "discalced," a recommended form of attire of many religious groups and symbolic of the Catholic Reformation. Indeed, going barefoot was by no means the most important feature of the Discalced Provinces, especially as they developed under the influence of Pedro Alcántara.

In 1524, the same year that Pedro Alcántara was ordained in Spain, twelve Discalced Friars from his Province of San Gabriel were welcomed to Mexico City by Hernan Cortés. The Indians were amazed that Cortés and his officers greeted these barefoot, ragged friars with such deference and respect. These twelve men became known as the Twelve Apostles of Mexico and initiated the custody that would become the Province of the Holy Gospel, the primary Franciscan organization that brought Christianity to Mexico and New Mexico. But the Province did so only after severing all ties to the Discalced Provinces, largely due to the fact that Conventual obedience was not acceptable in New Spain. An interesting question is what course the history of the Franciscans in Mexico might have taken if the mother house of the original friars had not been encumbered with an inappropriate Conventual obedience.

San Pedro Alcántara grew up in Alcántara, near the Portuguese border, where his father was governor. He professed at Brozas, only a few miles from his home, one of about ten friaries that the Discalced Province of San Gabriel had scattered about Extramadura. After he was ordained, he traveled extensively throughout western Spain and Portugal holding many offices for the "Descalzos" such as guardian at Plasencia, provincial minister of the San Gabriel Province, and provincial minister for another province that he started *de novo*, the Province of San José. Always practicing many personal austerities, he preached that the friars in every aspect of their lives should have a material existence identical to that of very poor people, including their food, dress, shelter, lack of money and property, and even the vestments and altars for their chapels. Under San Pedro Alcántara, the Discalced Provinces can be thought of as a microcosmic repetition of the earlier evolution of the Franciscan Order during and immediately following the lifetime of St. Francis. By the time of his death in 1562 at Areñas, San Pedro Alcántara had become famous as a friend of St. Teresa of Ávila, and his influence on the Discalced Provinces was so pervasive that these provinces became known as the "Alcantarines" and were ready to venture to the New World and elsewhere.

The story of how the Alcantarines got to New Mexico is included in a book published in 1682. This chronicle by Baltazar Medina concerns the history of the Discalced Province of San Diego, which became the only Discalced Province in New Spain. As Medina points out, near the end of San Pedro Alcántara's life, the Discalced Provinces were reunited with the Observants but under conditions assuring their virtual independence. At this point they were poised to expand to the four corners of the world. Medina lists the Discalced Provinces, most of which came into existence by 1650. There were sixteen of them, many in Spain and Portugal but some in other places as well.

The accompanying diagram shows the somewhat complicated lineage of the Discalced Province of San Diego. While the main Franciscan province in Mexico, the Holy Gospel Province, was derived from the Descalzos, it no longer pursued the Descalzo

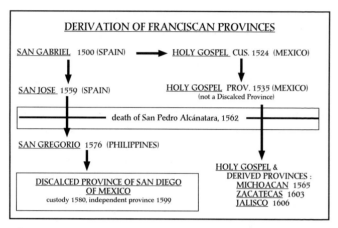

DERIVATION OF FRANCISCAN PROVINCES

SAN GABRIEL   1500 (SPAIN) ➡ HOLY GOSPEL CUS. 1524 (MEXICO)

SAN JOSE 1559 (SPAIN)   HOLY GOSPEL PROV. 1535 (MEXICO)
                                (not a Discalced Province)

death of San Pedro Alcánatara, 1562

SAN GREGORIO 1576 (PHILIPPINES)

                                HOLY GOSPEL &
                                DERIVED PROVINCES :
DISCALCED PROVINCE OF SAN DIEGO   MICHOACAN 1565
OF MEXICO   ZACATECAS 1603
custody 1580, independent province 1599   JALISCO 1606

reforms. However, in 1576, friars from the Discalced Province of San José (that is, the province founded by San Pedro Alcántara) sent twenty friars to establish the Province of San Gregorio in the Philippines. They used Mexico as an initial base for their operations and subsequently went on to Japan where a number of the friars were martyred. One of them, the Mexico City native San Felipe de Jesús, belonged to this province. In addition, friars of the San Gregorio Province renewed a Descalzo interest in Mexico, establishing a Custody of San Diego in 1580, which became the independent Province of San Diego in 1599.

In terms of the "spiritual conquest" of Mexico, the Descalzos started very late. Numerically, mendicant establishments in central Mexico about that time had reached saturation. In addition, Archbishop Montúfar had already made serious efforts to secularize many missions. And there were other problems. Internal dissension between gachupín and criollo friars had become a serious issue. But the most disconcerting issue was the massive die-offs of the Indians. Only about two and a half million Indians, from a precontact population some estimate to have been twenty-five million, survived the introduction of Old World diseases. As befitting their background as "God's Fools," the Descalzos ignored all these problems and simply went to work.

Franciscan provinces were largely defined geographically. However, the dozen or so friaries of the Province of San Diego were scattered over all of New Spain, totally ignoring any of the boundaries of the Holy Gospel Province as well as those of the three Provinces derived from the Holy Gospel Province (Michoacan, Zacatecas, and Jalisco). They could do so because all the popes of the sixteenth and seventeenth centuries supported their independence. In addition, it was clear that they merited considerable respect from other Franciscans. Their pattern of activity was to go out singly or in pairs or small groups to whatever place they were needed.

This table shows the size of the San Diego Province compared to the rest of the Franciscans. As can be seen, they were numerically much smaller, but they were not insignificant either. They maintained their numbers well into the nineteenth century, partly because they had their own college at Pachuca and partly because they continued to gain gachupín additions, priests that had already been ordained in Spain. They tended to be geographically scattered, working as chaplains to presidios or serving the Indians in the mining areas. Some even came to New Mexico.

Friar Population in Colonial Mexico				
	c.1680	1700s	1786	1825
Holy Gospel & deriv.	1457	1495	1061	733
San Diego Province	197	214	250	232

Eight Friars with 'Descalzo' Origins who Served in New Mexico
Fray Estévan Perea (1609-1639)
Fray Antonio de Arteaga (1629-1639)
Fray García de San Francisco (1629-1673)
Fray Thomás de San Diego (1629-1631+)
Fray Antonio Sánchez de Pro (1677-1680)
Fray Juan Muñoz de Castro (1680-1696+)
Fray Juan Alvarez (1665-1708+)
Fray Carlos Delgado (1710-1749)

Eight Franciscans who served in New Mexico can be identified as having Descalzo origins. Scanning this list we see that several of the names are immediately recognizable to people with general familiarity with New Mexican colonial history, names like Perea, García de San Francisco, Delgado. So the nub of this paper is that it wasn't some obscure Barefoot Friars that came to New Mexico. Rather, it was the relationship of an important group of friars to the Descalzo tradition that has been lost to our history books.

It would be beyond the scope of this paper to review in any detail the biographies of these eight friars. But a few statements that at least identify them seems appropriate. The first one, Father Estévan Perea, a gachupín , initially professed in the Discalced Province of San Gabriel, but when he came to New Spain in 1605, he affiliated with the Holy Gospel Province instead of the Province of San Diego. He came to New Mexico in 1609, and according to historian France Scholes, "for some thirty years, except for the brief period from 1626-1629, he was the dominant figure in the religious life of the province." He was also an aggressive antagonist in the church and state conflicts of his time and was the first to legally use the power of the Inquisition to promote his views.

Father Perea's *Relación* of 1629 is an important document on the condition of the New Mexico missions in the seventeenth century. It also describes how he returned with thirty new friars from Mexico. Three of them (the next three on the above list) were "Descalzos" from the San Diego Province whom Fray Estéban Perea assigned to the Piro Missions south of present day Socorro.

However, shortly thereafter we find Fray Tomás de San Diego as guardian of the convent at Santa Fe, where he got into the historical records by criticizing the armorer, Don Gaspar Pérez, for his intemperate speech. Pérez apparently avoided punishment for his heretical statements since the general view was that since Pérez was Flemish, well, what can you expect. Fray Tomás only stayed a few years in New Mexico before going back to Oaxaca where he wrote books and pursued other scholarly endeavors.

Fray Antonio de Arteaga, was highly regarded by his superiors in the San Diego Province. Medina devotes thirty-nine folios to Fray Antonio's biography in his *Chronicle*, and indeed, after ten years service at Senecú, he was called back to Mexico to serve in leadership positions, including Provincial Minister. During his stay in New Mexico he was known for his extreme austerities, going barefoot all winter in a land where rivers froze and totally abstaining from meat, chocolate, and table wine. Yet he was the first to introduce wine grapes to New Mexico and provided sacramental wine to the other convents.

Fray García de San Francisco spent the rest of his life in New Mexico and became the best known of the three. Originally he had come as a lay brother to assist Father Arteaga, but he took orders shortly after Arteaga left and was able to continue the work of converting the Piros, Mansos, and other tribes in the southern part of the Custody. In 1659 at the age of fifty-seven, his life got very complicated. On the negative side, he was appointed Vice-Custodian during the absence of the Custodian and thereby became embroiled in the conflicts between the Church and the notorious Governor Mendizábal. On the positive side, Fray García finally achieved the establishment of the first permanent mission in the El Paso area for the Manso Indians, an objective that had been sought since the early visit of Benavides in 1625. After nine more years the mission church was completed, a church considered magnificent for its time. Remnants are still at the present day Juárez Cathedral site. Fray García died in 1673 and was buried at Senecú. Thus his service overlaps the next group of three New Mexico Barefoot Friars.

These three, Fathers Sánchez de Pro, Muñoz de Castro, and Alvarez, were associated with events in the El Paso area just before the Pueblo Revolt. Fray Antonio Sánchez de Pro came with Father Ayeta's first mission caravan in 1677, was immediately assigned to the San Ildefonso mission, and was one of the twenty-one Franciscan martyrs killed during the Pueblo Revolt. At the time he was thirty-one years old.

Fray Muñoz de Castro came with the second relief expedition arriving in El Paso in 1680 just in time to give aid to the refugees of the Revolt. Fray Muñoz was an experienced Descalzo and had participated in the penetration of the Los Juntos and Tarahumara regions by the San Diego Province. He was named

Missionary President of all of the El Paso missions – there were as many as ten scattered along the river in 1684. One suspects that he had something to do with the naming of one of these missions San Pedro Alcántara. Later Fray Muñoz joined the reconquest in 1693 and worked closely with Vargas in the reestablishment of the missions. As a young priest, Fray Juan Alvarez had worked with Fray García de San Francisco, and he continued to serve in the El Paso area for almost 30 years. Finally, however, in 1696 he was elected custodian and later commissary of the Holy Office. He is well known for his investigations recorded in 1706.

Fray Carlos Delgado, last-mentioned in the above list, seems to be the only eighteenth century Barefoot Friar to be identified. He had an unusual life in that after serving dutifully for over twenty-five years as a typical eighteenth century mission priest, he retired and then suddenly became an apostolic ball of fire. First of all, in 1742 he went to the Hopi villages and brought back 441 Pueblo people who had been refugees since the Reconquest days. Then two years later he organized an expedition to the Navajo country and claimed to have made five thousand converts. This triumph made him famous all the way to the King of Spain himself. Finally, after he had retired again, he responded to criticisms of the Franciscans in New Mexico by writing a treatise of unparalleled harshness, almost reminiscent of Fray Estévan Perea's diatribes of the previous century.

Fray Carlos also had an artistic side. In many of the missions where he served he often embellished the title pages of the mission books. In fact, E. Boyd regarded Fray Carlos as a prime candidate to be the unknown hide painter referred to as "Franciscan B." "Franciscan B" was an important artist in the development of the New Mexican santero tradition.

If Father Delgado painted any representations of San Pedro Alcántara, none have been found. Indeed, no retablos or santos have been located of San Pedro Alcántara in any U.S. collection except for two at San Xavier del Bac in Arizona. A bulto of San Pedro Alcántara is mentioned in the will of Juana Luján in 1762, but no trace of it has been discovered so far. Nevertheless, there are numerous images in other countries that can be used to define the main iconographic attributes. St. Teresa's description of him is justly famous and worth repeating:

He told me that he slept but one hour and a half in twenty-four hours for forty years together ... that he never put up his hood, however hot the sun or heavy the rain, nor did he wear any other garment than his habit of thick coarse cloth or anything upon his feet .... It was usual for him to eat but once in three days .... When I came to know him, he was very old and his body so shriveled and weak that it seemed to be composed as if it were of the roots and dried bark of a tree rather than flesh.

With such a graphic description, one might suppose that artistic representations of San Pedro Alcántara would have many features in common. Actually there is considerable diversity. Only the later ones pay much attention to his austere lifestyle. For instance, at Areñas, next to his sepulcher, an earlier portrayal shows him lean but in glowing health and wearing a richly embroidered habit. This image shows a dove on his right shoulder to represent the Holy Ghost, a pen in his right hand, and a book in his left hand – the saint's common iconographic attributes. A statue at Barcelona has similar stylistic features. At Murcia, the addition of a whip for taking the discipline gives some recognition to the austerities of the "Descalzos."

One of the images at San Xavier del Bac was originally at Tumacácori and probably was brought up from Mexico in the late eighteenth century. It may have been in the same general style but the right hand is missing and there is no dove. The other one at Bac is labeled "San Pedro Alcántara" on the base, but the identity is nevertheless controversial.

Some examples give greater emphasis to San Pedro Alcántara's ascetic life style. A painting at La Paz, Bolivia, shows the influence of St. Teresa's famous description. It is titled "Jesús dando comer a San Pedro Alcántara" and shows Christ feeding a frail and weak friar. It also shows him wearing sandals, which was allowed when the "Descalzos" were very old or sick. A statue at Quito, Ecuador, shows him with an emaciated torso, the shortened habit prescribed by "Descalzo" rules, and a vicious-looking discipline.

From the available data on the Franciscans here identified as having "Descalzo" origins, what can be said in general about the

Alcantarine tradition in New Mexico? These friars with Descalzo backgrounds appear to have had more than their share of leadership qualities, including being custodians, Holy Office commissaries, and so forth, as well as a considerable intensity of purpose. They were not obscure friars; rather they were well known friars who shared what has become an obscure tradition.

The question arises, why has this tradition been largely ignored? One partial explanation concerns our sources of Franciscan history as it pertains to New Mexico. Our three most-used secondary sources have traditionally been the following: Mendieta's *Historia*, written in the last part of the seventeenth century, Torquemada's *Monarchia*, which is basically a reprint of Mendieta's book, and the *Teatro Mexicano* published by Vetancurt in 1697. But all of these are basically chronicles of the Holy Gospel Province and hardly mention the Descalced Province of San Diego.

Undoubtedly, there are other factors as well. Nonetheless, I think this study raises two interesting points; that Descalzo traditions were part of the apostolic equipment of a group of important friars during the colonial period and that these traditions might have influenced the gravity of the conflicts between Church and State during this period.

One final irony of this forgotten Descalzo tradition: hundreds of kitchens in New Mexico are decorated with a retablo of San Pascual, the patron saint of cooks in Mexico. Very few people seem aware of the fact that their San Pascual is actually a representation of San Pascual Bailón, a Spanish Barefoot Friar contemporary with San Pedro Alcántara.

Bibliographic Essay

A general treatment of the historical context of the development of the Franciscan Order can be found in Will Durant's *The Age of Faith* (Simon & Schuster, 1950; volume IV of "The Story of Civilization"). More specific information includes *A History of the Franciscan Order From its Origins to the Year 1517* by John Moorman (Franciscan Herald Press, Chicago, 1988) and *Franciscan History - The Three Orders of St. Francis of Assisi* by Lazaro Iriarte de Aspurz (also published by Franciscan Herald Press, 1982). Iriarte discusses the Discalced Reform within the context of other Franciscan reform movements. An internal view of this reform is related in

Baltazar Medina's *Chrónica de la Santa Provincia de San Diego de México, de Religiosos Descalzos* (Mexico, 1682; copies are in both UNM Zimmerman and Bancroft libraries).

Medina also gives some information on the life and contributions of San Pedro Alcántara, but the best source on this aspect of the study appears to be the result of a conference on San Pedro Alcántara held in Spain in 1962 to celebrate the four-hundredth year since his death. These papers were published in *Archivo Ibero-Americano* — *Revista de Estudios Históricos* 22 (1962). In particular, papers by Fidel Lejarza, "Orígenes de las descalcez franciscana"; Ángel Uribe, "Espiritualidad de la descalcez franciscana"; Pedro Borges, "San Pedro de Alcántara hasta su ingreso en la Orden franciscana"; and Arcángel Barrado "San Pedro de Alcántara en las provincias de San Gabriel, Las Arrábida y San José."

One of these papers, Manuel Castro's "San Pedro de Alcántara en el arte," is an extensive analysis of artistic representations of San Pedro Alcántara. Castro's analysis of the iconography of the saint makes use of about 250 examples from all over the world and includes paintings by a luminary such as Zubarán. Pictures of bultos of San Pedro Alcántara can be found in Richard Ahlborn's *Saints of San Xavier* (Southwestern Mission Research Center, Tucson, 1974) and in Pál Kelemen's *Baroque and Rococo in Latin America* (volume 2, Dover Publications, 1967). A general reference to New Mexico santero traditions is *Popular Arts of Spanish New Mexico* by E. Boyd (Museum of New Mexico Press, 1974).

Robert Ricard's classic study *The Spiritual Conquest of Mexico* (translated by Lesley Byrd Simpson, University of California Press, 1966) emphasizes the period in New Spain before the Province of San Diego was founded. The latter part of the 16th century involving the northward advance is considered in *Soldiers, Indians & Silver* by Philip Powell (University of California Press, 1969). We have already mentioned the important Holy Gospel Chronicles of the seventeenth century, which include such works as Augustín Vetancurt's *Teatro Mexicano*, Juan Torquemada's *Monarchia de Indiana*, and Gerónimo Mendieta's *Historia Eclesiástica Indiana*. Other important items concerning the Franciscans in New Spain include John Leddy Phelan's *The Millennial Kingdom of the Franciscans in the New World* (University of California Press, 1956), Marion Habig's "The Franciscan Provinces of Spanish North

America," *The Americas* 1-2 (1944), and *Franciscan Presence in the Americas,* a group of essays edited by Francisco Morales (Academy of American Franciscan History, 1983). In addition, two valuable dissertations are those by Edwin Sylvest, "Motifs of Franciscan Mission Theory" (Southern Methodist University, 1970), and Pius Barth, "Franciscan Education and the Social Order" (University of Chicago, 1945).

Much of the New Mexico part of the story is scattered throughout the papers of France Scholes and Lansing Bloom in *New Mexico Historical Review* as well as the specific translations in C.W. Hackett's works *Revolt of the Pueblo Indians* and *Historical Documents Relating to New Mexico, Volume III.* A dissertation and a paper by Jim Norris were also helpful "The Breakdown of Franciscan Hegemony in the Kingdom of New Mexico" (Tulane University, 1992) and "The Franciscans in New Mexico, 1692-1754: Toward a New Assessment," *The Americas* 51 (1994). Events in the El Paso area are covered by Anne Hughes's *The Beginnings of Spanish Settlement in the El Paso District* (University of California Press, 1914), Vina Walz's dissertation "History of the El Paso Area, 1680-1692," (University of New Mexico, 1951), and a paper by Ernest Burrus, "An Interlude in the Reconquest of New Mexico," *Manuscripta* 29 (1985).

La Plazuela de San Francisco: A Possible Case of Colonial Superposition?

David H. Snow

In a formal declaration sworn to and signed on February 21, 1824, Domingo Fernández de la Pedrera stated that he had received the deeds and other old documents from the "interested party" pertaining to a parcel of land on the west of the house of Juan de Abrego in Santa Fe. Except, he said, for the large patio of that house, the remainder of the parcel was formerly church property, "for having been the little plaza of the first church which, since the conquest, was rededicated by the settlers to their Patron – *por haber sido la plazuela de la Yglesia primera qe desde la conquista la rededicaron los pobladores a su Sor Patron*." It was, at the time he wrote, vacant and ownerless "so many years since they removed the church from it – *pues se halla dho pedaso de tierra llermo y sin dueno tantos años que se quito de alli la Yga*."[1]

In 1697, Governor Rodríguez Cubero granted land to the Franciscans at Santa Fe for a new *convento* (priest's house) already under construction, saying that it was sufficient for a new church as well. Although the dimensions are not provided, it appears that the lands included enough space for the plazuela referred to by Fernández. A point of reference for the argument presented herein is the west boundary, described as "the former plaza of this Villa."[2]

If I am correct, we must abandon the idea that the boundary cited formed the east edge of the original pre-1680 plaza of Santa Fe and consider the possibility that Rodríguez's grant extended some distance into that former plaza. Others have argued that the seventeenth-century church and convento were located easterly of the *parroquia* and convento described by Father Domínguez, in

1776;[3] sufficient space for a small plaza, or *atrio*, in front of the Reconquest *parroquia*, as a result, would have required an extension into the former plaza.

I suggest here that the Villa's seventeenth-century complex might have included a large open courtyard or *atrio* (as that space came to be called in the eighteenth century) fronting the church. Furthermore, I suggest that Governor Rodríguez, perhaps at the urging of the Franciscans, set aside enough space for a similar feature in the 1697 grant. Finally, I suggest that the *plazuela* was intended to obliterate the former south plaza of the Tano pueblo, with its single kiva in the center. Superposition, the concept of replacing pagan, non-Christian sites of worship with Christian temples, harks back to the frenzy of Catholic construction following the expulsion of the Moors.[4]

As yet unresolved are the implications of Domingo's statement that the church, apparently, once occupied the *plazuela*, or at least a portion of it. It has been accepted fact that the church and convent described in 1776 were those constructed during the early years of the eighteenth century. No evidence exists for rebuilding the Reconquest *parroquia* after its completion in 1717 and prior to about 1805, and it may be simply that Domingo had his facts wrong.[5]

The "Plazuela de San Francisco"

The property Domingo Fernández claimed was the *plazuela de la yglesia primera*, he wrote, "had been sold by Don Julian Rael [de Aguilar], together with the house of Domingo's grandfather, Bartolome de Fernández – in spite of the fact that over time this was no longer believed to be the case – *y aunque Don Julian Rael vendio dho pedaso de tierra con la casa de mi Abuelo con el tiempo se declaro no ser como llevo dho.*" Furthermore, Domingo cited a deed which, he said, clearly and legally described a transaction witnessed by the Alcalde Mayor, Don Francisco Guerrero, by which Don Antonio de Armijo sold the house in question to Bartolome. "In that deed," said Domingo, "it was declared that the property to the west did not belong to said house – *en la qe se declara qe dha tierra no es perteneciente a la mencionada casa.*"

It appears, therefore, that the house of Juan de Abrego, lying immediately to the east of the former plazuela, in 1824, was the same house (or lot) purchased by Domingo's grandfather, Bartolome Fernández, from Antonio [Duran] de Armijo. Unfortunately, the deed recording that transaction – once, presumably, in the hands of Domingo – has not been found. If Domingo's information were correct, Armijo must have purchased the property, later selling it to Bartolome Fernández. The date of Bartolome's death is not known, but his last child was baptized in 1767; and it seems likely that the house indicated on the 1767 map of Santa Fe by Joseph de Urrutia (Fig. 1) is the one referred to by Domingo.

Upon the death of Alonso Rael de Aguilar about 1745, witnesses in a suit brought by the heirs described the home Alonso had purchased for his second wife as being contiguous with the convento and church of the Villa, and it was this property that Julian Rael de Aguilar, Alonso's grandson, sold without the consent of his siblings sometime prior to 1750. By order of Governor Cachupin, the sale was declared null and void, and the property was put up at an auction conducted by Alcalde Mayor, Francisco Guerrero.[6] Bartolome Fernández cannot have owned the house prior to 1750; thus, Domingo's claim that Rael sold his grandfather's house and the plazuela refers to the house that would become Bartolome's following the auction.

The location of Juan de Abrego's house (he was married to Domingo's aunt, Juana Fernández) is further clarified by Domingo's statement that the property could not have belonged to Don Juan de Alari "since he cites as his boundary the street that runs in front of said house – *pues esta cita la calle por lindero que es el camino qe va delante de dha casa.*" The property of Juan de Alari[d], husband of Guadalupe Baca, is identified as number 3 on *Calle del Granero*, today's East Palace Avenue, in an 1836 property list of the plaza vicinity. Guadalupe Baca y Terrus was the daughter of José Francisco Baca y Terrus, whose property, listed as number 2, was adjacent to that of Alari (the easternmost property in that list is number 1, counting west to the *"granero de la tropa"* at the present intersection of Palace Avenue with Washington Street at the northeast corner of Santa Fe's plaza; Fig. 2).[7]

In 1856, Baca y Terrus sold to Bishop Lamy a house lot and piece of land east of the Santa Fe plaza which was bounded east by the *cienega*, north by a street leading to the *cienega*, south by the cemetery of the *parroquia*, a new house, and a piece of land belonging to the church. On the west, that piece was bounded by the *"plazuela of San Francisco."*[8] That same year, Lamy also obtained from Alexandro Valles a piece of property bounded on the north by a street leading to the plazuela de San Francisco, on the east by the same plazuela, and on the south by San Francisco Street;

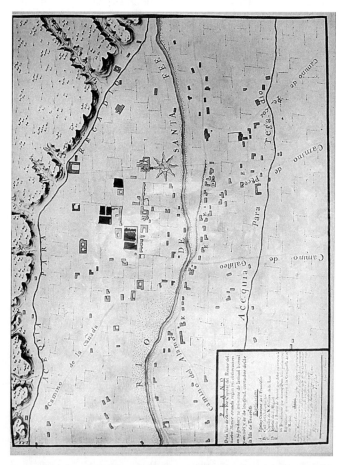

Figure 1. 1767 map of Santa Fe, New Mexico, prepared by Joseph de Urrutia. The parroquia is identified by the letter A. The little plaza cited by Fray Francisco Atanacio Domínguez in 1776 occupies the open area immediately northwest of the parroquia. Note the three houses bordering the plazuela on the east, north, and west, as stated by Domínguez.

to the west lay private property. That property was purchased by
Machebeuf at Lamy's request: "Casting about, Lamy fixed upon a
large house belonging to a rich Frenchman of St. Louis which
would be a suitable residence and convent school." The location
had the advantage, from Lamy's perspective, of having streets on
three sides for its boundaries. For many years the location of the
Federal Post Office in Santa Fe, the site is now occupied by the

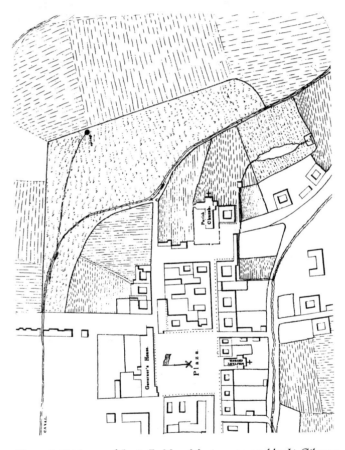

Figure 2. 1846 map of Santa Fe, New Mexico, prepared by Lt. Gilmore
(US Topographic Engineers). The constriction of the former plazuela is
almost complete by this time. Note that the houses on the east and
north (Prince Plaza), although somewhat modified, remain.

Museum of American Indian Arts, directly opposite the Cathedral.[9]

By about mid-nineteenth century, then, the little plaza once belonging to the *parroquia* following the Reconquest lay adjacent to, and immediately west of, the cemetery, bounded on the south by San Francisco Street, on the north by today's Prince and Sena Plazas and East Palace Avenue, and on the west by private properties (Figs. 1-2). On the east, along the north side of the *parroquia*, was also private land which Lamy purchased from Baca y Terrus, a parcel that is today's Cathedral Park.

The Pre-Revolt Templo Mayor

Small open forecourts called *plazas* attached to Mexican churches of the sixteenth century are mentioned briefly by McAndrew,[10] but their function and uses are not specifically identified. That such spaces differed, certainly in size and perhaps in use, from the ubiquitous sixteenth-century Mexican church *atrios* seems clear, and those generally are associated with churches constructed for the express purpose of converting masses of local Native American populations, so those churches were frequently very large indeed. Churches in towns and cities intended for Spanish populations frequently also had an *atrio*, but reduced in size, since conversions, indoctrination, and mass baptisms of Indians were not their primary function. Santa Fe, in New Mexico, certainly falls into this category, a town established solely for Spaniards (not a mission); but to paraphrase a well-known Southwestern archeologist, "When is an *atrio?*"[11]

Atrios, with their outdoor chapels and other features, were characteristic aspects of New World Spanish church architecture, serving not only as a place in which mass was celebrated for large congregations of Native American converts, but for religious and moral plays, Via Crucis and other holy processions, as well as for mass baptisms. McAndrew speculated that the word *atrio* was not used in sixteenth century Mexico since, in contemporary Spain, it might refer to a cemetery or to a raised garth adjacent to the church, "though often at one side."[12]

According to Fray Mendieta, writing in the last decades of the sixteenth century, "All the monasteries here in New Spain have a large walled patio in front of the church made to be used mainly on holy days, so that when all the townspeople are gathered together, they can hear Mass and be preached to in the patio, for they will not fit inside the body of the church, which they use only when, through piety, they come to hear Mass on weekdays." When the *atrio* was the scene of processions and plays, they were bedecked with flowers and ramadas erected by the local indigenous populations.[13]

So too in Santa Fe, for in July 1716 Governor Juan Flores Mogollon ordered that the pueblos send sufficient men to the Villa to erect the ramadas and decorate them for Corpus, adding that

> by this order those pueblos that pertain to Mexico, together, bring the flowers that each pueblo might gather for the two days referred to, and that they name the dancers they want in order that they dance in the procession before the Blessed Sacrament, striving to dress themselves as decently as they can.[14]

In August, however, the *cabildo* informed Flores Mogollon that the former streets of the Villa should be restored to their former width (prior to the 1680 Revolt) because of encroachment by residences and gardens, complaining that

> this capital Villa finds itself reduced to only a single exit which is that of San Francisco Street, on the west, such that the Mother Church of this kingdom, which is the convent of Our Father San Francisco, [is] left with no exit for its processions to walk, as happened this year for Corpus, which went coming and going by the same way.[15]

The possibility that Santa Fe's seventeenth-century *parroquia* was the scene of similar activities is suggested by Fray Alonso de Benavides, who said of the church he established at the Villa in the 1620s that it was where Indians and Spaniards were taught to "read, write, and play musical instruments, sing, and to practice all the arts of civilized society."[16] Surely some of those activities took place in an open courtyard – *atrio* or plazuela – similar to those then current throughout Mexico.

In the absence of data to the contrary it can be argued that the site of the new Villa's church in 1609-10 was chosen with an eye to the 1573 *Ordenanzas Reales*. Whether (or to what extent) Pedro de Peralta might have been guided by that document, of course, is not known;[17] but, if he were, the *templo mayor* should have been situated away from the main plaza of the town, so as to be elevated above and set off from the lesser constructions of administrative authorities and the homes of residents.[18]

A church existed in the Villa in 1613, when Governor Peralta was excommunicated and his chair tossed out onto the street.[19] Sometime between 1617 and 1620, his successor proposed to relocate, to "square up" the Villa for defensive purposes, and to erect, as a result, a new church. The Viceroy demurred, stating that "inasmuch as there is already there a church and convent of San Francisco which seems sufficient," he saw no reason for the change.[20]

In 1622, Fray Alonso Peinado reported that in Santa Fe the foundations had been laid for a church and convento that, he said, "will be the best in this land."[21] Fray Alonso de Benavides noted that the only thing lacking in Santa Fe in 1623 was a church. The one they had, he said, "was a miserable hut," and he began construction of a new church and friary. In his Revised Memorial of 1634, he claimed specifically that "I built a very fine church *for the Spaniards of the Villa.*[22]

Fray Gerónimo de Zárate Salmerón, following his tour of duty in New Mexico from 1621 to about 1626, wrote that Santa Fe had a "very good church [and that] everything pertaining to public worship is very complete and well arranged"; there were, he said, "two hundred Indians under its administration who are capable of receiving the sacraments."[23] Presumably by then the small *hermita* of San Miguel had been built to serve the Mexican Indian population of the *barrio* south of the river – except, perhaps, on feast days, for which the *parroquia* must have drawn on the Villa's total population. The possibility that those two hundred Indians might have been recent converts attached to Spanish families of the Villa is a strong one, particularly since, as Zárate indicated, they were under the spiritual administration of the *parroquia* and not of San Miguel.[24] Perhaps an *atrio* or plazuela was deemed appropriate for their indoctrination and continuing education?

Plaza de Armas

In 1628, a gunpowder tower attached to the *casas reales* was stated to be *"en cubierto con el convento y iglesia,"*[25] and unless we are willing to believe that the *parroquia* in 1628 was situated on the east side of the present plaza adjacent to today's Palace of Governors, we must seriously reconsider the pre-Revolt layout of the Villa.

During the siege of Santa Fe in 1680, Otermin and his men went out to meet the enemy above the convento, but the attackers retreated to a point near the hills to gain an eminence which *"comes down behind the house of the maese de campo, Francisco Gómez [Robledo]."*[26] Otermin was fearful that the enemy might burn the church, and on Friday August 17, the expected full assault occurred. The besieged soldiers went out into the *"streets leading to the convent,"* to find that the Holy Temple was burned to the ground.[27]

In 1662, Francisco Gómez Robledo was arrested by the Inquisition in his house "on the plaza" which "faced on the corner of the royal plaza of this Villa," and from there he was conducted *"across to a cell"* in the *convento*, where he was held pending trial in Mexico City.[28]

The eminence noted by Otermin was also described by Vargas in 1692, who observed a contingent of the [Pueblo] enemy "on the mesa at the *right corner* of the stronghold" which, said Vargas, comprised the "major portion of the palace and royal houses of the governor."[29] That eminence can only have been a spur from Fort Marcy Hill, a remnant of which remains behind present Holy Faith Episcopal church on East Palace Ave.

We are accustomed to think of only one street, that of San Francisco, leading to the *parroquia* in colonial times. Other streets, nevertheless, whose borders were examined in 1715, also led to the church prior to the Revolt: one from the *cienega* along the north and another along the south side of the *parroquia*.[30] As for the cienega, said Vargas in a letter to the viceroy,

> Besides, in La Cienega and its lowland, the waters gather from the surrounding mountains and mesas, and the said stronghold being near by, it is in the shade, and for that reason it is hidden from the sun in the morning, and in the afternoon it is also without out the sun's rays.[31]

A 1712 dispute over property in the vicinity of the *parroquia*, specifically to its north and east, described the *west* boundary as the "street that went to the house of Francisco Gómez [Robledo]" and, on the north, "the cienega."[32]

Prior to his replacement by Governor Rodríguez Cubero, Vargas had refurbished the north plaza of the Tano village, reclaiming the Pueblo house block for his *casas reales*, with its *plaza de armas* in front, that is, to the south. A review of Vargas' account of the recapture of Santa Fe in 1693 indicates that the Tano Pueblo established there contained two plazas aligned, not as tradition has it from east to west, but from north to south. Each contained a kiva, and in the north one was the famous kiva-tower whose use by the Franciscans for a chapel, prior to the opening of hostilities in December 1693, was initially rejected for its having been a pagan temple.[33]

The entire *casas reales* complex − Vargas' "stronghold" − was razed by Rodríguez Cubero, for in 1703 Vargas accused his successor before the cabildo of having done just that; and in their stead he had erected six low and six high buildings.[34] Having set aside land for a plazuela for church use, bounded north by an *acequia* − presumably the one that formerly ran down Palace Ave and was cut off both by the besieging Indians during the 1680 Rebellion as well as by Vargas in 1692 − it is unlikely that Rodríguez' new buildings fronted the plazuela now owned by the Franciscans.

Alonso Rael de Aguilar's house, said the witnesses in 1750 (in the suit referred to above, p. 83), was "contiguous with the church" of the Villa *and faced the "plaza de armas".*[35] As I have noted above, that same house seems to have been in 1824 the residence of Juan de Abrego fronted by the plazuela cited by Domingo Fernández.

What was considered the military plaza in 1693 was the northernmost of two Tano Pueblo plazas, aligned north to south and separated by a room block. Into these and the adjacent room blocks Vargas temporarily established his settlers in 1693. Preoccupied with the threat of yet another uprising, which occurred in 1696, it could well be possible that those former pueblo house blocks had yet to be completely (if at all) replaced prior to the appointment of his successor, Pedro Rodríguez Cubero. That

Rodríguez did replace them seems likely since he destroyed the stronghold, granting its plaza de armas to the church and resettling the residents on lands in nearby locations.

This is, of course, speculation, but it allows for the fact that as late as 1750 residents still referred to the northern plaza of the former pueblo as the plaza de armas. If Rodríguez ordered the former residents of the house block on the south end of Vargas' military plaza to settle elsewhere, his statement that any claims to that land were null and void at the time he granted it to the Franciscans makes sense.

The west boundary of Rodríguez Cubero's grant to the Franciscans, the former plaza, may not have been – as seems to have been inferred by previous investigators – the east *edge* of that pre-Revolt feature. If not – and the meaning is open to interpretation – and if the new convento property was configured such that *it was intended to intrude into, and to occupy a portion of the former plaza space*, we are left to speculate about the motives for such largess. Could the intention have been to superimpose re-established Christianity over the former Tano pueblo's south plaza, with its pagan kiva?

No documents so far known refer to an open chapel associated with the *parroquia* (even though Kubler has suggested that the balcony of the eigtheenth-century facade, over the main entrance, might have served the analogous function),[36] but it may be worth considering that if the church, according to Domingo's statement, had been relocated (or drastically renovated) at some unknown period in the eighteenth century, perhaps we should look to the west of the present *parroquia* for earlier structural remains.[37]

Santa Fe's public plaza, when seen in 1776 by Fray Atanasio Domínguez, was separated from the *parroquia*:

> In spite of what has been said, there is a semblance of a street in this villa. It begins on the left facing north shortly after one leaves the west gate of the cemetery and extends down about 400 or 500 varas. I point out that this quasi-street not only lacks orderly rows, or blocks of houses, but at its very beginning *it forms one side of a little plaza in front of the church.* The other three sides are three houses of settlers with

alleys between them. The entrance to the main plaza
is down through these (Adams and Chávez 1954:40;
my emphasis. See Figs. 3-6).

That arrangement is apparent on the Urrutia Map (Fig. 1), but it
had become considerably reduced by 1846 (Fig. 2). According to
the 1767 scale used by Urrutia, the open space lying between
what would today be Prince Plaza and San Francisco Street was
about 245 feet from north to south, Urrutia's *toesa* being equal to
5.5 feet, while the east-to-west distance from the cemetery to a
structure west of it was 220 feet, making a space containing about
1.3 acres total (incidentally, the approximate size of today's Santa
Fe plaza).

Figure 3. The *parroquia* in 1867. Photograph courtesy of the Museum of
New Mexico Neg. no. 10059.

Figure 4. Cathedral Place, north. The west end of Sena Plaza (the two-story building) and the north end of the house purchased by Bishop Lamy in 1856 form the center of the photograph. Property formerly of José Francisco Baca y Terrus, purchased by Bishop Lamy, also in 1856, is at the bottom left-center. Photograph courtesy of the Museum of New Mexico Neg. no. 15834.

Figure 5. Looking south along Cathedral Place from Palace Ave. The first school and residence for Bishop Lamy's nuns is on the left end of the building at the right, purchased from Alexandro Valles in 1856. Photograph courtesy of the Museum of New Mexico Neg. no. 61449.

Figure 6. Prince and Sena Plazas, East Palace Avenue; the view is northeast from the site of the former nuns' residence and first school, 1921, removed for construction of the US Federal Post Office building. This provides an impression of how the former plazuela may have appeared in the eighteenth century. Photograph courtesy of the Museum of New Mexico Neg. no. 150010.

Notes

1. New Mexico State Records Center and Archives (SRCA), Misc. Coll., Ortiz Family Papers. My original oral presentation at the Conference has been revised and somewhat refocused for publication here. See also Snow 1992.
2. SRCA, Archives of the Archdiocese of Santa Fe (AASF), Loose Docs., 1697, No. 1.
3. Chávez 1949; Ellis 1976; Adams and Chávez 1956; AASF, ibid.
4. Ivey 1988:415-21; Montgomery, Gordon, Smith, and Brew 1949:64-67. Ivey defined superposition as "symbolic overbuilding to indicate the dominence of Christianity over the pagan religion of the Indians."
5. Nevertheless, between about 1731 and 1737, an earthquake ("*terremoto*") leveled some adobe houses east of the *parroquia* (SRCA, Ortiz Family Papers, 1737). Severe enough to knock those down, what might have been the effect on the *parroquia*? Domínguez noted ruined portions of former structures east of the convento walls in 1776. In his 1737 residencia, Governor Cruzat y Gongora claimed that he had rebuilt the fortifications and the palace of the Villa. SRCA, Spanish Archives of New Mexico (SANM) Series II, No. 420. His reasons are not stated, beyond the fact that they had fallen to ruin.
6. SANM I:31.
7. The street in question must be, therefore, East Palace Avenue, and its edge, said Domingo, was visible by the footing stones. The inventory of properties is from SANM I:1314. Guadalupe Baca's house was inherited by her daughter, Carmen Benavides de Roubidoux, and subsequently sold by her to Josepha Salazar de Manderfield. Carmen was baptized María del Carmen Alarid, daughter of Juan and Guadalupe Baca. That property is today Prince Plaza, adjoining Sena Plaza on the west.
8. Santa Fe County Deeds (SFCD), Book C:17.
9. SFCD Book C:21-22; Horgan 1975:173.
10. McAndrew 1965:234.
11. Smith 1952.
12. McAndrew, op. cit.
13. McAndrew, ibid., pp. 216-18.
14. SANM II:251; author's translation.
15. SANM I:169; author's translation.
16. Hodge, Hammond, and Rey 1945:68
17. Governor Peralta's instructions from the Viceroy, in 1609, are silent concerning details of the layout of the new Villa (Chávez 1929).

18. Archivo General de Indias de Seville. *"De manera que ningun otro edificio se les arrime sino el perteneciente a su comodidad y ornato"* (No. 118). *"No se ponga [el templo mayor] en la plaza sino distante della y en parte que este separado del edificio que a el se llegue, que no se tocante a el, y que de todas partes sea visto porque se pueda ornar mejor y tenga mas autoridad; asi de procurar que sea algo levantado del suelo de manera que se aya de entrar en el por gradas, y cerca del entre la plaza mayor"* (No. 119).

19. Scholes 1936:38.

20. Bloom 1928:370

21. Kessell 1987:123

22. Hodge, Hammond, and Rey, op. cit.

23. Scholes 1929:46. The claims of Peinado, Benavides, and Zarate concerning the Villa's church in 1622-29 remain to be resolved.

24. Benavides reported a population of 750 Indian servants and 250 Spaniards in the Villa. If all were to fit into the nave for mass, the seventeenth century *parroquia* must have been nearly as large as today's cathedral, which will seat, in the nave, some 1200 persons (Marina Ochoa, pers. comm., Dec. 1997). Lamy estimated that the *parroquia* he razed must have held some 2000 people – clearly an overestimation, given its dimensions, scarcely larger than the chapel of San Miguel. Pedro Lucero de Godoy, testifying before Vargas in 1693, stated that the Villa, prior to the Revolt, held only 70 families, presumably referring only to "Spanish" families (Kessell, Hendricks, and Dodge 1995:509). Very rough estimates of family size at the time of the Revolt suggest a mean of 7.5 for both "Spaniards" and Mexican Indians (Snow and Stoller 1987). If the *hermita* of San Miguel served the needs of the Mexican Indians of the Villa, the *parroquia* – given the dimensions cited by Domínguez and by subsequent observers (Ellis 1985) – could easily have provided space for Lucero's 70 families, plus the 200 Indians cited by Zarate Salmeron.

25. Scholes 1935:204

26. *Proceso contra Gómez Robledo*, AGN, Inq., 583.

27. Hackett and Shelby 1942:100

28. *Proceso contra Gómez Robledo*, ibid.

29. Espinosa 1940:90

30. SANM I:169.

31. Hackett and Shelby, ibid., p. 282.

32. SANM I:491. Testimony therein identifies land owned by Diego de Duran adjacent to the church then being built, on the north side. In the 1715 examination of the former streets of the Villa, Duran's house was described as "well set back" from the street running in front of the *parroquia* (SANM I:169). Duran sold his

house and adjacent garden in 1721 to Alonso Rael de Aguilar (SANM I:744); this was the same house to which Aguilar added new rooms upon taking a second wife.

33. Ritch Coll. Huntington Library, Document RI 25. "Battle of Santa Fe, 1693" (copy courtesy of Rick Hendricks and John Kessel); von Wuthenau 1935.

34. SANM II:94a; Twitchell 1914.

35. SANM I:31

36. Kubler 1940:75-76; Ellis (1985:80) cites a passage from Guevara's 1817 report of his visitation of the *parroquia*, who described "*un atrio o cementerio que le sirve.*"

37. Might not the church Domingo described as having been removed from the plazuela have been an outdoor chapel?

38. Adams and Chávez 1956:40.

References Cited

Archivo General de Indias de Sevilla.
1973 *Las Ordenanzas de Descubrimiento, Nueva Poblacion y Pacificacion de las Indias Dadas Por Felipe II, el 13 de Julio de 1573, en el Bosque de Segovia.* Madrid: Ministerio de Viviendas, Servicio Central de Publicaciones.

Archivo General de la Nacion. Mexico
1662 *Proceso contra Francisco Gómez Robledo.* Inq., 583.

Adams, Eleanor B., and Fray Angélico Chávez (editors and translators)
1956 *The Missions of New Mexico, 1776.* Albuquerque: The University of New Mexico Press

Bloom, Lansing B.
1928 "A Glimpse of New Mexico in 1620." *NMHR* III/4 (Oct.), pp. 357-389.

Chávez, Fray Angélico
1949 "Santa Fe Church and Convent Site in the Seventeenth and Eighteenth Centuries." *NMHR* XXIV/2, 1949, pp. 84-93

Chávez, Ireneo L.
1929 "Instructions to Peralta by the Vice-Roy," *NMHR* IV/2:179-187.

Ellis, Bruce T.
1976 "Santa Fe's Seventeent Century Plaza, Parish Church, and Convent Reconsidered." IN, *Collected Papers in Honor of Marjorie Ferguson Lambert* (Ed., Albert H. Schroeder), pp. 183-198. Albuquerque: Albuquerque Archaeological Society Press.

1985 *Bishop Lamy's Santa Fe Cathedral.* Albuquerque: University of New Mexico Press.

Espinosa, J. Manuel

1940 *First Expedition of De Vargas into New Mexico.* Coronado Cuatro Centennial Publication, Vol. X. Albuquerque: University of New Mexico Press.

1942 *Crusaders of the Rio Grande.* Chicago: Institute of Jesuit History.

Forrestal, Peter P.

1954 *Benavides' Memorial of 1630.* Washington: Academy of American Franciscan History.

Hackett, Charles W., and Charmion C. Shelby

1942 *Revolt of the Pueblo Indians of New Mexico and Otermin's Attempted Reconquest, 1680-1682.* Albuquerque: University of New Mexico Press.

Hodge, Frederick W., George P. Hammond, and Agapito Rey

1945 *Fray Alonso de Benavides' Revised Memorial of 1634.* Albuquerque: University of New Mexico Press.

Horgan, Paul

1975 *Lamy of Santa Fe.* New York: Farrar, Straus and Giroux.

Ivey, James E.

1988 *In the Midst of a Loneliness: The Architectural History of the Salinas Missions.* Southwest Cultural Resources Center Professional Papers No. 15. US National Park Service, Southwest Regional Office. Santa Fe.

Kessell, John L.

1980 *The Missions of New Mexico Since 1776.* Albuquerque: University of New Mexico Press.

Kessel, John L., Rick Hendricks, and Meredith Dodge (editors)

1995 *To the Royal Crown Restored: The Journals of Don Diego de Vargas, New Mexico, 1692-1694.* Albuquerque: The University of New Mexico Press.

Kubler, George

1940 *The Religious Architecture of New Mexico in the Colonial Period and Since the American Occupation.* Colorado Springs: The Taylor Museum.

McAndrew, John

1965 *The Open-air Churches of Sixteenth-Century Mexico.* Cambridge: Harvard University Press.

Montgomery, Ross G., Watson Smith, and John O. Brew

1949 *Franciscan Awotovi: The Excavation and Conjectural Reconstruction of a Seventeenth-Century Spanish Mission Establishment at a Hopi Town in Northeastern Arizona.* Reports of the Awatovi Expedition, No. 3. Papers of the Peabody Museum of American Archaeology and Ethnology, Vol. 36. Cambridge: Peabody Museum of American Archeology and Ethnology.

New Mexico State Records Center and Archives. Santa Fe (as cited)
Ritch Collection
1693 "Battle of Santa Fe, 1693." Huntington Library, Document RI 25.
Santa Fe, County of
n. d.   Deed books (as cited)
Scholes, France V.
1929 "Documents for the History of New Mexican Mission in the Seventeenth Century, I. *NMHR* IV/1 (Jan.), pp. 45-58. n
1935 "The First Decade of the Inquisition in New Mexico." *NMHR* X/3 (July), pp. 195-241.
1936 "Church and State in New Mexico, 1610-1650." *NMHR* XI/1 (Jan.), pp. 9-76.
Smith, Watson
1952 *Excavations in Big Hawk Valley, Wupatki National Monument, Arizona.* Museum of Northern Arizona Bulletin 24. Flagstaff: Northern Arizona Society of Science and Art, Inc.
Snow, David H.
1992 "Archeological and Historical Investigations, Santa Fe Archdiocesan Historic-Artistic Patrimony and Archives Office Building, Santa Fe, New Mexico." Ms., submitted to the Archdiocese of Santa Fe.
Snow, David H., and Marianne L. Stoller
1987 "Outside Santa Fe in the Seventeenth Century." Paper presented at the "Ethnic Relations in the Southwest." American Society for Ethnohistory, Berkeley (November 5-7, 1987).
von Wuthenau, A.
1935 "The Spanish Military Chapels in Santa Fe and the Reredos of our Lady of Light." *NMHR* X/3 (July), pp. 175-194.

The Church in El Paso del Norte in the Eighteenth Century

Rick Hendricks

Introduction

As a result of the reconquest of New Mexico and the reconsolidation of the Spanish presence in the upriver colony in the 1690s, the Paso del Norte area lost importance as a population center and declined as a political force relative to the newly reestablished capital in Santa Fe. Although they were diminished in size, however, the communities of Ysleta, Senecú, San Lorenzo, and Socorro, which stretched downriver from the mission of Nuestra Señora de Guadalupe del Paso, constituted a firm base for the remarkable recovery of eighteenth-century El Paso. Scarcely three decades into the eighteenth century, the Paso del Norte area rivaled all the rest of the colony in economic importance. For much of the eighteenth century, El Paso also served as the de facto headquarters of the Franciscan Custody of St. Paul, since the custos often resided there for long periods of time.

El Paso also emerged in the period from 1730 to 1750 as a focal point in the struggle between the bishop of Durango and the Franciscan order in New Mexico for spiritual control of the colony, as the diocesan see pushed the transition from missions to secular parishes and the Franciscans insisted that the predominance of Indian populations created mitigating circumstances. As a matter of fact (rather than mere jurisdiction), the people of the riverine communities of the Paso del Norte area were frequently under the control of both diocesan officials who reported directly to Durango and regular, Franciscan church officials who responded to their provincial in Mexico City. Even though the Bishop of Durango placed a diocesan priest in New Mexico's

capital during this period, the situation in El Paso made it a logical site for diocesan priests from Durango to establish a firm foot-
hold in formerly Franciscan territory, and the experiment there
was more complex, including as it did the short-lived curacy of
Las Caldas to minister to the rebellious Sumas. The presence of
secular churchmen in El Paso in positions of authority also presented some new and interesting avenues for the increasingly
conflictive Franciscans to explore, which on occasion led to surprising cooperative efforts.

Beyond competition and cooperation between secular and
regular clergy particular to New Mexico, the situation of the church
in the colony reflected two other trends, one of long standing in
New Mexico and another that had become generalized in the
Spanish Indies. First, by the last quarter of the eighteenth century,
civil-military authorities in New Mexico had become determined
to wrest control of the colony from ecclesiastical authorities and
missionaries alike. This attitude reflected a battle as old as the
colony, but it was being fought with renewed vigor at this time.
Second, the growing creole resentment of peninsulars in the society at large had become manifest within the Franciscan order
as well. While this basic difference was often at the heart of the
internecine struggles within the order in New Mexico, the lines
were not always drawn as expected, and tensions among
Franciscans of all stripes erupted all too frequently in the last
quarter of the eighteenth century and the early part of the nineteenth. These currents moved through area churches, though they
were certainly not limited exclusively to the southern reaches of
New Mexico. By examining them we can learn more of church
life in El Paso del Norte in the eighteenth century, defined here
as the period between 1693 and 1817, from the departure of Diego de Vargas northward to the visit of Juan Bautista Ladrón
Niño de Guevara.

El Paso After Vargas (1693-1725)

When Diego de Vargas conducted a census of prospective
New Mexico colonists living in the El Paso area in late December 1692 and early January 1693, he found almost a thousand
individuals in the five communities of El Paso, San Lorenzo, Ysleta,
Senecú, and Socorro. The people enumerated consisted of 73

married couples, 115 widowers, widows, single men, and single women, 448 boys and girls, and 250 domestic servants. To Vargas's way of reckoning, these individuals formed the basis of his upcoming colonizing effort. In order to understand fully the size of the El Paso district in the winter of 1692-93, though, it would be necessary to add to the census the several hundred mission Indians whom Vargas did not count. While he expressed no interest in relocating such El Paso groups as the Mansos or Sumas, Vargas did plan for the Tiwas and Piros to return upriver to New Mexico. In the event, however, they did not.

By the time the colonizing expedition got under way in October 1693, Vargas had added a number of soldiers and their families whom he had recruited in Nueva Vizcaya to the pool of potential colonists formed by the New Mexico colony-in-exile in El Paso. These new arrivals probably swelled the population to as many as twelve hundred or more on the eve of departure. Since he neither held muster for the departing colonists nor conducted another census of the El Paso district, it is impossible to ascertain with certainty how many left and how many remained. What is known is that more than seventy families, among whom were many widows, single men and women, children, and servants totaling more than eight hundred individuals, and an unspecified number of Indians struck out upriver for Santa Fe. Vargas indicated that a few additional people, including the Piros and Tiwas, were waiting for spring to travel to New Mexico. It would seem that in the wake of Vargas's recolonizing expedition, only a handful of Spanish citizens remained in the company of several hundred mission Indians. Although some Franciscans accompanied the expedition north, others remained in the El Paso missions to provide for the spiritual needs of both Spaniard and Indian.[1]

Remarkably little is known about El Paso in the late 1690s after the departure of Vargas's colonists, when attention was focused on the upriver colony's desperate struggle for survival. Surviving documents provide a glimpse of Franciscan activity in El Paso in this otherwise obscure period.

Pedro Rodríguez Cubero briefly enjoyed good relations with the Franciscans after taking possession of the governorship in

July 1697. As he pursued legal action against Diego de Vargas and the former Governor's backers, the relationship soured and then turned ugly. In May 1698 Governor Rodríguez Cubero learned that Juan Páez Hurtado, one of Vargas's closest associates, had taken refuge in the convento of Nuestra Señora de Guadalupe in El Paso to escape prosecution in a pending lawsuit and criminal proceeding against him for defrauding the royal treasury. Páez Hurtado was disturbing the peace and trying to cause unrest by frightening the soldiers and citizens of El Paso with the false statements he issued from the safety of the church. The father guardian in El Paso, fray José García Marín, publicly supported Páez Hurtado and Vargas. According to El Paso presidial soldier Juan Roque Gutiérrez, Father García Marín cajoled him to retract his sworn statements against Páez Hurtado and grew angry and withheld absolution when he refused. Only when he saw there was no way to change Gutiérrez's mind did fray José grant him absolution. Other individuals reported similar actions by the father guardian. One said Father García Marín vehemently refused to baptize his son. A visiting military official stated that he missed mass on a feast day because the priest had rescheduled it to keep him from attending. For as long as the official stayed in El Paso, he had to go to Socorro to hear mass. All this was done because the individuals involved were allied with Governor Rodríguez Cubero. In addition, fray José preached from the pulpit that even those who had made false statements under oath against their neighbor could retract them without harm or dishonor and without burdening their consciences. Governor Rodríguez Cubero brought the matter of denying the holy sacraments of penance and baptism and Father García Marín's preaching to the attention of the Vice-Custos, fray Antonio Guerra, who was serving in Socorro. It is safe to assume that the Franciscan's response was not what the Governor had hoped.

Father Guerra quickly reported receipt of the Governor's letter to the Custos, fray Juan Álvarez, noting that the accusations against Father García Marín made Rodríguez Cubero subject to major excommunication. The Custos concurred, declaring that the Governor, the priest's accusers, and those who had criticized his preaching were excommunicated. Though the Custos referred the matter to the Holy Office, the Inquisition's action, if any, is not part of the record. As this case clearly illustrates, Franciscans in El Paso participated actively in the bitter struggle that followed Vargas's first term in the governorship. It also demonstrates how readily the Franciscans sought recourse to the Holy Office to further a political end when Rodríguez Cubero unwittingly presented them with the opportunity.[2]

Another of the very few documents bearing on El Paso in this period recounts the tale of Tomás Gutiérrez Carrera and the three little pigs of the mission of Nuestra Señora de Guadalupe. In October 1699 Captain Tiburcio de Ortega appeared before the captain and justicia mayor of the El Paso district, Captain Juan de Ulibarrí, to bring a civil suit against Alferez Gutiérrez Carrera. Acting in his capacity as syndic of the convento of Nuestra Señora de Guadalupe, Ortega alleged that the alferez had shot with an harquebus and killed three swine belonging to the Franciscans and failed to offer recompense. Gutiérrez Carrera countered that he had killed only two swine for which he would pay if he received ten fanegas of maize to replace what the swine had eaten from his field. He had removed ten animals more than twenty times. At one sack lost for each occurrence, that came to ten fanegas. Three times he had taken the animals to the father guardian and asked to be paid for damages, and twice more he had taken them to Captain Ulibarrí, but the Franciscans had neither paid for any damage nor controlled their swine. Finally, as Gutiérrez Carrera admitted, he lost his temper:

> I began to pick what little maize the swine had left me, having to pick it green so that they would not eat it all. When I was picking, the swine came while the maize was spread out in the milpa. After I had run them off twice and pulled a tendon in my foot chasing them, they returned. I became angry when I saw that they had eaten the rest of the milpa and I could not stop them. That was when I grabbed my harquebus and shot and killed them.

A compromise was reached, which apparently called for payment for the Franciscans' slain swine and compensation to the alferez of one sack of maize. With the unseemly affair concluded, the father guardian requested the return to both parties of all documents relating to the case. A rather indignant sounding Captain Ulibarrí stated that that was against the law and he could do no such thing. He would, however, give either party an exact, attested copy of the proceedings free of charge.

This incident offers additional evidence of how the church participated within the community. No Franciscan executed a document related to this case; such temporal matters fell to the syndic. It would also seem that the situation deteriorated to "porcuscide" largely because the friars declined to take steps to pen up their livestock. This otherwise minor episode is actually fairly typical of controversies that erupted in the El Paso area every so often, usually pitting the fathers against the Spanish citizenry and not their Indian charges.[3]

The first surviving report on the El Paso area in the post-Vargas era came in 1706. In January of that year Father Juan Alvarez noted that the mission of Nuestra Señora de Guadalupe was ministering to Mansos and Piros, a few Spaniards, and those soldiers from the El Paso presidio actually serving in the district. The real of San Lorenzo, a largely Spanish settlement, was served by the mission to the Piros at Senecú. Ysleta had a predominately Tiwa population, and Socorro was made up in the main of Sumas and Piros. Fray Juan also mentioned a previously unnamed mission, Santa María Magdalena, for another group of Sumas.[4]

The Sumas and the Franciscans both played a role in early events of the eighteenth century that brought El Paso to the attention of the rest of New Mexico. On 9 November 1711 Gen. Antonio de Valverde Cosío, who was in command in the El Paso district, received word from fray Gonzalo Sobens Barreda, minister of Socorro, informing him that after mass on that very morning, two Suma women had come to his cell. They had told him to tell Valverde that all the Sumas living in the pueblos wanted to depart that night with the Mansos and the Janos. Fray Gonzalo had seen the Sumas selling the blankets they had been weaving and gathering their things. They had been threatened with death at the Spaniards' hands if they did not go with the other Indians. A Manso had come to tell them that the night of the ninth was the night and went on to San Antonio to tell those there to go to

El Paso on the pretext of buying pots. Fray Gonzalo added that the Indians were not to be underestimated. Father Sobens had clearly earned the loyalty of at least some of the Indians to whom he ministered. Unlike Diego de Vargas, who ignored warnings that another revolt was about to occur in 1696, Valverde heeded the warning of the Franciscan, who was his friend and paisano, and he thereby averted a full-blown rebellion by dint of his personal diplomacy.[5] This incident was but one of several that demonstrated Valverde's willingness to work with church authorities in El Paso, particularly when it came to dealing with the challenge the Sumas presented. This attitude made it possible for him to take advantage in 1725 of the almost unprecedented opportunity that grew out of the first visit to New Mexico by a bishop from Durango.

Attempts to Establish Diocesan Authority over New Mexico (1725-60)

In 1725 Bishop Benito Crespo y Monroy traveled as far as El Paso on an official tour of his diocese. That year Valverde requested of the Bishop that a mission for the Suma Indians be established near his hacienda of San Antonio.[6] Valverde's desire for a solution to the Suma problem gave Bishop Crespo a chance to further the diocese's claim to jurisdiction over the province of New Mexico. On a number of occasions since the early seventeenth century, bishops in Durango had made halfhearted attempts to assert their authority over New Mexico and had always met with Franciscan resistance, but Bishop Crespo began to pursue the matter in earnest. In 1728 he placed Santiago Roybal in Santa Fe as vicar. A royal cedula issued in Madrid on 7 December 1729 seemed to resolve the matter; it mandated that Durango be recognized as diocesan authority over New Mexico. This brought a stinging rejoinder from the Franciscan commissary general in Mexico City. Recalling the martyrs of 1680, he stated that twenty-three missionaries had already fallen in that province and no bishop had. He added that were it not for the Franciscans those regions would have already been lost. This opposition notwithstanding, Bishop Crespo named fray Salvador López vicar and ecclesiastical judge in El Paso on the basis of the cedula. The other Franciscans refused to recognize him as such, and he had to leave the province. Bishop Crespo then informed the Custos, fray Andrés Varo, that he intended to conduct a visitation of the province, which he initiated in July 1730. The visit did not settle matters, however, and a viceregal decree in 1731 revoked Roybal's appointment. But another viceregal decree in 1733 upheld the Durango's diocesan jurisdiction over New Mexico, and the struggle continued.[7]

Meanwhile, although Valverde had died of illness in 1728, Crespo had not forgotten his idea of building a mission to the Sumas. It came to fruition in 1731 in an interesting variation on the mission idea. Before his death Valverde had established a *capellanía*, or benefice, in the amount of six thousand pesos of principal yielding three hundred pesos of income on his hacienda, San Antonio de Padua, located two leagues from Socorro. The *capellán* was obligated to say mass twice a month at a place Valverde Cosío or his heirs chose. In exchange he was to receive an annual income of three hundred pesos. The family also enjoyed the right to select the capellán, and Father Roybal was the first chosen. Viceroy Casafuerte directed the Bishop of Durango to dispatch a title to the holder of the benefice of the hacienda of San Antonio in early 1731 so that he could administer the sacraments to the Suma Indians who had gathered at a place called Palo Clavado. This directive resulted from information that the Bishop and José Valentín de Aganza, captain of the El Paso presidio (and Valverde's son-in-law), had provided to the viceroy. They had reported that some 250 roving Sumas had formed a pueblo and begun planting crops. The Sumas had asked for a priest, insisting that he not be a Franciscan. A secular parish was soon established with the title Santa María de las Caldas to serve the Sumas of Palo Clavado and the workers of the Hacienda de San Antonio. Aganza was responsible for reducing the Sumas to a sedentary state and recruiting settlers for the pueblo, many of whom relocated from Los Tiburcios. He purchased the land for the Sumas, built their house blocks, provided tools, seeds, and yokes of oxen, dug an acequia from the Rio Grande to the pueblo, and supplied them until they harvested their first crop. Aganza also provided suitable adornments, vestments, and sacred vessels for the church.

The experiment with the curacy of Las Caldas lasted almost fourteen years. For most of that time, secular diocesan priests from Durango served Las Caldas, although a Franciscan in Socorro ministered to the pueblo for a brief period. Disaster threatened in 1745 when the Sumas revolted. The rebellion was quickly snuffed, but it drove home just how vulnerable Las Caldas and the hacienda of San Antonio were. Although close in geographical terms to other area settlements, both pueblo and hacienda were isolated, especially when the river ran high, and exposed to Apache raiders from the neighboring mountains. As the rebellion also demonstrated, they were out of the reach of defenders during certain times of the year in the event of another uprising. This came with finality in 1749 when the Sumas destroyed Las Caldas and caused the abandonment of the hacienda of San Antonio.[8]

If matters were not going so well for the Bishop of Durango in El Paso, everything seemed to be doing fine in the largest part of the district, which remained firmly in Franciscan hands. Two detailed if somewhat idealized reports, fray Miguel Menchero's of 1744 and fray Manuel San Juan Nepomuceno's of 1754, described the local missions almost as though they were nestled in a Biblical land flowing with milk and honey, or perhaps more appropriate in this case, a land of fine wine and abundant grain.[9]

Despite the loss of Las Caldas, however, the Bishop ushered in a fundamental change for the church in El Paso in 1754 when he sent two priests there from Durango. As his vicar and ecclesiastical judge, the Bishop chose José Lorenzo de Rivera. Rivera remained at his post in El Paso almost continually until his death twenty-five years later in 1779. Accompanying Father Rivera was Nicolás Téllez Girón, who was selected to fill the benefice established on the hacienda of Nuestra Señora de los Dolores de Carrizal. Father Téllez Girón lived and worked in El Paso for thirty years as resident priest from the Durango diocese until his death in 1784. In selecting Fathers Rivera and Téllez Girón, the Bishop accomplished two things, by chance or design, one of which the Franciscans seldom achieved and the other which they never did. First, both priests ministered in the same community for decades, permitting them to establish remarkable continuity of service. This contrasted dramatically with the Franciscan tendency

throughout the eighteenth century to transfer priests from one
mission to another very frequently. Second, while Father Téllez
Girón was not the first New Mexican to become a priest and
serve in his home province, he was a native son serving in his
hometown among his friends and neighbors. The community,
moreover, could scarcely have failed to respect him, as he was
also a member of the local El Paso elite. His status would have
been very different from that of the Franciscans, all of whom
were outsiders and many of whom had great difficulty adapting
to life on the frontier.[10]

From Bishop Tamarón to Fray Francisco Atanasio Domínguez (1760-76)

Despite years of squabbling over jurisdiction, Bishop Pedro
de Tamarón y Romeral was, by all accounts, warmly received
when he arrived in El Paso in April 1760 on his official visit of his
diocese. There to greet him were El Paso's religious personnel,
two Franciscans, Custos fray Jacobo de Castro and one other priest,
and two diocesan priests, one of whom served as vicar and ecclesiastical judge. While there, the Bishop appointed the Custos to
these offices, apparently in an effort to smooth relations between
the Franciscans and the see in Durango. In addition to the priests
serving in El Paso proper, four more Franciscans served other
area churches, one each at San Lorenzo, Senecú, Ysleta, and
Socorro.[11]

Four years after the Bishop's visit to El Paso, the Christian
Sumas living in the real of San Lorenzo informed Gov. Tomás
Vélez Cachupín that their brethren were scattered among Senecú,
Ysleta, and Socorro where they had settled after the destruction
of Las Caldas. The San Lorenzo Sumas suggested that it would be
advantageous to have these people join them in their pueblo.
The Governor also learned that an additional thirty-five to forty
heathen Sumas were living in the Los Tiburcios area. In order to
implement the proposed resettlement, Vélez Cachupín notified
this latter group of his plan and offered them the opportunity to
relocate to San Lorenzo where fray José Páez would instruct them
in Christian doctrine.[12]

Also in 1764, at Bishop Tamarón's insistence, the villas of
Santa Fe, Santa Cruz de la Cañada, Albuquerque, and El Paso
were secularized by royal order and erected as curacies. After a

time the inability to find suitable priests to fill all these posts led to another royal order returning these communities to the Franciscans as missions, but without the annual stipend of 330 pesos they had traditionally enjoyed. As it had on numerous occasions in the past, El Paso served in this period as headquarters of the Franciscan custody of New Mexico. Father Juan de Hinojosa was serving as Custos in early September 1775 when fray Francisco Atanasio Domínguez arrived in El Paso en route upriver to conduct his formal inspection of the missions of New Mexico. Father Domínguez tarried in El Paso until March of the following year, dealing with personnel matters related to his position as canonical visitor and preparing for his journey north. History is much the poorer because he left no detailed description of the churches in the El Paso district as he did for the rest of the custody.[13]

Conflict: Church v. State, and Diocesan Clergy and Franciscans and the Transition to Secularization (1777-1817)

Church v. State

The office of commandant general, created in 1776, brought with it the associated title of vice-patron of the church and the power of exercising the Patronato Real throughout the northern frontier. With this authority the commandant general could place in curacies and benefices clergy whom prelates (or ecclesiastical cabildos, when an episcopal see was vacant) proposed. Because it was within the jurisdiction of the diocese of Durango, the bishop of Durango had the right to propose priests for vacant posts in New Mexico. The Caballero de Croix, the first commandant general, reserved for himself certain powers of the Patronato Real. Appeals from *juzgados ordinarios*, or local courts, except for matters relating to the Patronato Real, were to be forwarded to the Audiencia of Guadalajara.

The new commandant general, Felipe de Neve formally extended patronage rights to Gov. Juan de Bautista de Anza, and in the summer of 1781, the Governor informed the Franciscans that he was worried about adult Indians' ignorance of Christian doctrine and proposed a solution. Adult Indians would henceforth attend religious instruction twice weekly. He directed that absenteeism for males be punished with a week in jail and time in the

stocks on the first occurrence, two weeks of the same punishment on the second, and time in the Santa Fe jail on the third. As
for women, their punishment would be mandatory daily classes.
Anza ordered the alcaldes, *tenientes*, and the *justicias* to conduct a
census of every mission. He also placed on them the burden of
seeing to it that his orders were obeyed. For the Franciscans Anza's
meddling in mission administration and the teaching of the gospel was an outrage. Custos José de la Prada complained about
Governor Anza's interference in his administration to his fellow
friars in New Mexico and to the provincial in Mexico City, particularly regarding the assignment of priests.[14]

Franciscans and Diocesan Clergy and the Transition to Secularization
    Perhaps the most notable aspect of the Franciscan Order in
late eighteenth-century New Mexico was how seriously it was
divided against itself. By the last quarter of the century, tension
between peninsular Spaniards and creoles within the order had
reached levels comparable to those of the society at large. In 1782
a number of European friars accused American-born Governor
Anza and the Custos, fray Juan Bermejo, a peninsular Spaniard,
of discrimination. The Europeans made this claim even though
they constituted the majority of Franciscans in New Mexico at
the time.[15]
    In 1797 the Bishop of Durango selected five secular priests to
serve in New Mexican parishes, Gregorio Olidén, José Vivián
Ortega, Juan José Lombide, Juan José de Sida, and José Serampión
Prado. In general, the Franciscans resented the coming of the
diocesan clergy and resisted the transition from mission to secular parishes. On occasion, however, the presence of diocesan priests
in El Paso presented opportunities for local Franciscans. One such
instance involved Father Prado, the vicar and ecclesiastical judge
of El Paso, in a serious Franciscan jurisdictional dispute, details of
which he reported to his Bishop in Durango.[16]
    In December 1802, Father Prado wrote to the Bishop that he
had recently received a midnight visitor in the person of fray
Rafael Benavides, the priest of the Ysleta and Socorro missions.
Some time before, Custos Mariano José Sánchez Vergara had traveled to El Paso and removed fray Antonio Molina as vice-custos,
naming Benavides in his stead. Father Molina was a new arrival

in New Mexico, having been sent north from Mexico City by
the provincial at the end of 1801 with the title of vice-custos and
as president of a mission of nine Franciscans headed for the New
Mexico mission field. Thinking the Custos's actions unjust, Molina
apparently appealed to the provincial. By November 1802 he
had his response. Claiming that Father Molina had been improp-
erly treated and should be Vice-Custos, the Provincial suspended
Custos Sánchez Vergara, required him to explain himself, and
named fray José de la Prada as Vice-Custos while the matter was
sorted out.[17]

As soon as Molina had the provincial's favorable decision,
he summoned Benavides to appear before him, but the good
father refused to appear. Father Molina then enlisted the help of
the Lieutenant-Governor, who ordered men to Ysleta to force
Benavides to comply, even if it meant taking him in handcuffs.
When Benavides learned of this order, he fled to Father Prado's
house to seek refuge. A thoroughly shocked Father Prado shared
his thoughts with his Bishop:

> I shall leave it to your well-known prudence, most
> illustrious sir, to imagine how I felt upon hearing
> this explanation. It occurred to me that had this priest
> not found out in time and come to seek refuge in
> my house, what a scandal there would have been to
> see a priest with twenty-two years of service, and
> honorable ones so I have been informed, taken off
> bound on a day when there are so many people
> about, because there are bullfights now in this juris-
> diction. I have wondered what the people of this
> jurisdiction whom we call neophytes would think
> seeing a minister of Jesus Christ, an old priest from
> whom they have received instruction in the gospel,
> bound like a common criminal, the same as men
> without character. Having been persuaded that they
> owed priests their respect, the Indians would doubt-
> less think that the priests lived a deception.

Father Prado went on to tell the Bishop that he had scolded fray
Antonio for his rash actions against a fellow priest but that he
had made little impression on the Franciscan. Should similar

matters arise in the future, Prado wanted a clarification from the Bishop. When, he asked, were the Franciscans to recognize his authority and when were they to obey their regular prelate in matters of jurisdiction? Fray Rafael might have wondered the same thing or seen in the Bishop an avenue of appeal. At any rate, he asked the Bishop to intervene on his behalf with the provincial. The Bishop would understand, he wrote, that he could not travel to Mexico City to defend himself. He was not well, he was serving two missions and the presidio of San Elizario, and it was a very long journey to repeat what he had already communicated three times.

Writing to the Bishop in support of fray Rafael's petition, Father Prado put his finger on what he thought was the cause of the problem among the Franciscans: the generation gap. There was no hint of conflict between creoles and peninsulars or diocesan and regular priests in his analysis. If fact, this was the first time he had ever had any difficulty with them. Together he and the mature Franciscans got along with a great spirit of brotherhood, but this did not happen with the young ones. The most recent group to arrive in New Mexico, among them Father Molina, had upset the whole kingdom, opposing their superiors in everything and fighting especially with the vicar in Santa Fe. What they needed to attend to, thought Father Prado, was to fulfil their religious duties and to stop giving scandal. It is unclear whether the Bishop acted on these petitions, but fray Antonio Molina apparently departed New Mexico, perhaps to offer his side of the story to his superiors in Mexico City, and did not return. Meanwhile in El Paso, both regular and secular priests continued to serve the growing area communities.[18]

In 1812 Bishop José Miguel de Irigoyen named Juan Tomás Terrazas as interim priest of Nuestra Señora de Guadalupe. He was replaced in 1814 when Juan Rafael Rascón was selected as vicar of El Paso. Soon after, Terrazas became chaplain of the presidial company at nearby San Elizario. The new Bishop of Durango, Juan Francisco de Castañiza, commissioned Juan Bautista Ladrón Niño de Guevara to inspect the missions of New Mexico in 1817. The inspector found Father Rascón in the former Guadalupe mission church and the Franciscan Custos, fray Isidoro Barcenilla, serving the remaining area missions. Guevara's report was a scathing indictment of the Franciscans in New Mexico. Father Barcenilla came in for particularly harsh criticism. The area Indians were still ignorant and unfaithful to their Christian duties, and the churches were a disgrace. This woeful situation was the result of fray Isodoro's neglect. Presumably the diocesan clergy would do a better job when the remaining missions were eventually secularized.[19]

Conclusion

Although scholars have often erroneously assigned eighteenth-century El Paso to New Biscay, made it marginal in a colony with its capital in distant Santa Fe, or simply forgotten it altogether, the role the area played in the history of the church in New Mexico during that critical era was pivotal. Even though the El Paso population decreased markedly after Diego de Vargas's recolonization efforts upriver, churchmen in El Paso continued to be actively involved in the colony's governance. This became particularly apparent during the struggle between Vargas and his successor, Pedro Rodríguez Cubero, when the Franciscans sided with the former against the latter. At other times, such as when Father Sobens Barreda gave his timely warning to General Valverde Cosío, the priests' proximity to and understanding of the Indians in the area averted a rebellion that could have been very bloody.

Beginning in the second decade of the eighteenth century, successive bishops of the see of Durango renewed their claim to authority over the church in New Mexico. At Las Caldas, in 1731, the Bishop began a new parish where a secular priest sent from Durango ministered to voluntarily reduced Suma Indians. From that time on too, the bishops tried to maintain priests to represent them in the El Paso area. The Las Caldas experiment lasted for fourteen years, during most of which time secular priests served there. By around midcentury the bishop had established a more permanent presence in El Paso in the person of two long-serving representatives, José Lorenzo de Rivera and Nicolás Téllez Girón.

The fruits of these continued efforts in El Paso can be seen from the fact that after years of Franciscan protest against interference from Durango, Bishop Tamarón was warmly received in area churches when he paid his official visit in 1760. This did not mean, however, that the struggle between secular and regular in New Mexico was over. On the contrary, in the last quarter of the eighteenth century the struggle intensified in some respects and took on new dimensions, even though it occasionally offered new opportunities for cooperation. The arrival of Governor Anza ushered in a period of heated conflict between the church (both secular and regular clergy) and the state over control of the populace, both Indian and Spaniard. At the same time, the Franciscans were divided against themselves as peninsulars clashed with creoles and the younger priests showed a lack of respect for their elders. This was the backdrop for the inevitable, long-overdue secularization of the missions of the El Paso area, a process that was still very much incomplete – if well on the way – as the second decade of the nineteenth century came to a close.[20]

Notes

1.   John L. Kessell, Rick Hendricks, and Meredith D. Dodge, eds., *To the Royal Crown Restored: The Journals of don Diego de Vargas, New Mexico, 1693-1694*. Albuquerque: University of New Mexico Press, 1995), 65, 375-85.

2.   The Inquisition v. Pedro Rodríguez Cubero (Archivo General de la Nación, Mexico City, Inquisición 710) will be published by the University of New Mexico Press in volume five of the Vargas Project series.

3.   Tiburcio de Ortega v. Tomás Gutiérrez Carrera, El Paso, 8-13 Oct. 1699, Juárez Archive I (JA I, University of Texas El Paso, first filming), 1798, r. 48, f. 180-89.

4.   W.H. Timmons, *El Paso: A Borderlands History* (El Paso: Texas Western Press, 1990), 23.

5.   Antonio de Valverde Cosío, Proceedings, El Paso del Norte, 6 Nov. 1711-27 Feb. 1713, JA I, 1770, r. 45, f. 400-81. An incomplete copy is in Biblioteca Nacional de México (BNM), 25/419.1). Rick Hendricks, "Spanish-Indian Relations in El Paso del Norte in the Early Eighteenth Century: The Suma Rebellion of 1711" (Paper delivered at the Annual Meeting of the Society for American Archaeology, New Orleans, 1995), 2.

6.   Robert Nelson, "Unlocking Southwest History in Durango's Archives," *El Paso Times*, Sunday, 16 Aug. 1992, section F. Eleanor B. Adams, ed., *Bishop Tamarón's Visitation of New Mexico* (Albuquerque: Historical Society of New Mexico, 1954), 14.

7.   Adams, *Bishop Tamarón's Visitation*, 14-16. Guillermo Porras Muñoz, *Iglesia y Estado en Nueva Vizcaya, 1562-1821* (Mexico City: Universidad Nacional Autónoma de México, 1980), 38.

8.   Antonio de Valverde Cosío, Establishment of a capellanía, El Paso, 26 Apr. 1726, JA I, 1774, r. 45, f. 352-60. The Marqués de Casafuerte to the Bishop of Durango, Mexico City, 10 Feb. 1731, Archivos Históricos del Arzobispado de Durango, Rio Grande Historical Collections, New Mexico State University Library (AHAD)-39. Manuel Antonio San Juan, Testimony taken at the request of Domingo de Aganza relative to the service record of José Valentín de Aganza and Antonio de Valverde Cosío, El Paso, 14 July 1761, Juárez Archive, second filming (JA II), r. 7, bk. 1, 1761, f. 219-85. Documents related to the Suma revolt at Las Caldas, Las Caldas and El Paso, 24 Apr.-11 Sept. 1745, JA II, r. 10, bk. 1, 1770, f. 464-81. Liquidation of the Hacienda de San Antonio, El Paso, 1 Oct. 1749-24 Apr. 1751, JA II, r. 3, bk. 1, 1757, f. 1-400, continued on r. 4, bk. 1, 1757, f. 1-66. Rick Hendricks, "Santa María de las Caldas and the Hacienda de San Antonio: Diligencias Matrimoniales from the Lost Curacy, 1733-1739," *Nuestras Raíces* 6:3 (Fall 1994): 115-25.

9.   Timmons, *El Paso*, 34, 37.

10.   Rivera died in August 1779 and Téllez Girón on 22 June 1784. Documents relating to the death and estate of José Lorenzo de Rivera, El Paso, 18 Aug. 1779-19 May 1780, JA II, bk. 1, 1774, f. 62-87. Eugenio Fernández, Proceedings, El Paso, 23 June-23 July 1784, r. 11, bk. 1, 1784, f. 109-50. Br. José Lorenzo de Rivera, Report, El Paso, 11 July-24 September 1754, JA II, r. 4, bk. 1, 1757, f. 694-97. Referring to first half of the period under discussion in this paper, Norris computed that the average Franciscan served five missions and remained in each for 2.6 years. While I have not made a similarly precise calculation, it is clear that the policy of frequent transfers continued throughout the century. Jim Norris, "The Franciscans in New Mexico, 1692-1754: Toward a New Assessment," *The Americas* 51:2 (Oct. 1994): 166.

11.   Adams, *Bishop Tamarón's Visitation*, 29, 34.

12.   Tomás Vélez Cachupín, Proceedings in the demarcation and measurement of lands to the Suma Indians at the real of San Lorenzo, 18 Oct. 1764-31 Oct. 1765, SANM I:1350.

13.   Eleanor B. Adams and Fray Angélico Chávez, trans. and eds., *The Missions of New Mexico, 1776: A Description by Fray Francisco Atanasio Domínguez with other Contemporary Documents* (Albuquerque: University of New Mexico Press, 1956), xv. State of the missions of the custodies of New Mexico and Tampico, 1778-1813, BNM 10:52.

14.   Marc Simmons, *Spanish Government in New Mexico* (Albuquerque: University of New Mexico Press, 1990), 68. Rick Hendricks, "Church-State Relations in Anza's New Mexico, 1777-1778," Second Annual World Conference in Celebration of the Life of Juan Bautista de Anza, Arizpe, Sonora, 1997, 5-6. Juan Bautista de Anza, Edict, Santa Fe, 25 Aug. 1781, Archives of the Archdiocese of Santa Fe (AASF), Loose Documents (LD), Missions (M), 1781:5.

15.   The conflict within the order revolved around the *alternativa*. This system, established in 1711, provided for the alternation of ecclesiastical offices between peninsulars and creoles, who thought the Spanish-born friars were unduly favored. When a mission of forty-six Franciscans began to arrive in Mexico City in 1778, the *hijos de provincia* (those penisulars who had joined the order in the province) had sixteen Europeans sent to New Mexico, thereby tipping the balance in the custody heavily in the penisulars' favor. Hendricks, "Church-State Relations," 9-10. Rick Hendricks, "The Exile and Return of Fray Isidro Cadelo, 1793-1810," *New Mexico Historical Review* 70:2 (Apr. 1995): 132. Fray Angélico Chávez, *Archives of the Archdiocese of Santa Fe, 1678-1900* (Washington, D.C.: Academy of American Franciscan History, 1957), 43.

16.   Chávez, *Archives*, 61, 65. State of the missions of the custodies of New Mexico and Tampico, 1778-1813, BNM 10:52. José Serampión Prado to Francisco Gabriel de Olivares y Benito, El Paso, 30 Dec. 1802, AHAD-209, f. 314-16. Fray Rafael Benavides, Petition, Ysleta, 27 Sept. 1803, AHAD-209, f. 319-20. José Serampión Prado to Francisco Gabriel de Olivares y Benito, El Paso, 29 Sept. 1803, AHAD-209, f. 321-23.

17.   Fray José Angel Dorrego to fray José Mariano Sánchez Vergara, Mexico City, 25 Dec. 1801, AASF, LD, M, 1801:29. Chávez, *Archives*, 61.

18.   Prado to Olivares y Benito, El Paso, 30 Dec. 1802, AHAD-209, f. 314-16. Benavides, Petition, Ysleta, 27 Sept. 1803, AHAD-209, f. 319-20. Prado to Olivares y Benito, El Paso, 29 Sept. 1803, AHAD-209, f. 321-23.

19.   Timmons, *El Paso*, 67-68.

20.   The Custos and Vice-Provincial, fray Antonio de Jesús Camacho, relinquished the title of vicar of El Paso to Father Ramón Ortiz and instructed fray Francisco García Pérez of Ysleta to hand over the lower valley missions to Father Antonio Borrajo in late 1851. Gerarde Decorme, S.J., "Las misiones del Valle del Paso, 1659-1960," Tomo 2, "Epoca moderna, 1821-1960," unpublished manuscript, University of Texas at El Paso, microfilm.

Local Devotion to St. Michael: Examining Expressions of Popular Catholicism in Socorro, Texas

Lois Stanford

Introduction

Recent research on Latino religious practices and beliefs has furthered scholars' understanding of pluralistic identities and religious practices among the Latino immigrant community (Figueroa Deck 1992; Sandoval 1990; and Sandoval, ed. 1983). Among these peoples, the Catholic Church has often played an important role in assimilation. In contrast, Hispanos and Tejanos in the Southwest remained in their historic communities while the U.S. incorporated them (Montejano 1987; Nostrand 1992). Some scholars now reinterpret popular religious practices and organizations in this region as a form of resistance that expressed ethnic and community identity in the face of the American Catholic Church's attempts to impose official religiosity. From this perspective, popular religious practices often develop in response to official church doctrine and are often opposed by the institutional church (Matovina 1993). Still, within the U.S. Southwest, ethnohistorical research has demonstrated variation in the persistence and significance of popular Catholicism. The active persecution of the Penitentes during the late nineteenth century (Weigle 1976) presents a different situation than the Tejano experience in San Antonio, in which parishioners continued traditional rituals and processions despite pressures to desist (Matovina 1995).

Other scholars have cautioned against drawing rigid distinctions between popular and official religiosity, noting that this conceptual opposition often leads scholars to overlook the complex and dynamic relationship between the institutional Church and its parishioners (Wright 1994:52). Throughout the history of the U.S. Southwest, the Church itself actively shaped and instilled popular participation in Catholic rituals, although the nature and degree of this support varied at different times and in different parishes. In turn, popular practices and beliefs themselves shaped the nature of the Church, albeit often at the local level. In this paper, I examine three "historic" events, in 1838, 1877, and 1938, respectively, all related to the local devotion towards St. Michael in the U.S.-Mexico border community of Socorro, Texas. Drawing on both oral histories and documentary research,[1] analysis of these three historic events indicates some of the problems in interpreting local historical expressions of popular Catholicism. In this community, popular Catholic practices cannot be explained accurately by applying "some principle of separation between popular reliogisity and elite religiosity" (Wright 1994:55). Rather, interpretation of these specific events reflects the complex and dynamic history of a community situated in the middle of international political and ecclesiastical boundaries.

Historical Background

Spanish colonists and some Native American groups first established major settlements in the Lower Valley of El Paso, Texas, after fleeing New Mexico from the Pueblo Revolt of 1680. In 1682, Ysleta was established as a Franciscan mission to the Tigua Indians. By 1684, Socorro was established as a Franciscan mission to the Piro and Manso Indians, although there were Spaniards in both communities. After 1680, the San Elizario area was the site of rancho Nuestra Señora de la Soledad de los Tiburcios, and later, in 1789, the Spanish government relocated the San Elizario presidio to Los Tiburcios (Hendricks and Timmons, in press). These towns represent classic Spanish Colonial institutions; Ysleta and Socorro were Indian missions, and San Elizario was a presidio. Furthermore, two of the communities have been continuously occupied since the end of the seventeenth century. During the Spanish Colonial and Mexican periods, the communities were political and commercial centers, but by the mid-nineteenth century, residents found themselves caught in the middle of boundary disputes.

With the 1828 flood of the Rio Grande, Texas independence, and U.S.-Mexico treaties, the Hispano residents of these border communities found themselves incorporated into the United States, as did other Tejano communities throughout Texas (Castañeda 1936; Montejano 1987). When Bishop Zubiría made his first ecclesiastical visit to the El Paso Valley in 1833, he found two priests ministering to an estimated 15,000 parishioners in El Paso del Norte and the Lower Valley (DeCorme n.d.:6). By his second visit in 1845, the Diocese of Durango had established a greater presence in the Lower Valley, and Franciscan priests ministered to these parishes. Paralleling the U.S.-Mexican political disputes of this period, the Mexican and American Catholic Churches also contested ecclesiastical boundaries and frequently changed local parish priests. In 1851 Archbishop Lamy and Bishop Zubiría had agreed that Mexican priests would be allowed to minister temporarily to the Lower Valley parishes, but Archbishop Lamy never waived the Diocese of Santa Fe's rights of ecclesiastical jurisdiction over the Ysleta, Socorro, and San Elizario missions. On 20 June 1869 the U.S. Catholic church divided the Santa Fe diocese, granting the Bishopric of Tucson ecclesiastical jurisdiction over southern New Mexico and El Paso's Lower Valley. The Bishop of Durango at the time, J. Vicente Salinas, ignored the boundary changes and continued to send Mexican priests. For the parishioners of Ysleta, Socorro, and San Elizario, the consequences were that priests were changed frequently and that priests often ministered to several parishes. In 1873 the American Catholic Church assumed permanent charge, but the Church faced the persistent problem of placing Spanish-speaking priests in these rural, isolated parishes. Desperate to find clergy, in 1879, Bishop Salpointe turned to the Jesuits (Owens 1950; Steele 1983), and on 16 October 1881 the Jesuits assumed responsbility for Ysleta and acquired property to build a college, and in 1894 the Jesuits took charge of the Socorro and San Elizario parishes. Jesuit priests ministered to the Lower Valley parishes from 1881 to 1980, when the last Jesuit left Socorro.

From 1854 to 1870, increased Anglo settlement in El Paso undermined the traditional political and commercial power of these Hispano communities. The ecclesiastical conflicts also disrupted the continuity of religious practices and traditions. Facing the decline of their economic status and political influence, parishioners from Ysleta, Socorro, and San Elizario turned to the Catholic rituals and processions that expressed their community and ethnic identity. Several factors distinguish these communities' experiences. First, ecclesiastical boundary shifts resulted in frequent changes of parish authorities and religious doctrinal instruction, depending on whether Spanish Franciscans, Mexican secular clergy, U.S. secular clergy, or Italian Jesuits ministered to the parishes. Second, in general, from 1869 to 1915, parish priests were not Hispanic; Juan Córdova, S.J., Socorro parish priest from 1896 to 1913, was the lone exception. Reflecting their own cultural background and their seminary training, priests introduced new Catholic practices, often discouraging the ritual practices asssociated with popular Catholicism. However, under the Jesuits, the parishioners revived old practices and introduced new forms of community involvement. Unlike non-Latino priests in other Southwestern parishes, Jesuit priests encouraged community participation in processions, ritual plays, and cofradías as means of fostering religious faith and community integration (DeCorme n.d.). Thus, through the Jesuit presence, Hispano parishioners maintained, revived, and constructed beliefs and practices that affirmed their ties to Spanish Catholicism and to their communities.

Popular Catholicism in Socorro: The Case of St. Michael

Saint Michael the Archangel is repeatedly recorded as the angel protector of the Jews in numerous biblical passages, as an example in Daniel 12.1, appearing in apocalyptic situations as the Jews' source of comfort and strength. Michael became an important figure in early Christian cults. In the East, he was reputed to heal the sick, while in the West, Michael was recognized as "the head of heavenly armies and the patron of soldiers" (*New Catholic Encyclopedia*, 1967:9:794). He is commonly depicted as "youthful, strong, clothed in full armor, bare-legged, and wearing sandals," and often "raising the sword of victory over the dragon, on whom he treads" (*New Catholic Encyclopedia*, 1967:9:794). In Socorro, the church is dedicated to the Immaculate Conception, but St. Michael occupies an important role as the secondary and unofficial patron saint of the parish. The devotion to St. Michael and the legends repeated as to his miraculous apparitions in times of need are consistent with Michael's symbolic role as a protector in the early Christian church.

At various times of crisis in the history of the early Christian church, Michael has appeared in battle as a savior. In the fifth or sixth century, there was a reported apparition of Michael when the Goths invaded Gargano, on the coast of southeastern Italy (*New Catholic Encyclopedia*, 1967:9:794). It is this date to which Socorro residents refer as the first feast day for St. Michael, on May 8. In addition, Michael was the only individual angel with a liturgical feast before the ninth century, which was held at the end of September since at least the sixth century. The feast marks the dedication of the basilica in honor of St. Michael on the Salarian way, north of Rome (Thurston and Attwater, eds. 1962:679). This date also corresponds to the second feast day in Socorro, September 29, the only feast day currently celebrated in Socorro from the traditional liturgical cycle.

In El Paso's Lower Valley, the 1830s brought natural disasters to the communities. The 1829 flood of the Rio Grande destroyed the Socorro mission. The flood also shifted the main river channel, leaving Ysleta, Socorro, and San Elizario, on an island known locally as La Isla, separated from both Mexican and Texan territories by separate river channels (Timmons 1990:274). In rebuilding the Socorro church, residents turned to the titular patron saint, the Immaculate Conception, to plead for protection for the new church and the reestablished community. The 1834 flood shifted the Rio Grande once more, leaving the communities permanently on the north side of the main channel and within the state of Texas.

St. Michael's Miraculous Selection of Socorro (1838)

The mission's destruction, the altered international political boundary, and the absence of parish authorities created a crisis within Socorro, mitigated by St. Michael's arrival in 1838. Records indicate that the statue of St. Michael was given to the parish as a gift by the Holguín family and transferred to the new church on October 29, 1845 (Burrus 1984:149). The legend of St. Michael's miraculous arrival persists into the current day, while residents have long forgotten the documentary evidence. St. Michael's arrival and subsequent protection of Socorro symbolically reinforces the common perception of Socorro's unique and rich heritage.

During the early nineteenth century, annual caravans of New Mexican merchants passed through the El Paso Valley on their way to the markets of central Mexico. As the legend is retold, on one return trip, merchants carried with them a life-size wooden statue of St. Michael. The caravan stopped one night in Socorro. Upon arising the next morning, the merchants could not force the oxen to move. Socorro residents took this as a miraculous sign that the saint's image wanted to stay in Socorro. They paid the merchants in money, goats, and yearling sheep so that St. Michael might remain. Parishioners cite this legend as a demonstration of the unique cultural heritage of their community. As retold by Santiago Frésquez,

> When St. Michael arrived here, he was not carried directly here. Some people were taking him to Socorro, New Mexico. They arrived and spent the night in front of the church, near the Camino Real, as it is called. The Camino Real was just a dirt road then. They had carried San Miguel in a two-wheeled cart, pulled by a yoke of oxen. On the morning that they were going to leave, the oxen could not move with the Saint. They tried. When they had been traveling, St. Michael had not weighed too much to haul with a pair of oxen. But, the cart was locked! The merchants even put on another pair of oxen, but those oxen could not move the cart either. Then, one of the men turned towards the Socorro church and said, "Listen, I think the *santo* wants to visit the church. Let's go carry him so that he can make a visit, and then we shall take him." Well … . They no more than turned the cart at the side of the church, and the oxen walked alone to the church. The merchants arrived at the mission and they took the saint out of the cart. They were reciting prayers there with the *santo* beside them.

Afterwards, they took St. Michael and put him in
the cart again. They no more than started … . The
oxen would not move, not backwards, not forwards
… . The cart was tied. The men who came with St.
Michael cried a lot because he had power over them.
Finally, one man said to the other, "Look, what is
happening here is that the *santo* likes this town and
he wants to stay here." So, they took St. Michael out
of the cart and gave him to the Socorro church.

This oral tradition demonstrates the special and unique nature of
Socorro's religious and cultural heritage. Other studies of miracle
legends in Spanish popular Catholicism cite similar patterns in
the event as retold in Socorro. Legends of miraculous apparition
of Christ or other male saints often follow a similar genre, in
which the image is being carried to another community in a cart
drawn by oxen or on the back of a mule. At the "chosen" community, the oxen or mule refuse to move, the saint's image is discovered to have become so heavy to preclude moving, and parishioners in the "chosen" community recognize the image's expression of his desire to remain (Foster 1960:159-160). The legend
somehow became integrated into Socorro's religious tradition, and
it would be impossible to determine whether the retelling reflects the persistence of a religious tale carried by the original
Spanish Colonial settlers or later introduced by local priests, either Franciscan or secular clergy. By repeating this genre, in some
manner, Socorro parishioners express a persistence of a Spanish
Catholicism first introduced during the Colonial period. Furthermore, local residents defer to certain designated parishioners, those
descended from the original families, as the holders and tellers of
this legend. In turn, these residents present the legend as authoritative evidence of their families' and community's heritage.

By 1870 Fr. Antonio Severo Borrajo, under the direction of
the Durango Diocese, ministered to the parish despite the ecclesiastical boundary disputes mentioned above. In this year, the
image of St. Michael, carried out for religious feast day processions on May 8 and September 29, had been damaged by rain. In
attempting to renovate the image, the priest had the saint's image
submerged in water to remove the old paint. St. Michael was

repainted, and the arms and wings were repaired. Some Socorro parishioners contested the repairs, contending that it was blasphemy to change the image and that any modifications would reduce the saint's spiritual power and virtue (DeCorme n.d.:26).

St. Michael's Second Miraculous Appearance (1877)

Increased Anglo presence and El Paso's growth threatened the political and economic autonomy of Socorro, as well as that of other Hispanic communities in El Paso's Lower Valley. By 1874, recently elected to the Texas Senate, Albert J. Fountain presented a proposal at a citizen's meeting in San Elizario, situated further down in the valley from Socorro. Fountain proposed that the Texas Senate concede the Guadalupe salt flats as communal property to El Paso County residents, thus granting Socorro and San Elizario residents collective use rights to a regional resource exploited since the Colonial period. However, Mexican residents on the Rio Grande's south side, also traditional users of the salt flats, were concerned that Texas' recognition would exclude their access to the salt flats. Supported by Borrajo, by then a parish priest on the Mexican side of the border, Mexicans persuaded San Elizario residents to reject this proposal. In response to Fountain's proposal, San Elizario residents presented a petition signed by four hundred citizens who rejected the proposed law (DeCorme n.d.:34). In not staking a collective legal claim to the flats, San Elizario residents could not prevent private acquisition of the salt flats and jeopardized access for all Lower Valley communities, including Socorro.

In 1877, Charles H. Howard, an Anglo speculator, obtained private ownership of the salt flats with a Texas land script and tried to make San Elizario residents pay for a resource they had traditionally used for free (Porter 1973:51). On October 17, 1877, Charles Howard assassinated Luis Cardis, a local politician and political rival (Sonnichsen 1961:33). In retaliation, a mob of Mexican nationals and Lower Valley residents executed Howard in San Elizario and looted the stores and homes of several local Anglo businessmen. That night they fled back across the border to safety in Mexico. In response, Texas sent state soldiers to punish the residents of San Elizario. When Texas military reinforcements arrived, they began a vengeful killing of innocent resi-

dents. Ultimately, they arrested those they claimed were the principal organizers of the revolt, but no one came forward to accuse
them (DeCorme n.d.:45). Anglo Texans viewed all Lower Valley
residents with equal suspicion, not distinguishing between Mexican residents and Hispanic residents of the Lower Valley communities.

When Socorro residents recall the second legend of St.
Michael, they draw on the biblical and historical role of St. Michael
as protector of oppressed peoples in the early Christian church.
As retold by Francisco Holguín,

> After Howard was killed, the government soldiers
> came up the valley. They came with orders from the
> government to kill everyone, even the dogs, here in
> the Lower Valley. They were against all the people
> and wanted to kill them. The soldiers carried orders
> to kill everyone they met in the way because the
> soldiers claimed that revolutionaries had killed
> Howard.
>
> When the soldiers came to Socorro, they saw the
> people leaving the church. The people of Socorro
> had gone to the church to pray to St. Michael for
> protection. The soldiers fired a cannon shot at the
> church because they had seen people in the church.
> The cannon shot passed overhead, nothing more. It
> did hit the cross, though. That is why, to this day, it is
> to one side like that.
>
> Suddenly, a troop of pure white horses appeared from
> the inside of the church, led by the gleaming sword
> of a captain who was out front. It was St. Michael.
> The American soldiers were so frightened that they
> ran away. They mounted their horses and fled. They
> told their captain that they could not fight against
> an escort like that, that there were more soldiers pour-
> ing out of the church than were with them. There
> were pure white horses, very beautiful, and the heav-
> enly soldiers were very well armed. The Americans
> said, "They carried swords. Right at us."
> It was only him, St. Michael. And the Americans
> came back no more.

By retelling St. Michael's miraculous appearance, Socorro parishioners validate the survival of their community despite the on-
slaught by U.S. soldiers. No Socorro resident was killed during
the fighting that erupted over the Salt Flats, although several lives
were lost in neighboring San Elizario. St. Michael appeared in
time of need to save the oppressed from their oppressors. For
Socorro, the late nineteenth century represented an insecure and
hostile environment, as Anglo entrepreneurs and settlers threatened local control over land resources and political sovereignty.
Through this legend, parishioners appropriate the symbolic message of St. Michael, applying it to their own local history in order
to reaffirm their persistence in the face of major historical and
political changes.

St. Michael was able to save Socorro from invasion by U.S.
soldiers, but the saint's image could not alter history. In 1878, the
El Paso County seat was transferred from San Elizario to Ysleta,
now with 1,400 inhabitants (Timmons 1990:174). In May 1881,
the Southern Pacific Railroad arrived in El Paso, bypassing the
Lower Valley Hispanic communities to the Anglo community of
El Paso. In 1883, El Paso proposed to move the El Paso County
seat from Ysleta to El Paso (Timmons 1990:175). The 1877 Salt
War, the arrival of the Southern Pacific in El Paso, and El Paso's
appropriation of the county seat marked the permanent transfer
of county political power to El Paso. In the years following, El
Paso grew into a metropolis while Socorro and the neighboring
Lower Valley communities continued their rural agricultural traditions.

In 1891, the U.S. Catholic Church separated El Paso from the
Bishopric of Arizona, delivering the El Paso parishes, including
those of the Lower Valley, to the newly formed Bishopric of Dallas. In 1893, Bishop Dunne ordered the French priests of El Paso
to return the Ysleta, Socorro, and San Elizario parishes to the Society of Jesus, and on April 15, 1894, the Jesuits received charge
of the Socorro and San Elizario parishes (DeCorme n.d.:67-68). In
ministering to the Lower Valley parishes, the Jesuits introduced
new religious practices, including devotional associations such
as the Union of St. Joseph, Apostolate of Prayer, and the Daughters of Mary (DeCorme 1960). Through these congregations, the
Jesuits intended to encourage and teach religious doctrine to the

parishioners of these small, isolated rural communities. In addition, the order also attempted to "conserve ancient Mexican traditions in the celebration of the Christmas *pastorelas* and the ceremonies of the Pharisees during Holy Week" (DeCorme n.d.:84). The Jesuits were not aware of the specific historical origin of local and popular expressions of religious faith; they viewed these traditions as public expressions of devotion and encouraged their practice. The early twentieth century brought more stability following the ecclesiastical boundary disputes of the late nineteenth century. In Socorro, from 1915 to 1942, only two parish priests ministered to the parish, Leon Dupont, S.J. (1915-1925) and Gerarde DeCorme (1925-1942). Life in the small rural community centered around agricultural production and the church.

Local Appropriation of St. Michael (1938)

In 1938, Gerarde DeCorme, then parish priest, decided to restore the statue of St. Michael in honor of the centennial of his reported arrival in Socorro. DeCorme noted that the first renovation conducted in 1879 by Borrajo had actually disfigured the image, and he planned to remove the image from the church. According to DeCorme, "a few fanatics of the town opposed to the idea of the Saint leaving his town, fearing who knows what punishments" threatened DeCorme if he removed St. Michael (DeCorme n.d.:116). The confrontation between DeCorme and local parishioners was reported in newspapers as a local conflict in which community members signed a petition to prevent the statue from being removed, protesting that they feared the statue would never be returned.[2] The statue was temporarily removed, despite local protests. A religious procession accompanied the statue to the Jesuit seminary in Ysleta, and Catholic officials returned the saint to the mission after the procession passed through the valley.[3]

The explanation of the source of this conflict and its resolution must be based on local interpretation. As recalled by Santiago Frésquez,

> There are so many legends about St. Michael, but I do not tell you legends …. I tell you things I know about, and I tell you where I got them from. It is up to you if you want to believe them or not, but I do

tell you what I know. At that time, the saint needed repair.

Some people did not want the Jesuits to take St. Michael because they believed he was filled with gold. They said that the Jesuits wanted to take the statue to get the gold out. They also said that a disaster would come to Socorro if St. Michael was ever taken out of the church.

But what really happened was that the priest, Father DeCorme had made plans with the Ysleta seminarists to repair St. Michael. One man did not want them to take the saint just like that. He wanted to make an ox cart. So, some men built an ox cart so they could place St. Michael on it and carry him. This man, who lived in the house that belonged to my grandfather, was one of the men who worked with the ox cart.

So the other people found out what DeCorme was doing, and they opposed him. These other people went to Father DeCorme to tell him that he could not take the saint out of Socorro.

Father DeCorme went to the bishop and told him the story. He told the bishop about everything that was going on, about the men making the ox cart and everything else. He told the bishop that there were people in Socorro who were afraid and they were against St. Michael leaving Socorro, that some were afraid of it being filled with gold. Then, Decorme told the bishop, "What if the saint doesn't go?" The bishop said that the reason for having the procession was to find out if St. Michael would leave Socorro or not.

In order to maintain local composure within the parish, DeCorme decided to organize a procession of the ox cart, cars, and bicycles to accompany St. Michael to the Ysleta seminary, returning on the same day. Despite these concessions, some parishioners remained opposed to any attempt to remove the saint's image from the church. Other parishioners threw their support with DeCorme. As Santiago Frésquez continues,

> Then, my father, my uncle, another man whose name was Don Antonio Márquez, and about fifteen other ones had to go on the night of the procession to keep guard around where the father lived. Then, after the opponents saw that the guards were there, no one appeared. The men were carrying weapons with them. They did not know whom they had to confront. When there were processions here, they always fired shots. Generally, if they did not find blanks, they would take out real ammunition. But when they were going to do this, they did not take them out. They were going to take the rifles with ammunition, just in case these people wanted to stop them.

> The priest told them when they were going to get into the cars. Some went in trucks. Decorme then told them, "Okay, then get in the cars. Be careful that you do not drop anything because we are not going to stop for anything. If you drop your shoe, you drop it, and you leave it there."

The procession was carried out without further conflict. St. Michael was removed for one day and returned, without bringing down disaster upon the community of Socorro. For the El Paso newspapers, the reported conflict represented an exotic and violent confrontation between "Mexican" fanatics and the priest. For some local parishioners, the situation invoked fears of spiritual reprisal, drawing on the legacy of devotion to St. Michael. DeCorme's perspective and actions in this situation do not reflect an elite religiosity unsympathetic to local beliefs and practices. DeCorme originally intended to repair St. Michael in order to prepare the saint's image for the September 29 feast day procession, which in 1938 was the centennial of St. Michael's miraculous arrival in Socorro. DeCorme's interest in commemorating this historic event precipitated the local conflict. In describing the 1938 incident, DeCorme himself refers to the opposition as "a few fanatics," but he skillfully reconciled the local factions through his actions. He removed the saint's image for only one day, accompanied by a procession of local parishioners to reassure those concerned, and at the same time he employed the ox cart constructed by the faction that originally supported his intent to repair St. Michael.

Conclusions

By the 1950s, urban El Paso's government moved to take control of the unincorporated Lower Valley communities. In 1955, El Paso forcibly annexed Ysleta, over the protest of Ysleta residents. In 1963, under the Chamizal Convention, the U.S. and Mexico divided disputed territory and resettled 4,500 U.S. citizens of Mexican descent living in what would become Mexican territory. Most were placed in hastily constructed subdivisions in the Socorro area (Timmons 1990). Mexican-American and Mexican residents of recent origin pressured the diocese to reorganize parish activities to fit their spiritual needs and beliefs. The reforms under Vatican II and the Jesuits' departure left the original residents facing a new and different Church, not the one that they remembered from their childhood. By 1970 Hispano residents became a minority in what had once been their community. What remains of their Church now is found in old photographs and their historical memory.

In oral history interviews, the texts document integration of old and new practices, in turn presented by parishioners as authoritative evidence of their traditional faith and community identity (Tonkins 1992). In these communities, Catholic traditions have not persisted unchanged from the Colonial Period. Instead, the late nineteenth and early twentieth century rituals and lay organizations reflect a dynamic, complex history in which the parishioners of the time appropriated and reinterpreted practices and beliefs. In many instances, informants refer to the important role of cofradías, or religious sodalities, such as the Union of St. Joseph and the Daughters of Mary. Although the Jesuits introduced these specific devotional associations in the 1880s, parishioners' oral tradition links the cofradías of their historical memory to those of their Spanish Colonial ancestors. In regard to other events such as St. Michael's miraculous apparitions in Socorro, the oral tradition closely replicates the telling of similar appearances in rural Spanish communities (Foster 1960). As revealed through the oral texts, the construction of the local form of popular Catholicism reflects historical changes and influences experienced by this border community from the late nineteenth century to the present.

Notes

1.   The tapes, Spanish language transcripts, and English language transcripts of the original interviews are archived at the Institute of Oral History, University of Texas, El Paso. The author acknowledges the cooperation of Francisco Holguin and Santiago Frésquez, former residents of Socorro, who provided the testimonies upon which this paper is based. The English translations were done by the author; in these cases, I have translated for meaning, attempting to represent most accurately how the speaker would have told the legend in English, rather than presenting a literal translation.
2.   El Paso *Herald*, 6 May 1938.
3.   El Paso *Times*, 9 May 1938; El Paso *Herald*, 9 May 1938.

References Cited

Blake, Robert. *History of the Catholic Church in El Paso*. Unpublished M.A. thesis. University of Texas, El Paso, 1942.

Burrus, Ernest, S.J. An Historical Outline of the Socorro Mission. *Password* 29(3):145-150, 1984.

Castañeda, Carlos. *Our Catholic Heritage, 1519-1936*. 7 Volumes. Austin: Von Boeckman-Jones Co, 1936.

DeCorme, Gerarde, S.J. *Epoca moderna, 1821-1950, Tomo II*. in *Las misiones del Valle del Paso, 1659-1960*. Unpublished document.

_____ . *Con motivo de las bodas de diamante de una humilde congregación Mariana en Socorro, Texas, 1885-1960*. Unpublished report, 1960.

Figueroa Deck, Allan, S.J. *Frontiers of Hispanic Theology in the US*. Maryknoll: Orbis, 1992.

Fitzmorris, Sister Mary Angela, A.M. *Four Decades of Catholicism in Texas, 1820-1860*. Ph.D. dissertation. Washington: The Catholic University of America, 1926.

Foster, George M. *Culture and Conquest: America's Spanish Heritage*. New York: Wenner-Gren Foundation for Anthropological Research, 1960.

García, Mario. *Desert Immigrants: The Mexicans of El Paso, 1880-1920*. New Haven: Yale University Press, 1981.

Hendricks, Rick, and William Timmons. *San Elizario: Presidio to County Seat.* El Paso: Texas Western Press (in press, 1998).

Matovina, Timothy. *Tejano Religion and Ethnicity: San Antonio, 1821-1860.* Austin: University of Texas Press, 1995.

Montejano, David. *Anglos and Mexicans in the Making of Texas, 1836-1986.* Austin: University of Texas Press, 1987.

New Catholic Encyclopedia. New York: McGraw-Hill, 1967.

Nostrand, Richard L. *The Hispano Homeland.* Norman: University of Oklahoma Press, 1992.

Owens, Sister M. Lilliana, S.L. *Jesuit Beginnings in the Southwest.* Jesuit Studies - Southwest, Number One. El Paso: Revista Católica Press, 1950.

Porter, Eugene O. *San Elizario: A History.* Austin: Jenkins Publishing Company, the Pemberton Press, 1973.

Sandoval, Moisés. *On the Move: A History of the Hispanic Church in the United States.* Maryknoll: Orbis, 1990.

_____ . ed. *A History of the Latin American Church in the USA Since 1513.* San Antonio: Mexican American Cultural Center Press, 1983.

Sonnichsen, C.L. *The El Paso Salt War of 1877.* El Paso: Texas Western Press, 1961.

Society of Jesus. *On Sodalities of Our Lady.* El Paso: Revista Católica Press, 1948.

Steele, Thomas J. *Works and Days: A History of San Felipe Neri Church 1867-1895.* Albuquerque: Albuquerque Museum, 1983.

Thurston, Herbert, S.J., and Donald Attwater, editors. *Butler's Lives of the Saints,* all volumes. New York: P.J. Kennedy and Sons.

Timmons, William. *El Paso: A Borderlands History.* El Paso: Texas Western Press, 1990.

Tonkins, Elizabeth. *Narrating Our Pasts: the Social Construction of Oral History.* New York: Cambridge University Press, 1992.

Weigle, Marta. *Brothers of Light, Brothers of Blood: The Penitentes of the Southwest.* Santa Fe: Ancient City Press, 1976.

Wright, Robert E. If It's Official, It Can't Be Popular? Reflections on Popular and Folk Religion. *Journal of Hispanic/Latino Theology* 1(3):47-67, 1994.

The Contributions of the Jesuit Order in the New Mexico-Colorado-West Texas Area as the Rocky Mountain Mission, 1867-1919

Eduardo C. Fernández, S.J.

In 1867, a small group of five exiled Neapolitan Jesuits arrived in Santa Fe, the capital of New Mexico. Establishing what came to be known as the Rocky Mountain Mission, which later included native-born Jesuits and those from other countries, they came as a response to Bishop Lamy's plea for Jesuits. For fifteen years, the French prelate, making his case in San Francisco, Los Angeles, St. Louis, and finally Rome, had sought out these sons of St. Ignatius of Loyola for various ministries in his mission territory.[1]

In 1871, the New Mexican legislature allowed Jesuits and members of other religious institutes to teach in public schools. Some time later, this arrangement was declared unconstitutional. In 1873, the Jesuits opened a novitiate in Albuquerque with a total of three novices, one Neapolitan, one Nuevomejicano, and one Anglo. The Revista Católica Press was launched there during the same year. It produced an uninterrupted weekly for eighty-seven years and was responsible for innumerable publications such as books, manuals, and entire Bibles. After having been moved to Las Vegas, New Mexico, in 1874, it was transferred to El Paso in 1918.

The above are only a sampling of the works of the Jesuit mission in this designated period. A systematic examination of the various contributions of the Jesuits in a specific region and time, the greater El Paso-Ciudad Juárez area during 1881 through 1919, yields a more complete picture of how they were able to contribute to the religious and cultural life of the towns and cities in question. The period marks their arrival to this part of the Southwest and ends with the incorporation of the mission territory into two established Jesuit provinces. These contributions will be explored under four general areas, although naturally they overlap: evangelization and church leadership, education, social services, and historical documentation.

Evangelization and Church Leadership

Over the centuries since its founding in 1540, the two primary apostolates of the Jesuit Order have been evangelization, which used to be known as "parish mission work," and formal education. The same is true even today. At the time of the arrival of the first Jesuits in the El Paso Valley in 1881, the Franciscans had already evangelized the area, having established a mission in 1659, Nuestra Señora de Guadalupe del Paso del Norte, today downtown Ciudad Juárez, Chihuahua. In 1680, the Spanish survivors of the Pueblo Indian Revolt sought refuge there. Around that time, they established several other missions, such as those of Socorro and Ysleta del Sur, along the Rio Grande for the Indians who had accompanied them downriver.

In 1852, the Franciscan friars, having worked in the lower valley towns for 172 years, were replaced by diocesan clergy assigned there by Bishop Zubiría of Durango.[2] In 1879 two Jesuits had preached popular parish missions in the Lower Rio Grande Valley. As Ernest Burrus notes of the entire El Paso region,

> The valley had always remained far from the diocesan centers which claimed it: Mexico City, Guadalajara, Durango, Galveston, Santa Fe, Durango again, and now [1881] Tucson, Arizona. As a result the valley always seemed the last area to be provided for.[3]

Before Pius X made the large area which encompassed southern New Mexico and West Texas into an independent see on March 3, 1914, it came under the jurisdiction of Joseph P. Lynch, Bishop of Dallas. Anthony Schuler, S.J., served as the first Bishop of the new El Paso Diocese.[4] Burrus, writing in 1981, summarizes the accomplishments of the Jesuits:

One hundred years ago when the first two Jesuits stepped off the train at El Paso, an area where there had already been Catholic communities for three centuries, they hardly imagined that they and the Jesuits to follow them would eventually build and staff over thirty parishes, set up an El Paso Diocese with one of the Jesuits as the first Bishop, and operate a large international printing press.[5]

Education

From 1893, when Bishop Edward J. Dunne of Dallas named Italian-born Father Carlos Pinto as his Vicar General for El Paso, the area witnessed an intensification of Jesuit initiative. The energetic Jesuit superior, fifty-one years old at the time, set up his headquarters near what is today downtown El Paso. Burrus relates how quickly the Italian went to work.

Simultaneously he [Pinto] built three parish churches, a central rectory, and a parochial school: Sagrado Corazón in Juárez, and in El Paso Sacred Heart Church with a Jesuit Residence and a Grade School for the Spanish-speaking and the Immaculate Conception Church for the English-speaking.[6]

Having built Sacred Heart Parochial School for Mexican children in south El Paso, he staffed it with a group of religious woman by then familiar with the Southwest, the Sisters of Loretto at the Foot of the Cross. Next to it, as mentioned above, he later built Sacred Heart Church. What is noteworthy here is the priority given to education. Sister Lilliana Owens, S.L., explains his reasons: "Father Pinto realized the great need for a Catholic church in South El Paso, but he felt the education of the children of this district was by far the greater need."[7]

The same author relates a diary account from the school's first principal, Sister Magdalen Dietz, S.L.

My first experience at the Sacred Heart was with eighty overgrown Mexican boys, some of them wearing mustaches, unkempt, untidy, with shirt tails hanging out. They knew absolutely nothing of order or discipline. After a morning or two, I managed to explain to them that three signals of the bell would be given. Accordingly at the next dismissal the three taps were given and much to my amazement I saw the boys leaping from every window. They were *passing out.* I had not thought to state they were to pass out *through the door.*[8]

Figure 1. Young Father Carlos M. Pinto, S.J. Photograph courtesy Jesuit New Orleans Province Archives.

The much needed school began with an enrollment of two hundred which jumped to the four hundred mark by 1899, at which time a second story for the edifice was completed.[9] Other parishes followed and a parochial school generally stood beside each new church.

Pinto, a tireless worker, was not without a sense of humor. Owens quotes a Loretto Archive manuscript which relates a story told by a friend of his, Doctor Francis Gallagher:

Figure 2. Sacred Heart Church as Fr. Pinto, S.J. built it in 1892. Photograph courtesy Jesuit New Orleans Province Archives.

In 1896 El Paso was off the main line of the Santa
Fe. The train which in those days ran through to the
city of Mexico, arrived ordinarily at two in the afternoon. One Sunday, Cardinal Satolli, who was in this
country as a special representative of Leo XIII, of
happy memory, arrived on that train and was met
by Father Pinto and taken to the Jesuit residence on
North Oregon street. After cleaning up from the dirt
of the journey from the north, Father Pinto decided
to take the Cardinal to lunch in the refectory, which
was in charge of a lay brother ... The Cardinal demurred, as he hadn't as yet said Mass. Father Pinto
explained that in this country Mass was not said (at
this time) after noon. The Cardinal assured Father
Pinto that he was aware of this but that he desired to
say Mass. Father Pinto countered with the answer
that he understood quite well but that it was Sunday and that there would be visitors in the Church.
They were simple people of Faith, who would be
scandalized to see anyone celebrating Mass in the
afternoon. The Cardinal then intimated that the scandal was largely in Father Pinto's imagination. Father
Pinto was still not ready to admit defeat and so with
a patronizing air he suggested that this was the first
intimation he had that the Cardinal was not actually an Italian, but a Sicilian.[10]

Figure 3. A view of the Sacred Heart Church, rectory, and school as
Father Carlos M. Pinto, S.J. left it in 1919 Photograph courtesy Jesuit
New Orleans Province Archives.

Another large school and church complex which Pinto oversaw was that of St. Ignatius, also built in the poor area of south El Paso. Working with the then aging Pinto in 1918 was a young, spirited Italian Jesuit by the name of Carmelo Tranchese. Tranchese also showed much interest in education, building a large school in 1919 with a capacity of a thousand students. The Loretto Sis-

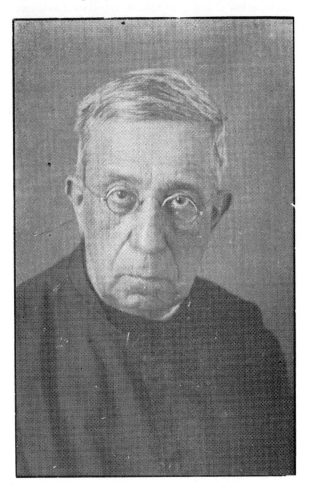

Figure 4. Father Carlos M. Pinto, S.J. Photograph courtesy Jesuit New Orleans Province Archives.

ters also spearheaded this teaching staff and eventually became responsible for about seven parochial schools in the area.

Cleofas Calleros, an El Paso historian, has nothing but praise for the enthusiastic Tranchese who, decades later, caught the national limelight for his work among poor immigrants in San Antonio, Texas.[11]

> He was a young, Italian priest who, during his short stay, had accomplished excellent work in Albuquerque, New Mexico. [He was] bursting with youth and enthusiasm, interested in the youth and their education, progressive in thinking, a builder and financial planner, a great lover of music and the arts.[12]

The Italian Jesuits, following in the tradition of the creative Franciscans who had not hesitated to use art and music to evangelize and educate, took a very holistic view of the human person. In the tradition of St. Ignatius, the "care of souls" meant more than tending to the sacramental needs of their parishioners. Influenced by the humanist trends of their day, the early Jesuits were convinced that the liberal arts were essential for the betterment of society. The Jesuit historian John O'Malley says of the early Jesuits:

> When they urged the bishop of Murcia in 1555 to establish a college, they said it would be of great benefit to the "republic" by producing good priests, good civic officials, and good citizens of every status. This was of course standard humanist talk, but its employment by the Jesuits indicates the breadth that marked their desire to "help souls." As with their other *opera caritatis* [works of charity], their ministry of education had civic and societal dimensions that carried the Jesuits beyond the evangelical models that principally inspired them.[13]

In the same way, the Jesuits made use of visual art, drama, music, and sports to form the youth under their care, even those who were not in the parochial schools. Tranchese turned the old chapel of St. Ignatius into an auditorium, furnishing it with a stage, comfortable seating, and appealing wall decorations. The "Hijas de María" had a good library, and the "Luises," a boys' organization named for San Luis Gonzaga, had their athletic center. The parish plant included various meeting rooms, and on occasion these groups sponsored parties, dances, picnics, and other types of gatherings. St. Ignatius Parish was quite proud of its Boy Scout group and of its large orchestra, which had been organized in 1912 by Father Modesto Izaguirre, S.J.[14] Calleros describes the type of "Pied Piper" effect which this large band had on the neighborhood children.

> Playing melodious music, the band of San Ignacio Parish passed through the streets of the Segundo Barrio, inviting hundreds of children to march back with them to the "children's Mass."[15]

One of the most important educational works of the Society of Jesus, not only in this part of the American Southwest but also throughout Spanish-speaking Latin America, was the previously mentioned Revista Católica Press. Since its 1873 inception in Las Vegas, New Mexico, to that of its demise in El Paso, 1962, it produced Catholic and civic literature in the Spanish language for a population that was growing by leaps and bounds. One of its most important functions in early days was to combat anti-Catholicism, an attitude quite prevalent in the "Old West" due to the Know Nothing movement of the middle of the nineteenth century. In the most comprehensive article written about the *Revista Católica* newspaper, Edward Vollmar describes the religious and philosophical climate of the Southwest:

> The Mexican War had been fought by the frontiersmen of the West. They considered the territory acquired by the Treaty of Guadalupe Hidalgo as theirs. Many had deserted from the army to settle in the region; others came from western settlements seeking land. One characteristic shared by many of these new settlers was a long tradition of anti-Catholicism. To them Manifest Destiny meant the extension of WASP civilization. They considered the natives they met as indolent, ignorant "greasers." The Catholicism of the Mexicans, weak as it was, was another obstacle to be wiped out. This attitude was encouraged by some Protestant ministers, whose virulence was matched only by their ignorance.[16]

Having started the press with $1,650 which he obtained by donations and loans, Father Donato Maria Gasparri, S.J., the second Superior of the Mission, was convinced that, although the preached missions were very successful, their effect was only temporary.[17] The printed word went much further. What were needed were leaflets, books, and periodicals. Burrus summarizes how the Revista Católica Press met this need over its eighty-seven years of existence:

> It furnished world-wide religious news, imparted systematic and solid religious instruction, refuted calumnies, cleared up misunderstandings, and even ran in serial fashion popular novels. It not only edited school and religious books but acted as agent for numerous publishing houses in the New and Old World.[18]

For many years, the *Revista Católica* was the only weekly Spanish Catholic periodical in all the Americas. The press also published catechisms, church bulletins, and some serious religious and historical books.[19] Writing in 1912, Benjamin Read, a Catholic historian, gave *Revista Católica* credit for preserving the Roman Catholic Faith in the territory.[20]

Social Services

It is obvious that the Jesuits, in their educational endeavors, provided a great social service to the people of the greater El Paso area. They were convinced, as had been their early Jesuit predecessors in Europe, that the way to reform an entire society was to direct one's energy towards its youth:

> At the urging of Ignatius, Pedro de Ribadeneira wrote to Philip II of Spain on 14 February 1556 to explain why the Society was so deeply committed to its colleges. One sentence jumps from the page: "All the well-being of Christianity and of the whole world depends on the proper education of youth."[21]

An excerpt from the *Memoirs* of Sister Mary Berchmans García, S.L., who taught at the recently opened Sacred Heart School, reveals the same conviction in Father Pinto.

> Father Carlos M. Pinto came often to our [class]rooms
> to speak with us about the progress of the children
> and to encourage us in our work for the Sacred Heart
> and the people of South El Paso. He always wanted
> us to have the best and most advanced means of
> furthering the education of the children. He bought
> as many of these things as his limited resources
> would permit him to do. He always said, *"Hermanas,
> we must build for the future and not just for to-day."*[22]

Having said that educational work is also social work, however, we must also mention some of the other social works of the Jesuits who focused more on the immediate needs of the people, for example, the dire need of housing for the elderly, care for refugees, job training, and mutual aid societies.

In 1910, the Mexican Revolution broke out. During this entire "decada trágica" thousands of refugees, seeking relief from hunger, bloodshed, and religious intolerance, came across the Rio Grande around the El Paso area. Since both Sacred Heart and St. Ignatius parishes were extremely close to the river, they provided a gateway into the United States. Owens, narrating the 1918 arrival of a new pastor at Sacred Heart, Father Cruz Garde, comments that

> Father Garde's assignment of the Sacred Heart church
> came at a critical time. The Revolution and religious
> persecution in Mexico were raging. He offered hos-
> pitality to many refugees, priests and laymen, flee-
> ing from Mexico. During the years of his pastorate
> the parishioners at Sacred Heart church increased
> as almost all the people of *Juárez*, eager to assist at
> Holy Mass and to receive the various sacraments,
> came to the Sacred Heart. Many Congregations and
> Associations were organized during these years.[23]

Even as late as the 1930s, Mexico was still experiencing church-state tension, so there were several periods in which Catholics in Juárez did not have public access to the sacraments.[24] Burrus notes that the El Paso Diocese incurred a heavy debt in caring for the refugees, among them many Mexican Jesuits, one which took many years to pay off.[25]

As early as 1903, the "Unión Católica de San José," a mutual aid society whose rallying theme was "Religión, Protección y Trabajo," had formed in Sacred Heart Parish under the direction of Jesuit Father Pascual Tomassini, led by the initiative of Reynaldo Pérez.[26]

Although the Rocky Mountain Mission had already been dissolved by 1929, it is significant to note that Bishop Schuler, complementing the Sacred Heart parishioners for paying off their church expansion debt, makes mention of two of the people's goals at the time.

> Organize yourselves anew and do not cease to work until with a School of Arts and Sciences, a home for the aged, you will have completed the work that has been planned. God Bless You![27]

Historical Documentation

The information provided above could not have been written without the necessary documentation, so abundant for the period. Thanks to the Jesuit custom of sending frequent reports to Rome, the keeping of house diaries, and the existence of eighty-seven years of the *Revista Católica*, there is ample written material for writing the history of the period.[28] As Sister Lilliana's research has shown, another valuable source are letters and the diaries and memoirs of the Sisters of Loretto.

In 1919, its task of having helped to establish the Church in this vast part of the Southwest completed, the Rocky Mountain Mission, made up of 158 Jesuits, of whom a large part were native born, was dismantled. All in all, it lasted for fifty-two years. The territory was divided among existing Jesuit provinces: the New Orleans Province assumed responsibility for New Mexico and Texas while the Missouri Province added the Colorado apostolates to its jurisdiction. As historians and anthropolgists explore the contributions of this group of men, it is clear that these irreplaceable accounts reveal fascinating details not only about the works of the Jesuits at the time but also about the People of God with whom they were privileged to work.

Notes

1. For a detailed description of the reason for their exile, as well as vivid details of the perilous journey, see Thomas J. Steele, S.J.'s *Works and Days: A History of San Felipe Neri Church, 1867-1895* (Albuquerque: The Albuquerque Museum, 1983), 2-20. Steele incorporates eighteen primary accounts of the trek.

2. Gerard Decorme, S.J., ms. *Las Misiones del valle del Paso, Texas.*

3. Ernest J. Burrus, S.J., "Jesuits Came Late, But Built with El Paso for 100 Years," *The Southern Jesuit*, Vol. 1, No. 2, Dec., 1981: 5.

4. Having been the Denver Jesuit Superior, he administered the diocese until 1942. He died in 1944.

5. Burrus, *op. cit.*, 4.

6. Burrus, *op. cit.*, 5.

7. Lilliana Owens, S.L., *Reverend Carlos M. Pinto, S.J., Apostle of El Paso, 1892-1919* (El Paso, Revista Católica Press, 1951.

8. Quoted in *ibid.*, 81.

9. *Ibid.*, 84.

10. *Ibid.*, 92.

11. See "Rumpled Angel of the Slums," *Saturday Evening Post*, August 21, 1948. Tranchese became a personal friend of Eleanor Roosevelt, through whom he was able to secure much housing for the poor in San Antonio's westside district.

12. "Era éste un jóven sacerdote Italiano que había presentado excelentes servicios en Albuquerque, Nuevo México, durante el corto período de su permanencia en aquella ciudad. Rebosante de juventud y entusiasmo, interesado por la juventud y su educación, de ideas progresistas, constructor y económico, muy amante del arte y de la música." Cleofas Calleros, *Jubileo de Oro de mi Parroquia, 1905-1955* (El Paso, Texas: American Printing Company, 1955), 26.

13. John W. O'Malley, S.J., *The First Jesuits* (Cambridge: Harvard University Press, 1993), 210.

14. Cleofas Calleros, *op. cit.*, 16-17.

15. "La Banda de San Ignacio recorría las calles del Segundo Barrio, tocando música melodiosa, y cienes de niños la seguian para asistir a la 'misa de los niños." *Ibid.*, 20.

16. Edward R. Vollmar, S.J., "La Revista Católica," *Mid-America: An Historical Review*, Vol. 58, No. 2, 88-89.

17. *Ibid.*, 86-87.

18. Found in "The Jesuits Come to the American Southwest," *Archivum Historicum Societatis Jesu*, Vol. XLIX, Fasc. 97, 1980, pp. 433-448. This article is among the most concise, yet scholarly pieces written

about this subject. Besides primary sources, Burrus draws from the work of Giuseppe M. Sorrentino, S.J., *Dalle Montagne Rocciose al Río Bravo* (Naples: Federico & Ardia, 1948) and from that of Gerardo Decorme, S.J, *op. cit.*

19.   Burrus (1981), *op. cit.*, 6. For example, the Revista Católica Press put out a "Jesuit Studies-Southwest" series of which the previously cited book written by Sr. Lilliana Owens' on Father Pinto is the second in the series, the first being her *Jesuit Beginnings in New Mexico, 1867-1882* (El Paso: Revista Católica Press, 1950). Her third book in the series was the biography *Most Reverend Anthony J. Schuler, S.J., D.D., First Bishop of El Paso* (El Paso: Revista Católica Press, 1953).

20.   Benjamin Read, as cited in Randi Jones Walker, *Protestantism in the Sangre de Cristos* (Albuquerque: University of New Mexico Press, 1991), 101. Walker concludes, "When *Revista Católica* left the field in 1918, Roman Catholicism was still the form of religion practiced by the Hispanic New Mexicans" (*Ibid.*, 105).

21.   O'Malley, *op. cit.*, 209.

22.   Quoted in Owens, *op. cit.*, 82.

23.   Owens, *op. cit.*, 97.

24.   See David Charles Bailey, *Viva Cristo Rey! The Cristero Rebellion and the Church-State Conflict in Mexico* (Austin: University of Texas Press, 1974).

25.   Burrus (1981), *op. cit.*, 6.

26.   *"Reglas y Constitucion: Union Católica de San José, 1991, El Paso, Texas."*

27.   Recorded in Owens, *op. cit.*, 100. In the same book, Owens, writing in 1951, mentions the project proposal for the School of Arts and Trades, then under the leadership of the new pastor of Sacred Heart, Joseph M. Walsh, S.J. See pages 85-88.

28.   Together with interviews of older persons in some of these communities, this periodical is serving as an irreplaceable historical source for the anthropologist Lois Stanford. For some other research sources see Burrus' appendix in "The Jesuits Come to the American Southwest," *op. cit.*, 447.

Perseverance and Renewal:
The Missions of Tomé

John M. Taylor

Introduction

The Church of the Immaculate Conception in Tomé, New Mexico, has served the spiritual needs of the people of the Rio Abajo for nearly two hundred fifty years. During that time, the parish's "domain" extended as far east as Manzano and Tajique, south to Casa Colorada, and north to Bosque de Los Pinos and Isleta – a sprawling, untamed area encompassing nearly six hundred square miles. At one time or another this church was responsible for up to ten missions or *visitas* throughout this region, requiring the priests to travel long distances over dangerous, unprotected trails to serve their flock. The story of Tomé and its missions, one of perseverance and renewal, typifies the Catholic mission heritage of early New Mexico.

Tomé

In about 1660, Tomé Domínguez de Mendoza, the son of a Spaniard of the same name who had come north sometime after Oñate's *entrada*, received an *encomienda* grant to the area south and west of the hill now known as El Cerro de Tomé. The family built a large *estancia* where they lived for about twenty years.[1] During the Pueblo Revolt of 1680, thirty-eight members of the Domínguez de Mendoza family were killed, and Tomé and the remainder of his household fled south, never to return. Even after De Vargas reestablished Spanish control over the area, it continued to be victimized by the nomadic Indians, so no large-scale resettlement was attempted. However, in 1739 a group of *genízaros* petitioned Juan Gonzales Bas, the *alcalde* of Albuquerque, for permission to settle the area, to which they referred as "lo de Tomé," or Tomé's place. This petition was approved on July 30, 1739.[2]

During the Spanish Colonial and Mexican Territorial periods, diocesan oversight for Catholic affairs in New Mexico came from Durango, Mexico.[3] In 1742 the Bishop of Durango, Martín de Elizacoechea, granted permission for the first church to be built

Figure 1. Our Lady of the Immaculate Conception Church, Tomé, ca. 1915. Photograph courtesy of the Museum of New Mexico Neg. no. 28686.

Figure 2. Our Lady of the Immaculate Conception Church, Tomé, ca. 1947. Photograph by Paul A. Wilson, courtesy of the Museum of New Mexico Neg. no. 86712.

in Tomé. The structure was completed in 1750, and in 1754 it was dedicated to the Immaculate Conception by Santiago Roybal, vicar of Pedro Anselmo Sánchez de Tagle, Elizacoechea's successor as Bishop of Durango.[4] When Sánchez de Tagle's successor, Pedro Tamaron y Romeral, visited the area in 1760 he noted, "a decent church already built … with a transept and three altars … dedicated to the Immaculate Conception."[5]

Initially, the mission church at Tomé was attended by Franciscan priests from Isleta, Belén, or Albuquerque. However, on July 6, 1821, Father Rubi, the Franciscan Superior in Belén, acting on instructions from Bishop Juan Francisco Márquez de Castañiza, directed Fray José Ignacio Sánchez, the pastor of Isleta, to turn Tomé over to Manuel de Madariaga as the first parish priest.[6]

Oversight for Catholic churches in New Mexico continued to come from Durango until 1851, when Jean Baptiste Lamy was appointed bishop of the newly formed see of Santa Fe. Lamy's "inventory" of parishes and missions in 1852 served as one of the earliest listings of New Mexico churches.[7]

Sangre de Cristo, Valencia[8]

The area now known as Valencia was originally settled between 1630 and 1640 by Francisco de Valencia, the son of Blas de Valencia, one of Oñate's soldiers. Francisco and his family built a large *hacienda*, which almost certainly included a small chapel, on the site of an abandoned Tiwa pueblo. The family remained there until they were driven out during the Pueblo Revolt and the *hacienda* was burned. Although the area was eventually resettled, the namesake Valencia family, like the Domínguez de Mendozas of Tomé, never returned.

In 1740 another group of *genízaros* from the Albuquerque area was given permission to relocate in the Valencia area, and by 1744 the area was home to about fifty families. Although it is very likely that one or more small chapels existed in the area from 1744 on, construction of the structure that would eventually evolve into today's chapel probably occurred between 1800 and 1801.[9] One story of the construction and dedication of this church goes as follows:

Figure 3. Sangre de Cristo Church, Valencia, pre-1941. National Archives Neg. no. 114-G-NM-11254.

Figure 4. Sangre de Cristo Church, Valencia, 1947. Photograph by Paul A. Wilson, courtesy of the Museum of New Mexico Neg. no. 86713.

... there lived two brothers who developed a bitter hatred for each other; and, as the years went by, this hatred became so great that on one occasion much human blood was shed by these two brothers. The parents, relatives, and even neighbors tried in every way possible to appease the hatred existing between these two brothers, but to no avail. Finally, the older of the two, evidently touched by the Guidance and Sympathy of the Divine Providence, came to the younger and offered terms of peace between them. It was decided that a Catholic church be erected, naming it Sangre de Cristo in commemoration and repentance for the blood that each one had shed in their bitterness and hatred for each other.[10]

Priests of Tomé

Diocese/Archdiocese of Durango, Mexico

Manuel Madariaga	July 1821 – November 1838
Mariano de Jesús Lucero	Nov. 1838 – Sept. 1839
Rafael Ortiz	September 1839 – October 1845
José de Jesús Cabeza de Baca	October 1845 – March 1853

Diocese/Archdiocese of Santa Fe

Vicente Montano	March 1853 – June 1855
Carlos Brun	June 1855 – June 1858
Jean Baptiste Rallière	June 1858 – April 1913
Albert Castanie	April 1913 – May 1939
Joseph Assenmacher	May 1939 – June 1952
Joseph Mueller	June 1952 – September 1965
Robert Auman	September 1965 – July 1976
Robert Beach	July 1976 – September 1992
Clarence Mays	October 1992 – May 1994
Greg Neuzel	September 1994 – September 1995
Robert Sánchez (Deacon)	September 1995 – August 1996
Carl File	August 1996 – present

Although direct documentation of the Sangre de Cristo mission is sparse for the first half of the nineteenth century, it is noted as a mission of Tomé as early as 1821 when that parish was officially designated. During these early years, it was probably a simple, flat-roofed structure, occupying about the same area as the main portion of the church does today.

Despite continual attention, years of flooding and summer rains took their toll; and on a Sunday afternoon in the spring of 1941, part of the northeast wall of the chapel collapsed. While Father Joseph Assenmacher and a three-man commission debated repair alternatives, the remainder of the north wall fell in under somewhat mysterious circumstances. As a result, the structure was completely razed and rebuilt on a concrete foundation, using the original floor plan. Although the total reconstruction effort took over two years, Mass was first celebrated in the partially rebuilt structure in 1942. Finally in late 1942 or early 1943, the renovated structure, originally dedicated to peace among families, was rededicated to world peace by Archbishop Rudolph Gerken.[11]

The mission church at Valencia was assigned to the parish of Our Lady of Guadalupe at Peralta when that parish was formally established in April of 1971.

Figure 5. Our Lady of the Immaculate Conception Church, Casa Colorada, pre-renovation, circa 1940. Photograph courtesy Ben Otero.

Our Lady of the Immaculate Conception, Casa Colorada
The Casa Colorada area was probably occupied in the late
eighteenth century since there are references to the location in
several Spanish documents. Although the Casa Colorada land

Figure 6. Interior of Our Lady of the Immaculate Conception Church,
Casa Colorada, pre-renovation. Photograph courtesy Ben Otero.

grant dates from 1823, permission to erect a church in the area had been granted some two years earlier in 1821.[12] This chapel is associated with Tomé on Lamy's 1852 list and has been a mission since that time.

The building was in ruins by the 1940s and Father Assenmacher had the original structure torn down and rebuilt in 1949.[13] It remains the sole mission of Tomé today and is used primarily for special devotions and funerals.

Our Lady of Sorrows, Manzano

The mountains east of the Rio Grande and south of Tijeras Canyon take their name from the village of Manzano, one of the settlements in the area. The word, which means apple tree, described an area where conditions were favorable for fruit orchards in the early part of the nineteenth century.

The village of Manzano is located near Quaraí, a Piro pueblo abandoned because of drought in the late 1670s and never reoccupied.[14] José M. Trujillo and several other residents of Valencia, Tomé, and Adelino petitioned Rio Abajo officials for permission to homestead the land on September 22, 1829. The claim included the square "where the chapel is to be constructed" and further noted that "permission [to construct the chapel] has been

Figure 7. Our Lady of the Immaculate Conception Church, Casa Colorada, 1990. Photograph by author.

granted us."[15] The site of the original structure was at or near the location of the ruins of the former Franciscan mission at Quaraí.

In 1830 the citizens of Manzano abandoned the Quaraí site for reasons of "protection from enemy [presumably Indian] invasion,"[16] and a committee of three citizens requested permission from Father Madariaga of Tomé to build a new church at Plaza de Apodaca (the site of the present Manzano church) which was "near a copious spring."[17] Bishop José Antonio Laureano Zubiría visited the relocated Manazano chapel, dedicated to Nuestra Señora de los Dolores, during his 1833 "tour" of New Mexico churches.

Archbishop Lamy did not note Manzano as a mission of Tomé in either of his first two diocesan inventories (1852 and 1853).[18] Whether this is an oversight or whether the priests at Tomé were not serving the mission during this era remains an open question, although in 1853 Manzano was credited with a "dilapidated church."[19]

In 1854, Manzano does appear on the list of missions associated with Tomé, and in 1859 it was separated from Tomé, becoming a separate parish under the leadership of Reverend Alexander Grzelachowski, taking with it the mission churches at Chililí (formerly attended from San Felipe Neri in Albuquerque), Tajique,

Figure 8. Our Lady of Sorrows Church, Manzano, ca. 1935. Photograph by De Castro, courtesy of the Museum of New Mexico Neg. no. 55475.

Torreon, and Punta de Agua.[20] According to Kajencki, Grzelachowski moved to Manzano in 1857. However, the Archdiocesan records show him at Santo Domingo through 1858. He remained at Manzano until 1860 when he left the priesthood and began a career as a merchant in the village of Puerto de Luna.[21]

The document that separates Manzano from Tomé credits Manzano with a "fine stone church," a definite improvement over the earlier assessment. The present church structure dates from 1885.[22] In 1877, Manzano and its four missions were again attended from Tomé due to a priest vacancy, although it retained its

Figure 9. José Antonio Laureano Zubiría, Bishop of Durango. Museum of New Mexico.

parish status. Manzano continued as a separate parish until 1973 when it became a mission of the parish of Saint Alice in Mountainair.

San Antonio, Tajique

Tajique was the site of a Piro pueblo and large Franciscan mission church abandoned in 1672.[23] Manuel Sánchez and nineteen other claimants from Valencia and Tomé gained title to a tract of land a few miles north of Manzano on March 17, 1834, and the area was officially demarked by Vicente Otero on April 9 of that year. The actual record of demarcation notes the existence of "a temple," suggesting that a church existed almost from the start.[24]

A mission at "Tassique," a spelling used in some early records, is mentioned by Lamy in 1852 as being attended from Tomé. Although similarly noted 1853, Tajique drops from the list until 1859 when it reappears as a mission of the new parish of Nuestra Señora de los Dolores at Manzano. The present chapel at Tajique, built in 1915 and now a mission of Saint Alice in Mountainair, is dedicated to San Antonio and earlier chapels at that site may have been similarly dedicated.

Figure 10. San Antonio Church, Tajique, 1989. Photograph by author.

Saint Anthony and the Holy Family, Torreon

Torreon, an area between Tajique and Manzano, was settled by "Niño Antonio Montoya and others" according to an October 16, 1841 petition.[25] No further details are available until Lamy's 1852 inventory which lists "Peralta (Torreon), Mexicans."[26] The notation is unclear since Peralta and Torreon are distinct geographic entities and probably had separate missions in 1852. After an identical entry in 1853, Torreon is not mentioned again until the Manzano parish separation in 1859.

The present chapel at Torreon, a mission of Saint Alice, dates to 1912 and is dedicated to Saint Anthony and the Holy Family, suggesting that the original settlers may have come from (or had family ties) to Tajique.

Our Lady of Guadalupe, Peralta[27]

Peralta, a settlement which probably consisted of a few large *haciendas* between Los Pinos and Valencia, seems to have acquired its own separate identity rather gradually in the 1830s and 1840s. Prior to this time, residents of the area probably considered themselves to be residents of Valencia, a mile or so to the south. Although there are several candidates for the area's namesake, the leading one appears to be the large pear trees (*pera alta*) known to have been cultivated in the area.

Figure 11. Saint Anthony and the Holy Family Church, Torreon, 1989. Photograph by author.

Since Lamy's 1852 survey refers to a chapel at Peralta and since construction on the present-day church did not begin until 1879, there clearly was a chapel, very likely the *hacienda* chapel at the estate of Juan Antonio Otero, prior to this time. In fact, when the county seat of Valencia County was relocated to Peralta in 1848, the offices were housed in a structure which is said to have been "used as a church" before being used by the county and which apparently reverted to use as a church after the county government moved to Tomé in 1852.[28] This structure may very well date to the original settlement of the area by the Oteros in the mid-1830s.

Figure 12. Our Lady of Guadalupe Church, Peralta, circa 1900. Photograph courtesy the author.

Father Jean Baptiste Rallière, affectionately known as "El Padre Eterno" because of his fifty-five year tenure as pastor of Tomé, began saying Mass in Peralta on a regular basis in 1872, and construction of the present-day church was begun in 1879 on land donated by Mercedes Otero, widow of Juan Antontio. The construction, periodically interrupted by floods and no doubt

Figure 13. Interior view of Our Lady of Guadalupe Church, Peralta, decorated for fiestas, circa 1920. Photograph courtesy Emma Gabaldon.

Figure 14. Our Lady of Guadalupe Church, Peralta, 1916. Photograph by Witter Bynner, courtesy of the Museum of New Mexico Neg. no. 124379.

chronically short of funds, was probably completed sometime in 1888. The chapel was officially dedicated by Father Rallière and two Jesuit priests from Denver on March 13, 1892. The older portion of the structure, known as the *sacristia*, was torn down in the early part of the twentieth century and the remaining church structure was renovated in 1987 under the guidance of Monsignor Sipio Salas.

Figure 15. Father John Baptiste Rallière, "El Padre Eterno." Photograph courtesy Emma Gabaldon.

The church of Our Lady of Guadalupe was designated the mother church of a new parish under Father Albert Chávez on April 1, 1971.

San José de Los Pínos[29]

The area which was known as Bosque de Los Pinos and which is now known as Bosque Farms was created by a change in the course of the Rio Grande during the flood of 1769. The tract, previously part of the Gutiérrez, Sedillo, and Lo de Padilla land grants,[30] was purchased by Francisco Xavier Chávez of Los Padillas, an early governor of New Mexico, in a series of transactions with the heirs of Clemente Gutiérrez. In the early to mid-1830s, Chávez built a large *hacienda* on the property and one of his sons, José Mariano Chávez, moved to the area with his wife and four children in 1837 or 1838.

The large *hacienda* included a chapel dedicated to Saint Joseph as was the Chávez family custom.[31] Being from Los Padillas, the clan had strong religious ties with the church of San Augustine at Isleta and, not surprisingly, maintained those ties at Los Pinos. San José de Los Pinos was being served by priests from

Figure 16. San José de Los Pinos Church, Los Pinos. National Archives Neg # 111-SL-87943.

Isleta when Lamy inventoried the diocese in 1852 and continued to be a mission of that parish until 1858.[32] In that year Father
Rallière was assigned to Tomé, a pastorship which included responsibility for the parish of San Augustine at Isleta and its missions through 1859. A new priest, Father Dámaso Taladrid, was
assigned to Isleta in 1859, and Father Rallière was relieved of that
portion of his pastoral responsibility. During this shift of assignments, the mission at Los Pinos was attached to Tomé.[33] By this
time, Francisco Xavier Chávez and his sons were dead and José
Mariano's widow, Dolores Perea de Chávez, had married Dr. Henry
Connelly, soon to become the governor of the New Mexico Territory. This union effectively severed the Los Padillas-Isleta-Los
Pinos ties.

The Connellys abandoned Los Pinos in 1862 during the brief
Confederate incursion into New Mexico, and the *hacienda* was
used by the U.S. government until 1867 for Indian control and
relocation operations. Dolores Connelly, once again a widow, and
her son, José Francisco Chávez, returned to the *hacienda* in 1867
and lived there for several years. After her death, the estate was
sold to Eduardo Otero of Los Lunas. Throughout this period, the
chapel of San José continued to be served by Father Rallière of
Tomé.

The condition of the *hacienda* and chapel deteriorated near
the end of the century and the mission was dropped from the list
of Tomé missions in 1891. They were torn down in 1898 and
Father Rallière used the chapel's vigas to reroof a barn.[34]

Santa Ana, La Ladera

A chapel dedicated to either Saint Ann or Saint Joseph was
served by priests from Tomé from 1867 until 1891.[35] The chapel,
located on the grounds of the Sánchez *hacienda* near the present-
day intersection of Jerome and La Ladera Roads in Valencia, was
probably a small, flat-roofed, rectangular structure constructed from
terrones or adobe brick. According to some long-time residents of
the area, it was also filled with the statues of many saints. Unfortunately, the mission burned to the ground in the 1920s. A few
older residents of the area still recall attending the summer-time
fiesta of Saint Ann there as children, and others remember seeing the charred walls of the burned-out structure in their youth.

Santa Ana, El Cerro

In 1941, Father Assenmacher of Tomé acquired a piece of
land on the East El Cerro Loop and erected a small chapel to
serve the growing population in that area. Perhaps in fond recollection of the former mission at La Ladera, the new chapel was
dedicated to Saint Ann. The chapel continued to be served from
Tomé until 1964 when it was determined that, in light of flagging
attendance, resources were being overtaxed by its continued use.
In addition, vagrants were breaking into the building, raising the
specter of desecration of the structure and its furnishings. In accordance with the 1941 donation agreement, ownership reverted
to the original landowners and the structure was torn down.[36]
The artifacts (crucifixes, statutes, stations of the cross, bell, etc.)
were either returned to Tomé (where the bell is still on display) or
were kept by those who had donated them to the church.

Others

The venerable church of San Augustine at Isleta served as
the mother church for Tomé off and on prior to the establishment
of Immaculate Conception Parish in 1821. From 1858 to 1860,
Isleta was designated as a mission of Tomé, and Father Rallière
returned the favor of years past, providing priestly service to the
pueblo's Catholic population.

Figure 17. Santa Ana Church, El Cerro. Photograph courtesy Ben Otero.

It is possible that mission chapels served sporadically by priests from Tomé also existed at Punta de Agua, La Constancia, and Adelino. Punta de Agua is noted in 1859 as a mission of Manzano, although there are no prior mentions by Lamy. A church dating from 1874 and dedicated to Saint Vincent de Paul presently stands in Punta de Agua. Pearce says that this area was settled in the "late 19th century," so overlap with Tomé may have been relatively short.[37]

Ellis mentions in passing a church dedicated to San Lorenzo at Adelino.[38] Some older residents recall a building used as a church located on Patricio Road, east of the present-day Route 47, which may have been that church. Ellis also describes Father Rallière as "saying Mass in the big hall, otherwise used for dances, across from the saloon at La Constancia." It is probable that this "big hall" was on the grounds of the Otero estate at La Constancia, although it is unlikely that it ever achieved mission status. Some older residents claim that this chapel was dedicated to Saint Francis. No mention of Adelino or La Constancia appears in any of Lamy's inventories.

Conclusions

Today Our Lady of the Immaculate Conception at Tomé is a small country parish serving a few hundred families from a single church and a seldom-used mission. This is not enormously different from the situation in 1821 when the parish was originally established. However, it is certainly a far cry from the halcyon days of the mid-nineteenth century when Tomé was one of the political, economic, and religious centers of central New Mexico and when priests from this area journeyed to as many as ten missions spread over six hundred square miles of dangerous terrain as they served the pastoral needs of their flock. The history of Tomé and its missions is representative of the mission heritage of early New Mexico: mother churches in population centers served missions and *visitas* scattered all along the "roads less traveled."

In its nearly two hundred fifty years, the church at Tomé and its family of missions have survived floods, fires, time, and cycles of growth and decline in their local populations. Throughout all of this growth and change, Tomé's mission heritage has persevered, anchoring and renewing the Catholic traditions of thousands of New Mexicans.

Notes

1. The early history of Tomé is documented in Roberto de la Vega, *Three Centuries of Tomé, New Mexico* (Los Lunas: Saint Clement's Catholic Church, 1976); Florence H. Ellis, "Tomé and Father J. B. R.," *New Mexico Historical Review* 30 (1955), 89-114 and 195-220; and Gilberto Espinosa and Tibo Chávez, *El Rio Abajo* (Portales: Bishop Publishing Co., 1967).

2. A copy of the Tomé land grant is given in the Spanish Archives of New Mexico, #956. Genízaros, nomadic and pueblo Indians who had taken Spanish surnames and lost most or all of their Indian heritage, are discussed in Marc Simmons, *Albuquerque – A Narrative History* (Albuquerque: University of New Mexico Press, 1989), p. 104.

3. The Franciscan Province of the Holy Gospel, headquartered in Mexico City, also had jurisdiction over parts of New Mexico. However, Tomé was under diocesan control for most of its lifetime.

4. The early Tomé church is described by de la Vega, *Tomé*, and John Kessell, *The Missions of New Mexico Since 1776* (Albuquerque: University of New Mexico Press, 1980). A complete listing of the bishops of the diocese is given by Fray Angélico Chávez, "Lamy Memorial – Centenary of the Archdiocese of Santa Fe" (Santa Fe: Archdiocese of Santa Fe, 1950).

5. E. B. Adams, "Bishop Tamaron's Vistation to New Mexico – 1760," Historical Society of New Mexico, 1954 and Ellis, "Father J.B.R."

6. The date of the establishment of the parish of the Immaculate Conception is noted in several places, including documents on display at the Tomé museum and in de la Vega, *Tomé*.

7. Lamy's "inventory" is given in the 1852 edition of the *Metropolitan Catholic Almanac and Laity Directory* (Baltimore: Fielding Lucas, 1852).

8. The history of Valencia and the Church of Sangre de Cristo is taken from John Taylor, *Our Lady of Guadalupe Parish History Project* (Peralta: Our Lady of Guadalupe Parish, 1989), pp. 11-12 and 39-40.

9. There was almost certainly no significant chapel in Valencia either during the 1760 visit of Bishop Tamaron (Adams, "Bishop Tamaron"); during the 1777 mapping expedition of Miera y Pacheco (Bernardo Miera y Pacheco, "Plano Geographica de la Tierra Descuber la Neubamete a los Rumbos Norte, Noro-este, y Oeste, de Nuevo Mexico," 1777-1778); or during the 1799 visit of Father Guerra (Kessell, *Missions of New Mexico*) since no chapel is noted in any of the reports. However, the area was definitely known as Sangre de Cristo by 1802 as noted in V. L. Olmstead, *Spanish and*

Mexican Censuses of New Mexico – 1750 to 1830 (Albuquerque: New Mexico Genealogical Society, 1981).

10. This quote is taken from a petition circulated by Manuel Sánchez of Valencia during 1941 to raise funds for the Valencia reconstruction. Copy courtesy Ben Otero.

11. Ellis refers to the rededication of the chapel (Ellis, "Father J.B.R."). This must have occurred before March 2, 1943, when Gerken died in office (Chávez, "Lamy Memorial," p. 32).

12. The request to construct a church at Casa Colorada is given in Archives of the Archdiocese of Santa Fe, Loose Documents, 1821, #25. The petitioners for the Casa Colorada grant came from Manzano as described in David V. Whiting's translation of the grant papers (University of New Mexico Special Collections, Surveyor General Report #5, file #29, Frames 8-10). Prior occupation of the area is suggested by Bishop Tamaron's visit (Adams, "Bishop Tamaron") and in a reference by Governor Fernando de la Concha as noted in Valencia County Historical Society, "Rio Abajo Heritage – A History of Valencia County" (Belén: Valencia County Historical Society, n.d.) pp. 10-11.

13. Chávez, "Lamy Memorial," p. 83.

14. Alfonso Ortiz, ed., *Handbook of the North American Indians – Volume 9, The Southwest* (Washington, D.C.: Smithsonian Institution, 1979), p. 241.

15. A record of the original claim is given in House of Representatives Executive Document #14, First Session – 36th Congress (1859-1860) pp. 63-74: New Mexico Private Land Claims, Claim #23, Town of Manzano. The petition requesting permission from Father Madariaga of Tomé to build a church at Manzano dated August 25, 1829, and his reply dated September 4, 1829, are contained in the Archives of the Archdiocese of Santa Fe, Loose Documents, 1829, #11.

16. Archives of the Archdiocese of Santa Fe, Loose Documents, 1830, #8 (August 3), #10 (August 10).

17. Archives of the Archdiocese of Santa Fe, Loose Documents, 1830, #10 (August 10).

18. *Metropolitan Catholic Almanac*, 1852 and 1853.

19. Father Stanley Crocchiola, "The Manzano New Mexico Story," undated.

20. *Metropolitan Catholic Almanac*, 1854, 1857; *Metropolitan Catholic Almanac and Laity Directory for the United States* (Baltimore: John Murphy and Co., 1859); Edward Dunigan, ed., *Dunigan's American Catholic Almanac* (New York: Dunigan and Brother, 1858, 1859, 1861).

21.   Francis Kajencki, "Alexander Grzelachowski: Pioneer Merchant of Puerto de Luna, New Mexico," *Arizona and the West* 26 (1984), 243-260.

22.   Chávez, "Lamy Memorial," p. 67.

23.   Ortiz, *Handbook*, p. 241.

24.   House of Representatives Executive Document #14, First Session, 36th Congress (1859-1860) pp. 46-52: New Mexico Private Land Claims, Claim #21, Town of Tajique.

25.   T. M. Pearce, ed., *New Mexico Place Names*, (Albuquerque: University of New Mexico Press, 1965), p. 168.

26.   House of Representatives Executive Document #14, First Session, 36th Congress (1859-1860) pp. 53-63: New Mexico Private Land Claims, Claim #22, Town of Torreon. At least one early map of the area produced by Domínguez in 1778 shows a "Torreon" on the east bank of the Rio Grande between Isleta and Valencia. The "Map of the Territory of New Mexico by order of Brigadier General S. W. Kearny" (prepared in 1846-1847 by W. H. Emory, J. W. Abel, and W. G. Peck) shows Torreon located on the east side of the Manzano mountains between the villages of "Tassique" and Manzano.

27.   The history of Peralta and the Church of Our Lady of Guadalupe is given in Taylor, *Our Lady of Guadalupe*, pp. 13-19 and 40-43.

28.   *Valencia News Bulletin* 51, no. 35, August 31, 1960, article on Los Lunas Courthouse.

29.   The history of Los Pinos is documented in Taylor, *Our Lady of Guadalupe*, pp. 19-22.

30.   The land grants are shown on maps produced for the Court of Private Land Claims in 1899 (Lo de Padilla Grant) and 1902 (Gutiérrez and Sedillo Grants).

31.   This custom is discussed in an unpublished, annotated Chávez genealogy by Jaquelyn Otero, "A Chávez Family Genealogy."

32.   Metropolitan, 1858; Dunigan, 1858. In these references, Los Pinos is referred to as "Bosquet."

33.   Chávez, "Lamy Memorial," p. 83.

34.   Florence Ellis and Edwin Baca, "The Apuntes of Father J. B. Rallière," *New Mexico Historical Review* 32 (1957), 10-35 and 32, 259-273.

35.   In *Sadlier's Catholic Almanac and Ordo* (New York: D. J. Sadlier and Co., 1882 and 1883) the chapel at La Ladera is listed as being dedicated to San José, although local residents maintain that its dedication, at least in the early twentieth century, was to Saint Ann. The church location (without a name assigned) is also shown on a 1922 Middle Rio Grande Conservancy District Topographic Map (Sheet 17 of 39, 1:12,000).

36. Personal interview with Father Robert Auman, presently retired and living in Belén, New Mexico.
37. The date of construction of the present church at Punta de Agua is given as 1878 in Chávez, "Lamy Memorial," p. 67, although a mission at Punta de Agua is listed in Sadlier's 1874 Almanac. See also Pearce, *New Mexico Place Names*, p. 167.
38. Ellis, "Father J. B. R.," p. 106. Rallière is also said to have had jurisdiction as far south as the Rio Bonito in Lincoln County. However, none of the Lamy inventories mention any locations this far south, and this reference may be to some sort of oversight responsibility (perhaps analogous to today's deanery assignments) given to Rallière by Lamy by virtue of his status as a senior priest.

Bibliography

Adams, E. B. "Bishop Tamaron's Visitation to New Mexico—1760." Historical Society of New Mexico. 1954.

Chávez, Fray Angélico. "Lamy Memorial—A Centenary of the Archdiocese of Santa Fe." Archdiocese of Santa Fe. 1950.

Crocchiola, Father Stanley. "The Manzano, New Mexico Story." undated.

de la Vega, Roberto. *Three Centuries of Tomé, New Mexico*. Los Lunas: Saint Clement's Catholic Church. 1976.

Dunigan, Edward, ed. *Dunigan's American Catholic Almanac*. New York: Edward Dunigan and Brother. 1858, 1859, 1860.

Ellis, Florence H. "Tomé and Father J. B. R." *New Mexico Historical Review* 30 (1955), 89-114, 195-220.

Ellis, Florence H. and Edwin Baca. "The Apuntes of Father J. B. Rallière." *New Mexico Historical Review* 32 (1957), 10-35 and 259-73.

Espinosa, Gilberto and Tibo Chávez. *El Rio Abajo*. Portales: Bishop Publishing Company. 1967.

Kajencki, Francis J. "Alexander Grzelachowski: Pioneer Merchant of Puerto de Luna, New Mexico." *Arizona and the West* 26 (1984), 243-60.

Kessell, John L. *The Missions of New Mexico Since 1776*. Albuquerque: University of New Mexico Press. 1980.

Metropolitan Catholic Almanac and Laity Directory. Baltimore: Fielding Lucas. 1852-1858.

Metropolitan Catholic Almanac and Laity Directory for the United States. Baltimore: John Murphy and Co. 1859-1862.

Miera y Pacheco, Bernardo de. "Plano Geographical de la Tierra Descuber la Neubamete a los Rumbos Norte, Noro-este, y Oeste, de Nuevo Mexico." Map surveyed in 1777-1778.

Olmstead, V. L. *Spanish and Mexican Censuses of New Mexico – 1750 to 1830.* Albuquerque: New Mexico Genealogical Society. 1981.

Ortiz, Alfonso, ed. *Handbook of the North American Indians – Volume 9: Southwest.* Washington, D.C.: Smithsonian Institution. 1979.

Otero, Jacquelyn. "A Chávez Family Genealogy." unpublished manuscript.

Pearce, T. M., ed. *New Mexico Place Names – A Geographical Dictionary.* Albuquerque: University of New Mexico Press. 1965.

Sadlier's Catholic Almanac and Ordo. New York: D. J. Sadlier and Co., 1867-1891.

Simmons, Marc. *Albuquerque – A Narrative History.* Albuquerque: University of New Mexico Press. 1982.

Taylor, John M. *Our Lady of Guadalupe Parish History Project, Part I: A History of the Parish and its Local Areas.* Peralta, NM: Our Lady of Guadalupe Parish. 1989.

Valencia County Historical Society. *Rio Abajo Heritage – A History of Valencia County.* undated.

Continuity of Commitment and Customs in La Capilla de San Antonio at Los Lentes, New Mexico

Patty Guggino

Eighteen miles south of Albuquerque, nestled among the majestic cottonwoods of the lower Rio Grande Valley, is an ancient settlement now called Los Lentes. Indians have lived here since time out of memory, and through the centuries they have been joined by other settlers. As Isleta Pueblo's southernmost encampment, this area has always been called *Be-jui Tu-ay* (Rainbow Village) by the Natives. They are the descendants of the Indians who in 1540 encountered Don Francisco Vásquez de Coronado's conquistadores as the newcomers searched for supplies.[1]

Later, in 1598, when Don Juan de Oñate entered New Mexico leading colonists who intended to stay, they commandeered Isleta for their soldier-settlers' southern headquarters. Reinforced with a *presidio* (garrison) and mission, Spanish control soon radiated from Isleta over the entire Río Abajo. During the Pueblo Revolt of 1680, it is no wonder neither the Tiwa speakers nor the Piro Indians further south, near Socorro, New Mexico, rose up against these strongly entrenched Spaniards.[2]

In recognition of the area's geographical and historical significance, the Rainbow Village was entered into the State Register of Cultural Properties in 1986 and recommended for the National Register of Historic Places in February of that same year.[3]

A few miles north, the church and mission the Indians constructed at Isleta for the Franciscan priests was judged "very fine — *excelentísima*" in the 1641 mission census.[4] That original chapel was dedicated to San Antonio,[5] and the humble saint came to occupy a special place in the Isletas' hearts. He inspired devotion to Christ and the Catholic Church among Natives and Hispanics alike.

Following the 1680 Revolt, as the last Spanish refugees staggered south seeking sanctuary, some Christian Isletas accompanied those exiles to the El Paso-Juárez area.[6] This mixed group of Hispanic and Indian survivors found they could agree both on their devotion to San Antonio and their faith in God. Accordingly, they built a church dedicated to their beloved San Antonio, named just as their previous house of worship at Isleta had been. Eventually an Indian Pueblo called *Ysleta del Sur* – Isleta of the South – evolved there.

During the twelve year interval before Spain's successful reconquest of New Mexico, many Pueblo Indians tried to eradicate all vestiges of Hispanic and Catholic influence. The Spanish language was not to be spoken. Sheep, cattle, fruit trees, vineyards, and other European additions to Indian life were to be destroyed. The corruption of baptism was to be scrubbed off in the rivers with yucca root soap, and Indian names were reinstated. Marriages blessed by the Catholic priests were invalidated, and of course church structures were destroyed. [7]

At Isleta, statues were decapitated, excrement was spread on the altar, and what remained of the burned church walls was eventually used as a corral.[8] And so life returned to the ancient ways, until 1692. Without Spanish protection, the sedentary Pueblos were doubly vulnerable to raiding Indians. Many now preferred that the Spanish return, and, with brokering help from Pueblo supporters, Don Diego de Vargas once again established Spain's control over all the land, including Isleta and its southernmost settlement, Rainbow Village.[9]

The returning Spaniards and the remaining Pueblos now sought to recover from the chaos and collapse experienced by both ethnicities in the wake of revolt. With the prudence to repair past injustices, they entered an era of accommodation. Instead of fighting each other, the two groups now united against their common enemy, the fierce Navajo and Apache.

By appointing a *capitan de guerra* – war captain – at each Pueblo, the Spaniards acknowledged the Indians' abilities. The chosen Natives then organized all able-bodied warriors into auxiliaries of mounted and armed troops who rode alongside the Spanish militia on forays against their nomadic foes. The Spaniards utilized the Pueblos' knowledge of terrain and their insights into battle strategy. Together they protected both Indian and Hispanic homes and families and came to respect each other.[10]

In an example of accommodation, the Franciscan *Custos* – friar in charge, along with a number of his missionaries, campaigned for the right of the Pueblo Indians to wear war paint when embarking on skirmishes against the hostiles. These clerics understood it was important to the Pueblos that they be prepared to meet the enemy in the tradition of their ancestors. So at a meeting with Governor Flores Mogollón in 1714, Fray Juan de Tagle pointed out that Spaniards painted their faces and often placed feathers in their hats when going to church, and requested official sanction of the same practices for the Indians going to war.[11] At this point, after almost 120 years of encounter, Hispanos and Pueblos were finally able to focus on their commonly held beliefs and goals while downplaying their differences. At Rainbow Village these adaptations were becoming increasingly more common.

As the eighteenth century went forward, a remarkable representative of Spanish presence in the Río Abajo was the extraordinary Ana de Sandoval y Manzanares. In 1715 Doña Ana petitioned Governor Félix Martínez to reissue a deed to the land grant south of Isleta Pueblo previously held by her father. This official action was necessary since all documentation had been destroyed during the Pueblo Revolt. That the governor failed to meet her request deterred this strong-willed woman not at all. With only a few servants accompanying her, she traveled by burro the 1,500 miles to Mexico City in search of clear title to her property.

Doña Ana was gone a total of two years, but she returned to New Mexico with a valid deed. She called the 110,000 acres recently restored to her control *La Merced de San Clemente* – St. Clement's Grant. Señora Sandoval was now the Rainbow Village's newest neighbor. Her grant's name, *San Clemente*, still today designates the main Catholic Church south of Rainbow Village, in the modern-day village of Los Lunas.

And so areas of similarity developed. The lands surrounding Isleta Pueblo were increasingly populated by persons, both Hispanic and Native, who shared common concerns and points of culture. Rainbow Village, or Los Lentes as the area would come to be called, now was home to Hispanic settlers, Isleta Indians, and the offspring of those who had intermarried.

Meanwhile as the eighteenth century continued, Apache raiders forced the Piro Indians to abandon their pueblos around Socorro. They then drifted north onto the southernmost outskirts of Isleta, or Rainbow Village. The Piros spoke a variation of Isleta's Tiwa dialect. Even though the Piros looked a little strange because they shaved all but the topmost part of their hair, the Isletas accepted the Piros and gave them refuge.[12] They joined the group of Isletas and Hispanos who had learned to live together at Rainbow Village – Los Lentes.

To this day there are families with the surname Piro and even a Piro Lane in the Rainbow Village of Los Lentes.[13] Albino and Jessie Piro were mayordomos for the Los Lentes Catholic Church in the 1940s, and Sara and Anthony Piro, Jr., served in that capacity during the 1980s. Both families still live on Los Lentes Road, a pathway at Rainbow Village eventually named for the Lente family. But who were the original Lentes?

The name Lente is an unusual one. In the Isleta language "ente" means "others," and "los entes" means "the other ones." This is possibly a reference to persons who are "not quite like us."[14] Still another view asserts that in eighteenth century colloquial Spanish "ente" meant "guy" and "los lentes" meant "those guys." This might also imply a cultural variance from the persons speaking.[15]

The Lente name, especially that of Matías Lente, appears many times in both church and archival land records. Sometimes the documents list Matías Clente as a major land buyer. This spelling is interestingly close to Clemente, the name of Doña Ana's nearby property that Matías Lente was systematically acquiring piecemeal. By the mid-eighteenth century, Doña Ana was no longer alive to object, and her sons were selling her land parcel by parcel.

Perhaps Lente's motivation for gaining control of this particular property can be found in an old Rainbow Village legend recounted by the prominent Isletan Pablo Abeita (1871-1940).[16]

Early folklore of the area told of the adventures of Matías Lente, an Isleta man, who fell in love with a woman from the San Clemente grant and subsequently moved south to be near her. The census record indicates that Matias married a woman from the grant named Juana and that they had a son Nicolás Andrés, who was born in 1730. In church records as late as 1771, the Lente family is listed as Indian by ethnicity. They were residing in an area south of the main Isleta Pueblo, at the exact location of today's Los Lentes/Rainbow Village, next door to the San Clemente Grant.[17]

According to land records, in 1744, Ana de Sandoval's heirs sold another part of her hard-won grant to Matías Elente. Even then there was confusion as to his ethnicity, perhaps indicating he was considered different. In census records he was variously listed as either a *genízaro* – a detribalized and hispanicized Native American – or an Isleta Pueblo Indian.[18] Again in 1760, the same Matías Elente purchased another part of Doña Ana's land, this one at Pueblo San Clemente.[19] The Lente family lives there still.

One of Los Lentes' most beloved *rezadoras* – prayer and song leaders – was Nellie Lente, who was active through the 1980s. She was the product of over two hundred years of Hispano-Indio adaptation and faith-keeping. Nellie was living proof that through the centuries differences between Pueblo and *vecino* – neighbor, settler – became increasingly less.

As Hispanos crept ever closer to the Indian towns for protection from the nomadic raiders, Pueblo peoples were conversely enticed into the Spanish settlements by the promise of work. Lifestyle preferences blended and became very similar. But where, in the 1780s, could the Isletas, Piros, Lentes, and their Hispano neighbors at Rainbow Village worship their God?

Although by 1730 many of the churches attended by both the Pueblos and the Hispanos had been restored from the destruction that was their fate from 1680 to 1692, none was in Los Lentes. The mission at Isleta was among those reconstructed, but for reasons still unknown, the newly refurbished church was now dedicated to the illustrious Church Father, Saint Augustine. Superseded in the transition was San Antonio, the humble and comfortably familiar friar for whom that church had originally been named.[20] Who now would lovingly care for the people as

San Antonio always had, and who would so willingly help them find their lost possessions?[21] Besides, Isleta was more that a league away from Rainbow Village, a long walk to visit an unfamiliar saint. The people needed a chapel of their own.

To further complicate spiritual matters, by the late eighteenth century, the number of priests was declining. Even as the Hispanos and Pueblos grew closer, the clergy was progressively more distant due to their diminished ranks. Throughout the eighteenth century, diocesan influence in New Mexico increased only a trifle while Franciscan influence weakened a great deal. Conversely, that frontier's importance as a military outpost against the nomadic tribes, the other European powers, and the Anglo-Americans was growing. Official visits from the church hierarchy were rare, and as the debate about whether the area should continue to be administered by the Franciscans or be taken over by the diocesan clergy continued, New Mexico's Catholics, both Native and Hispanic, were increasingly left with fewer and fewer shepherds.[22]

The first Episcopal visitation from the Diocese of Durango came in 1730 when Bishop Benito Crespo traveled north to review the New Mexican church now under his jurisdiction. This trip took place one year after that Diocese had officially claimed to be in charge of the New Mexico territory. It would actually be 1797, some sixty-seven years later, before the bishop at Durango would become actively involved in meeting the spiritual needs of New Mexicans.[23] Meanwhile, the faithful were left on their own to maintain and foster what devotion to God they could.

Consequently, the people at Rainbow Village established their own chapel in 1789. The Spanish Census of 1790 listed Blas Lente, Matías' son, along with a Pedro and a Manuel Lente and their families, as residents of *El Pueblo de San Antonio de Los Lentes*. The people's beloved San Antonio once again was honored in the name of their plaza. Juana Lente was recorded then as a ninety-one-year-old Indian widow, and the industrious Matías was no longer alive. Also in this document are found the surnames Padilla, Perea, Piro, Samora, Gallego, Olgin, Gutiérrez, Brito, Sedello, García, Guerro, Saens, Moreno, and Chávez with a mixture of ethnic designations that included Mexican, *castizo* – pureblooded Spanish, and Indian.[24]

Rainbow Village was now called El Pueblo de Los Lentes, after its leading land owner. This area was most probably also recorded as San Antonio in the census because a church, dedicated to the familiar saint supplanted by Saint Augustine in the restored church at Isleta, had already been built at Rainbow Village. It seems entirely logical that Los Lentans of the eighteenth century, persons who carved their names and the date 1789 on a church *viga* still visible today, would want to reinstall that humble friar as patron of their new church south of Isleta.

A century before, the Los Lentes' ancestors had been devoted to San Antonio, patron of the Church at Isleta. The transplanted Isletas and Hispanics, settled at Ysleta del Sur in El Paso-Juárez after the Revolt, had also chosen that familiar Franciscan as the patron to whom they dedicated their church. Later on, in 1864, an even more official reference to the Los Lentes chapel is recorded.

By 1851, soon after the United States took over Mexico's northern frontier, Jean Baptiste Lamy became Bishop of the New Mexico Territory. Lamy sent to France for what he considered properly trained and dedicated priests. They came to serve the newly American frontier church in New Mexico. One such cleric answering Lamy's call was Felix Jouvet.

Fr. Jouvet came to New Mexico from his native France in 1861 and was assigned to San Augustine Church at Isleta Pueblo in February of 1862.[25] According to his notation in Isleta's baptismal book, Fr. Jouvet blessed La Capilla de San Antonio de Los Lentes in 1864. Cataloging that event, he created a delightful and official notation of the occasion by drawing a small picture of the chapel above his official entry.[26] This record assured that posterity would know of the church (fig. 1).

But the people of Los Lentes have other ways of recalling what this church, and saint, have meant to them through the centuries. History and traditions surrounding the San Antonio Chapel at Los Lentes have been handed down orally from one generation to the next. They are packed with meaning and provide a way of viewing the importance of this devotion to the mostly *mestizo* – but by now partly Anglo – population of the area. One relative newcomer recalled what her grandparents told her about the San Antonio Chapel as they first saw it in 1864:

The church had a flat roof supported by vigas and dirt floor, they had no pews just hand made benches and no kneelers, it had the stations of the cross, statue of St. Anthony and a baby Jesus, statue of our blessed mother, a big picture of St. Joseph. The church was always kept so clean, the Padre assigned 2 couples every year as mayordomos … to keep the church clean and in order(;) this assignment was for a whole year then at fiesta time June 13th he would appoint 2 new couples for the following year.[27]

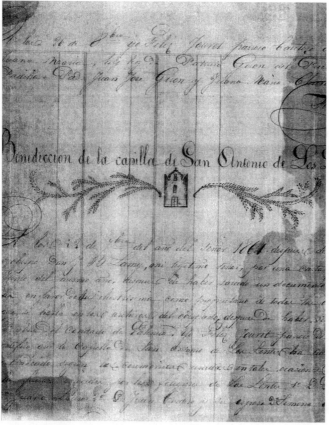

Figure 1. Record in San Agustín Baptismal Book by Fr. Felix Jouvet.

Through the years the beliefs and customs have remained essentially unchanged. Two couples are still appointed as *mayordomos* (stewards) in charge of keeping the chapel clean. They also are responsible for planning the fiesta that is today celebrated on the weekend closest to June 13th, San Antonio's feast day. Previously, fiestas were held on that exact date, no matter what day of the week it might be.[28] Each family has special memories of what those celebrations have meant to them and their relatives.

Excitement always ran high and preparations were extensive. First the grounds were cleared of weeds. Then the church itself refurbished with a *yeso* – gypsum – whitewash that was applied to the inside walls with a *saleita* – sheepskin – while the exterior was similarly spruced up with a new coat of mud plaster.[29] The wood stove that heated the church no doubt also left a smoky residue on the walls, and the whitewash would make them bright again. Today the chapel remains white, although by dint of stucco and paint instead of the *yeso* of yesterday.

The priest collected donations from every family as he went from house to house requesting that each group be responsible for specific cleaning chores.[30] The greatest generosity possible was encouraged by the realization that during the Fiesta Mass the padre would announce from the pulpit the amount each family had given.

The stations of the cross, the statues, and the altar-linens all had to be in perfect shape for the feast day. The responsibility for cleaning and repairing them was an honor that is still enjoyed today. Traditionally, certain women have handled these activities, and then passed on their duties to daughters and god-daughters.

During the first part of this century Emilia Perea was charged with beautifying the altar. Her daughter Juanita Griego followed in her footsteps. Doña Juanita yearly provided a new *hábito* – religious habit – for San Antonio, and she also changed the decorations for the *andita* or carriage upon which the santo was paraded through the village (fig. 2). These embellishments assumed many styles, types of cloth and colors, depending on the ladies' preferences and availability of materials.

Not only did the designated women decorate San Antonio and the other statues in the church, they also repaired the occasional cracks and broken fingers suffered by the saints. That responsibility is tended to today by Sally López, who lives directly south of the chapel, and who is Doña Emilia's god-daughter.[31] In a bygone era of illiteracy, when the stations of the cross were once again placed on the newly white washed walls, it was the proud duty of Mrs. Atilano (Carmelita) Chávez to make sure they were numbered correctly.[32]

Preparations at this little chapel for the yearly fiesta are still extensive, as are the refurbishment for Christmas and monthly Mass. Ever-changing styles are reflected in the church's altar, window casings, frames around the stations of the cross, and *nicho* – niche – holding the *bulto* – statue – of San Antonio and baby Jesus. All are examples of the "Folk Federal Style" popular in the United States around 1776. This trend did not reach isolated areas like Los Lentes until a later date, and it probably replaced many indigenous decorations and artifacts when it finally did arrive in New Mexico.[33]

Figure 2. Doña Juanita Griego (on the right) fixes the *hábito* of San Antonio.

The pictorial representations of the stations of the cross are consistent with a style encouraged from Bishop Lamy's time on. They, as well as the smaller statues of the Infant of Prague, San Lorenzo, St. Jude, and the Virgin Mary were probably brought to the church in the 1860s. The presence of these statues is an indication that the local people accepted the Bishop's request that they adapt European or American styles to replace the more primitive art of their ancestors.

An indication of redecoration in the chapel prior to Lamy's arrival is the type of glass that protects the stations of the cross. It could have arrived around 1840, earlier than either the pictures it covers or Bishop Lamy.[34] Also from an earlier time, the bulto of San Antonio is carved from wood and has two rough-hewn legs ending in plaster feet. The head and shoulders of the statue are plaster also, as are the hands. They are affixed to the wooden body with a variety of tapes and glue. The Infant Jesus cradled by San Antonio is constructed in the same manner. They were not replaced by more modern representations and are still cared for lovingly.

No matter the decor or design of the statues, people came and still come, bringing food and drink with them. Many planned to spend the entire day, or perhaps several days, cleaning and refurbishing their chapel and its contents. Some years are more notable than others for the amount of work required at *la capilla*.

In the spring of 1906 the Rio Grande overflowed. In spite of the many sandbags stacked along the river bank, the sacristy and part of the church's east wall were swept away.[35] All the sacred vessels, linens, statues, stations of the cross and vestments were then housed in a room at the Tondre ranch, just west of the chapel. These quarters had been reserved for Fr. Anton Docher's visits to this mission from the main church he pastored at Isleta.[36]

Improvements continued to be made. In 1912 parishioners covered the dirt floor with wooden planks and also replaced the old roof with a galvanized one (fig. 3). In 1917 water seeped up from the ground (no doubt the reason for calling this area *los charcos* – the puddles) necessitating work on the west wall that was weakened by the rising moisture.[37] In 1926 Walter and Willie Gómez refurbished the main altar and constructed the side altars from sawmill planks. Proud of helping in this project, Martín

Ryan inscribed his name on the back of the altars. The windows were framed by the grandfather of the noted *santero* Alcario Otero. Private pews were also constructed by many families at this time, an undeniable improvement over those left since 1864.[38]

New statues are still added periodically. In June of 1937 Hermenes José Baca carried the figure of San Antonio now guarding the holy water font all the way from Belén.[39] Writing at the base of the Holy Family statue on the right altar indicates that it was brought to the chapel in June of 1959 to fulfill a *promesa* (vow or promise).

Through the years many renovations of the chapel have been carried out. The bell, dedicated in 1893, remains and still is joyfully rung for fiestas.[40] It used to be an important part of keeping Los Lentens informed, whether for happy events or sad. When a member of the community died the bells were sounded twice, then held still and rung twice more. This was called *doblando las campanas* (ringing the bells twice) and the *vecinos* knew then that there had been a death. Everyone would come to the chapel to hear who had passed away. That custom is less useful now since

Figure 3. La Capilla de San Antonio de los Lentes circa 1912.

most residents work some distance from their homes and the chapel.

Today, San Antonio de Los Lentes is the property of the Archdiocese of Santa Fe. That office has officially controlled *la capilla* ever since the people deeded it to Archbishop Chapelle in 1894. In doing so, they were represented by Fred Tondre, Nicolás Aguirre, Pilar Aguirre, Juan Rey Jojolá, Luis Sais, and Narciso Carasco.[41] This same Narciso Carasco would be pleased that the 1997 Fiesta Queen is his great-great-granddaughter, Paula Jean Walker (fig.4). And so threads binding the present to the past are enduringly interwoven.

Renovations of the chapel have continued. The last major one was in 1975, when the wooden floor was replaced with cement and the west tower torn down and rebuilt in an effort to overcome the effects of the underground river still trying to reach the surface. New pews were also built by the Industrial Arts students at Los Lunas High School and installed by Jerry Gabaldon, their teacher and a member of the Los Lentes community.

The June weekend nearest the thirteenth continues to be the high point of the year for the people of Los Lentes, and their relatives who return from places near and far. It is a time for reunion and celebration of what was and what still is.

People come back to their roots, and all dress in their finest to enter the shining *capilla* – little chapel. A *rompida del nombre* – breaking of the name – signals the beginning of festivities with rifles fired into the air (fig. 5) as San Antonio is reverently carried to homes wishing his presence for recitation of the rosary (fig. 6). New *mayordomos* are chosen and a queen is crowned while the Knights of Columbus stand at attention.

On the practical side, yesterday's *matanza* – slaughtering and cooking of a pig or a steer – has given way to hundreds of hamburgers, broiled over a National Guard grill and quickly consumed (fig. 7). Isleta and Los Lunas *vecinos* congregate under the shade of a *carpa* – tarp. Children play games and have their faces painted, not unlike both their warrior and church-going ancestors of nearly three centuries ago.

Isletans perform their traditional dances (fig. 8) and sell fry bread. Anglos call out bingo numbers to the strains of vibrant Hispanic music once again filling the plaza in accompaniment to Spanish dancers (fig. 9). Traditional *vihuelas, guitarons* – large guitars, and squeeze boxes make room for electric guitars and drums. Still, at some time during the celebrations all stop to visit the *santo*, give thanks, and spend time in prayer.

This scenario, ever evolving, yet always the same, is the concrete expression of faith and continuity. It reflects the persistence of a New Mexican community that was ruled first by Spain, then by Mexico, and now by the United States. The multi-hued Rainbow Village community is a living example of a people who have survived several governments and kept their Catholic faith alive and glowing. Through over two hundred years of turmoil and unavoidable neglect, the loyal residents of *El Pueblo de San Antonio de Los Lentes* have remained together under their *santo's* kindly gaze, safely tucked within the mantle of the Catholic Church (fig. 10).

Figure 4. 1997 Fiesta Queen and her Royal Court. The 1997 Queen was Paula Jean Walker (second from right).

Figure 5. Bullets and bells mark the start of fiesta, 1979.

Figure 6. Procession of the San Antonio statue led by Mayordomos Mr. and Mrs. Moises Griego, 1974.

Figure 7. Food preparation for the fiesta.

Figure 8. Traditional dances at Fiesta. The Buffalo Dancers from Isleta Pueblo are led by Mr. Jerome Shupa.

With the music stilled, the dancing done and San Antonio once more returned to his special place at the front of the altar, Los Lentes families gather in their homes to share a pot of chili. Basking in the warmth of Christ's love, everyone agrees that the present celebrations are "the best ever" — just as their remote *antepasados* — ancestors, their grandparents, and their parents have agreed since 1789.

Figure 9. Traditional dancers from Regina's Dance Studio.

Figure 10. Fr. Rick Zerwas at 1997 Fiesta.

Notes

1. Elsie Clews Parsons, *The Pueblo of Isleta* (Albuquerque: Calvin Horn Publishers, 1974), p. 205.
2. Joseph P. Sánchez, *The Rio Abajo Frontier: 1540-1692* (Albuquerque: The Albuquerque Museum, 1987), p. 136.
3. Letter from State of New Mexico Historic Preservation Division Office of Cultural Affairs to Patty Guggino, March 25, 1997.
4. France V. Scholes, "Documents for the History of the New Mexican Missions in the Seventeenth Century," *New Mexico Historical Review* 4 (1929), 46-51.
5. Sánchez, op. cit. p. 103: "By 1626, the T(e)wa area had two convents… The first was at San Antonio de Isleta and the second at San Francisco de Sandía."
6. David J. Weber, *The Spanish Frontier in North America* (New Haven: Yale University Press, 1992), p. 135.
7. Ibid., p. 136.
8. L. Bradford Prince, *Spanish Mission Churches of New Mexico* (Cedar Rapids: The Torch Press, 1915), p. 192.
9. John L. Kessell, ed., *Remote Beyond Compare: Letters of don Diego de Vargas to His Family from New Spain and New Mexico, 1675-1706* (Albuquerque: University of New Mexico Press, 1989), pp. 174-183.
10. Ramón A. Gutiérrez, *When Jesus Came the Corn Mothers Went Away: Marriage, Sexuality, and Power in New Mexico 1500-1846* (Stanford: Stanford University Press, 1991), p.151.
11. Joe S. Sando, *Pueblo Nations: Eight Centuries of Pueblo Indian History* (Santa Fe: Clear Light Publishers, 1992), p.79.
12. Sando, op. cit., p. 78. Also, Patty Guggino interview with Ted Jojolá, Ph.D., of Isleta Pueblo, March 5, 1990.
13. Patty Guggino, interview with Anthony Piro, Sr., June 8, 1997. He related that his grandfather's great-great-great-grandfather had moved to the Isleta Pueblo from the south and that he had then established the family on a farm in the Los Lentes area. His family lives on Piro Lane.
14. Jojolá, op. cit.
15. T.M. Pearce, *New Mexico Place Names* (Albuquerque: University of New Mexico Press, 1977), p. 91.
16. Katherine Powers Gallegos, ed., *The Indio and Hispano Child: Improving His Self Image* (Los Lunas: United States Office of Education, 1970), p. 72.
17. Fray Angélico Chávez, *Origins of New Mexico Families* (Santa Fe: William Gannon, 1975), p. 205. Also U.S. West Directory for Valencia County, Belén, Bosque Farms, Isleta, and Los Lunas lists thirty-one

phones under the surname "Lente." Most reside at Isleta and Bosque Farms.

18. Pauline Jaramillo, *A Small History and Folklore: El Pueblo de San Antonio de Los Lentes New Mexico* (Los Lunas: San Clemente Parish, 1990), p. 10, citing San Clemente Land Grant Records, New Mexico State Archives, Santa Fe, New Mexico.

19. Ibid.

20. Joe L. Montoya, *Isleta Pueblo and the Church of St. Augustine* (Isleta: St. Augustine Church, 1978), pp. 9-22. According to Montoya, the Isleta Church was rebuilt by 1710.

21. Prince, op. cit., p. 193. "St. Augustine is the patron saint of Isleta. . . . [he] is honored now by being the chief figure in the procession; but a good priest told me that the people had not transferred their affection to the new image, and mournfully insisted that it did not hear their prayers so well as the old one of their fathers."

22. Marta Weigle, *Brothers of Light, Brothers of Blood: The Penitentes of the Southwest* (Albuquerque: University of New Mexico Press, 1976), pp. 19-21.

23. Ibid., p. 20.

24. Virginia L. Olmstead, *Spanish and Mexican Census of New Mexico, 1750-1830* (Albuquerque: New Mexico Genealogical Society, 1981).

25. *Sadlier's Catholic Almanac and Ordo*, 1867-1891. Also Archdiocese of New Mexico Archives, Santa Fe, as per Marina Ochoa, archivist.

26. New Mexico Marriages and Baptisms, San Augustín de la Isleta Church, Isleta Pueblo, New Mexico, June 13, 1864, p. 256. Also Montoya, op. cit., pp. 9-22.

27. Letter from Stella Tondre Cunningham to Patty Guggino, June 6, 1976.

28. Patty Guggino, interview with Moisés Griego, May 2, 1997.

29. Cunningham letter, op. cit.

30. Griego interview, op. cit.

31. Ibid.

32. Pauline Jaramillo, op. cit., p. 10.

33. Opinion of Thomas J. Steele, S.J., in conversation with Patty Guggino, May 22, 1997.

34. Ibid. All these articles reflect the impact of trade from America over the Santa Fe Trail.

35. Cunningham letter, op. cit.

36. Ibid.

37. Ibid., and Griego interview, op. cit.

38. Jaramillo, op. cit.

39. Patty Guggino, conversation with his son Oswaldo Baca, Ph.D., May 5, 1997.

40. Montoya, op. cit., pp. 9-22. Fr. Anton Docher, a native of Le Crest, Clermont, France, was responsible for the bell.

41. Valencia County Records for 1894, Warranty Deed, recorded on December 24, 1894, p. 37, Valencia County Court House, Los Lunas, New Mexico.

The Community Influence and Cultural Power of Nuestra Señora de Belén

Margaret Espinosa McDonald

The Rio Grande del Norte has drained the southern watershed of the Rocky Mountains for eons leaving a river valley ripe for agricultural development. It is no wonder that Juan de Oñate chose to follow this river north. An upper portion of the Rio Abajo, known today as Valencia County, has been inhabited by humans for ten thousand years. However few Spanish settlements occurred in this area until the eighteenth century.

In 1740, a group of thirty-two men and women settlers led by Diego de Torres applied and received a royal land grant from the Governor and Captain General, Don Domingo Gaspar de Mendoza.[1] The grant's name was Nuestra Señora de Belén, or Our Lady of Bethlehem.

The site the future citizens of Belén eyed with favor for their grant was certainly desirable for agriculture. The village was to be situated in the flat valley on the west side of the Río Grande. To the west and east of the valley and elevated some three hundred feet above its floor were the dry tablelands. Covering this tableland were native grasses that became the pasture for the flocks and herds of the Belén settlers. Though the Río Grande was a slow-moving river by the time it reached Belén, it deposited sediments in the valleys around Belén for centuries, thus contributing to a rich farm land. Belén's section of the river valley remains today some of the finest agricultural lands in New Mexico. The plains area surrounding Belén was ideal for stock raising, which was to figure prominently in the economy of the Río Abajo.

The Belén community began to develop with little difficulty. As a community land grant, Belén welcomed additional settlers

with the *Alcalde* assigning them unallocated land. Subsidiary ham-
lets began to grow around the original settlement on the west
side of the river.[2] To the north was the plaza of Sausal; to the
south of the original plaza were the villages of *Plaza de Nuestra
Señora de Dolores de los Genízaros, Plaza de Nuestro Salvador de Pilar,* and
Plaza de Nuestro Padre de Jarales.[3]

The Catholic religion provided the structure and focus for
the citizenry of New Mexico. The work of the fields and home
was eased by the church festivals, masses, baptisms, marriages,
processions, wakes, and burials. Entertainment was found at fiestas with their dances and songs. In addition to providing a diver-
sion from the daily work schedule, the church provided a cultural framework that mediated between the past and the future
during periods of rapid social change in Belén.

When the Belén Land Grant was awarded in 1740, Belén
became a *visita* or mission of San Agustín at Isleta. In 1793, Nuestra
Senora de Belén was built on the plaza of Belén and the church
was elevated to the status of a full parish equal to Isleta.[4] The
status of full parish allowed for a resident pastor and more frequent services in Belén. Tomé, though established a year before
Belén, became a *visita* of Belén. Most of the chapels north of Tomé
were under the ecclesiastical jurisdiction of Isleta.[5]

The Territorial Assembly of New Mexico asked the Bishop
of Durango to secularize the mission of Taos, Abiquiú, Belén, San
Juan, and San Miguel del Vado with Belén secularized in 1826.[6]
Secularization refers to the transference of a parish from the control of a religious order, in this case the Franciscans, to that of the
secular or diocesan clergy. The religious orders are under the authority of the provincial superior of their order while the secular
clergy are under the authority of the bishop of the area.

New Mexico and Belén both continued to grow. Don Juan
Rafael Rascon, the Vicar General of the Diocese of Durango, visited Belén in 1829, and by reason of his authority as Vicar General, he conferred the sacrament of Confirmation to over a hundred people in Belén.[7] Following Rascon's visit, Rt. Rev. José Antonio de Zubiría, Bishop of Durango, made a *visita,* or inspection,
to New Mexico in 1833. While in Belén on Tuesday, August 14,

1833, Bishop Zubiría reprimanded Father Luis de Lujan for his lack of diligence in keeping strict records.[8]

By 1837, the first of many incidents of conflict by the parishioners of Belén with the priest was recorded. Apparently, the citizens of Belén were angry at Father Lujan and had forced the priest to flee south to the nearby village of Sabinal. Father Lujan wrote to Bishop Zubiría that he was so intimidated by the parishioners of Belén that he was "prostrate in bed without moving."[9] The Bishop told Lujan it would be better if Lujan were to remain in Sabinal. He was to "help Belén when they ask you for your help with their souls."[10] Lujan felt he could do better in Sabinal since "all but five [Belén parishioners] hate me."[11]

Belén appeared to settle down until the appointment of Father Nicolás Valencia on August 15, 1845. This was to be a trial period for Father Valencia. Early on, according to Bishop Zubiría, Father Valencia began to display his "penchant for acting independently as if the church's canons and his bishop's regulations counted for nothing."[12] These difficulties led Bishop Zubiría to suspend Valencia later in 1845 on the grounds of insubordination. The suspension did not have much impact on Valencia, who remained in Belén until March 13, 1850. Later, all marriages performed by Valencia were decreed invalid.[13] By August 14, Valencia was in Sabinal and remained there for the next four years.[14] When Bishop Zubiría visited for the last time, he wrote "a history of said schism and concluded the books were stained by the sacrilegious hand of Father Valencia."[15] During the period that Valencia had been ousted, an apostate Franciscan priest, Benigno Cárdenas, arrived in the Belén-Tomé area. He had been defrocked by the church authorities in Mexico City. In just a few months time, Cárdenas managed to charm the people of Belén, took over their entire parish, and began to preach. Cárdenas was finally ousted after a year and left the area, but he returned the next year from Europe as an ordained Methodist minister.[16]

While in Belén, Zubiría granted permission to Don Juan Cristóbal Chaves of Sausal for the construction of an oratorio or chapel the northern most plaza of Belén. Permission was granted because of the distance between Sausal and the church of Nuestra Señora de Belén, a distance of about three miles. The chapel was to be dedicated to *Nuestra Señora de Refugio,* Our Lady of Refuge.[17]

With the Anglo-American takeover of New Mexico in 1846 came not only political change but also a religious jurisdictional change. Until the Anglo-American takeover, New Mexico had been under the ecclesiastical jurisdiction of the Mexican Synod and the Bishop of Durango. In 1850, jurisdiction was transferred to the Council of Baltimore in the United States. Pope Pius IX appointed a young French priest, Father Jean Baptiste Lamy, to be the bishop of the newly formed Vicariate-Apostolic of New Mexico.

Bishop Lamy, realizing the lack of priests in New Mexico, brought many young French priests. This had long ranging effects on Belén. The first priest to be assigned to Belén in 1853, though only as a temporary pastorate, was Bishop Lamy's good friend and the future bishop of Colorado, Father Joseph Machebeuf.

Meanwhile, many problems occurred with the church structure as a result of deterioration and flooding. The church was situated on low ground in the rich, fertile floodplain of the Río Grande. Flooding of the Belén plaza was a frequent problem. Flood control measures had been adopted in an attempt to save the church, including the reinforcement of walls by placing flat rocks against them. The parishioners had also made an effort to raise the ground level surrounding the church.

Don José Dolores Córdova recollected an episode of 1855 which his mother related to him:

> When she was a young girl, she was taken to the church for confirmation. Bishop Lamy was the officiating priest. While the ceremonies were being held, the entire ceiling plaster fell. All the worshipers fled the building.[18]

According to Hays, Bishop Lamy was visiting on May 17, 1855, when the two exterior towers collapsed. As the tower began to fall, the plaster on the ceiling also began to fall.[19] By June of 1855, the spring runoff had destroyed the church. The only thing saved was a wooden altar depicting Calvary.[20]

The destruction of the church led to a fierce disagreement as to the future location of the new church. With the construction of the Chamizal Ditch in 1827, irrigation was possible further west than when Belén was initially settled. By 1846, American occupation, many people had begun moving into these new, fertile farmlands. One of the new villages was named Bacaville. Patricio Baca and his son, Josè Maria Baca, were both leaders in moving the church west. Rafael Córdova of Jarales led the opposition.[21] Those favoring the move were, for some unknown reason, called "karanklanes," a cheap grade of calico from which women of that time made their blouses.[22]

When Father Eugenio Paulet, a young French priest, arrived in Belén in December of 1856, he began saying Mass in the home of Vicente Baca—another Karanklan. This angered the people of the Belén plaza who wanted the church rebuilt on the original spot. In retaliation, they took the santos, vestments, and holy vessels. Bishop Lamy finally stepped in and decreed that "the church would be in New Town, as his Vicar General, Father Machebeuf, had selected a much better place to locate the new church."[23] The Bishop threatened to excommunicate anyone who said Mass in the old church, anyone who persisted in the intention to rebuild the new church, and anyone who refused to return the stolen religious articles.[24] Father Paulet was given permission by Bishop Lamy to absolve all from excommunication if they would retract before witnesses. Those who did not would be refused the sacraments.

The new rectory was built first, beginning in May 1857. Work on the church started in September 1858 when the Bacas, Castillos, and Chaveses of New Town sent their hired men and many other parishioners lent a helping hand. Since the building materials were quite valuable, Father Paulet bought two Colt revolvers in May of 1860 from Don Rafael Armijo to use in guarding the supplies.[25]

The new church was blessed on November 19, 1860, by Bishop Lamy. The *mayordomos* – caretakers of the church – were Don Juan Cruz Baca, Don Juan Cristóbal Chávez, and Don Francisco Chávez of Jarales.[26] As such, they were assigned pews in the front of the church and were allowed to keep those pews for the next five years. Both Baca and Chávez, since they were from Belén, were to be allowed to be buried in the church upon their death.[27] The new bell was donated by Don Antonio Chávez and his wife, the *padrinos* – symbolic godparents, for the Christ Child at Christmas. The bell had been brought over the Santa Fe Trail from Cincinnati, Ohio, and was blessed on August 15, 1861, the feast day of *Nuestra Señora de Belén*.[28] Stations of the Cross were erected in 1863, and the following year a chapel was built on the north side of the church. The chapel, dedicated to St. Francis Xavier, was for members of the Society for the Propagation of the Faith. The altar scene of Calvary, saved from the flood at the original church, became part of the altar in the chapel.

By 1875, problems began to develop with the two adobe towers and it was decided to replace them with one central tower. The first stone, hauled by the parishioners from a quarry in El Cerro near Los Lunas, was laid on June 22, 1876, and the new tower was completed eight months later. Francisco Folenfant, a French carpenter who had settled in Belén, directed the work. The tower reflected the strong French influence sweeping New Mexico churches.[29]

Nuestra Señora de Belén continued to be staffed by the French clergy introduced by Bishop Lamy. In 1885, Father Francisco Gatignol was assigned to the church. In 1888, he brought the Sisters of Mercy to teach in Belén. The first term lasted only three months, but the following year was a nine-month term. However, for reasons unknown, the nuns left that summer.

By the turn of the century, the church was remodeled. The church's altar was remodeled to reflect a French gothic style with plaster of Paris angels. The roof was pitched, the interior *vigas* – exposed beams – were covered over with banting, and more pews were installed.

Father Juan Anthony Picard, a very well-liked priest, served from 1901 to 1916. Not only was he an active pastor, he was a member of the Commercial Club, served on the first public school board, and was even the town marshal.[30]

With the Belén Cut-Off, John Becker's business necessitated the increased use of Becker Avenue, which linked his store to the railroad depot. With spring rains, Becker Avenue was often impossible to use. Becker approached Father Picard to sell the adobes from the ruins of the old Catholic Church in the area commonly referred to as *Plaza Vieja,* or the Old Plaza. Becker, after buying the adobes, used them to raise the street level of Becker Avenue.

In 1917, Father Antonio Cellier, the new pastor, recognized that due to the large influx of Catholics with the Belén Cut-off, the community had outgrown the church. Pillars were put in the original walls' place with the existing roof intact. Then new exterior walls were built about twenty feet out from the original walls on either side. The original roof was pitched, and the roofs of the additions were flat. The original tower of 1876 remained intact. The floor was cement. All the church furnishings were new. Bishop Pitaval blessed the church on October 19, 1919. The church had the largest seating capacity of any church in the state – 1,128.[31]

Work began on a parochial school and a sisters' convent in 1926. St. Mary's School opened in September of 1927 under the Ursuline Nuns of the Roman Union. The Ursuline Nuns remained in Belén until 1932 when they were replaced by the Dominican Nuns of Grand Rapids, Michigan.

Also in 1927, Archbishop A.T. Daeger petitioned Father Brosnahan, the Provincial of the American Province of Servites, for the Servites, a Religious Order, to take charge of the parish. *Nuestra Señora de Belén* had originally been under the auspices of the Franciscans; it was transferred to the auspices of the secular clergy in 1826, and in 1927 it was turned over to the Servites.[32]

Father Pietro Biondi, Apostolic Delegate, visited Belén in April of 1928 with the message to increase the native clergy. Accordingly, the Servites built a combination seminary and rectory adjacent to the church. Eventually, seven men from Our Lady of Belén, as it was beginning to be known, became either priests or brothers.[33]

The church continued to grow and improvements were added. The Knights of Columbus were established in 1928 and the Catholic Daughters began in 1944. Hardwood floors were installed to cover the cement floor in 1929, a loudspeaker was added in 1939 and a cooling system was added in 1942.[34]

Religion is an organized system of beliefs, ceremonies, practices and worship that centers for some on numerous deities and for others on a unique supreme God. For the Hispanic residents of New Mexico, Catholicism was the all-encompassing religion:

> The Spanish were immersed in a highly familial
> religion, in a peasant-type extended family appro-

priate to their economy of subsistence agriculture,
and in a view of time that de-emphasized the future
as something controllable less by man than by God
and the saints and validated the present through its
relation with events in the historical past or with
eternal entities.[35]

As part of the peasant culture, Hispanic Catholics had a intimate
relationship with the land that had been passed down from generation to generation: "The religion which came to be associated
… with the peasant is … practical and directed to very particular
social roles and the duties that one who occupies a social role
must perform faithfully if the social order is to retain its stability."[36] As in other Hispanic communities throughout New Mexico,
Belén's activities revolved around and were dictated by the Catholic Church. Baptism, First Communion, marriage, and death customs were patterned after Catholic customs throughout the state.
The customs were reinforced through religious dramas, the
Penitentes, who supervised most of the Holy Week ceremonies,
and the celebration of the Belén feast day, August 15.

Today in Belén the Catholic Church and its festivals and
saints' days continue to be an integral part of the *Hispano* family
and to be the center of their spiritual and cultural world.

Notes

1.   The land was granted to Captain Torres and twenty-seven other
      men and five women from Albuquerque though evidence sug-
      gests that some were from the *Río Arriba*. It appears that Torres
      was originally from the Abiquiú area and had been illegally sell-
      ing guns to the Indians of the area. In an effort to elude the law, he
      and his family moved to the Río Abajo. John and Christina Van
      Ness, *Spanish and Mexican Land Grants in New Mexico and Colorado
      Their Origins and Extent,* (Manhattan: Sunflower Press, 1980) 41.

2.   Gilberto Espinosa and Tibo J. Chávez, *El Río Abajo* (Pampa: Pampa
      Press, 1976), 17.

3.   *Plaza de Nuestra Señora de Dolores de los Genízaros* is in the area today
      called Los Trujillos. *Plaza de Nuestra Salvador de Pilar* location is un-
      known. *Plaza de Nuestra Padre de Jarales* known today simply as
      Jarales.

With time, additional villages developed. For the purposes of this work, the cultural area of Belèn in the present day will be used. The area defined as the cultural area comprises communities to which the people of Belèn are closely tied spiritually and physically. Belèn itself is included and the following villages: to the north on the west side, Old Town, Los Cháves, Sausal, and Los Lecos; to the north on the east side of the river, San Fernando, Tomè, Adelino, Los Enlames and La Constancia; to the south on the west side of the river, Bacaville, Los Garcias, Upper and Lower Pueblitos, Los Trujillos, Jarales, Bosque, Sabinal, Abeytas, and Bernardo; to the south on the east side are Rio Communities, Casa Colorada, Veguita (formerly San Juan), Las Nutrias, Contreras, and La Joya.

4. Ignacio Chávez, a resident of Belén, remembered from his boyhood the church in ruins about 1880. "The walls were made of black rocks at the base and the flat rocks on top, were from four to five feet thick and the two towers, flanking the front entrance, were from ten to fifteen feet thick. Fr. Andrew Hays, *150th Anniversary of the Founding of the Parish of Our Lady of Belén, 1793-1943* (N.p., 1943), 7.

5. Later, it was discovered that two of Belén's distinguished citizens were buried in the church towers at about this time. When the church was torn down in 1884, the skeletons were found. No one knows who they were, though this was a popular custom to bury important personages in the walls of the church at the time. It has been said that the closer the burial site was to the altar, the more important the individual. Author's interview with Catherine D. Espinosa, Belén, May, 1985.

6. *Seminarío de Nuestra Señora de Guadalupe* (Albuquerque: Ward Press, n.d.), 16.

7. *Seminarío de Nuestra Señora de Guadalupe,* 17. The see was vacant at the time, so Rascon was the representative of the cathedral chapter.

8. *Seminarío de Nuestra Senora de Guadalupe,* 17.

9. *Taylor Varíos, June 27, 1837,* Mary Taylor Collection, Las Cruces.

10. *Taylor Varíos, Oct. 18, 1837,* Mary Taylor Collection, Las Cruces.

11. *Taylor Varíos, Oct. 18, 1837,* Mary Taylor Collection, Las Cruces.

12. Florence Ellis and Edwin Baca, "The Apuntes of Father J.B. Ralliere" in *New Mexico Historical Review* 32 (1957), 37.

13. *Bishop's Visita, 1850,* Mary Taylor Collection, Las Cruces.

14. *Taylor Varíos, August 14, 1850,* Mary Taylor Collection, Las Cruces.

15. *Taylor Varíos, March 1, 1848,* Mary Taylor Collection, Las Cruces.

16.   Cárdenas left New Mexico in early 1850 but returned as an ordained Methodist minister in 1853. He helped to organize the Methodist community in Peralta. According to folklore, Cárdenas was gravely ill in 1856 when a pig dragged him out of his bed. He became convinced that this was a sign from God and quickly renounced his Protestantism and begged Bishop Lamy for acceptance back into the priesthood. Lamy finally relented and sent Cardenas to Havana, Cuba, where he died in 1860. See Ellis, "The Apuntes of Father J.B. Rallière," 272-273; John Taylor, *Our Lady of Guadalupe Parish History Project* (n.p., 1990), 16.

17.   On September 13, 1877, Don Juan Cristobal Chávez was granted permission to move the chapel to La Ladera since he had moved his home and store there. Again, in 1905, the chapel was moved to the Castillo settlement. Mass was open only to the family of Felipe Castillo, whose wife was an adopted daughter of Juan Cristobal Chávez. The only exception was on July 4th when there was a large fiesta open to the public. Alejandro Castillo, interview with author, Belèn, June, 1985.

18.   Espinosa, *El Río Abajo*, 189.

19.   Hays, *Seminario de Nuestra Señora de Guadalupe*, 15.

20.   *Seminario de Nuestra Señora de Guadalupe*, 15.

21.   Espinosa and Chávez, *El Río Abajo*, 190. Josè Maria Baca was a descendent of this particular Baca family. Rafael Cordóva was the grandfather of José Dolores Cordóva who built the Jarales flour mill and is the grandfather of the Cordóva family of Jarales today.

22.   The term "karanklanes" is still commonly heard in Belèn when referring to the people of the west side of Belèn.

23.   *Seminarío de Nuestra de Guadalupe*, 19.

24.   After the bishop approved the move, several parishioners, led by Juan Domingo Valencia, sought to halt the building by filing an "action in chancery" against Bishop Lamy. Kirby Benedict, one of the first judges of the Superior Court (today called the Supreme Court) named by General Kearny, heard the case. Benedict rendered his decision in favor of the Karanklanes. Some of the people were so bitter they moved to Corrales, N.M. Espinosa and Chávez, *El Rio Abajo*, 189.

25.   *Seminarío de Nuestra de Guadalupe*, 19.

26.   Being selected as a *mayordomo* for the church is considered a great honor within the Belèn community. The *mayordomos* were, and still are, responsible for keeping the church clean and in good repair and for taking care of the *santos* – statues of saints – in the church. They were responsible for providing wood to keep the

church warm in the winter, opening the church, and preparing the articles needed by the priest to say mass. *Mayordomos* served for one year.

Today, the *mayordomos* are generally a husband and wife, and it is not unusual to have two husband and wife teams. In the last few years, the individuals in charge of the *fiesta* in August have generally become the *mayordomos*.

27.   Hays, *150th Anniversary of the Founding of Our Lay of Belèn, 1793-1943*, 17.

28.   In 1935, the bell was found to have developed a deep crack but was repaired by an Albuquerque firm.

29.   Hays, *The 150th Anniversary of the Founding of Our Lady of Belèn, 1793-1943*, 17.
      One of the reasons cited by the Church's engineers for demolishing the church in the early 1960s was that the tower was separating from the building. Since the tower had been built at a different time than the building, it was only natural that they would be separating. The building was not deteriorating.

30.   He was reported to be quite large and over six feet tall. If two men began brawling, he simply put each of the combatant's heads under each of his own arms and knocked their heads together. Author's interview with Gertrude L. Delgado, August, 1983, Belèn.

31.   Hays, *150th Anniversary of the Founding of Our Lay of Belèn, 1793-1943*, 21; *Seminario de Nuestra Señora de Guadalupe*, 19.

32.   *Nuestra Señora de Belèn* would again return to secular jurisdiction in 1973.

33.   The most notable of these individuals was Fr. John Castillo. He was born Andrés Castillo on Jan 1, 1913, the son of Mauricio Castillo and Francisquita Chávez y Peña de Castillo. He attended St. Mary's School through the eighth grade and completed his education at Belèn High School. In 1931, he made his novitiate in Granville, Wisconsin, and finished his seminary in Hillside, Illinois. He was ordained at the Chapel of Quigley Seminary in Chicago. He served the order in Detroit, Chicago, Commerce City in Colorado, and Belèn. He was instrumental in the destruction of the old church and the building of the present church in Belèn. *Río Abajo Heritage*, 76.

34.   It is important to note that Protestant groups entered Belén as early as 1888 with the incorporation of the Evangelical Lutheran Church of Zion by the German merchants and their families in the area. With the completion of the Belén Cut-off, additional Protestants came to the Belén area, resulting in the Methodists

opening a church in 1905, and the Episcopalians and the First
Christian Church opening churches in 1908. By 1922, all the Protestant churches were having difficulty not only with finances but
with a waning membership. The solution, a practice that was oc-
curring all over the United States, was to combine the churches
to form the Federated Church. Nine different denominations were
originally represented with the Federated Church eventually having nineteen different denominations participating.

With all the different church memberships available, the author
has not found a single Hispanic in the Belèn community who
converted to Protestantism before World War II.

35.   Thomas J. Steele, *Santos and Saints: The Religious Folk Art of Hispanic
New Mexico* (Santa Fe: Ancient City Press, 1982), 6.

36.   Steele, *Santos and Saints,* 74.

In the Shadow of the Miter: New Mexico's Quest for Diocesan Status

Marc Simmons

On December 22, 1602, Don Juan de Oñate, founding father and first governor of the Kingdom of New Mexico, wrote a letter to King Phillip III containing an earnest request. Mentioning the services that he had rendered to the crown, Oñate asked as a reward, should he merit one, "the sending to these provinces by your majesty of a chief prelate-bishop who would organize and set them in order. The land could easily support him ... and your majesty would be well served."[1]

The creation of a diocese on the upper Rio Grande Governor Oñate would have found personally rewarding for two reasons. First, as he well knew, it could prove a huge boost to the recently launched program of converting the Pueblo Indians, a matter in which he had a sincere and pious interest. To date, however, his relations with the Franciscan missionaries had been marred by petty jurisdictional conflicts and by complaints from some of the fathers concerning his policies, especially toward the Indians. Indeed, the previous year six disaffected Franciscans joined a large body of settlers who deserted New Mexico and fled south. The governor obviously hoped that a bishop, vested with full canonical powers, might "set things in order," as he phrased it in his letter to the king. A second reward in the obtaining of a diocese would have been immense prestige added to Oñate's kingdom, which at that moment was desperately struggling to survive and stood in need of any aid, material or spiritual, that it could find.

In reality, the Count of Monterrey, Viceroy of New Spain, had first raised the possibility of a diocese for New Mexico a year earlier. In a communication with the king, he stated that Governor Oñate had asked him to allow other religious orders, in addition to the Franciscans, to enter and work freely in his new kingdom. Probably Oñate thought that a bit of competition might help the Franciscans focus on their work of evangelization, leaving them less time for their squabbles with him.

The viceroy in his letter to Phillip III foresaw something other than competition. He wrote: "Even if Oñate's request [for other orders] should be granted, it would be necessary ... that his holiness create first a bishopric, abbey, or vicariate-general with jurisdiction over them so as to prevent quarrels among the various groups."[2] Oñate, when he addressed the king on this subject, tactfully recommended his personal religious adviser, Fray Francisco de Velasco, for the office of New Mexico's first bishop. "He possesses all the qualifications," said the governor.[3] Velasco was chief among a small pro-Oñate faction of New Mexico's Franciscan missionaries. He also happened to be the governor's cousin.

Neither of Juan de Oñate's appeals, for a bishopric and for an open-door policy in regard to religious orders, met with royal approval. Whether they were simply ignored or were pointedly rejected in writing has not been determined. To the end of the colonial period, the Franciscans were the only religious order in the New Mexican missionary field. And as is well known, in spite of repeated attempts that followed in the wake of Oñate's initial recommendation, New Mexico never managed to achieve its long-sought goal of diocesan status while under the Spanish regime, or for that matter while subject for a quarter of a century to the Republic of Mexico.

This essay will outline in summary form the main landmarks in New Mexico's prolonged quest to become a bishopric, noting in particular the arguments of supporters and opponents and giving my assessment of why the effort continually failed.

The direction and shape of events in this story are guided by several important historical realities. One has to do with the *patronato real* (royal patronage) defined in a series of papal bulls, or decrees, which granted to the monarchs of Spain extensive privileges and obligations that allowed them control over the temporal or administrative affairs of the Spanish Church, but not over matters of doctrine. The result was a close-linking between the

Church and State, so that the two became inextricably related. In the view of Catholic historian Carlos Eduardo Castañeda, "It is impossible to separate one from the other without presenting an imperfect and incomplete picture of history."[4]

Under the ecclesiastical *patronato*, the Spanish crown nominated archbishops and bishops, the candidates' names being sent to Rome for pro forma approval by the Pope. Lesser church offices were filled by the viceroys and provincial governors, acting as vice-patrons in the name of the king. Patronage also permitted the crown, or more specifically the royal treasury, to collect church tithes. The funds so gathered were turned back to pious purposes, such as paying the expenses of missionaries and providing for the construction of new cathedrals and churches. Further, members of the clergy had to get licenses from the king before they could come to the New World.[5]

These and other privileges associated with the *patronato* were zealously guarded by the Spanish crown, none more so than the right to erect new dioceses and parishes and set their territorial boundaries, with approval of the Supreme Pontiff. Therefore, it can be seen why Governor Oñate submitted his petition to the king rather than to the Church hierarchy when he began seeking a diocese for his New Mexico.

Another significant historical fact that colors our story has to do with the status of the Franciscan Order in New Mexico, which owing to its extreme isolation managed to govern its own affairs with considerable independence, particularly in the seventeenth century before the Pueblo Revolt. The Order was organized into provinces, each managed by a father provincial and a committee of definitors. Some provinces in turn supported subsidiary appendages called custodies (Lat. *custodiae*) New Spain's important Province of the Holy Gospel, headquartered at its Convento Grande de San Francisco in Mexico City, had two such custodies. One was the custody of San Salvador de Tampico on the Mexican Gulf coast, and the second was the custody of the Conversion of San Pablo in New Mexico.[6]

The founding of New Mexico's Franciscan custody occurred in 1616. The first man to serve as custodian (Lat. *custos*) or head of the missionary unit was Fray Estévan de Perea, and not the better known Fray Alonso de Benavides as is sometimes claimed.[7] During the 1600s, the residence of the custodian came to be the mission at Santo Domingo Pueblo, which became known, consequently, as New Mexico's ecclesiastical capital. But in the next century, the custodian moved around, as did a vice-custodian. In 1782 Fray Juan Agustín de Morfi mentions that, as of that date, one or the other of the custodians was always stationed at the mission of Nuestra Señora de Guadalupe in El Paso.[8]

Beginning in the sixteenth century, a series of papal bulls had conceded to prelates of the missionary Orders extraordinary powers, especially when they worked in remote frontier zones far from a bishop. The custodian of New Mexico, for instance, initially collected tithes, assigned friars to mission stations as he saw fit, excommunicated parishioners, and served as judge ordinary for the ecclesiastical court. In effect, he enjoyed quasi-episcopal authority over his chapter.[9]

Not surprisingly, the custodian and the missionaries tended to expand their authority beyond the original limits imposed by papal bulls and the *patronato real*. In 1642, to cite one case, the king complained to Rome that "the fathers of the Order of St. Francis who serve in New Mexico use the crosier and mitre and perform confirmations and ordinations."[10] In other words, they were acting too bishop-like in administering these sacraments, and the crown wanted it stopped. In fact, frontier missionaries had successfully appealed for the faculty to administer the rite of confirmation, but the matter remained in dispute, with the trend being toward reserving the privilege to prelates of episcopal rank.[11]

As of 1620 the Bishop of Guadalajara had ecclesiastical jurisdiction over all of northern New Spain, a diocese too vast for one prelate to handle. To relieve the situation, the king issued a royal *cédula* in 1621 creating a new diocese in northwestern New Spain and establishing a cathedral at Durango, capital of the province of Nueva Vizcaya. The same edict also directed the Audiencia of Guadalajara to define the boundaries of the newly formed Diocese of Durango, or Guadiana as it was sometimes called.[12]

The formal description of boundaries encompassed the modern Mexican states of Durango, Chihuahua, Sonora, and Sinaloa in their entirety, as well as parts of Coahuila and Zacatecas. Strangely, no specific mention was made of New Mexico, although a vague reference stated that the diocese should extend to the North Sea. The first Bishop of Durango, Fray Gonzalo de Hermosillo y Rodríguez, and all of his successors interpreted that to mean that New Mexico fell under their authority.[13]

The Franciscans of New Mexico's Custody of the Coversion of San Pablo, however, stoutly resisted the expansion of the bishop's control into their area, claiming that papal and royal concessions granted them a monopoly over the missionary program in New Mexico along with considerable autonomy. In fact, a jurisdictional struggle between the bishops of Durango and the Order continued intermittently for the next two centuries, with the missionaries gradually losing ground. The conflict forms a sub-theme in the story of New Mexico's efforts to win a bishopric of its own, but it will not be dealt with here because the subject has already been treated by other scholars in detail.[14]

The new Durangan diocese, as it turned out, had the same problem as the older bishopric of Guadalajara: it was simply too large to be administered effectively. Back in 1570, Mexico's Archbishop Fray Alonso de Montúfar had observed that the dioceses of New Spain were so vast in extent that their bishops were unable to visit all parishes and missions, with the result that administration of the sacraments suffered.[15] It was precisely New Mexico's isolation and its great distance from the cathedral of Durango that generated periodic petitions in support of another diocese on the upper Rio Grande.

One of the earliest and most vigorous proponents of that idea was the celebrated Alonso de Benavides, who served as Franciscan custodian in New Mexico from 1626 until his departure in late 1629. By 1630 he was in Madrid, giving a first-hand report of his missionary experiences to the King and the Council of the Indies and also recommending the creation of a diocese in New Mexico. A formal memorial to that effect was submitted to Don Juan de Solórzano, legal adviser for the Council, who gave the opinion that "the bishopric should be established and that the man appointed by your Majesty ought to be a friar of the order of St. Francis."[16] In reality, Father Benavides had been quietly lobbying government officials in hopes of obtaining for himself the nomination of bishop for the proposed episcopal see of New Mexico. Instead, in 1636 he was appointed auxiliary bishop of Goa in Portuguese India, and he never saw New Mexico again.

Fray Francisco de Sosa, secretary general of the Franciscan Order in Spain, in 1631 had quickly endorsed Solorzano's recommendation for a new bishopric on the Rio Grande with a friar as its ordinary.[17] But even with these supporting statements, the crown was not fully convinced, and it ordered officials in New Spain to conduct an inquiry into the advisability of setting up a separate diocese for New Mexico. Owing to the inevitable bureaucratic delays, this particular inquiry dragged on for almost a decade.

As late as 1638-1639 the viceroy was still collecting information from missionaries who had served in New Mexico and corresponding with the bishop of Durango on the matter. But finally in the latter year, a viceregal letter went to His Majesty, affirming that New Mexico deserved diocesan status and proposing two qualified Franciscans as nominees for bishop.[18]

In May of 1641 the Council of the Indies began a formal review of the sizeable body of documentation that had accumulated concerning this question. In the end, it presented an adverse report to the king, showing that New Mexico's resources were inadequate to sustain the minimal costs of an episcopal organization. That should have settled the matter, perhaps, but in fact the issue kept periodically bubbling to the surface throughout the remainder of the colonial period.[19]

In 1656, for instance, a royal order went to the Archbishop of Mexico instructing him to study the New Mexico situation and render an opinion as to whether it would be feasible or not to erect a cathedral, inasmuch as the Holy Catholic faith had been flourishing there for more than thirty years.[20] The Franciscans again made the case in 1666, asking that their custody on the Rio Grande be transformed into a diocese.[21] Once more, nothing was done.

Several times during the eighteenth century, the idea of a New Mexican bishopric reappeared. Juan de Oliván Rebolledo, legal adviser to the viceroyalty, in 1724 suggested placing an auxiliary bishop in New Mexico with a salary of 6,000 pesos to be paid by one of the more affluent dioceses of New Spain.[22] Prominent missionary Fray Juan Miguel Menchero apparently authored the 1748 document "Instrucciones para la erección de obispado en Nuevo México."[23] And in 1789 another report was circulated concerning the founding of a bishopric and seminary at New Mexico's capital, the Villa of Santa Fe.[24]

All of these assorted efforts to gain diocesan status for New Mexico were grounded in the following three assumptions: that a local bishop could improve the efficiency and effectiveness of evangelization among the Indians, that he could exercise tighter administrative and economic control over the temporal functions of the missionary program, and that his presence would end juris-dictional disputes between the bishops of Durango and the Franciscans, which for so long had plagued the Church in New Mexico.

As persuasive as these considerations may have been, they were insufficient to override a single, weighty reality: that is, New Mexico's economic impoverishment would preclude a diocese being able to raise enough funds, through tithes and other sources, to maintain properly a bishop and cathedral chapter. Such an ecclesiastical development would require an outside subsidy.

Another negative factor serving as an impediment was a provision in Spanish law providing that a new cathedral could only be established in a *ciudad*, a royal city with a charter and a coat of arms. Santa Fe, holding the lesser rank of a *villa*, fell far short, in terms of population and municipal resources, of the re-quirements needed to qualify for elevation to *ciudad* status.[25] In the end the bleak economic picture in New Mexico furnished the key reason causing rejection of a diocese for the province.

Notwithstanding, there were diocese advocates who disputed that New Mexico was too poor. Best known of these was Pedro Baptista Pino, who in 1811 went to Spain to represent his native province in the Spanish *cortes* (or parliament), then convening at the southern city of Cádiz. As part of his official duties, Pino pre-pared and had published an extensive report, *The Exposition on the Province New Mexico*, which contained petitions for aid and reforms addressed to the king and delegates of the *cortes*.[26] Pino complained that during the past half century no prelate of Durango had con-ducted a formal ecclesiastical visit in New Mexico, so that most of his fellow citizens had no idea how a bishop looked or dressed. Thus, he pointedly asked the king for "the establishment of a bishopric in Santa Fe and the founding of a seminary college."[27]

Pino claimed that foundation of the seminary had been authorized back in 1777 by His Holiness Pope Innocent XI, and land
set aside and buildings put up in Santa Fe. But the school never
opened, he said, because of the failure to organize a diocese.[28]

Don Pedro alleged that the tithes of New Mexico annually
produced a revenue of nine to ten thousand pesos. Therefore, the
new bishop could be given five thousand pesos (the amount the
bishop of Sonora received) and the remainder of the tithes could
be applied to the seminary and other expenses. Using this formula, he noted, the diocese would not have to be subsidized by
the royal treasury.[29]

Other observers over the years had consistently given a much
lower figure for the tithes, so the estimate submitted by Pino was
probably exaggerated, in hopes that it would help New Mexico
gain at last its coveted diocese.[30] In his petition, don Pedro asked
the king to nominate a Franciscan as New Mexico's first bishop,
saying that the inhabitants were so accustomed to seeing that
order's habit that anyone else, in all likelihood, would not be
welcomed in the province. The brash nature of that suggestion,
addressed to His Majesty, reflects the independent spirit of frontier New Mexicans.[31]

In fact, the *cortes* on January 26, 1813, issued a decree authorizing the creation of a diocese and *colegio seminario* for Santa Fe in
the province of New Mexico. Later that year, the cathedral chapter of Durango formally notified New Mexico's governor of the
action of the *cortes*.[32]

However, elation over the news in Santa Fe turned out to be
premature. Back in 1808 the French forces of Napoleon had invaded Spain and deposed King Ferdinand VII. In the years following, the *cortes* in exile at Cádiz attempted to govern the unoc-
cupied portions of the mother country as well as the overseas
empire in the name of the legitimate monarch. Hence, the ruling
body, upon authorizing a diocese for New Mexico, took the same
step the king would have taken; it referred its action to Rome for
confirmation. His Holiness, Pius VII, however, declined to grant
approval, evidently because he was unwilling to recognize the
right of the *cortes* to exercise the *patronato real*.[33]

The following year, 1814, Napoleon was defeated and
Ferdinand VII returned to the throne. At once he began review-

ing the decrees of the *cortes* to determine which ones he should approve and which ought to be abrogated. On January 27, 1815, he issued a royal *cédula* requiring officials in New Spain to update him on the matter of the New Mexico diocese, recommended by Pino and authorized by the *cortes* in 1813.[34]

From all that can be learned, the king took no further action. An 1816 document originating in Santa Fe mentions that New Mexico was still in need of a bishop.[35] And when independence was won five years later, in 1821, the province had not yet gained diocesan status. The struggle, lasting two and a quarter centuries under the Spanish regime, had failed.

When Mexico launched itself on the sea of independent nationhood, it proclaimed that the laws passed by the Spanish *cortes* and a liberal constitution it had promulgated in 1812 should remain in effect until the new country could adopt its own constitution.[36] That will explain the action of the Mexican congress when in 1823 it announced that in conformity with the 1813 decree of the Spanish *cortes*, it was authorizing the erection of a bishopric in New Mexico. But that action was never implemented, in part no doubt because of the long-lasting problems with Rome over the transfer of the old rights and privileges of the *patronato real* to the successor government in Mexico.[37]

Four years after New Mexico was seized by the United States, Pope Pius IX in a decree of July 19, 1850, designated the territory a Vicariate Apostolic, which the late Fray Angélico Chávez defined as a provisional bishopric.[38] The Most Reverend Jean Baptiste Lamy, then a missionary in Kentucky within the Diocese of Cincinnati, was appointed Vicar Apostolic. Exactly three years later, the Vicariate of New Mexico was elevated to the rank of an episcopal see, and in 1875 it became an archdiocese.[39] With the latter development, the Church closed a chapter in its history that had begun early in the colonial period.

Notes

The author wishes to thank Dr. Félix D. Almaráz, Jr. and Thomas J. Steele, S.J. for reading early drafts of this paper.

1. George P. Hammond and Agapito Rey, eds. and trans., *Don Juan de Oñate, Colonizer of New Mexico, 1598-1628* (2 vols., Albuquerque: University of New Mexico Press, 1953), 2: 986.

2. *Ibid.,* 2: 670. The "vicariate-general" would probably have been what was later called a vicariate-apostolic – a provisional diocese.

3. *Ibid.,* 2: 986.

4. Carlos E. Castañeda, *Our Catholic Heritage in Texas,* 1519-1936 (7 vols.; Austin: Von Boeckman-Jones Co., 1936-1958), 7: Preface (unpaginated). Standard works on the subject include W. Eugene Shiels, S. J., *King and Church, The Rise and Fall of the Patronato* (Chicago: Loyola University Press, 1961) and Jesús García Gutiérrez, *Apuntes Para la Historia del Origin y Desenvolvimiento del Regio Patronato Indiano, Hasta 1857* (Mexico: Editorial Jus, 1941).

5. Lillian Estelle Fisher, *Viceregal Administration in the Spanish-American Colonies* (Berkeley: University of California Press, 1926), 183-89. In making nominations to the Pope, the Spanish king customarily submitted a list of three candidates with the expectation that the first name would be approved.

6. Benito López-Velarde López, *Expansión Geográfica Franciscana* (Mexico: Universidad Pontífica Urbana de Propaganda Fide, 1964), 22-23, 39.

7. France V. Scholes, "Problems in the Early Ecclesiastical History of New Mexico," *New Mexico Historical Review,* 7 (January, 1932): 61. Benavides was elected custodian in 1623.

8. "Geographical Description of New Mexico, 1782," translated by Alfred B. Thomas, *Forgotten Frontiers* (Norman: University of Oklanoma Press, 1932), 109. For reference to appointment of a vice-custodian at El Paso, see Letter of Gov. Fernando Chacón, Santa Fe, November 18, 1798, Spanish Archives of New Mexico [SANM], II, no. 1430a, New Mexico State Records Center and Archives [NMSRCA], Santa Fe.

9. Jim Norris, "The Struggle Over Diocesan Control in New Mexico, 1715-1737," *New Mexico Historical Review,* 70 (April, 1995): 111.

10. Royal Cédula, June 12, 1642, Archivo General de Indias. Indiferente General, leg. 2873, cited in Eleanor B. Adams, *Bishop Tamaron's Visitation of New Mexico, 1760* (Albuquerque: Historical Society of New Mexico, 1954), 7.

11. Charles W. Polzer, S. J., "Roman Catholicism: Spanish," in Jacob Ernest Cooke, ed., *Encyclopedia of the North American Colonies* (3 vols.;

New York: Charles Scribner's Sons, 1993), 3: 536; Robert Ricard, *The Spiritual Conquest of Mexico* (Berkeley: University of California Press, 1982), 109. A papal bull of 1522, known as the *Omnimoda*, granted friars certain powers equivalent to those of bishops. See Stafford Poole, "The Spanish Legacy in the United States," *Catholic Southwest*, 8 (1997): 160

12. Adams, *Bishop Tamarón's Visitation*, 1-2; León Lopetegui, S. J., and Félix Zubillaga, S. J., *Historia de la Iglesia en la América Española* (2 vols.; Madrid: Biblioteca de Autores Cristianos, 1965), 1: 662-64, and Guillermo Porras Munoz, *Iglesia y Estado en Nueva Vizcaya, 1562-1821* (Pamplona: Universidad de Navarra, 1966), 33-34.

13. José Bravo Ugarte, S. J., *Diócesis y Obispados de la Iglesia Mexicana* (Mexico: Editorial Jus, 1965), 47.

14. Norris, "The Struggle over Diocesan Control," 113-24. Also, Lino Gómez Canedo, *El Reformismo Misional en Nuevo México, 1760-1768* (Guadaiajara: Universidad de Guadalajara, 1981), *passim.*

15. Quoted in Ernesto de la Torre Villar, "Erección de Obispados en el Siglo XVIII," *Estudios de Historia Novohispana,* (1970): 180.

16. Frederick Webb Hodge, George P. Hammond, and Agapito Rey, eds., *Fray Alonso de Benavides' Revised Memorial of 1634* (Albuquerque: University of New Mexico Press, 1945), 11.

17. *Ibid.,* 150.

18. Letter of the Marquis of Cadereyta, Mexico, Feb. 28, 1639, translated in Charles Wilson Hackett, *Historical Documents Relating to New Mexico, Nueva Vizcaya, and Approaches Thereto, to 1773* (3 vols.; Washington: Carnegie Institution, 1923-1937), 3: 89.

19. *Ibid.,* 93; France V. Scholes, "Royal Treasury Records Relating to the Province of New Mexico, 1596-1683," *New Mexico Historical Review,* 50 (April, 1975): 164.

20. Royal order to the Archbishop of Mexico, Dec. 22, 1656, Archivo General de las Indias [AGI], Sevilla, leg. 234, folios 112-13.

21. Charles J. G. M. Piette, O.F.M., "Missions of Colonial New Mexico," *The Americas,* 4 (October, 1947): 251.

22. Charles Wilson Hackett, ed. and trans., *Pichardo's Treatise on the Limits of Louisiana and Texas* (3 vols.; Austin: University of Texas Press, 1941), 3: 231.

23. This document, from Mexico's Biblioteca Nacional, is cited by Piette, "Missions of Colonial New Mexico," 25. It has not been examined by the author.

24. AGI, Audiencia de Guadalajara, leg. 561.

25. Oakah L. Jones, Jr., *Nueva Vizcaya, Heartland of the Spanish Frontier* (Albuquerque: University of New Mexico Press, 1988), 83.

218 Seeds of Struggle/Harvest of Faith

Seeds

26. Adrian Bustamante and Marc Simmons, trans., *The Exposition on New Mexico, 1812* (Albuquerque: University of New Mexico Press, 1995).
27. *Ibid.,* 28-29.
28. *Ibid.,* 30-31. Each diocese in New Spain came to have its own seminary. See José Bravo Ugarte, S. J., "Datos Sobre la Fundación de los Seminarios de México y Sus Confiscaciones," *Memorias de la Academia Mexicana de la Historia,* 9 (1952): 140-41.
29. Pino, *Exposition,* 30.
30. For example, Father Juan Agustín de Morfi in 1778 placed the sum of tithes collected yearly in New Mexico at just under 4,000 pesos. Marc Simmons, *Coronado's Land* (Albuquerque: University of New Mexico Press, 1991), 141.
31. Pino, *Exposition,* 32.
32. José Miguel de Yrigoyen to Gov. José Manrrique, Dec. 7, 1813, Archivo General de la Nación, México, Reales Cédulas, vol. 208, exp. 29. Also, letter of Yrigoyen, SANM, Benjamin Read Coll., NMSRCA.
33. David J. Weber, *The Mexican Frontier, 1821-1846* (Albuquerque: University of New Mexico Press, 1982), 70.
34. A copy of the *cédula* can be seen in SANM, II, no. 2577. Ferdinand VII's predecessor, Charles IV, also showed an interest in New Mexico's diocesan status, requesting information on the matter in 1800. See SANM, II, nos. 1500a and 1517a (5).
35. Letter of Fray Isidro Barcenilla, San Juan Pueblo, 1816, Archives of the Archdiocese of Santa Fe, Loose Documents, Mission, no. 6.
36. Felipe Tena Ramírez, *Leyes Fundamentales de México, 1808-1973* (Mexico: Editorial Porrúa, 1973), 59. In 1820 a liberal revolt had forced Ferdinand VII to restore the constitution and decrees of the *cortes,* so they were the laws of the Empire when Mexico broke away.
37. José M. Ponce de León, *Reseñas Históricas del Estado de Chihuahua* (Chihuahua: Imprenta del Gobierro, 1913), 158-59.
38. *But Time and Chance* (Santa Fe: Sunstone Press, 1981), 94.
39. J. B. Salpointe, *Soldiers of the Cross* (Reprint ed.; Albuquerque: Calvin Horn, Publisher, 1967), 194, 206, 265.

How Many Are "A Few"?
Catholic Clergy in Central and
Northern New Mexico, 1780-1851

Robert E. Wright, O.M.I.

It has been my contention for several years that the standard portrayal of the Catholic Church in New Mexico and indeed throughout the northern Borderlands between 1780 and 1850 is a classic example of a prejudicial historical memory. It is prejudicial in that it presents far too negative a picture of the actual presence of the Catholic Church in New Mexico during the final seventy years when that Church was under Hispanic direction. The standard picture has thus served to help justify the political takeover of New Mexico by the United States, the ecclesiastical takeover by the United States Catholic Church, and the crusading arrival of Protestantism.[1]

Upon their arrival in New Mexico, all three of these groups – the United States, the Catholic Church in the United States, and the various representatives of Protestantism – were content to allow their historical prejudices against the Hispanic Catholic Church to be confirmed by weaknesses which they perceived or about which they were told in New Mexico.[2] No one – I emphasize *no one* – has undertaken a scholarly historical study of the Catholic Church in New Mexico during the period from 1780 to 1851. This has not been due to a willful desire to suppress the truth. Rather, I would venture, it is the result of a general complacency with the standard picture on the part of the dominant groups. The conventional picture has been repeated again and again with no dissent by all the important historical works on New Mexico for the past one hundred and fifty years. It has become so embedded in the literature that new works by very reputable scholars take it for granted as the general ecclesiastical background for their studies.[3]

In historical surveys, New Mexican church history usually disappears after the Domínguez visitation of 1776, only to re-emerge with the arrival of Bishop Lamy in 1851. The intervening period is dismissed with a few very generic statements about decline, neglect, and scandal. A general Church decline is said to have begun in the last decades of the 1700s if not sooner, followed by terrible neglect in the 1800s and near-total collapse by the 1840s. This scenario not only invites but begs the newcomers after 1846, whether Catholic or Protestant, to re-establish religion in New Mexico on a new institutional basis, since the previous efforts of the Hispanic Church are alleged to have resulted in such failure.

I hope this essay will gain a hearing and allies for a more balanced understanding of the Catholic Church in central and northern New Mexico[4] from 1780 to 1851. This is a multi-faceted question, involving the numbers of Catholic clergy and laity, their mission and parish institutions, their religious commitment and their conduct. Given the solidity of the established historical tradition and the limitations of an essay, I can only hope to address one aspect of this question. Since one of the fundamental cornerstones of the standard thesis of neglect and abandonment by the institutional Church is that of a great lack of clergy beginning in 1800 or even earlier, I will seek to shed some light on that one issue.

An immediate question which should strike anyone familiar with the literature on the Church in New Mexico in the nineteenth century is the following: how can Bishop Lamy upon his arrival in 1851 be portrayed as having to engage in a protracted struggle over the direction of the Church with a strongly entrenched Mexican clergy, if that clergy have previously been portrayed as non-existent or minimally present for decades?! The question begs an answer, but none is ever given.[5]

In response to that and similar questions, I will try to identify how many priests were ministering in central and northern New Mexico from 1780 to 1851.[6] At the same time, I will seek to clarify where they were ministering. Finally, I will offer some explanations on why certain changes in the number and location of clergy occurred at different important junctures of the period under investigation. This research is still in process, and certain data or conclusions may need to be modified. Nevertheless, I believe that there is very solid evidence for a quite different picture than the standard thesis of neglect and abandonment.

The Colonial Government's Clergy Planning, 1780-1812

From the outset, it is extremely important to realize that during the colonial period it was the viceregal government, and not the Church, which determined the number of priests who could be assigned to New Mexico and the places which were to have resident priests. For the greater part of the eighteenth century, the number of Franciscans who were to minister in central and northern New Mexico and receive governmental subsidies was set at twenty-four. Missionaries were allotted to eighteen *pueblos*, with Zuñi having an additional Franciscan due to its isolation and large population.

Tesuque and Pojoaque near Santa Fe were normally *visitas* of nearby missionary centers, and thus did not have resident Franciscans. The three *villas* of Santa Fe, Santa Cruz, and Albuquerque each had a subsidized pastor. A second subsidized Franciscan at Santa Fe and an additional one at Pecos were eventually reallocated to provide priests at the new *pueblo* of Sandía above Albuquerque and at the new *genízaro* settlement of Abiquiú on the northwestern frontier. From the 1740s until 1782 the number of Franciscan missionaries actually present in central and northern New Mexico usually remained fairly close to this set number of twenty-four.[7]

In an economizing measure by the viceregal government, the subsidies of the Franciscan pastors in the three major towns – Santa Fe, Santa Cruz, and Albuquerque – were withdrawn in 1768.[8] While this reduced the number of subsidized missionaries to twenty-one, the Franciscans were still expected to provide all twenty-four priests. In 1779 a military chaplaincy was established in Santa Fe, staffed by an additional Franciscan who was paid out of the military budget and not that of the missions.[9] Around this same time, Galisteo ceased to exist as a *pueblo* and Tesuque or Pojoaque took its place on the list of subsidized missions.[10]

During his governorship (1778-1787), Juan Bautista de Anza tried to improve the defenses of New Mexico, which was being besieged by raiding Apaches, Utes, and Comanches, by consolidating the settlements on all fronts, including the missions. But whereas the consolidation of Hispanic settlements attempted to relocate several communities into more physically compact centers, the "consolidation" of the missions merely reduced the number of missionaries, leaving one missionary caring for a much larger territory than before.[11] Anza and his immediate superior, the Commandant General of the Interior Provinces, were happy to report to the savings-conscious Bourbon regime that by thus combining the missions they were reducing expenses for the royal treasury. In spite of strong protests by the Franciscans, the government ordered major reductions in the number of staffed missionary centers and thus in the number of missionaries.

In the restructured mission alignment which was gradually implemented between 1781 and 1784, one friar ministered to Zia, Santa Ana, Jémez, and the Hispanics at Vallecillo. Another Franciscan cared for Santo Domingo, Cochití, San Felipe and the Hispanic settlements of La Cañada and Peña Blanca. Tesuque reverted to a *visita*. One priest cared for Santa Clara, San Ildefonso, and the Hispanic villages in their area. Ácoma and Laguna were entrusted to one Franciscan, while Zuñi remained with two missionaries. In this way seven missionary residences were abolished, resulting in seven fewer subsidies.[12] This reduced the clergy allowed for central and northern New Mexico from twenty-five to eighteen, including the presidial chaplain at Santa Fe.[13]

Unfortunately, this governmental "downsizing" of the clergy occurred at exactly the time when the Hispanic settlers were beginning to increase rapidly. Contrary to Anza's defensive plans, they were developing new settlements at greater distances from the old ecclesiastical centers. During the last decades of the 1700s and the first half of the 1800s, the Hispanic population of New Mexico far surpassed that of the Pueblo nations served by mission churches. With the significant increase in population, settlement began to spread in all four directions. Above Santa Fe, this meant moving into various mountain valleys and elevations of more difficult access.[14]

After Anza and the other frontier military leaders succeeded in making peace with the Utes and the Comanches and could thus concentrate on their campaigns against the Apaches, the expansion of settlements took on new life. But as a result of the mandated clergy reduction, the Franciscans had allowed their numbers to diminish through the regular attrition of deaths and returns to central Mexico or Spain. Suddenly, however, with the deaths of three friars in succession in early 1785, they were two men short of the expected number of eighteen priests.[15]

In the latter part of 1786 the Franciscan Provincial in Mexico City was ordered to send more friars to fill the vacancies in New Mexico.[16] But the Provincial complained that, while he was still held responsible for maintaining the proper number of missionaries, the friars there had been removed from his supervision. The administration of the New Mexican Custody had been temporarily taken away from the Santo Evangelio Province by the government and given to the Bishop of Sonora under a plan proposed by that latter prelate. The Franciscan provincial thus had much less knowledge of what was transpiring in New Mexico and consequently less ability to respond adequately to it. He also objected to the fact that the Commandant General in Chihuahua had taken it upon himself to transfer several missionaries from work in the New Mexico Custody to service as military chaplains elsewhere in the Interior Provinces.[17]

Certain past and future governors of New Mexico would also claim a right to transfer missionaries by virtue of the *patronato real*, a claim always contested by the Franciscan superiors as infringing upon the internal discipline of their religious institute. The Franciscans did not question the government's prerogative to decide how many friars could be assigned to each designated missionary post, but they insisted that it was their own decision as to which friar would be assigned to any specific post.[18]

While this debate was going on through a very time-consuming exchange of letters between Mexico City and Chihuahua, there was yet another missionary death in New Mexico and two friars returned to their home province.[19] By the end of 1788 there were only thirteen Franciscans in northern New Mexico, five fewer than specified in the consolidated mission plan.[20] The Provincial held firm in arguing that the four friars serving chaplaincies elsewhere in the Interior Provinces should be returned to New Mexico. But the Commandant General countered that there were no secular priests to fill the chaplaincies.[21] Finally in late 1789 the Viceroy overruled the Commandant General and decreed that the Franciscan chaplains be reassigned to the New Mexico missions.[22]

There were actually eight new Franciscans who finally arrived with the convoy in August 1790. Six were employed to fill the vacancies, which by then had increased by yet one more. The "extra" two friars were placed in San Ildefonso and Tesuque, where the governor judged there was an urgent need of resident ministers. Governor Concha, who had succeeded Anza, even asked that the governmental subsidy be increased to include stipends for these two posts.[23]

Furthermore, Concha also advocated re-establishing Cochití as a subsidized mission center. In July 1791 he proposed placing a resident priest in the developing Hispano-*genízaro* district of Belén, with a half-subsidy for its missionary, in response to the southward expansion of settlement along the Rio Grande. Governor Concha even argued that it would be better to have two missionaries at every post, but he realized that the royal treasury would never agree. In all, his proposal called for increasing the quota of priests in central and northern New Mexico from eighteen to twenty-two, with nineteen of them receiving subsidies including the presidial chaplain.[24]

While this latest clergy plan was still being reviewed by viceregal authorities, the number of Franciscans temporarily dipped back down to seventeen, one less than the current quota.[25] In January 1792 the Commandant General ordered the implementation of Concha's new plan, and the Viceroy promptly gave his approval. Both royal officials sought to present this decision as a savings to the royal treasury by the ruse of comparing the new quota of nineteen subsidized Franciscans with the pre-1768 quota of twenty-four.[26] In this new plan, there was a positive recognition of the needs of the growing population in both the old and new areas of settlement. Belén received a resident priest in 1793.[27] On the other hand, the urge to economize which pervaded the Bourbon regime meant that the clergy quota was still below what it had been in much less populous and expansive times.

In 1792 the first wave of a new royally-approved reinforcement of fifty Franciscans from Spain arrived in New Spain. They
were meant to bolster the ranks of the Santo Evangelio Province
in order to staff its missions and military chaplaincies. Six of the
first contingent were assigned to New Mexico.[28] Groups of friars
began the journey northward from Mexico City toward Chihuahua in late 1792. Experiencing long delays for convoys at certain
points, five of these friars had finally arrived in central and northern New Mexico by late 1794.[29] In the meantime, however, two
friars had been expelled by the governor as troublemakers.[30] Thus
even with the new arrivals there were only twenty priests, two
fewer than specified, leaving Pecos and Tesuque without resident
priests.[31]

In late 1795 there were still twenty priests. However, the
Franciscan *Custos* advocated expanding the number of clergy in
keeping with his recommendations for strengthening the defensive perimeter of New Mexico against the continued raids of the
Apaches. He encouraged supporting the new village of San
Miguel del Vado near Pecos. He also suggested that a new mission center or at least a settlement be established in the Mora
Valley. Since Truchas was too distant for the priest at Santa Cruz
to provide prompt pastoral care, he recommended that a second
priest be assigned to that area. Finally, he proposed that a military
post of *genízaros* be established at the old site of Socorro at the
southern edge of the central Rio Grande valley above the Jornada
del Muerto.[32] All these settlements would eventually develop.
But in early 1796 there were still only twenty friars, two fewer
than specified, caring for the same posts as before.[33]

In 1798 the Diocese of Durango finally fulfilled a long-cher-
ished desire to introduce diocesan pastors into New Mexico. Two
secular priests arrived bearing a letter from the new Bishop of
Durango stating that they were taking over the parishes of Santa
Fe and Santa Cruz. One of the new priests was also named Visitor of the Church in New Mexico. Immediately there surfaced
various points of tension between the new priests and the
Franciscans, who had steadfastly resisted the introduction of secular clergy. By October one of the secular priests left New Mexico,

but Father Ortega remained as pastor of Santa Fe and the Bishop's Visitor and Administrator.[34]

In 1802 two new diocesan priests joined Ortega in New Mexico, taking over the pastorates of Santa Cruz and Albuquerque, but by the end of 1803 all three secular priests had departed.[35] These priests had not found the *villa* pastorates anywhere near as financially sound as previous governors and bishops had claimed. Their repeated attempts to extend their jurisdiction at the expense of the Franciscan missions in order to improve their financial situation were disallowed by the bishop. Governor Chacón complained about the turmoil they occasioned and their alleged highhandedness with the people.[36] Once again the Franciscans were the sole clergy in central and northern New Mexico. Nevertheless, the three *villas* remained officially secular pastorates, with the Franciscans liable to be replaced by diocesan clergy as soon as any became available.[37]

Although the records are somewhat confusing, apparently there was no change in the approved missionary plan of 1792, which called for twenty-two priests.[38] During these years which witnessed the first attempt to introduce secular pastors, the number of priests went from twenty in late 1798 to twenty-four at the end of 1802.[39] In the latter year there were momentarily two more clergy than specified due to the arrival that year of the two new secular priests at the very same time that the Franciscans had bolstered their numbers to provide for all the mandated posts.[40] After the departure of all three diocesan pastors the following year, the Franciscans managed to provide twenty-one or twenty-two priests up through 1806.[41]

The disparity between the expanding population and the limited number of priests was becoming more and more evident. When the new governor, Joaquín del Real Alencaster, arrived in the spring of 1805, he immediately remarked upon the "notable lack" of clergy and lamented "how long it will take to replace those who are lacking, even though I will leave no stone unturned to bring this about." His effort to improve the plan for the provision of clergy included writing to the highest colonial and ecclesiastical authorities.[42] He was unsuccessful, since by the end of his governership in 1808 there were even fewer priests, eighteen Franciscans in all.[43]

The numbers began to increase again with the arrival of a new diocesan pastor in Santa Fe, who lasted from Fall 1809 to early 1813.[44] In 1811-1812 the number of clergy stood at twenty or twenty-one, a priest or two short of the specified twenty-two.[45] In the latter year of 1812 the people of San Miguel del Vado succeeded in having the priest's place of residence moved from the declining pueblo of Pecos to their new settlement on the eastern frontier of New Mexico.[46]

As one reviews this history of clergy presence in central and northern New Mexico from 1780 to 1812, it becomes clear that the governmental plans for supplying the settlements with priests had a major and indeed decisive impact. Whereas in 1780 there were twenty-five priests allotted by the government, by 1784 there were only eighteen. This rose to twenty-two in 1792, which was apparently the figure for the remaining years of the colonial period up through 1820. The number of clergy actually present throughout the 1780-1812 period (see Table 1) usually remained one or two below the designated number, with the exception of the late 1780s when the Franciscans were insisting that their members assigned elsewhere by the government be returned to New Mexico. At times the number of priests exceeded the quota. The frequent lack of one or two clergy was due to the time factor involved in replacing friars and eventually secular clergy who died, returned to the home province or the Durango diocese, or were expelled as troublemakers by the governor.

Unfortunately, the government-ordered reduction in the number of priests occurred at precisely the time when population trends required the opposite policy. As the Hispanic population began to increase significantly and expand in all directions, the Franciscans and the first diocesan priests found their work multiplying. The distances from their prescribed residences to the outlying settlements were becoming greater. The New Mexican delegate to the Cortes of Cádiz in 1812 stated the situation clearly:

> Las distancias que hai desde los pueblos donde
> residen los párrocos a las plazas de habitantes
> españoles, deben llamar la atención; pues siendo
> algunas de 8 y 10 leguas, ni pueden concurrir a oir
> misa en un mismo pueblo, ni puede el párroco decir

> dos misas en un dia con tan largo viaje; ni pueden
> poner vicarios, porque no alcanzan las rentas o
> sinodos señalados puramente para la administracion
> espiritual de aquellos pueblos; cuya dotacion fue
> hecha sin contar en aquel tiempo con aquellas 102
> plazas que la necesidad obligó a construir desde el
> año de 1780, para conservar el todo de la provincia.[47]

Given the restricted number of clergy, judicious decisions appear to have been made in their allocation. In the tough choices over which former mission residences would no longer be staffed, the ones which were left without a resident priest were *pueblos* such as Pojoaque and Santa Ana which were of relatively easier access from other missionary residences. Two mission centers of questionable value – that in Pecos where the population was dramatically decreasing and that in Zuñi where there was great isolation and little response to mission efforts – were deemphasized but not abandoned. This helped to make possible the establishment of the new Hispano-*genízaro* parish centers of Belén and San Miguel del Vado on the southern and eastern frontiers.

The one zone which was clearly understaffed was the northern mountain district. The priests residing in the arc of settlements extending from Abiquiú in the northwest through San Juan, Santa Cruz, Taos and Picurís to Pecos or San Miguel del Vado in the northeast had extensive territories. They were composed largely of very small *plazas* or settlements which were difficult of access, with the possible exception of those in the Taos district.

Nevertheless, considering the overall population pattern of New Mexico, it seems clearly unwarranted to claim that

> by the early nineteenth century the church in New
> Mexico had become for a majority of New Mexicans a church without clergy. That condition of neglect, more than any other, gave it its special character.[48]

To the contrary, it is demonstrable that the vast majority of both the Pueblo Indians and the Hispanics still had a resident priest within relatively easy access to them.

The year 1811, when there were twenty priests, is a representative example.[49] Of the reported population of 36,700 (26,950 Hispanics, 9750 "Indians") in central and northern New Mexico in 1811, the 5950 persons in the relatively compact environs of Santa Fe were served by two priests. The 950 people in Nambé, Pojoaque and Tesuque were pastored by a priest at Nambé and one of those from Santa Fe. The rapidly growing central Valley district of Sandía, Albuquerque, Ysleta, Tomé, and Belén had an impressive 8100 people served by four priests. The large populations which each of these priests had to serve in this central district were compensated by the accessible terrain.

The 1,950 people in the Taos Valley had a priest, as did a similar number in Santa Clara and San Ildefonso jointly served by one priest. The 800 mostly Hispanic settlers of the Pecos district had their pastor. The western central district of Cochití, Santo Domingo, San Felipe, Santa Ana, Zia, and Jémez with a population of 5150 had four priests located in all the most populated areas except Santo Domingo. Another priest served the Laguna district's 1350 inhabitants. Even Zuñi's 1600 Pueblo Indians had a resident Franciscan at this time.

While there was a priest in each of the populous northern districts of Abiquiú (2150), San Juan (2250), Santa Cruz (2500), and Picurís (1150), the extensive mountainous territory of these parishes made it more difficult to provide regular service to those persons living away from the parish centers. Along with Santo Domingo (1250) and Ácoma (800), which were both without resident priests in 1811, the outlying northern mountain villages were probably those most poorly attended. In years when there were more than twenty priests, the additional clergy were not assigned to the northern arc of settlements.

In the rest of central and northern New Mexico, however, as well as in the settlements of Abiquiú, San Juan, Santa Cruz, and Picurís themselves, there was not a remarkable absence of priests. At least in terms of clergy numbers and residences, it does not seem appropriate to characterize the period from 1790 to 1812 in New Mexico as one of neglect on the part of the Church. Rather, by spreading its government-allotted personnel ever thinner, the Church continued to provide priests for the vast majority of New Mexicans. On the other hand, the governmental reduction in the

number of clergy at the same time that the population was significantly expanding was indeed causing an increasingly notable disparity between the number of priests and the pastoral
needs of the people of New Mexico.

The Secular Takeover, 1813-1828

Although there was a continual and growing need for more
clergy, the real crunch did not arrive until the late 1820s. It was
the unforeseen result of a combination of circumstances: the continually proliferating Hispanic settlements, the sustained effort of
the Durango diocese to replace the Franciscans with secular clergy
in the more viable Hispanic parishes, the expulsion of Spanish
clergy from independent Mexico, and the clergy crisis which
developed in Mexico beginning in the late 1820s.

Not only were the old settlements of New Mexico steadily
growing, the Hispanic frontier continued to expand beyond the
established mission and parish centers. In 1815 the people founding Socorro on the southern frontier requested a priest. That same
year the Trampas community in the mountains above Picurís
offered to pay for the services of a Franciscan. Around 1818 the
people of Mora on the eastern edge of the Sangre de Cristo mountains asked for a pastor.[50]

The Durango diocese finally succeeded in establishing a permanent presence in central and northern New Mexico beginning in 1816. In that year a secular pastor returned to the Santa
Fe parish, which had been under Franciscan administration again
since 1813. Albuquerque and Santa Cruz received secular pastors in 1817-1818.[51] The ecclesiastical Visitor and Vicar who arrived from Durango to direct the Church in New Mexico during
those same years signaled the beginning of a decade of severe
and sustained criticism of the Franciscans by diocesan officials.[52]

At the conclusion of the Vicar's stay in 1818 there were
twenty-four priests – the three secular clergy and twenty-one
Franciscans – in central and northern New Mexico, not including the Vicar himself. This number temporarily exceeded the
quota, since the Franciscans, unaware that new secular priests
would be arriving, had just sent four new Spanish Franciscans to
provide for all the specified posts.[53] Two years later, in 1820, there
were two fewer Franciscans for a total of twenty-two priests.[54]

Whatever weight the clergy plan still carried, it probably disappeared after Mexican independence in 1821. Already in 1820 the struggling and financially-strapped colonial government decided to abolish or cut in half eight of the missionary subsidies in central and northern New Mexico. The viceroy pointed to the increased Hispanic population, but also admitted the urgent need to eliminate all but "absolutely indispensable" expenses.[55] In actual practice, after Mexican independence in 1821 the new national government ceased to pay any missionary subsidies in New Mexico due to its serious financial straits and its different priorities.[56]

Within New Mexico itself, any concern over clergy quotas and subsidies appears to have given way to the determination to bring about the consolidation and growth of diocesan control in what had been an entrenched Franciscan stronghold. At the end of 1821 there were twenty-four priests, only four of whom were secular clergy, in central and northern New Mexico.[57] In that year a new parish staffed by a secular priest had finally been inaugurated in Tomé.[58] For their part, the Franciscans had begun a new parish at Socorro.[59] In spite of continued significant population growth in the years ahead, these would be the last new parishes to be established for thirty years.[60] Unbeknownst to anyone at the time, the challenge for the Church in the next three decades would be survival, not expansion.

At the time, however, things appeared very promising from the diocesan point of view. No sooner had secular clergy returned to pastor the *villas* and the energetic Vicar from Durango made his presence felt than several young Hispanic men native to the area entered the seminary in Durango to study for the diocesan priesthood. Between 1823 and 1826 four had already returned as priests, joined by another born in Puebla.[61] Since the four parishes which had been secularized were already staffed, the diocesan clergy were naturally intent upon finding other openings for these new priests. Rather than begin any more new parishes or occupy one of the non-staffed Pueblo towns, the secular clergy had their eyes on the more established and solvent parishes among those administered by the Franciscans.

Upon the death of the long-term Franciscan military chaplain in Santa Fe in 1823, the diocesan clergy assumed that responsibility.[62] The parish of Socorro was secularized in 1824.[63] Still short on available posts and apparently not finding it desirable to remain as assistants in one of the already secularized parishes, the diocesan clergy persuaded the local Provincial Deputation to petition the Bishop to transfer five more of the principally Hispanic parishes – Abiquiú, Belén, San Juan, San Miguel del Vado, and Taos – to the secular clergy.[64] This was actually two more parishes than there were priests with whom to staff them!

For their part, the Franciscans realized that they were under siege, but they had no idea just how bad things would become.[65] The blows which they absorbed in the 1820s would reduce their presence to a mere shadow in a land where the Church had been practically synonymous with the Order. Between September 1823 and January 1825 they lost five friars, at least three of them through death.[66] During the same period they only received one new friar, while another returned to them after a brief assignment in the El Paso district.[67] Previously the Franciscans had always managed to recoup their personnel losses within two or three years. But in the new political era of Mexican independence, the Santo Evangelio Province to which they looked for new missionaries was itself entering very difficult times.[68]

Upon the arrival of another Vicar of the Durango diocese in April 1826, there were twenty-three priests in central and northern New Mexico. But by then there were only fourteen Franciscans in comparison to nine secular clergy.[69] By August 1826 the five desired parishes had been secularized, even though two – Abiquiú and El Vado – were left temporarily under the care of the Franciscans due to the insufficient number of diocesan priests.[70] The transfers stirred up some strong feelings.[71] The Vicar attempted to expel the two Franciscans who were stationed at San Juan and Picurís; but their absence, if any, was brief due to their support by civil officials.[72] The Franciscan pastor of Taos may have been temporarily removed from the territory (he was at Picurís by May 1827), and the friar at Belén apparently departed after the Vicar ignored the people's petition that the town not be secularized.[73]

Once the dust settled, it appears that only one Franciscan had been lost permanently. The death of the secular pastor of Santa Fe in December dropped the total clergy number to twenty at the end of 1826.[74] All of the principally Hispanic parishes continued to be staffed. But the decades spent under the clergy restrictions of the Anza and Concha mission plans had brought about a lasting pattern among the Pueblo towns, where in more than one area several *pueblos* and the Hispanic settlements in their vicinity were being pastored by one Franciscan. Tesuque, Nambé, and Pojoaque were all stations of San Ildefonso, Santa Ana and Zia of Jémez, Ácoma and Zuñi of Laguna, and San Felipe of Sandía.[75]

If the Franciscans harbored any hopes that they had successfully weathered yet one more storm, they were sadly mistaken. In 1827 the Mexican government enacted anti-Spanish legislation expelling from the country, among others, Spanish priests who did not qualify under certain exemptions. Manuel Armijo, the *jefe político* in Santa Fe at the time, was not inclined to give the Spanish Franciscans much leniency. One friar was removed immediately in mid-1827, and at least three others by early 1828. Only two Spaniards who were sixty years of age or older were allowed to remain.[76] For whatever reasons, probably not all unrelated to the expulsions, four other friars ceased to minister in the territory during these same months.[77]

Thus in less than a year the Franciscans had seen their numbers reduced drastically. Suddenly the numerical tables were dramatically reversed: there were only five Franciscans, at least two of whom were quite elderly, while there were eight secular clergy of whom half were New Mexicans and quite young. Seldom can the passage from one era to another in the life of a Church be so precisely dated. Now there were only thirteen priests in all of central and northern New Mexico,[78] whereas in early 1826 there had been twenty-three. The critical shortage of clergy in the territory did not occur in the 1790s, nor 1810s, nor even the early 1820s, as has so often been asserted. New Mexico's clergy crisis can be clearly dated to the two years 1827 and 1828.

The Resilient Local Church, 1829-1851

The Durango diocese and powerful political factions in New Mexico had finally succeeded in establishing the dominance of the secular and increasingly native-born clergy in that territory. It is one of those historical ironies, however, that this came about as a result of the replacement and even the expulsion of many Franciscans, just before people became aware that there was an alarming clergy shortage developing throughout Mexico. This shortage became especially acute in northern territories such as the diocese of Durango, which had never been well staffed.

The Franciscan leadership in Mexico City desired to help address the situation and sought to reassure the small handful of their friars left in New Mexico, hundreds of leagues from the rest of their members. The provincial authorities sent word in 1828 that they had decided to send six "American" friars to replace the Spaniards who had left the New Mexico Custody.[79] The reality was that no new priest had been sent since 1823, and the only one to join the little group of five thereafter would be a "demented" friar who came in 1831 and stayed less than a year.[80]

For their part, the secular priests fared no better until 1833. The new priest who took the place of Manuel Rada, who departed for the National Congress in fall 1828 and never returned, was himself gone by the middle of the next year.[81] There was thus one less secular priest until mid-1831, when a single new one arrived.[82] Meanwhile, the Hispanic population boom continued unabated, spurred on by the newly opened "Santa Fe trade" between Missouri and Chihuahua. Independent Mexico's policies also allowed foreign immigration, which added a new element to the priests' pastoral care.[83]

Perhaps in recognition of the very difficult challenges faced by the mostly recently ordained secular priests and the remnant of Franciscans, the Durango diocese sent a new Vicar to oversee Church affairs during the years 1829 to 1832.[84] Those were years which truly launched a new era for the Church in New Mexico. The whole clerical scene, one might say, had changed. Secular priests and Franciscans suddenly found themselves very much in need of coming to each other's aid, given the vast field and huge numbers they were charged to pastor.

There was a recognizable basic division of labor, however. The Franciscans were left with ever-growing groupings of *pueblos* which at one time had each had its own missionary. By exception, one of the elderly friars resided in Santa Cruz, since the diocese was unable to provide a pastor for it; from there he ministered to four *pueblos* and several Hispanic settlements all along the route to Santa Fe. A young Franciscan at Isleta visited the vast western area of Laguna, Ácoma, and (rarely) Zuñi. Another younger friar at Sandía pastored the central *pueblos* of Santa Ana and San Felipe and the Hispanic settlements in those districts. The fourth friar, even though approaching old age, ministered not only to the *pueblos* and villages immediately below the Bajada (the district of Santo Domingo and Cochití), but also the mountainous country of Zia and Jémez to the west. The elderly fifth Franciscan, while still remaining responsible for Santa Clara, was required by the diocesan Vicar to pastor the rugged and extensive northern district belonging to San Juan after the secular pastor there departed in mid-1829.

Thus the secular priests had taken charge of all the principal concentrations of Hispanic settlement except the north-central Santa Cruz-San Juan districts. The diocesan clergy administered the Hispanic Rio Grande towns from Socorro all the way up to Albuquerque, Santa Fe and its military chaplaincy, the mountainous northwestern Hispanic frontier beyond Abiquiú, and the rugged northeastern frontier from Taos down to El Vado. This northeastern region contained the only *pueblos* administered by the secular clergy at this time: Taos, Picurís, and the fast-disappearing Pecos. The Picurís district including Mora to the east was visited from Taos, then from Santa Fe, and finally it reverted to Taos in late 1833.

Between December 1829 and March 1833 Tomé and Albuquerque had to share a priest, as did Belén and Socorro between February 1829 and April 1831. El Vado was temporarily a *visita* of Santa Fe from August 1832 to November 1833. The two new secular priests who arrived in 1831 and 1833 were assigned to Belén and Albuquerque respectively. Thereafter all the major Hispanic towns had their own resident priest up through 1851, except for Tomé and Belén which had a shared pastor from 1838 to mid-1841.[85]

In an oft-cited text from 1832, the lawyer Antonio Barreiro claimed that in New Mexico "there is an absolute lack of ministers, since almost all the parishes and missions of the territory are vacant." He then dwelt upon the alleged pathetic consequences for the people.[86] But there were actually thirteen clergy still present, who among themselves assumed responsibility for all the *pueblos* and Hispanic settlements.[87] Certainly it was much harder for the priests to attend to all the people on a regular basis, especially those who were more difficult to reach from the priests' residences. But most appear to have applied themselves to the task.[88]

Barreiro's picture is too bleak and in fact greatly misrepresents the actual number of clergy. Apprised of the facts, one cannot help but think that the lawyer was exaggerating the gravity of the situation in hopes of stimulating the government to approve several of his proposed initiatives in favor of New Mexico. He advocated a bishopric and a college for the territory, as well as a clerical preferment program for those who volunteered to serve there.

In 1831 the Diocese of Durango received a new bishop, José Antonio Laureano de Zubiría. Zubiría did his best to provide direction for the New Mexico Church. He appointed Juan Felipe Ortiz, one of the native New Mexican priests, as his Vicar for the territory in 1832.[89] The following year the bishop made the first of his three pastoral visits to New Mexico.[90] He abolished the Santa Fe military chaplaincy.[91] He also authorized Father Martínez of Taos to begin a preparatory seminary to ready local youth for subsequent clerical studies in Durango. About a dozen young men from New Mexico who received their initial training locally – mostly in Taos – between 1833 and 1845 would return from very abbreviated further studies in Durango to serve their people as priests.[92]

It was this New Mexican clergy and their four compatriots ordained in the 1820s who would insure that their people continued to have priests for the next two decades. In 1833 the leader of the few remaining Franciscans acknowledged that there was only "the remotest chance that [more] friars will ever come."[93] He was proven right. Two Franciscans died in 1834 and the other three in 1840.[94] The bishop assigned a priest from elsewhere in the diocese to New Mexico in 1833, but by the end of 1838 that priest and two out of the other four secular clergy who were nonnative to the territory were gone. In 1843 another non-native secular priest arrived to join the two still serving there.[95]

Thus it was almost entirely due to the periodic arrival of native New Mexican clergy that the diocese of Durango was able to counter the loss of the Franciscans and non-native priests.

In this manner the total number of clergy in central and northern New Mexico between 1833 and 1844 remained fairly stable, averaging twelve to fourteen. With the death of the Franciscan at Santa Cruz in 1834, a secular priest assumed that pastorate and its attached *pueblos* and Hispanic villages along the road to Santa Fe.

On the other hand, the district of Sandía-San Felipe-Santa Ana left vacant by the death of a second Franciscan that same year was split between the parishes below and above it, mainly because the aging Franciscan who covered everything from Jémez to Santo Domingo balked when the Vicar directed him to add the entire district to his care. The friar ended up pastoring all but Sandía (including Bernalillo), which was attached to the secular pastorate of Albuquerque.[96]

The territory hit its all-time low in clergy from November 1838 to June 1839. Even though three of Father Martínez's alumni had already returned as priests by early 1837,[97] three secular priests originally from outside New Mexico ceased to minister there by the end of the following year.[98] Additionally, Vicar Ortiz, who had left for the National Congress in mid-1837, did not return until June 1839.[99] Thus for seven months there were only eleven priests. The additional vacancy was addressed by having one priest take care of both Tomé and Belén, an arrangement which actually continued until mid-1841.[100]

With the death of the remaining three Franciscans in 1840, the large central zone of six *pueblos* and the four others stretching from Isleta to Zuñi, plus the San Juan district, all became the responsibility of the secular clergy. They were able to shoulder that task thanks to another group of three Martínez alumni who began ministering that same year.[101] Thereafter the clergy numbers began steadily increasing (see Table 1).

Bishop Zubiría's second visit in 1845 marked the arrival of four more priests: two ordained New Mexicans, a secular priest possibly from outside New Mexico, and a single Franciscan. Another native New Mexican priest returned in 1846 after an absence of several years. This actually jumped the number of clergy up to nineteen by March 1846. The death of the lone Franciscan in 1848 made for one less priest up through 1850. One native New Mexican priest ceased to minister in the territory in the

Table 1
Priests in Central and Northern New Mexico, 1780-1851

Year	Clergy Plan				Actual Clergy			
	Total	OFM		Dioc.	Total	OFM		Dioc.
1776	24	24			22	22		
1784	18	18			19	19		
1785	18	18			16	16		
1788	18	18			15	15		
1789	18	18			12-13	12-13		
1790	18	18			20	20		
1791	18	18			17	17		
1792	22	22			17	17		
1794	22	22			20	20		
1795	22	22			20	20		
1796	22	22			20	20		
1798	22	20	+	2	20	19	+	1
1799	22	20	+	2	21	20	+	1
1800	22	20	+	2	19	18	+	1
1802	22	19	+	3	24	21	+	3
1804	22	19	+	3	22	22	+	0
1805	22	19	+	3	22	22	+	0
1806	22	19	+	3	21	21	+	0
1808	22	19	+	3	18	18	+	0
1810	22	19	+	3	19	18	+	1
1811	22	19	+	3	20	19	+	1
1812	22	19	+	3	20	19	+	1
1818	22	19	+	3	24	21	+	3
1820	22	19	+	3	22	19	+	3
1821				4	24	20	+	4
1826 May				6	23	14	+	9
1826 Dec.				11	20	12	+	8
1827				11	17	9	+	8
1828				11	13	5	+	8
1829					12	5	+	7
1832					13	5	+	8
1834					12	3	+	9
1837					13	3	+	10
1838					11	3	+	8
1839					12	3	+	9
1841					13			13
1843					14			14
1845					18	1	+	17
1846					19	1	+	18
1848					18			18
1851					17			17

spring of 1851, just a few months before the arrival of Bishop Lamy to take over the direction of the church in New Mexico.[102]

The surprising result, completely ignored by the conventional historiography of ecclesiastical desolation, was that the eight or so diocesan priests of the late 1820s and the 1830s had doubled to seventeen by the time of Bishop Lamy's arrival in 1851 (see Table 1).[103] There had even been at least one more priest during the six years just prior to the bishop's coming.[104] Even when one assesses *where* these clergy served when their numbers were lowest, only once, for a period of a year and a half, were there two major Hispanic population centers simultaneously without a resident priest.[105]

Clearly the Church experienced serious difficulties during the period from 1826 onward. Institutional resources, in particular the number of clergy as well as church finances, were seriously weakened. But the Hispanic Catholic Church in New Mexico, aided by their bishop, resolutely faced the crises rather than collapsing under them. They fostered their own native clergy, found ways to build and adorn their chapels, and welcomed into those chapels and into their families those foreigners who were so disposed.

Conclusion

While in some respects the period from 1780 to 1851 in central and northern New Mexico can indeed be viewed as a "period of decline" for the Catholic Church – particularly in terms of the number of clergy – it can also from other points of view be called a period of expansion. Certainly it should not be described as a period of neglect and abandonment by the Church. While the institutional Church was at first not allowed, and later unable, to keep pace with the settlement expansion in terms of placing a priest within relatively convenient access to every village, the Church did somehow manage to establish new parishes with resident priests in San Miguel del Vado to the east (1812), and Belén (1793), Tomé (1821), and Socorro (1821) to the south.

A determined effort to introduce diocesan clergy finally took hold when native New Mexicans began to be trained for the ministry in a way adapted to their needs and the urgencies of the times. This allowed the beleaguered Church during the Mexican period to continue to staff all the mainly Hispanic parish centers (Santa Fe, Albuquerque, Tomé, Belén, Socorro, Santa Cruz, Abiquiú, San Miguel del Vado, San Fernando de Taos). On the other hand, it did not have the resources to establish other needed new parishes after 1821. And for decades, ever since the 1780s, there was only one priest to take care of more and more Pueblo missions as well as the Hispanic settlers in their districts.

Under independent Mexico, it was the secular clergy and the few remaining Franciscans after 1828 who had to find a way through new economic and political challenges. Shorn of major traditional sources of Church support, they had to try to develop a new system of financing. With the introduction of some non-Mexican immigrants, some of whom were very anti-Catholic, the traditionally Catholic Hispanics had to assess more profoundly their sociocultural paths.

It was the mostly native New Mexican clergy, to the surprising number of nineteen, who remained with their people in central and northern New Mexico to face the conquering United States army. Five years later they would number seventeen as they greeted Bishop Lamy and his assistant Father Machebeuf with a still strong Hispanic Catholicism as well as a varied Pueblo Catholicism. In whatever way the newcomers might seek to educate the Hispanic New Mexicans, the roots of their faith would remain solidly Hispanic Catholic. And their native sons would continue to minister among them, although in rapidly decreasing numbers, for several decades more. But that is another story!

Notes

1.   For a critical survey of the reigning historiography up through 1989, see Robert E. Wright, O.M.I., "Local Church Emergence and Mission Decline: The Historiography of the Catholic Church in the Southwest During the Spanish and Mexican Periods," *U.S. Catholic Historian* 9:1-2 (Winter/Spring 1990), 27-48. I sketch the principal conclusions of that survey in the first paragraphs of this essay.

The only published author of whom I am aware who has seriously challenged the standard negative historiography of the institutional Church in New Mexico during the late colonial and Mexican periods is Gerald Theisen. His brief essay attacked the

conventional interpretations as unsubstantiated opinions coming from opponents of the Mexican-era clergy, but he did very
little to effectively counteract those interpretations: Gerald Theisen,
"The Catholic Church in the Mexican Period of New Mexican
History: Interpretations and Archival Source Material," in *Religion
in Latin American Life and Literature*, ed. by Lyle C. Brown and William F. Cooper (Waco: Markham Press Fund, 1980), 83-89.

2.   A good example of the first perceptions left to posterity by the
incoming Catholic clergy from the United States are those of Bishop
Lamy's companion, Father Machebeuf: "There are but fifteen priests,
and six of these are worn out by age and have no energy. The
others have not a spark of zeal, and their lives are scandalous
beyond description. ... If the few remaining Mexican priests who
have still the force of youth in them were animated with any
good intentions, it would be the easiest thing in the world to
bring these people back to the practice of their religion. But, alas!
the great obstacle to the good which the Bishop is disposed to do
among them, does not come from the people but from the priests
themselves, who do not want the Bishop, for they dread a reform
in their morals, or a change in their selfish relations with their
parishioners. One of the great neglects of the priests of New Mexico
is that they seldom or never preach. But how could such priests
preach?" W.J. Howlett, *Life of the Right Reverend Joseph P. Machebeuf...*
(Pueblo: privately printed, 1908), 164-165.

3.   For publications up until 1989, see again my essay, "Local Church
Emergence." The comments of Myra Ellen Jenkins and Albert H.
Schroeder in their *A Brief History of New Mexico* are milder than
most, but still typical: "The decline of the Franciscan Order apparent in the last decades of Spanish rule continued and as the friars
died or were recalled, they were replaced by secular priests
reponsible to the Bishop of Durango.... Many parishes and missions were vacant throughout the period due to a shortage of
secular priests.... The few parish priests were mostly New Mexicans trained in Durango" (Albuquerque: University of New
Mexico Press for the Cultural Properties Review Committee, 1974),
37, 40.

Even a scholar as intimate with the church records of New Mexico
as Fray Angélico Chávez succumbed to the "centuries of neglect"
paradigm: *But Time and Chance: The Story of Padre Martínez of Taos,
1793-1867* (Santa Fe: Sunstone, 1981), 46. Earlier Chávez had written of the Franciscan ministries in the 1700s as "in a steady decline," due in part to "a dearth of missionary replacements." He

concluded: "Several native New Mexicans were ordained after 1800, but these and the last few aging friars were unable to meet the demands of so vast and impoverished a region... By the time the U.S. took over, the Church in New Mexico was in a sorry state": "Santa Fe, Archdiocese of (Sanctae Fidei), N. Mex.," *New Catholic Encyclopedia* (New York: McGraw-Hill, 1967), vol. 12, 1062.

In his monumental *The Spanish Frontier in North America* (New Haven: Yale University, 1992), David J. Weber completely ignored the development of the institutional Church among the Hispanics themselves in New Mexico and the introduction of secular clergy in the final years. His remarks on the Church in New Mexico after 1750 were reduced to a portrayal of the Franciscans as living in concubinage (332) and the single comment: "By the mid-eighteenth century, the missions had lost their vigor and the number of Franciscans had declined" (195).

Although Jim Norris' research dealt with the preceding period, his revisionary upgrading of the Franciscans before 1750 did not prevent him from leaving the post-1750 group in a very negative light. Besides the usual charges of misbehavior, he faulted these friars for making "only a single effort, in the 1770s, to expand the mission operation": "The Franciscans in New Mexico, 1692-1754: Toward a New Assessment," *The Americas* 51:2 (October 1994), 170. In his fascinating *Sabino's Map: Life in Chimayo's Old Plaza* (Santa Fe: Museum of New Mexico, 1995), 184, Don J. Usner stated: "The scarcity of clergy became particularly acute in 1800, when the Franciscans were expelled from New Mexico, leaving a void of priests."

4.   I thank Margaret Espinosa McDonald for alerting me to the fact that within New Mexico "northern New Mexico" only refers to the Rio Arriba region (Santa Fe and above). This essay encompasses both central (the Rio Abajo) and northern New Mexico. It does not include the El Paso district or southern New Mexico, even though those areas were a part of New Mexico until 1824, when they became northern Chihuahua, and even though they remained under the Franciscan Custody of New Mexico throughout the colonial and Mexican periods. I do not include those areas since the historical accounts of New Mexico which I am addressing almost never included them, and in fact have often spoken of today's New Mexico and colonial New Mexico as if they were the same territories. This has often resulted in confusing or incorrect statements and comparisons in regard to clergy presence in New Mexico. To have included the El Paso district would

also have required enlarging this study beyond the size requested for the oral presentation and eventual publication.

5. A very similar contradiction is encountered in those Protestant authors whose religious prejudices have led them to portray New Mexico during the Mexican period (1821-1848), on the one hand, as having a clergyless folk Catholicism and yet, on the other hand, as absolutely dominated by the local clergy! See, for example, Richard L. Hough, "Religion and Pluralism Among the Spanish-Speaking Groups of the Southwest," in *Politics and Society in the Southwest: Ethnicity and Chicano Pluralism*, ed. by Z. Anthony Kruszewski, Richard L. Hough, and Jacob Ornstein-Galicia (Boulder: Westview, 1982), 169-195.

6. The only attempt, to my knowledge, to list the clergy who served for any significant part of this period was that of J.B. Salpointe in his *Soldiers of the Cross: Notes on the Ecclesiastical History of New Mexico, Arizona and Colorado* (Banning, CA: St. Boniface's Industrial School, 1898), 179. But his list of the priests from 1821 to 1850 omits at least sixteen clergy and is faulty in several other respects.

7. For the governmental missionary plan allocating twenty-four Franciscans to various places in central and northern New Mexico, see the report of Bishop Crespo in 1730 in Eleanor B. Adams, ed. and trans., *Bishop Tamarón's Visitation of New Mexico, 1760* (Albuquerque: University of New Mexico, 1954), 99-100. This same plan allotted six missionaries to the El Paso district. In spite of Crespo's detailed list of the missionary plan, John L. Kessell, *Kiva, Cross, and Crown: The Pecos Indians and New Mexico, 1540-1840* (Washington, D.C.: National Park Service, U.S. Department of the Interior, 1979), 327, reported forty royal allowances for "New Mexico" in 1730 with no further explanation.

At various points in this essay I will note agreements and divergences from Kessell's published work. I do this out of great respect and indeed admiration for his impressive research and fluid writing. Precisely because his books have a deserved reputation as the best scholarly works to address both the general history of the Church in New Mexico as well as the particular history of a single New Mexico mission, they seem most appropriate as points of reference in this discussion.

In 1744 there were twenty-four priests: twenty residing at seventeen pueblos (since there was a second friar at Taos, Pecos, and Zuñi). The friar at San Ildefonso also took care of the mission of Santa Clara. There were two friars at Santa Fe (who also took care of the nearby *visitas* of Tesuque and Pojoaque), and one each at

Albuquerque and Santa Cruz: Charles Wilson Hackett, ed. and trans., *Historical Documents Relating to New Mexico, Nueva Vizcaya, and Approaches Thereto, to 1773*, collected by Adolph F. A. Bandelier and Fanny R. Bandelier, Volume III (Washington, D.C.: Carnegie Institution, 1937), 398-406.

In 1749 there were twenty-four priests (and one brother) staffing the three *villas* (with Santa Fe and Albuquerque having two priests each) and all twenty-one pueblos (Sandía being a new foundation) except Galisteo and Pojoaque (with Zuñi having only one priest): census report by Andrés Varo transcribed in Henry W. Kelly, *Franciscan Missions of New Mexico, 1740-1760* (Albuquerque: University of New Mexico, 1941), 19. Father Varo complained that this prescribed number of priests was insufficient "because most of [the missions] have only one minister, even when they extend long distances and have a large population" (Adams, *Bishop Tamarón*, 27).

In 1760 there were twenty-four priests – two in Santa Fe and one everywhere else except the *visitas* of Tesuque and Pojoaque. By this time Abiquiú had a priest, and the Bishop noted that the new settlement of Tomé should have one (El Paso still had six priests) (ibid. 43-71, 77). Citing a Mexico City document, Kessell, *Kiva*, 301, reported without clarification that there were thirty-four Franciscan priests for "New Mexico." This must have included the El Paso and La Junta districts.

When Father Domínguez made his famous visitation of northern New Mexico in 1776, there were twenty-two Franciscans; Pecos and Galisteo were without their allotted missionaries at that time. Abiquiú continued to have a priest but Tomé remained a station: Eleanor B. Adams and Fray Angélico Chávez, trans. and annot., *The Missions of New Mexico, 1776: A Description by Fray Francisco Atanasio Domínguez with Other Contemporary Documents* (Albuquerque: University of New Mexico, 1956).

8.   Lino Gómez Canedo, *El reformismo misional en Nuevo México (1760-1768): ilusiones secularizadoras del Obispo Tamarón* (Guadalajara: Dirección de Bibliotecas, Universidad Autónoma de Guadalajara, 1981), 55-60.

9.   Juan Agustín de Morfi, "Geographical Description of New Mexico," in *Forgotten Frontiers: A Study of the Spanish Indian Policy of Don Juan Bautista de Anza, Governor of New Mexico, 1777-1787*, trans. and ed. by Alfred Barnaby Thomas (Norman: University of Oklahoma, 1932), 91. For a brief period before his death in 1781, a diocesan vicar stationed in Santa Fe took over the military chaplaincy: Angélico

Chávez, O.F.M., *Archives of the Archdiocese of Santa Fe, 1678-1900* (Washington, D.C.: Academy of American Franciscan History, 1957), 43, entry 1782:7.

Kessell cited documents indicating thirty-five Franciscans in the Custody [including the El Paso district] around 1779, "leaving three as extras on hand to fill vacancies as has been customary" (Kessell, *Kiva*, 348).

10. Kessell, *Kiva*, 543 n. 60.
11. Thomas, *Forgotten Frontiers*, 379-380 n. 59. Already in 1730, the visiting Bishop Crespo had recommended a very similar mission retrenchment (Adams, *Tamarón*, 95-100). The same basic plan, advocating even two further reductions than Anza would in the 1780s, was again proposed in 1749 by a visiting government official very hostile to the Franciscans (Hackett, *Historical Documents*, 3:451-452). The friars were more successful in dissuading the colonial administration in those earlier decades than they were during the heydays of the Bourbon efforts to economize. Adding weight to Anza's arguments for a mission consolidation was the devastating reduction of the population by a quarter or more in the great smallpox epidemic of 1780-1781 (Kessell, *Kiva*, 348).
12. For the Hispanic settlements in the districts of the various missions by 1780, see Morfi, "Geographical Description," 92-106. The consolidations happened over a three-year period, from 1781 to 1784, during which time some rearrangements were made. See Pedro Galindo Navarro to Comandante General, August 6, 1781 (Spanish Archives of New Mexico [hereafter cited as SANM] microfilm series II, roll 11, 269-271, State of New Mexico Records Center, Santa Fe); Croix to Anza, September 15, 1781 (SANM II, roll 11, 324); Fray Juan Bermejo circular, October 15, 1782 (Archives of the Archdiocese of Santa Fe [hereafter cited as AASF] microfilm series, roll 48, 1070); Croix to Anza, January 27, 1783 (SANM II, roll 11, 519); Fray Santiago Fernández de Sierra to Comandante General [ca. 1783] (AASF, roll 52, 715-716); Custos to Anza [after April 26, 1784] (AASF, roll 52, 711-712); Anza to Custos Prada, May 13, 1784 (AASF, roll 52, 727). Anza summarized this whole history in a list he sent to Chihuahua on July 20, 1784 (Anza, "Lista de los nombres," Archivo General de la Nación [hereafter cited as AGN], Prov. Int., roll 52, legajo 5, 81-82). In actuality, in contrast to Anza's mission plan, Acoma had a resident missionary for a while rather than Zuñi, which the Franciscans found very difficult to staff (see, for example, Chávez, *Archives*, 46, entry 1785:10; 47, entry 1786:3; 48, entry 1787:1).

13. Kessell reported that the number of missions in New Mexico subsidized by the crown was reduced to twenty (Kessell, *Kiva*, 348). He erred in that four of these "missions" were the *villas* including El Paso which were no longer receiving subsidies. He also did not clarify that four of these Franciscan residences were in the El Paso district, leaving only sixteen residences, including the three *villas*, in central and northern New Mexico. Kessell stated that in this consolidation Pecos was formally attached to Santa Fe as a *visita* (ibid., 349). On the contrary, Pecos remained listed as one of the subsidized missionary residences (see previous note, Anza, "Lista de los nombres," July 20, 1784).

14. Peter Gerhard, *The North Frontier of New Spain* (Princeton: Yale University, 1982; revised edition Norman: University of Oklahoma, 1993), 24, Table B; Richard L. Nostrand, "The Century of Hispano Expansion," *New Mexico Historical Review* [hereafter *NMHR*] 62:4 (October 1987), 361-386.

15. For the three deaths, including one missionary for Zuñi and one at Picurís, see Chávez, *Archives*, 46, entries 1785:1,5,6. For at least 16 Franciscans in central and northern New Mexico in September 1785, see *ibid.*, 46, entry 1785:10. This circular sent by the Custos in Pojoaque was signed by Franciscans at the three *villas*, the presidio, Abiquiú, and ten pueblos besides Pojoaque.

16. Anza to Custos Prada, March 5, 1787 (Chávez, *Archives*, 48, entry 1787:1).

17. Ylzarbe to Flores, December 21, 1787, M-M 431 no. 39, Bancroft Library, University of California at Berkeley.

18. For one of the first disputes of this kind in 1749, see Hackett, *Historical Documents*, 3:442-444, and Kelly, *Missions*, 59-60, 64. Custos Prada in 1783 complained about Anza's interference in placing missionaries (Kessell, *Kiva*, 351). Governor Chacón in 1802 would accuse the Franciscan *custos* of causing "scandals" when the latter sought to uphold his right to transfer Franciscans without Chacón's approval (Chacón to Audiencia de Guadalajara, June 15, 1802, SANM II, roll 14, 985-986; Arroyo de Anda to Chacón, July 22, 1802, SANM II, roll 14, 1007; Chacón to Com. Gen. Salcedo, November 19, 1802, SANM II, roll 14, 1041-1046). Seriously undermining the claims of the governor in church affairs, the Audiencia of Guadalajara ruled that he was not invested with the *patronato real subdelegado* which he claimed to have received from the previous Commandant General. The governor appealed this ruling (Chacón to Salcedo, March 28, 1804, and July 26, 1804, SANM II, roll 15, 225-227 and 309-310). See also Rick Hendricks, "The Exile and Return of Fray Isidro Cadelo, 1793-1810," *NMHR* 70:2 (April

1995), 139-152. Oftentimes a Franciscan *custos* would give in to the governor under pressure (Hackett, *Historical Documents*, 3:430). The ecclesiastical Visitor of the Durango diocese wrote from Santa Fe in 1818 that "una de las mayores disgracias de Provincias Internas es la extraordinaria extención a que por mala inteligencia se han prolongado los carácteres y términos del Vice Regio Patronato" (Guevara to Bishop Castañiza, February 17, 1818, AASF roll 47, 540).

19. Two friars had left New Mexico between 1786 and late 1788, and the Franciscan pastor (Burgos) of Santa Fe died around October 1788 (Concha to Ugarte, November 10, 1788, SANM II, roll 12, 102-103).

20. In early 1789 the new Bishop of Durango stated that the Custos of New Mexico had informed him that "en las dos misiones de Zuni y Taos faltan los dos Padres de la primera y el Padre de la segunda" (Estevan Lorenzo [de Tristán] to Manuel Antonio Flores, March 10, 1789, M-M 431 no. 5, Bancroft Library). The Custos must have written his note to the bishop before November 1788, since he indicated that only three Franciscans were lacking. Writing in mid-November 1788, the New Mexico governor reported the death of the Franciscan pastor at Santa Fe, the lack of the two priests at Zuñi, of the one at Picurís (rather than Taos), and also of one at Pecos (Concha to Ugarte, November 10, 1788, SANM II, roll 12, 102-103). This made a shortage of five priests, leaving only thirteen in northern New Mexico. The situation was unchanged in the fall of 1789, when twelve priests, to whom must be added the military chaplain, submitted the inventories of all the parishes and missions in central and northern New Mexico. Picurís and Taos were still sharing a minister, Zuñi was still lacking its two, Pecos its one, and Santa Fe was staffed by having a priest take care of both Albuquerque and Sandía (Angélico Chávez, "Some Original New Mexico Documents in California Libraries," *NMHR* 25:3 [July 1950], 246-247).

21. Ugarte to Governor, June 4, 1789 (SANM II, roll 12, 176-178).

22. Revilla Gigedo to Governor Concha, January 5, 1790 (SANM II, roll 12, 250).

23. Concha to Ugarte, November 1, 1790 (AGN, Prov. Int., roll 52, 84v) and November 12, 1790 (SANM II, roll 12, 409).

24. Concha to Comandante General, November 1, 1790, and July 12, 1791 (AGN, Prov. Internas, roll 52, 84-86v, 88v-90, 104). Kessell interpreted these events in a very different fashion. He portrayed Concha as reluctantly forced to raise the number of allotted and subsidized missionaries solely due to the arrival in 1790 of the

new band of missionaries. Thus he said that under pressure from the Franciscans Concha "compromised" in slightly altering the Anza plan (Kessell, *Kiva*, 352-353).

25.   Fifteen Franciscans signed circulars during the Lenten season of 1791 and also indicated that they had passed the news on to the mission of Zuñi (with its two friars). The friar officially assigned to Pecos was temporarily also caring for both the Santa Fe parish and the presidio, and Tesuque no longer had its own priest (AASF, roll 53, 34-35). There was still the same number of seventeen Franciscans in September 1792. By then two friars had departed (Vilchez and Villanueva), but a new one (Canals) had arrived and the chaplain had returned. By leaving only one missionary at Zuñi, all the posts specified in the Anza mission plan were staffed except Pojoaque and Sandía, which were vacant in order to maintain missionaries at the additional posts of Cochití and San Ildefonso as proposed in the new plan of Governor Concha ("Estado de las Misiones," copied September 30, 1792 in Durango: AGN, Prov. Internas, roll 52, expediente # 5).

26.   The various officials actually wrote as if the pre-1768 level of subsidies was still current in 1778, failing to note the removal of subsidies from the *villas*: Galindo Navarro to Comandante General Nava, January 9, 1792 (AGN, Prov. Internas, roll 52, 90-92v); Nava to Governor, January 16, 1792 (SANM II, roll 13, 3-5); Nava to Viceroy el Conde de Revilla Gigedo, January 20, 1792 (AGN, Prov. Internas, roll 52, 94-96v); Conde de Revilla Gigedo, *Informe sobre las misiones, 1793, e Instrucción reservada al Marqués de Branciforte, 1794*, ed. by José Bravo Ugarte (México, D.F.: Editorial Jus, 1966), 53, 56-57.

27.   Margaret Espinosa McDonald, "The Community Influence and Cultural Power of Nuestra Señora de Belén," presentation at the Conference on the History of the Catholic Church in New Mexico, sponsored by the Archdiocese of Santa Fe Catholic Cuarto Centennial Commission, Santuario de Guadalupe, Santa Fe, September 8, 1997.

28.   Hendricks, "Exile," 129; Royal order, April 20, 1793 (Chávez, *Archives*, 51, entry 1793:5).

29.   Nava to Governor, February 2, 1796 (AASF, roll 53, 161-163).

30.   Chávez, *Archives*, 51, entry 1793:2 (Patero) and ibid., 246, "Fernández de Sierra"; Hendricks, "Exile," 134, 136, 137; Chávez, *Archives*, 56, entry 1798:11.

31.   Chacón, "Provincia del Nuevo Mexico," November 18, 1794 (SANM II, roll 13, 561); "Certificaciones de las misiones .. 1794" (AASF, roll 53, 108-114, 116). The anonymous Franciscan author of this latter document claimed that all the missions were owed a

government subsidy, even those five districts which he noted as *visitas*, that is, places officially designated as stations to be visited by missionaries residing elsewhere. The *visitas* in 1794 were Pojoaque (rather than Nambé in the Concha plan), San Felipe, Santa Ana, Zia (rather than Jémez in the Concha plan), and Laguna (rather than Ácoma in the Concha plan). In subsequent reports, this attribution of subsidies to all the *pueblos* tends to be repeated, and the fact that five are officially *visitas* appears to be lost sight of (see below).

32. Transcriptions in November 1796 by Fray Ramón Antonio González of "Noticia de las Misiones," October 30 and November 3, 1795. The two sections of this very informative report are in two different archives, with the final pages of each section misplaced with the other section (AASF, roll 53, 153-156, and NMSRC, Read Collection, Series II, folder 8). In order to provide a priest for the Pecos area, one priest took care of both Albuquerque and Sandía. Just as in the 1794 *certificaciones* (see previous note), the Franciscans maintained that they should be receiving subsidies for the missions which they had to administer from other mission centers, since they still had to shoulder all the expenses: "todas las misiones .. están dotadas con 330 pesos cada una, aunque en la actualidad se hallen sin ministros las que son administradas por los ministros en las otras, sin darles por ello gratificación alguna" (AASF, roll 53, 154-155). For the founding of El Vado near Pecos in late 1794, see Kessell, *Kiva*, 415-417.

33. The number of clergy can be ascertained from Chávez, *Archives*, 54, entries 1796:6-7, and Robert W. Delaney and Myra Ellen Jenkins, *Guide to the "Lost" Records of the Mission of Nuestra Señora de Guadalupe de Zuni, 1755-1858* (Santa Fe: New Mexico State Records Center and Archives, 1988), 14, for Pereyro at Zuñi.

34. Chávez, *Archives*, 55, entries 1797:7 and 1798:2-3; 56, entries 1798:4-14; 260, entries on Olidén and Ortega.

35. Chávez, *Archives*, 259-261, entries on Lombide, Ortega, and Sida.

36. On the financial support of the secular pastors since 1798 and their alleged difficult characters, see Chacón to Bishop Olivárez, 13 May 1798, 18 November 1798, 20 July 1799 (SANM II, roll 14, 272-273, 329-330, 403); Nava to Chacón, 10 June 1800 (SANM II, roll 14, 550-553); Chacón to Nava, 28 August 1800 (SANM II, roll 14, 597); Chacón to Audiencia de Guadalajara, 15 June 1802 and 10 October 1803 (SANM II, roll 14, 985-986; roll 15, 117).

37. Chacón to Salcedo, March 27, 1804 (SANM II, roll 15, 211).

38. The documentary record on the missionary plan during these years is ambivalent, since generally every *pueblo* is indicated as

being endowed with a subsidy for a missionary. Scholars such as Kessell have taken this to indicate that the governmental plan actually called for missionaries in every *pueblo*. I have already discussed in previous notes how the Franciscans in the 1790s claimed that they should receive subsidies for every *pueblo* including *visitas*. Thus they would indicate a subsidy for every mission on their mission lists, even though they were only paid for where they actually had resident missionaries. I have not as yet found any references in published works or original documentation to an official recommendation or approval of an increase in the number of priests from the Concha plan of 1792.

Furthermore, when the Franciscans received a major number of recruits from Spain for their missionary work, they usually tried to send enough new priests to New Mexico to have one or two extra for the vacancies which would inevitably arise (Kessell, *Kiva*, 348). The group of new recruits sent to New Mexico in 1802 were sufficient to fulfill the Concha plan, but not to provide a priest for every *pueblo* (see following note). Nevertheless, the documentary record does prove confusing. For lack of more conclusive evidence, and given the Bourbon emphasis on cutting back on mission expenses, I deem it more probable that the missionary plan was not increased after 1792.

39.   Assuming that the 1792 plan was still in effect, the documentary records indicate the following:

1798: 20 priests — 19 Franciscans and one diocesan,
leaving Pecos without its allotted minister and Zuñi with only one. Santa Fe's diocesan pastor and Franciscan military chaplain were not included on the list, which was only for Franciscan "mission" posts (Francisco de Hozio, "Noticia de las Misiones," 1798, in *Two Thousand Miles on Horseback: Santa Fé and Back,* by James F. Meline, 208-209. New York: Hurd and Houghton, 1867).
1799: 21 priests — 20 Franciscans and one diocesan
(Chacón report, July 18, 1799, in Meline, 210-211). Kessell cited a more detailed 1799 report which indicated to him that every *pueblo* was supposed to have a subsidized priest (probably like the 1800 report cited verbatim below); thus he stated that the missions, including the El Paso district, were nine friars short (Kessell, *Kiva*, 420).

1800: 19 priests — 18 Franciscans and one diocesan:
both friars were missing at Zuñi as well as the friars at Pecos and San Ildefonso. But there were two friars rather than one to cover Zia, Santa Ana, and Jémez. In regard to the missionary plan, the

document stated that all the Pueblo missions including those in the El Paso district were endowed with subsidies for a priest, and then commented:

Ninguna [misión de Indios] ha tenido ni tiene pueblos de Indios de visita, pues con las plazas de vecinos anexas se las ha considerado competente administración, y en algunas más de lo que regularmente pueden desempeñar. Estas 26 misiones [including the El Paso district but none of the 4 *villas*] que necesitan 27 ministros o religiosos para su administración, se hallan hoy asistidas por solos 18, a causa de estar encargadas las vacantes a los ministros de las mas cercanas que las tienen; pero por mucha que sea su vigilancia y esmero no dejan de tener sus faltas involuntarias, causadas unas veces por la mucha nieve que cae, y otras por estar los rios, arroyos y caminos [h]elados sin poderse transitar. A más de los 18 religiosos empleados en las 26 missiones como va dicho, están otros dos en las Villas de la Cañada y Albuquerque, pues los párrocos de Santa Fe y el Pueblo del Paso son curas seculares, resultando faltan para el completo nueve religiosos. ("Estado general," November 24, 1800, SANM II, roll 14, 651).

The first line of this quotation errs in stating that none of the Pueblo missions ever had another *pueblo* as a *visita*. Under a clergy plan which would have a missionary in every *pueblo*, there would have been 8 priests missing in central and northern New Mexico in 1800 (and one in the El Paso district); under the 1792 Concha plan, there would have been three missing (none missing in the El Paso district).

1802: 24 priests
(Gov. Chacón, "Noticia de las Misiones," December 31, 1804, in Kessell, *Kiva*, 423.

40.   For the departure of a new group of friars from Mexico City for the Custody in December 1801, including Esteban San Miguel, Sebastián Alvarez, Francisco Bragado, Jácome González, Gerónimo Riega, and José Castro, all six of whom arrived in central and northern New Mexico in 1802, see Chávez, *Archives*, 61, entry 1801:29.

41.   *1804: 22 Franciscans*: there were a total of two for the jurisdiction which included Jémez, Zia, and Santa Ana, but only one for Zuñi (Chacón, "Noticia," 1804).

1805: 22 Franciscans: same postings as 1804 (J. Rl. Alencaster, "Statement of the Missions and Curacies," November 20, 1805, in Meline, 212).

1806: 21 *Franciscans* (José Benito Pereyro, "Account of the Missions," December 30, 1808, in *The Missions of New Mexico since 1776*, by John L. Kessell, 241. Albuquerque: University of New Mexico, 1980).

42.   Real Alencaster to Bishop, May 28, 1805 (SANM II, roll 15, 644). In a letter to the bishop later that year, the governor stated that he was writing to the Commandant General, the Provincial, the Franciscan Minister General in Europe, and the King in regard to "el arreglo que espero entablar" for clergy placements (Real Alencaster to Bishop, November 20, 1805, SANM II, roll 15, 991). Due to lack of time, I had to halt my research in these civil documents at this point until my next opportunity. The subsequent correspondence could prove to be very informative in regard to the changing clergy plan in New Mexico.

43.   The Franciscan military chaplain pastored the Santa Fe parish left vacant by the secular clergy, and San Ildefonso and Zuñi were without their allocated priests. In Kessell's English translation of the document, the *Custos* is quoted as describing as "vacant" five out of the seven missions which were without resident priests, rather than calling any of them *visitas* (Pereyro, "Account," 1808, above, 241-245).

44.   For the Santa Fe pastor, see Chávez, *Archives*, 262 (Ybave). In 1810, besides the specified *visitas* in the 1792 plan, there were clergy vacancies at Tesuque, Pojoaque, San Ildefonso, and only one priest at Zuñi, but San Felipe had a priest. There were nineteen priests in all (Josef Benito Peyrero, "Noticia de las misiones," December 31, 1810, Henry E. Huntington Library, Pasadena, California).

45.   In 1811 there were twenty priests. Zuñi had only one friar, and Tesuque and San Ildefonso were without priests; but Santa Ana had a Franciscan (Antonio Cavallero, "Noticia de las misiones," end of 1811, Santa Barbara Mission Archives).

For 1812, see Pedro Baptista Pino, *Exposición sucinta y sencilla del Nuevo México* (Cadiz: Imprenta del Estado Mayor General, 1812), 7. He reported twenty-four priests, including secular pastors in Santa Fe and El Paso, for the Custody. Assuming four priests in the El Paso district, the other twenty would have been in the rest of New Mexico. He may or may not have included the Franciscan military chaplain at Santa Fe in his figures. Pino stated that all received a subsidy except the *villa* pastors. But later he gave the old pre-1782 number of thirty Franciscans as those who were supposed to be in New Mexico including the El Paso district, and contradicted his earlier statement in considering all thirty as still subsidized by the government (ibid., 26, note 15). The facsimile of

Pino's report is printed in H. Bailey Carroll and J. Villasana Haggard, ed. and trans., *Three New Mexico Chronicles: the Exposición of Don Pedro Bautista Pino 1812; the Ojeada of Lic. Antonio Barreiro 1832; and the Additions by Don José Agustín de Escudero, 1849* (Albuquerque: The Quivira Society, 1942), 211-261.

46. Chávez, *Archives,* 74, entry 1812:14; Kessell, *Kiva,* 426-427.

47. Pino, *Exposición,* 7.

48. Kessell, *Missions,* 14. This passage has since become a basic citation and reference for many. See also Kessell, *Kiva,* 420.

49. Cavallero, "Noticia de las misiones." In my presentation I have rounded off the population figures to the nearest multiple of 50.

50. Chávez, *Archives,* 75, entry 1815:6; 76, entry 1815:21; 82, entry 1818:32.

51. Chávez, *Archives,* 259-261, Terrazas entry (for Santa Fe in 1816 and Santa Cruz in 1818), Leyva entry (for Albuquerque in 1817), Madariaga entry (for Santa Fe in 1818).

52. See the administrative records of Vicar Juan Bautista Ladrón de Guevara in 1817-1818 (Chávez, *Archives,* 150-151, 156-157 [mistakenly attributed to Rascón], 189-190).

53. In his 1820 report on New Mexico, which reflected the situation as he knew it from his visit in 1818, Guevara reported twenty-three Franciscans and five secular clergy in the entire province including the El Paso district (Juan Bautista Guevara to Bishop Castaniza, October 23, 1820, Durango, AASF roll 45, 294). There were a secular pastor and his assistant in El Paso (294). There were two Franciscans caring for the four missions in the El Paso district (299). This left twenty-one Franciscans and three secular pastors in central and northern New Mexico. Four of the friars had just arrived from Spain (300).

Led astray by the entrenched historiography of neglect, even Angélico Chávez reported that there were "few Franciscans left" at the time of Guevara's visit (Chávez, *Martínez,* 21). In another book he wrote that "after 1800 [there were] few custodial friars left," and added that Guevara "saw the missions and parishes falling into saddest neglect with the steady decline in the number of the Franciscan padres, as well as the early departures of the more recent secular clergy from Durango": Chávez, *Très Macho—He Said: Padre Gallegos of Albuquerque, New Mexico's First Congressman* (Santa Fe: William Gannon, 1985), 8.

54. A circular letter among the Franciscans was directed from the *Custos'* residence at Belén to eighteen other posts, including the Santa Fe chaplaincy, Tesuque, Pecos, and Zuñi: Rubí Celis circular,

26 September 1820, transcribed in Gerald Theisen, "Opinions on the Newly Independent Mexican Nation: Documents from the Archives of the Archdiocese of Santa Fe, New Mexico, 1820-1843," *Revista de Historia de América* 72 (Julio-Diciembre 1971), 486-487. The report on the Franciscan-staffed posts in central and northern New Mexico in 1821 also indicated nineteen Franciscans in 1820: Lansing Bartlett Bloom, "New Mexico under Mexican Adminis-tration, 1821-1846," *Old Santa Fe* 1 (1913-1914), 28 n. 43. Adding the three secular pastors of the *villas* results in twenty-two priests at that time.

55.   In June 1820 the five subsidies for Taos, Isleta, Belén, San Juan, and Abiquiú were eliminated and the four of Picurís, Santa Clara, Jémez, and Pecos were halved (Francisco de Hozio circular, July 3, 1820, AASF roll 54, 217-219). The missionary at Santa Clara suc-cessfully appealed to have his full stipend restored: see his objec-tion in the above circular, and the full stipend assigned Santa Clara in the 1821 census report transcribed in Bloom, "New Mexico," 28 n. 43. In Rev. Bloom's zeal to prove the gross negli-gence and greed of the Catholic Church in his highly prejudiced study, he confused this actual report for central and northern New Mexico with a national budget estimate in 1828 which cited ear-lier colonial figures for the entire New Mexico Custody includ-ing the El Paso district (1: 258, 268, 271 n. 257).

56.   Marc Simmons, "New Mexico's Spanish Exiles," *NMHR* 59:1 (Janu-ary 1984), 71, cited the statement of the Franciscans in New Mexico in early 1828 that they had not received any of the budgeted subsidies for the past eight or nine years.

57.   Bloom, "New Mexico," 1:28 n. 43. The person who prepared the census report for publication apparently failed to note that it was only a report on the Franciscan posts, and therefore mistakenly "corrected" it to indicate priests at the three *villas*, which were actu-ally staffed by secular priests. Thus while the report correctly gave a total of twenty (Franciscan) priests, the column which it totalled indicated twenty-three priests. Furthermore, since this was only a report on Franciscan posts, it did not include the secular parish of Tomé. The total of twenty Franciscans correctly given by the re-port together with the four secular priests at the three *villas* and Tomé add up to twenty-four priests at the end of 1821.

58.   Chávez, *Archives*, 87, entry 1821:11. Madariaga, the first secular pastor of Tomé, was replaced in Santa Fe by Terrazas of Santa Cruz, who in turn was replaced by the newly arrived Manuel Rada. See the entries on Madariaga, Rada, and Terrazas in Chávez, *Archives*, 260-261.

59. Chávez, *Archives*, 228, book M-57 Socorro.

60. Bishop Lamy established the parish of Arroyo Hondo in 1852 (Chávez, *Martínez*, 99).

61. Among the first ordained native sons was the famous Antonio José Martínez, who entered the Durango seminary in 1817. Around the same time three members of the extended Ortiz family – Fernando, Rafael, and Juan Felipe – also joined the seminary. Martínez returned to New Mexico as a priest in April 1823. He was the first known native son of New Mexico to be ordained in 90 years (Chávez, *Martínez*, 20-24; Chávez, *Gallegos*, 8). Rafael Ortiz celebrated his solemn First Mass in Santa Fe on October 4, 1823 (Chávez, *Archives*, 91, entry 1823:16). José Vicente Chávez transferred from the Puebla diocese to that of Durango in early 1826 (ibid., 95, entry 1826:22). For the assignment listings of all five, see Chávez, *Archives*, 258-261.

62. Chávez, *Archives*, 213, B-66, Santa Fe Castrense (Box 57) 1798-1833; 238, Bur-51, Santa Fe Castrense (Box 28) 1779-1833; Bloom, "New Mexico," 1:246-247.

63. See the Socorro assignments of Manuel Martínez, O.F.M., and Rafael Ortiz in their respective entries in Chávez, *Archives*, 251 and 260.

64. Bloom, "New Mexico," 1:173, 247-248; Salpointe, 160.

65. Chávez, *Archives*, 83, entries 1819:5-6.

66. Chávez, *Archives*, 238 (death of Francisco de Hozio, the military chaplain); 239 (death of Ignacio Sánchez, pastor of Isleta); 248 (last extant record of Ambrosio Guerra, pastor of Sandía); 253 (last extant record of Mariano Peñon, pastor of Laguna); Kessell, *Kiva*, 503 (death of Francisco Bragado, pastor of El Vado).

67. For the new friar see the entry for Buenaventura Muro in Chávez, *Archives*, 252. For the return of Juan Caballero Toril, see 244 (his assignments) and 85, entry 1820:16 (minister at San Lorenzo el Real in 1820).

68. Not having at hand statistics on the Santo Evangelio Province from the early 1800s themselves, I merely cite here the comparison given in Fidel de Jesús Chauvet, O.F.M., *Los Franciscanos en México (1523-1980): Historia Breve* (2a ed. México: Provincia del Santo Evangelio de México, Editorial Tradición, 1989), 145, 148, in which he cited 476 Franciscans in the Santo Evangelio Province in 1785 compared to 171 in 1843. Chauvet briefly mentioned a few reasons for the decline on pages 147-148.

69. I have determined this through analyzing Chávez's notes on the Vicar's records (*Archives*, 190-192) and the clergy assignment lists he compiled in the Appendix to that work.

70.   Chávez, *Archives*, 191-192 (Vicar's record); first months of assign-
      ments of Antonio José Martínez to Abiquiú and then Taos, Juan
      Felipe Ortiz to San Juan, and José Vicente Chávez to Belén (ibid.,
      Appendix).

71.   See the administrative records of Vicar Agustín Fernández San
      Vicente in 1826 (Chávez, *Archives*, 157, 190-193). Connie Cortazar,
      "The *Santa Visita* of Agustín Fernández de San Vicente to New
      Mexico, 1826," *NMHR* 59:1 (January 1984), 33-48, embellished
      any negative criticism of the friars and the Church in general, but
      cited only one instance (40) of how the Durango cathedral records
      "contain numerous complaints regarding the vicar's dealings with
      the Franciscans" (39).

72.   Chávez, *Archives*, 157, Book LXXVIII (Vicar's record), entries on
      García del Valle and Bellido in ibid., Appendix.

73.   Chávez, *Archives*, 192 (Vicar's record), Buenaventura Muro and Juan
      Bruno González entries in ibid., Appendix.

74.   Chávez, *Archives*, 227, M-53, Santa Fe (Box 29), 1821-1836; 238,
      Bur-52, Santa Fe (Box 29) 1816-1834 (death of Terrazas).

75.   Census in Bloom, "New Mexico," 1:28 n. 43 (see note 57, above).
      For San Ildefonso and the three missions attached to it, see Chávez,
      Archives, 206, B-23 (Pojoaque) and 204, B-21 (Nambé). For San Felipe
      attached to Sandía, see 93, 1824:17 and Gerónimo Riega entry in
      Appendix. For Santa Ana and Zia attached to Jémez, see Simmons,
      "Spanish Exiles," 70. For Zuñi attached to Laguna, see Kessell, *Mis-
      sions*, 210.

76.   Marc Simmons, "Spanish Exiles," 69-72, describes the expulsion
      of four Spaniards and the exemption given to two. Simmons con-
      cluded that Manuel Bellido was not expelled from New Mexico
      until the latter part of 1828 (72), but Bellido's last extant entries in
      the territory were in May 1827, the month in which the first anti-
      Spanish legislation was enacted (Chávez, *Archives*, 243 Bellido en-
      try). That Bellido was already expelled in 1827 is proven by
      Armijo's statement in early 1828 that only five Spanish friars
      were in New Mexico by then, and those named did not include
      Bellido (Bloom, "New Mexico," 1:258). True to his anti-Catholic
      prejudice, Bloom stated that the three friars subsequently expelled
      "preferred to leave the country" (amply disproved by Simmons'
      article), and that "the so-called `expulsion of the Spaniards'" was
      only "incidental as affecting the number of clergy in our Territory."
      For the departure of one of these friars from El Vado, see Kessell,
      Kiva, 454. Chávez, *Martínez*, 29, was unaware of Bellido's expul-
      sion from Picurís.

77. Diego Martínez and Pedro Rubí de Celis were Mexicans (Kessell, *Kiva*, 503), and thus clearly not expelled as Spaniards. The last extant entries by them and Gerónimo Riega (birthplace?) in central and northern New Mexico were between November 1827 and February 1828 (Chávez, *Archives*, assignment listings in Appendix). Sebastián Alvarez, *Custos* at the time and still in Santa Fe in 1826, wrote from the El Paso district in March 1828 to appoint one of the friars as vice-custos in the central and northern area (ibid., 97, entry 1828:5).

78. The undated 1827 census by Narbona which was printed in Escudero's 1849 report and reproduced in Carroll and Haggard (*Chronicles*, 88) reflects the situation at the end of that year, when there were seventeen priests (nine Franciscans and eight secular clergy). The census total gave seventeen priests, but there were only sixteen itemized locations of clergy since the one at Picurís was not noted.

    For the clergy situation at the end of 1828, see Manuel de Jesús Rada, *Proposición hecha al Soberano Congreso General de la Nación*, 2, in *Northern Mexico on the Eve of the United States Invasion: Rare Imprints Concerning California, Arizona, New Mexico, and Texas, 1821-1846*, ed. by David J. Weber (New York: Arno, 1976). Rada correctly reported ten secular parishes (but not the military chaplaincy). However, the number of *pueblos* he gave, twenty-two, was inflated. Even counting Pecos as separate from El Vado, there were only eighteen. He probably double-counted San Juan, Taos, Abiquiú, and Belén, including them in both categories. The fifteen new priests whom Rada requested together with the thirteen clergy already present would have been the exact number to staff all eighteen *pueblos* and the ten secularized parishes.

79. Chávez, *Archives*, 97, entry 1828:6.

80. Buenaventura Muro's first extant entries were in 1823 (Chávez, *Archives*, Muro entry in Appendix). Juan Lejarzar was only in New Mexico for a few months in 1831 (ibid., 102, entry 1831:1; 103, entry 1831:4; 154, 1831 paragraph).

81. Entries for Manuel Rada and Manuel Murga in Appendix to Chávez, *Archives*; ibid., 99, entry 1829:8, for Murga's departure.

82. Luis Dias Luján entry in Appendix to Chávez, *Archives.*

83. For population growth in the Taos district at this time, see Chávez, *Martínez*, 27-28. For the foreign immigration, see ibid., 61, 66-77, especially 73-74.

84. See the New Mexico administrative journals of Vicar Juan Rafael Rascón (Chávez, *Archives*, 101-102, 152-154, 193-194).

85. These patterns have been determined from the Vicar's acts cited in the previous note and the clergy assignments compiled in the Appendix of Chávez, *Archives*. See also a document noting all the Franciscan placements in 1830 (ibid., 100, entry 1830:4). For the Vicar's requirement that the Franciscans replace the secular priest who departed San Juan, see ibid., 99 entry 1829:8, and 153 (1829).

86. Antonio Barreiro, *Ojeada sobre Nuevo-México* (Puebla, 1832), 39-41, in Carroll and Haggard, *Chronicles*. These remarks have often been misinterpreted to portray as negligent those priests who were actually still in New Mexico. Several historians have even inappropriately used this text to characterize the whole 1800-1850 period, if not even earlier.

87. I have identified the following priests in central and northern New Mexico in 1832:

> 1) Juan Felipe Ortiz (Vicar, Santa Fe parish, Picurís; plus San Miguel del Vado after July);
> 2) Fernando Ortiz (Santa Fe chaplaincy and Picurís);
> 3) Teodoro Alcina, O.F.M., (Santa Cruz up to July; San Ildefonso, Nambé, Pojoaque, and Tesuque);
> 4) José Francisco Leyva (San Miguel del Vado up to July; then Santa Cruz);
> 5) Antonio José Martínez (Taos);
> 6) José de Castro, O.F.M., (San Juan and Santa Clara);
> 7) Rafael Ortiz (Abiquiú);
> 8) Mariano José Sánchez Vergara, O.F.M., (Cochití, Santo Domingo, Zia, and Jémez);
> 9) Manuel Antonio García del Valle, O.F.M., (Sandía, Santa Ana, and San Felipe);
> 10) Francisco Ignacio de Madariaga (Albuquerque and Tomé);
> 11) Buenaventura Muro, O.F.M., (Isleta, Laguna, Acoma, and Zuñi);
> 12) Luis Dias Luján (Belén);
> 13) Vicente Chávez (Socorro).

The sources for this information are all from Chávez, *Archives*, at the following locations: Appendix, 241-262; 103-104 (loose document entries for 1831-1832); 153-154 (Vicar Rascón Book of Patentes); 196 (Vicar Ortiz book of administration).

88. The priests' entries in the various sacramental registers demonstrate their efforts to cover the districts assigned to them. For the commended pastoral care provided the Taos-Picurís-Mora district by the priest(s) of Taos, see Chávez, *Martínez*, 30-31, 33, 47, 65.

89. See the New Mexico administrative journals of Ortiz in 1832-1851 (Chávez, *Archives*, 195-197).

90. The bishop visited in 1833, 1845 (Chávez, *Archives*, 104-106, 111-112), and 1850 (Fray Angélico Chávez, "A Nineteenth-Century New Mexico Schism," *NMHR* 58:1, January 1983, 44-45). See also Chávez, *Martínez*, 41-43, 45-46, 74-75, 88-89.

91. Chávez, *Archives*, 212-213, B-66 Santa Fe Castrense; 238, Bur-51 Santa Fe Castrense.

92. Chávez, *Martínez*, 43-44. I do not include Nicolás Valencia in this number, since Chávez cited inconclusive evidence which he took to indicate Valencia's probable origin outside New Mexico (ibid., 44; Chávez, "Schism," 36-39).

93. Chávez, *Martínez*, 45.

94. For the deaths of Alcina and García del Valle in mid-1834, see Chávez, *Archives*, 237 (Bur-35, Santa Cruz), 196 (Accounts Book LXXVI); for Muro, Sánchez Vergara, and Castro in 1840, see ibid., 196 (Accounts Book LXXVI).

95. José Francisco Rodríguez only served from 1833-1837 (Chávez, *Archives*, Rodríguez entry in Appendix). For the death of Madariaga in November 1838, see ibid., 239, Bur-54 Tomé). For the last extant entries of Dias de Luján in February 1838, see ibid., 201, B-11 Belén, and under his name in the Appendix. This left only two non-native secular priests serving in the territory: José Francisco Leyva, one of the earliest to arrive in 1817 (ibid., Appendix), and José Vicente Chávez. José Vicente Saturnino Montaño was from the interior of Mexico (ibid., 110, entry 1842:4). He was a lay teacher in Father Martínez's school in Taos since August 1838 or earlier (Chávez, *Martínez*, 60, 63-64). Montaño must have then gone to the seminary in Durango, since he was back in New Mexico as a priest in 1843 (Chávez, *Archives*, 222, M-49 Isleta; see also Chávez, *Martínez*, 64). Chávez's entry on Montaño in his Appendix somehow erroneously included an 1834-1840 stint at Isleta. Fray Buenaventura Muro was still serving at Isleta during those years.

96. These conclusions are based upon an analysis of the clergy listings in the Appendix to Chávez, *Archives*, together with the information cited in the previous two notes. For the protest of the friar at Cochití about assuming the entire Sandía-Santa Ana-San Felipe district, see ibid., 196. For the attachment of Sandía to the Albuquerque parish, see ibid., 234, Bur-47 Sandía; for all the other *pueblos* falling to the one Franciscan's care, see ibid., 106-108, entries 1834:9,10; 1836:1,8; 1837:2-5.

97. Chávez reported that all three were ordained by October 1836 (Chávez, *Martínez*, 43), but their first extant entries are all as assistants to Martínez in Picurís in February-May 1837 (Chávez, *Archives*, Appendix entries for Trujillo, Valdez, and Lucero). Accordingly, I have counted them for the year 1837, but not for the year 1836.

98. See note 95, above.

99. See this gap in the Vicar's sacramental entries, in Chávez, *Archives*, Appendix, along with the *patentes* for 1837-1839 noted in ibid., 183-184. See also Chávez, *Martínez*, 51, 60.

100. See the assignments for Madariaga, then Lucero, and then Rafael Ortiz in Chávez, *Archives*, Appendix.

101. See the first extant entries for Abeyta, Gallegos, and Luján in Chávez, *Archives*, Appendix.

102. These changes are based upon an analysis of the clergy listings in the Appendix to Chávez, *Archives*. For these calculations I do not include the renegade priest Cárdenas, who never had permission to serve in the territory although he did minister there; but I do include the suspended Valencia who had begun his ministry legitimately in 1845 (see Chávez, "Schism"). For the lone Franciscan in 1845-1848, see Chávez, *Archives*, 196-197, 222, 233.

103. The clergy and their assignments upon Bishop Lamy's arrival in August 1851:

Vicar, Santa Fe	Juan Felipe Ortiz
Santa Fe assistant	José de Jesús Luján
Abiquiú	Antonio Salazar
San Juan	Fernando Ortiz
San Ildefonso (and S. Clara)	José Tomás Abeyta
Santa Cruz (and Nambé)	Juan de Jesús Trujillo
Taos	Antonio José Martínez
Picurís	Mariano de Jesús Lucero
San Miguel del Vado	José Francisco Leyva
Cochití (and San Felipe)	Ramón Salazar
Santo Domingo	Rafael Ortiz
Albuquerque (and Sandía)	José Manuel Gallegos
Isleta	José Vicente Saturnino Montaño
Tomé	José de Jesús Baca
Belén	Rafael Chávez
(suspended Nicolás Valencia in area)	
Socorro	José Antonio Otero

I have included Nicolás Valencia, both because he continued to minister even though suspended by Zubiría, and because Lamy reinstated him into the ministry (Chávez, "Schism," 44-45). This list is mostly derived from an analysis of the clergy entries in the Appendix of Chávez, *Archives*. Those entries are unclear in regard to San Ildefonso, but the fact that Abeyta was pastor there at the time is proven by ibid., 118, entries 1851:18 and 1852:10. The names and assignments of all the priests from Santa Fe northward, except the one in Abiquiú, are confirmed in the historical recollections of Demetrio Pérez published as "New Notes on Bishop Lamy's First Years in New Mexico," ed. by Bruce T. Ellis and trans. by Florence H. Ellis and Fred G. Hawley, *El Palacio* 65:1 (February 1958), 26-33. For Abiquiú, Pérez apparently confused Ramón with Antonio Salazar. Pérez also included Fathers Valdez and Vigil, but the latter had died in July 1850 (Chávez, *Archives*, 197), and the last extant entries of the former were for Santa Clara in April 1851 (ibid., Appendix). Consequently, Santa Clara was not on the distribution list when the Vicar sent out a circular about Lamy's approach in July 1851 (ibid., 117, entry 1851:9).

104. A much lesser number of priests, if any at all, has usually been given for the time of Lamy's arrival. Writers have been led into error by statements made by the newly-arrived French clergy after 1851 such as Lamy and Salpointe. In his 1866-1867 reports, Lamy stated that there had only been nine priests upon his arrival: Paul Horgan, *Lamy of Santa Fe: His Life and Times* (New York: Farrar, Straus and Giroux, 1975), 335. Salpointe later wrote that Lamy upon his arrival found "nine priests residing in as many Indian pueblos, and a few others who had charge of Mexican parishes" (Salpointe, *Soldiers*, 206). In the same publication, however, Salpointe stated that Lamy had only found ten priests, whom he listed (282). A private letter of Machebeuf a month after the arrival of Lamy and himself was closer to the mark, stating that they found fifteen priests (Howlett, *Machebeuf*, 164).

David Weber stated that there were only eleven secular clergy in New Mexico by 1846, rather than the actual eighteen present (plus one Franciscan). He also underestimated the impact of Martínez' preparatory seminary on these clergy numbers. Weber asserted that "the results of [Martínez'] work affected New Mexico chiefly following the United States invasion": David J. Weber, *The Mexican Frontier, 1821-1846: The American Southwest Under Mexico* (Alququerque: University of New Mexico, 1982), 74. Actually ten of Martínez' alumni were ministering in central and northern New Mexico by 1846.

105. See the analysis above for the period from December 1829 to April 1831.

La Guadalupana and La Conquistadora in the Catholic History of New Mexico

Pedro Ribera-Ortega

The time couldn't be better, both for the Catholic Church with its longing for the millennium and all that the Holy Father, Pope John Paul II, has dreamed and prayed for, and for the State of New Mexico as it readies itself statewide for the long-awaited coming of the Cuarto Centennial of the Oñate founding in 1598 and of the concomitant evangelization of the indigenous peoples of the Southwest. Even Venerable Madre María de Jesús de Ágreda, the enterprising mystical Conceptionist-Franciscan nun from Ágreda, Spain, came to help the Franciscan missionaries by her extraordinary bilocations to the Indians, telling them to seek the missionary padres for their eventual conversion. But that is only a mere fragment of our Catholic story of New Mexico, from which we will single out the unique Marian devotion that has preceded it and has lasted until now, in 1998.

As Mayordomo of the ancient Confraternity of La Conquistadora, I have been asked many questions about the characteristics that make our Hispanic-European Marian devotion something extraordinary, and many questions as well about our present Indo-Hispanic devotion to María Santísima, but always with a subtle – and sometimes a not-so-subtle – indication that we Santa Feans and New Mexicans whose ancestors came with Oñate have more public and private devotion to La Conquistadora than to Our Lady of Guadalupe, who is of Mexican origin, from 1531 onwards. We in Santa Fe and New Mexico can only explain this unfortunate presupposition by first assuming that such ignorance comes from lack of knowledge, as it philosophically does. And we remove that kind of Marian ignorance of our past in Santa Fe and New Mexico history by clarifying the whole story of our almost two thousand year devotion, that dates from apostolic times, from the days of Saint James the Greater, whom we prefer to call by the Galician name "Santiago" (San Yago), for his tomb and shrine are found at Compostela in green-coated Galicia, in the Celtic part of Spain, right next door to Portugal, where in 1917, Our Lady came to three shepherds at Fatima, and where Our Lady promised the world much-needed peace and the triumph of her Immaculate Heart.

If this presentation is going to be worth its salt, religion-wise, for us as Catholic New Mexicans of the Archdiocese of Santa Fe, let me first offer an overview of our Palestian-Spanish origin of our love and devotion to the Mother of Christ and our Mother from the time of Santiago's attempts at our Spanish-Roman conversion. From our Catholic upbringing, we all very well know that Christ our Divine Redeemer, before his Ascension to heaven, encouraged his Apostles and disciples time after time "to go throughout the entire world and baptize everyone in the name of the Father, the Son, and the Holy Spirit." Scriptural verses are abundant in this regard. And so, after Pentecost when the Blessed Mother and the Apostles were in the Cenacle at Jerusalem, Saint Peter and the other Apostles felt strong enough with the power of the Holy Spirit to preach the Gospel in Jerusalem and even to suffer persecution, as our Lord had predicted many times: "If they persecute Me," He said many times, "they will do the same to you!"

And so the time came when Saint Peter with the advice of the apostolic college sent out the chosen Apostles of Christ in all directions. In our Spanish-Roman case, it was Saint James – the older brother of the "Beloved Disciple," Saint John the Evangelist, who would go to Hispania, a province of great importance to Rome, and begin to convert us. Santiago valiantly went to Hispania, and he soon consecrated six bishops. But what we know about the stubbornness of our hard-headed Roman-Spanish ancestors leads us to believe that from the earliest days Santiago had great difficulties and that our ancestors, pagan Romans as they were and very individualistic in manners and temperament, demurred and caused him much difficulty. And so, discouraged after a few years, Saint James and his first converts and bishops headed back to Jerusalem to report back to Saint Peter, the first Pope of the Church. And on their way there they camped on the river-bank of Zaragosa, which was named after the Roman Emperor Caesar Augustus of the Christmas decree-mandate, remember? And as they camped on the fast-running Rio Ebro, lo and behold, here began our unique Marian devotion, extraordinary in its story and certainly most providential in its results for us as first Roman Spanish converts.

Today when one visits the magnificent Basilica de la Virgen del Pilar at Zaragoza, one marvels at the devotion of today to Our Lady: the image of Our Lady stands on a pillar, whence her name "Our Lady of the Pillar." But why a symbol of a hard-stoned pillar? Well, there's more to the story than the pillar, so let's briefly cover the background of our Lady's first intervention in apostolic times! The first title the Spaniards would know after the pillar-symbol was given by Our Lady herself to Saint James the Apostle is that of typical Spanish royal pageantry: Nuestra Señora María la Real de Jerusalén. Keep in mind that Our Lady was still very much alive (the year was 53 A.D., well before her death and Assumption to Heaven, and she was very well taken care of by Saint James' younger brother Saint John, the Apostle and Evangelist). The Spanish tradition very much alive today is that Our Blessed Mother, before the Apostles scattered world-wide, had privately or collectively counseled them, "If you ever need my help, at any time, dearest sons and apostles, pray to Our Divine Lord, and ask Him to send me to help you, anywhere, anytime!" Well, it seems that Santiago on the Rio Ebro at Zaragoza reminded his companion first converts and bishops to pray to Our Lord to send María Santísima la Real de Jerusalén to come to their aid before they left for Jerusalem to report to Saint Peter.

Well, lo and behold: from the sky came the vision of angels escorting la Virgen Santísima María, and they had a pillar with them! Our Lady must have greeted the surprised Santiago and his first converts with loving words and a message, and She gave Santiago the pillar as a symbol of the faith in Christ that would never die in Spain!

Thus from apostolic Santiago-times in the "Hispania" of Roman days, after countless heroic martyrdoms in all areas, the faith

in Christ has survived! Never did the faith falter, but in this century at a price of over a million casualties, and for the Church
over eight thousand martyred bishops, priests, and religious both
men and women, and four thousand lay persons! Every year,
every day, we New Mexicans should join Spain in remembrance;
Rome has beatified countless members of the ten thousand martyrs who died because of hatred of the faith between 1931 and
1939. Interestingly enough, the first three beatified were three
Discalced Carmelite nuns from the Carmel of Guadalajara, Spain,
who offered their lives for the cessation of the barbarous civil war
that tore their country apart. As a Hispanophilo, I have collected
many books in Spanish on the ten thousand martyrs of modern
Spain, and these are available for borrowing by my fellow New
Mexicans from my "Library of the Faith" at the Truchas Research
Center.

Zaragosa and Compostela, the Two Poles of the Faith in Spain

We New Mexicans have great devotion to Santiago, our
first teacher of the Christian faith, and it is well we do! That's how
we started our fervent and extraordinary devotion to María
Santísima, from the apostolic times of the Church. Other races
and cultures, assuredly, have their own apostolic background;
they venerate the Apostle Saint Thomas in India, and they venerate and love the Mother of Christ and our Mother! But if you
ever go on a delightfully educational pilgrimage in Spain, don't
forget the two shrines, the one in Zaragoza, the Marian shrine of
la Virgen del Pilar, her feast day being October 12 (shades of the
Columbus day of discovery of the New World, ¿verdad?), and
then across the country in the northwest, the other in Galicia at
Compostela; and here is the medieval shrine-tomb of Santiago
de Compostela, a tomb-city of truly great renown. In the Middle
Ages, there were three very important pilgrimage sites to all Christians who could travel there. First was Jerusalem in the Holy
Land of our Lord's life and death; then Rome, where the apostles
Saints Peter and Paul were martyred and are buried today; and
thirdly and not least, Santiago de Compostela in Galicia, Spain.
From Europe, especially France, there are still four major routes
through France and over the Pyrenees Mountains, and each of

them can be a very enjoyable but difficult pilgrimage route for
modern-day pilgrims.

La Virgen de Guadalupe de Extremadura, España, Siglo Trece

Christopher Columbus stubbornly appealed to Queen Isabella
of Castile; he needed to see her, and he begged her sponsorship
for some six years. He must have known from his friend, Isabella's
Franciscan confessor, that she had more important matters to consider such as the last ten years of constant battles in the Granada
area, where the last Moorish king, Boabdil the Unlucky, had refused to surrender at the Alhambra. So Queen Isabella and her
husband, King Fernando de Aragón, ignored poor disillusioned
Cristóbal Colón and kept on fighting in Granada.

And it should be of paramount interest to us Santafesiños
Neomexicanos that a serious, devastating fire burned her camp-
site to the ground. The Queen requested of her soldiers from all
parts of Spain that they should now rebuild not another tent-city
but a formidable city of stone, and so they did; they wanted to
name it after their favorite mistress, la Reina Doña Isabel de Castilla,
but she diplomatically reminded them that it had been a 774-
year-long Reconquista de la Cruz en España, from Covadonga,
near Oviedo, Asturias, to Granada in the south. And so Queen
Isabella named it for better reasons "Santa Fe de la Vega de
Granada" in 1491. This rebuilt city basks in the history of the
Reconquista of our ancestors from north to south for almost eight
long centuries of battle between the Islamic Crescent of
Mohammed and the Catholic Cross of Christ! We are the fourth
of thirteen official Santafeños in the New World that Columbus
encountered while trying to reach "las Indias" of his dreams.

Hernán Cortés, Bishop Zumárraga, Juan Diego, and Guadalupe: 1531

Well, we've finally reached 1531 and the Tepeyac apparitions of Our Blessed Mother to the newly-converted fifty-year-
old Juan Diego. We all know the story and wonder at its providential uniqueness, its varied hieroglyphic explanation to the
Aztecs and other Indians of Mexico, and the influence the apparitions and the portrait had on the conversion of the Indians.
There are innumerable books in Spanish and English, as well as

other languages, that in one way or other tell us the details, apart from the Spanish versions of the pastorelas at Christmastime amongst us in New Mexico. But as I get older, I have preferred three or four other storied books that now give me many more details of the apparitions, and I especially love the wonderful Aztec translations, which are sheer poetry, in contradistinction to the prose-minded Spanish versions.

Let me share the titles of these modern interpretations that I hope will be made better known and available for the twentieth century. Not that the older versions from 1531 to today are not good, but these favorite versions of today can give us more substance to better understand the period of 1531, the person of Juan Diego and his uncle Juan Bernardino, Archbishop Zumárraga (who privately before had asked for the impossibility of castillian roses, before the actual apparitions of December, 1531), and the message of hope in its world-wide uniqueness and applicability. And we have learned that she belongs to the entire Church, not just to Mexico or Latin America: ¿verdad?! And these three modern books can bring us up to date as to the scientific, hieroglyphic, and spiritual contents and applications so that we can marvel more and more as we venerate the sacred image of Guadalupe.

The first of these fine books is from Spain, from a unique source, from an author known there for his extraterrestrial works, who learned "all about Guadalupe" from scratch, and whose book has gone into twenty editions in Spain. I found it in Madrid, and it is *El Misterio de la Virgen de Guadalupe* by J.J. Benítez, published by Planeta, Barcelona, in 1982. One would say of it: "Everything you wanted to know about Guadalupe!" Secondly, from the Trappists (Cistercian Monks of the Strict Observance in Lafayette, Oregon, formerly in Pecos at the behest of our late Archbishop Edwin Vincent Byrne of Santa Fe), who have continued to do extremely valuable research of "things Guadalupan" like the translation not from the Spanish, but from the original language, Nahuatl, which Juan Diego spoke and to Our Lady and she spoke to him in reply. This poetic version, *The Nahuatl Guadalupe Story*, is a Godsend to us! Thirdly, the very new book entitled *A Handbook on Guadalupe*, now available from various sources, my version from the Family Fatima Apostolate, Redfield, SD 57469. This is a must for American English-speaking Catholics who love our Lady of Guadalupe, for it's a treasure-house with recent discoveries on hieroglyphics, images-in-the-eyes, and so forth. Priests and laity should place this book in parish libraries so it will be available for everyone. And in fourth place, the "Our Lady of Guadalupe" issue of the *Immaculate Heart Messenger*, April-June 1997, from the Family Fatima Apostolate, which is based in great part on the *Handbook*. This issue brings us details that make us want to read the *Handbook* with its many references. Father Robert J. Fox knows how to popularize not only the devotion of Our Lady of Fatima but now Guadalupe as well. And if other bibliographical titles are necessary, let me mention *The Wonders of Guadalupe* by Francis Johnston, from Tan Books and Publishers, Rockford, IL 11056, authentic and comprehensive even while inexpensive. In Spanish there are innumerable books of all kinds.

From Old Mexico to the New Mexico with Oñate in 1598

Here's our New Mexican connection with the apparitions and message and portrait of la Virgen Santísima de Guadalupe del Tepeyac. Many of our ancestors came from el Valle del Anáhuac, where the apparitions miraculously took place to Beato Juan Diego del Tepeyac, December 9 through 12 of 1531. This is our Mexican Marian heritage; this is part and parcel of our Indo-Hispanic history; this is also part and parcel of "la Nueva México" which our ancestors established under Governor Juan de Oñate in 1598. All of it is Our Lady's history: from Palestine to Roman-Spain to the New World, from "las Indias" beginnings in Old Mexico (called "la Nueva España") to "the Ancient Kingdom of la Nueva México" with its capital at Santa Fe.

It was the custom for our ancestors that they caravaned from Mexico City and up to the north – through Querétaro where they got supplies to Zacatecas, thence up to Durango and on to Santa Bárbara in "la Nueva Vizcaya," Parral in Chihuahua, and la Ciudad de Chihuahua de San Felipe el Real, then crossing el Rio Grande del Norte – the Rio Grande – where Don Juan de Oñate took formal possession de "las Tierra de Adentro," on the fiesta de las Ascensión del Señor al Cielo, 30 de Abril de 1598. Departing el Valle del Anáhuac of the Guadalupan shrine area, it was only natural that the Franciscan padres would insist on stopping at

Tepeyac and celebrating a mass of petition at the foot of la Guadalupana to beg her for a safe long journey to the Norte de Nueva México; and assuredly, countless were the estampas de la Virgen Guadalupana that our ancestors brought and saved for sharing in New Mexico later on. Some two thousand Spanish leagues they would travel, four months of hard journeying and many difficulties including deaths and frontier births, for "El Camino Real" was just a name for the harsh roads of a highway that went from south to north, from Mexico City to far-off Santa Fe. Even today, at the north end of the Camino Real, is found the Santuario de Guadalupe.

The Autobiography of an Ancient Statue, La Conquistadora

I challenge any New Mexican, Spanish-speaking or otherwise, from other cultures and devotions to Mary, to read carefully and devotionally the *Autobiography of La Conquistadora* by the late padre Fray Angélico Chávez, O.F.M., her "knight-errant of New Mexico", to understand Our Lady's place in our four-centuried history and its Mundo-Hispánico fame, and to claim that it doesn't belong also to "La Nueva México." Fray Angélico's book devotes its first chapter to Guadalupe, its apparitions, its message of hope for the world, and the details of the heavenly portrait. The story of La Conquistadora is the story of the founding and development of the faith in New Mexico. It even includes, perforce, the story of the evangelization of the Pueblo and other Indians of the Southwest. In 1940, on the June Sunday of the first public procession, Fray Angélico wrote an interesting historical-genealogical article for the Santa Fe *New Mexican*, "La Conquistadora Is Our Paisana" — she is one of us in faith, in history, and in New Mexican culture!

How the image from Spain called "La Conquistadora" came up from Mexico City, right along with the story of Guadalupe in all her glory, is yet another of the multifaceted characteristics of devotion to Our Blessed Mother Mary from Europe to the New World. And the Chávez *Autobiography* book tells the story in detail; it is definitely history in the widest sense, but it is also the genealogy of the ancestors of us New Mexicans, who came in 1598 with Don Juan de Oñate to stay definitively, to form a northern kingdom for Spain, to be frontier people of the best kind, to persevere in the Catholic faith, and to share that faith of ours with the Indians, our brothers!

"La Conquistadora" is aptly described by the late Archbishop Edwin Vincent Byrne (d. 1963), who prefaced the first of the Conquistadora books – the one full of researched documentation of the story. Archbishop Byrne loved "our Patroness and Heavenly Queen" as only a fervent priest-bishop with a Celtic or Irish persecution background could, and when he came to us from Philadelphia by way of bishoprics in the Puertorican cities of Ponce and San Juan, he quickly learned to appreciate just what our Indo-Hispanic devotion to Our Lady was all about. And so he wrote in the "Foreword":

> All who sincerely love the Southwest and its colorful history will concur with us in congratulating and blessing Dr. Sylvanus G. Morley for raising the true story of *Our Lady of the Conquest* from the relative obscurity of strictly historical pages, into a beautiful volume that will attract all and sundry. For perhaps more than any other work or stage study of New Mexico life and customs, this work reproduces the very soul of the Spanish Southwest, and of New Mexico in particular, by virtue of the very subject of which it treats – "Nuestra Señora, La Conquistadora." This *Our Lady of the Conquest* means much more than the ancient little image treasured for so long in our Cathedral of Saint Francis of Santa Fe; it means the spirit of deep-rooted Faith and Marian Devotion which characterized the Conquistadores of this land, no matter what their individual or collective faults, a spirit which united all alike, regardless of class or station, in conquering an enchanting but indomitable region because they themselves had been conquered by the grace and beauty of "our tainted nature's solitary boast"; she whom Don Diego de Vargas, the great Reconquistador, referred to as the "Queen and Patroness of this Kingdom of New Mexico and its Villa of the Holy Faith."

> May this knowledge not merely aid toward a fuller understanding of our land's wonderful history of

three centuries and a half, but also assist us, in the bettering of human relations, beneath the mantle of all that is good and beautiful.

The author merits the praise and gratitude of all lovers of history and true civilization. We of the Southwest owe him a tribute of devoted appreciation for shedding more light upon the grand past of a region of which Santa Fe is the heart and inspiration.

Archbishop Edwin V. Byrne

The out-of-print *Our Lady of the Conquest,* by our great Franciscan historian Fray Angélico Chávez, after whom the History Library and Photoarchives in downtown Santa Fe have been dedicated after his 1996 death, was the first documentary record of the history of La Conquistadora; it was published by the Historical Society of New Mexico in 1948 and reprinted in a handsome format, with Jean Charlot of Mexican lithographic fame doing the jacket and the fascinating sketch of Our Lady of the Conquest. It is a treasure-house of the story, the documentation, the interpretation of records, and the actual wording of the Spanish documentary fragments, all researched, studied, and interpreted by Fray Angélico Chávez. For example, Chávez interprets the Cofradía's inventories as documents drafted when one mayordomo turned over to another the wardrobe and accessories given to La Conquistadora by governors and other devout persons. And he describes the two chapels where the members of the Confraternity observe its festivities year-round, her special Lady Chapel attached to Saint Francis Cathedral and the Rosario Chapel. This is indeed Newmexicana at its documentary best, from the seventeenth century to the present, for La Cofradía continues to function.

The second Fray Angélico book, aptly entitled *The Autobiography of an Ancient Statue: La Conquistadora,* was first printed by the Saint Anthony Guild Press in 1954, Patterson, New Jersey, with Fray Angélico and La Conquistadora in regal robes as photographed by the late Laura Gilpin. This is the story as it were told by Our Lady herself, autobiographically, century after century, from Spain to Mexico to "la Nueva Mexico"; and it covers our ancestors in a flowing genealogical pattern, at a time when the Cofradía covered the entire "Ancient Kingdom of New Mexico" from the El Paso-Juárez area north to San Luis in southern border of Colorado, where our ancestors settled in the 1850s. Its membership still comes from this entire region of the Southwest plus other areas of the United States, being inclusionary in its membership of anyone who truly loves La Conquistadora, Our Lady of Peace.

Why La Conquistadora and La Guadalupe Are the Same

Here we are in 1998 celebrating the Cuarto Centennial of the Oñate founding of "la Nueva Mexico" by our conquistador and poblador ancestors of twenty generations past, and we have an obligation to thank Almighty God publicly, throughout the entire "Ancient Kingdom of the New Mexico and its Villa Capital called Santa Fe," for it is very important to say "thank you" graciously and proudly as active Catholics of the Archdiocese of Santa Fe, the Texas Diocese of El Paso, the Diocese of Las Cruces, the Diocese of Gallup, and the Colorado Diocese of Pueblo, all the regions comprised in 1598 by the "Kingdom and Provinces of Tierra Adentro del Norte." Our Lady is still Queen and Patroness of the entire region, and we continue to reverence her, to venerate both her image as Guadalupe of Tepeyac and her image as Our Lady of the Rosary, La Conquistadora. Many Indians of areas outside New Mexico were beginning to disapprove the ancient Spanish title "Conquistadora" because it derived from "conquistar," which they wrongly translated as "conquest by war and sword." But Dr. Thomas Chávez, Fray Angélico's historian-nephew and successor, explained at the Santa Fe Fiestas of 1990 that the correct translation of "conquistar" is "to unify," as in the 718-1492 Reconquista de España. And our good historian-priest, Rev. Jerome Martínez y Alire, current pastor of the unique mission-style modern parish church called in honor of La Conquistadora "Santa María de la Paz," also gave us beforehand the other interesting translation of "Conquistadora" that calls her in simple English, with lots of meaning and gusto, "Our Lady of Conquering Love of All Peoples, Our Lady of Peace." A good translation is a blessing in our modern times!

But for a better Christian approach to coexistence with the Pueblo Indians and others of the American Southwest, it was thought better not to change her title "La Conquistadora" but to add yet another title to fit the modern day. So Archbishop Roberto F. Sánchez *added* "de la Paz" to her ancient titles of The Assumption of Our Lady (1625), la Inmaculada, the Immaculate Conception (seventeenth century), and Our Lady of the Rosary (since the 1570 rosary victory at Lepanto when and Pius V, the saintly rosary pope, gave the Church the feast of the Holy Rosary).

Oración a la Madre de Dios:

Virgen santa, madre mía, con títulos del Pilar, Inmaculada, Guadalupana, Conquistadora, del Rosario y del Escapulario consagracional, victoriosa Reina de la Paz, esperando vuestro triunfante-corazón de la paz mundial, aquí pido, oh luz hermosa, claro día, sol y luna del cielo, abogada, patrona y reina nuestra, qué las tierras aragonesas del Pilar en Zaragoza, Monte del Tepeyac, oh madre santísima Guadalupana! En Nuevo México te amamos como reina y patrona de vuestro antiguo reino y de Santa Fe, todos estos te dignaste de visitar, estos pueblos qué te rezan, de tu amor celestial, muchos favores; te pedimos ahora y mañana, oh Madre nuestra, ruega por nosotros. Amen.

Prayer to the Mother of God:

Holy Virgen, our mother, with many titles of the Pillar, Immaculate, Guadalupana, Lady of Conquering Love, Lady of the Rosary, and Scapular of our Consecration! And waiting for the triumphant heart of world peace, we beg you, oh beautiful light, clearest day, sun, moon, and stars, advocate, our patroness and queen, may you deign to visit the Aragonese site of Our Lady of the Pillar, Mount Tepeyac, Juan Diego's site of the Guadalupana image, and in New Mexico your ancient Kingdom and Provinces and our City of the Holy Faith, and all of us; and thus we pray thee for help and the many favors we ask daily: oh sweet mother, pray for us all. Amen.

Why So Many Marian Titles?

For almost two thousand years Marian devotion has flourished in Spain and thus in todo el Mundo Hispánico, including the southwestern United States, and so we have been privileged to inherit as our Catholic Marian heritage from apostolic times, since 53 A.D. and Santiago, Saint James the Greater, a host of Marian titles that have great and providential meaning in our liturgical and scriptural and devotional lives so it will become that much more comprehensive of the life of the Gospel. We need these (and many more saints) to help us to emulate the life of Jesus Christ our Lord and Redeemer and the virtues and prerogatives of His and Our Blessed Mother – "our tainted nature's solitary boast" as the poet warns us. And so we the Indo-Hispanics are not in the least shy nor worried about our cumulative past, for each Marian title goes right along those of our Divine Lord; and, the many saints and blessed (and causes in Rome, as well, in our modern times); for we are "peregrinos hacia el Cielo – pilgrims on our journey to Heaven" and we need all the help we can get, unto our eventual salvation!

It is truly wise to explain briefly the variety of titles of Our Lord and Our Lady and some of our favorite intercessor saints as well:

Mother of God, Solemnity, January 1.

Our Lady's Annunciation to be the Mother of God, March 25.

Our Lady's Visitation to her cousin Elizabeth, plus Saint John the Baptist.

The Birth of Our Lord, Our Lady's Motherhood.

Nuestra Señora de la Leche, the Nursing Mother.

La Dolorosa, Our Lady at the Foot of the Cross, Friday before Good Friday, Viernes de Dolores.

Our Lady at the Resurrection, first Retreat Mistress at the Cenacle.

Feast of Pentecost, Our Lady and the Apostles and the Early Church.

Historical Titles of Spain's Conversion, 53 A.D. to 1998.

Santa María la Real de Jerusalén, to whom Santiago prayed at Zaragoza.

La Virgen del Pilar de Zaragoza, 53 A.D.

Santiago de Compostela, tomb, city, and pilgrimage center to Nuestro Primer Maestro de la Fe.

La Reina de los Mártires, from earliest times to present times.

Nuestra Señora de Covadonga, Asturias, beginning of "La Reconquista de España," 718-1492 A.D.

La Virgen de Guadalupe de Extremadura, thirteenth century, "The Reina de La Hispanidad."

La Virgen del Sagrario en Toledo, Diocesis Primicial de España.

Titulares de Regiones de España – por dondequiera.

Nuestra Señora de las Angustias, Granada, 1491.

La Rabida, en Colón.

Nuestra Señora La Antigua de Sevilla, Nuestra Señora de Buenos Aires.

Nuestra Señora del Santo Niño de Atocha, Madrid, eleventh century.

Nuestra Señora de Altagracia, Primer Diócesis en las Américas, 1494.

La Inmaculada Concepción de María, a Franciscan promotion everywhere.

Santa María de Guadalupe de México, 1531.

La Conquistadora de Santa Fe y de "la Nueva México," since 1598 and ongoing from 1625 to 1998.

Los Santos Patronos y Favoritas, en España y en las Américas:

Mártires de persecución en México (1910 sqq.) y en España (1934-39).

Santiago, San Juan Evangelists, los Apóstoles.

Mártires primeros: San Esteban de Jerusalén; San Lorenzo, mártir-diácono de España y Roma.

Millares de mártires de cada siglo de la Cristiandad en España.

Los Primeros Seis Obispos bajo Santiago, mártires todos.

Santa Teresa de Ávila, San Juan de la Cruz, San Pedro de Alcántara, sixteenth century.

San Francisco de Asís, San Antonio el Portugués y Santo Domingo Guzmán; San Juan de Ávila, San Ignacio del Loyola, San Francisco Javier, San Francisco de Borja, San Luis Gonzaga, San Juan de Ribera, San Juan de Ortega, San Millán, Santo Tomás Villanueva.

Los santos y mártires y causes en todas las Américas: Santa Rosa
de Lima, San Martín de Porres, San Juan Macías, San Pedro
Claver, Santa Mariana de Jesús del Ecuador, Hermano San
Miguel del Ecuador.

San Felipe de Jesús de México y Mártires de Japon y China, las
Filipinas.

Los 39 Mártires Franciscanos de la Nueva México.

Beato Juan Diego (1531).

Los Tres Ninos-Mártires de México 1545 en Taxcala.

Beato Miguel Pro, S.J.

Mártir Arzobispo Oscar Romero de San Salvador, y muchos
Compañeros.

En Sudamérica también: San Toribio de Mogrovejo, Arzobispo
de Lima; San Ezequiel, Obispo de Pasto, Colombia; San
Luis Beltran, Colombia; Los Mártires de Paraguay; San Francisco Solano.

Beata Laura, Niña-Mártir de Argentina-Chile, Santa Teresa de
Chile.

Beato Andrés Hurtado, S.J., de Chile; San Pedro de Betancurt de
Guatemala; y un sinnúmero de santos, beatos y millares
de causas.

The Arrival of the Catholic Faith and Its Growth in the Roswell and Chaves County Area

Josephine Gutiérrez

First of all I want to share with you how I first came to do the research from which this paper is taken. My parents are northern New Mexico natives, and all four of my grandparents have ancestral roots leading back to several of the Oñate colonists who came to New Mexico in 1598. I was three years old when my family moved to Roswell where I grew up, went to school, and have lived a large part of my life. In 1978 Father John Kramer, O.F.M., asked me to help with a seventy-fifth anniversary history project about St. John's Parish in Roswell.

Researching this project created as many or more questions than it answered for me. I was appalled at the lack of recorded information about the early Hispanic presence both in the church history and in the local Roswell and Chaves County histories. It was almost as if the Hispanic presence did not exist and had never existed in the southeastern New Mexico area.

Now let us set the stage, that is to say, the time and locale for the arrival, planting, and growth of the seed of Catholicism in what is today the Chaves County area of the Pecos Valley.

In 1582 the Antonio de Espejo expedition had traveled the route southward down the Pecos River taking them past the location of present day Roswell. In 1590 Gaspar Castaño de Sosa had crossed the area leading an ill-fated unauthorized expedition up the Pecos River.

It appears the first Hispanic settlement with any semblance of permanence in the southeastern New Mexico area was in the very late 1840s or early 1850s at Las Placitas del Rio Bonito (today known as Lincoln, maybe even better known as Billy the Kid country). It was not until the late 1840s, when New Mexico had come under the jurisdiction of the United States, that the conditions became favorable for settlement in southeastern New Mexico.[1]

In 1850 New Mexico had just become a part of the United States, and the area that is today Chaves County was uninhabited other than by nomadic Mescalero Apaches who had long roamed the southern part of New Mexico and adjoining land in Texas and Mexico from their "home area" in the White, Sacramento, and Guadalupe Mountains. On May 4, 1855, the United States Government established Fort Stanton, some seventy miles west of present day Roswell, to help control the Mescalero Apaches. Seeing an economic opportunity to supply meat and other foodstuffs for the fort, Hispanic colonists from the Manzano area began to drift down to the Hondo Valley and settled in the Rio Bonito area.

The 1860 census reflected that the Rio Bonito Precinct had a little over two hundred and ninety men, women, and children. Ninety-two percent of them were born in New Mexico. Immigrants from outside New Mexico included seventeen from Missouri and eleven from Canada.[2] In 1866 Bishop Lamy visited the Rio Bonito country.[3] The very next year the *Catholic Directory* indicated that the Rio Bonito chapel was under construction.

At about this same time, in 1866 and 1867, La Plaza de San José de Missouri (commonly referred to as "Missouri Plaza"), the first recorded settlement in present-day Chaves County, was started by a group of Hispanic settlers, many of them from Manzano. This settlement was located approximately fifteen miles west of what is today Roswell.

At that time the nearest settlement in the area was La Placita, later named Lincoln, on the Rio Bonito. There were no settlements east and southeast as far as Fort McKavett, Texas, a distance of about four hundred miles. At the time of the settlement of Missouri Plaza there were no ranches on the Pecos River between Fort Sumner and the Horsehead Crossing, a distance of about two hundred miles.[4]

Three reasons are usually given for the settlement of Missouri Plaza, that it was the first place and one of the best on the Rio Hondo where the land flattened enough that significant farming could be done, that coincidentally it was equidistant between Fort Sumner and Fort Stanton so that grain and meat could be supplied to both forts, and that other than Puerto de Luna further up the Pecos it was the easternmost settlement in New Mexico at that time.[5]

On September 25, 1868, the Vicariate Apostolic of Arizona was created. Lincoln County spent its first five years under Bishop Salpointe of Tucson, not Bishop Lamy in Santa Fe, and Lincoln County also included at that time the area that is today Chaves County. The Capilla del Rio Bonito (Lincoln) was again a mission chapel but attached at this time to Tularosa rather than Manzano. The Oratorio de San José appears on the Tularosa parish records in March 1870. The oratory was located at Missouri Plaza, which was the seat of Precinct Three, with its own justice of the peace, its own constable, and a store owned by Rufus C. Vose. If the number of baptisms administered at the oratory is any indication, Missouri Plaza had a very active quasi-parish for as long as the settlement lasted.[6]

However, the settlement of La Plaza de San José was shortlived. It lasted into the early or mid-1870s when the Hispanic settlers in the upper part of the Rio Hondo, Rio Bonito and Rio Ruidoso began irrigating to such an extent that the lower Rio Hondo began drying up. Many settlers living in La Plaza de San José (Missouri Plaza) moved to Picacho and to other settlements on the rivers.[7]

In about 1872, Van Smith, who was to name Roswell after his father Roswell Smith, arrived in the area. One historian describes the founding of Roswell in these words:

> Before the birth of the town of Roswell, there were some homes built in the area. Crude adobe shacks, but homes nevertheless, and the community Rio Hondo, later to become Roswell, was established. There was an acequia, or ditch, for irrigating small patches of gardens and fields, running from North Spring River and crossing that area on which later was to be built the Chaves County courthouse. Here along the Hondo was considerable cultivated land.[8]

On the head of the North Spring River in the vicinity immediately west of what is today Roswell was a large camp of Mexican
families, some of them quite well-to-do sheepmen, who had started
to dig a large irrigation ditch. For some reason they were forced to
abandon their project. Part of them returned to their homes on
the Rio Grande, but ten of these families joined the little settlement on the Berrendo.[9]

By 1880 there were four buildings in Roswell, two homes, a
blacksmith shop, and a combination general store and post office.[10] In 1880 Lincoln appeared in the *Catholic Directory* as a new
parish in the Santa Fe Archdiocese with the Reverend José
Sambrano Tafoya as pastor with responsibility for several new
settlements.

In 1894 activity in Roswell began to bustle when the first
passenger train arrived from Eddy (today known as Carlsbad).
Roswell now had one thousand residents, more than tripling the
population in a three-year period. By 1895 the *Catholic Directory*
indicates Lincoln as the parish of St. John the Baptist with Father
L. Migeon serving as pastor and also attending to San Patricio,
Torres Ranch, Ruidoso, Picacho, Picacho Abajo, Fort Stanton,
Roswell, White Oaks, Nogal, Bonito City, Las Palas, and Las Tablas.
Church records indicate that in 1896 the Archbishop visited the
area for confirmations. Roswell was at the end of the list with
forty-nine confirmations.

The Roswell *Register* for April 1, 1896, noted that "Father
Migeon of Lincoln conducted services last Sunday in Roswell.
The good father is a regular visitor to Roswell and is doing a
splendid work here. Roswell is soon to have a Catholic Church,
so we are informed."

In the years just prior to the turn of the century, the German
Carmelite fathers from Stanton, Texas, had been coming to Eddy
(Carlsbad) on the Pecos Valley Railroad and also made a few
visits to the Roswell area.[11]

At the turn of the century in 1900 the official U. S. Census
listed Chaves County with a population of 6,700 and Roswell as
having a population of 2,049, doubling its population in the previous six years.

On July 25, 1902, John Baptist Pitaval was consecrated Bishop
and appointed Auxiliary of Santa Fe. Later that same year, on

November 28, 1902, the following article appeared at the center of the front page of the Roswell *Register*:

CATHOLICS MAY ERECT PLACE OF WORSHIP
Project it is Said, Has Received Substantial
Encouragement. Sanitarium also Talked of.

The Rt. Rev. J. B. Pitoval [sic], bishop of Santa Fe, arrived here on Tuesday and was met by Father Giraund [sic] of Lincoln and Father Aultaman [sic] of Anton Chico, his visit here being for the purpose of ascertaining whether it is practicable to build a Catholic church here. It is understood that he has received such substantial encouragement that it is probable that a church will be built and that a sanitarium may be established here under the care of the Sisters of Mercy. The bishop celebrated mass at 8 a.m. yesterday and confirmed a class at 10 a.m. at the court house. The services were well attended by the Catholics of the city.

The Roswell confirmation record for this date lists 126 names with almost all the surnames being Hispanic. The confirmation records indicate the bishop visited and confirmed 658 Catholics in the extensive Lincoln-Chaves County area. No doubt this "survey" through the Confirmation trip led to serious consideration of establishing a parish in Roswell.

The establishment of area parishes at the time is best described by the account in Robert L. Wilken's *Anselm Weber, O.F.M., Missionary to the Navaho*:

The widening influence of the Navaho mission saw a new expression in Southwestern mission activity when in 1903 the Cincinnati Franciscans accepted the missions of southern New Mexico. ... Three Franciscans were appointed to the Roswell-Carlsbad mission.

The Roswell-Carlsbad news was not to have come out until Custos Raphael Hesse on April 21, 1903, accompanied Fathers Herbert, Eligius, and Brother Libor to Roswell. There they found scarcely a handful of Anglos who were Catholic, though Chihuahuita and the Berrendoes area were heavily populated by poor Mexican immigrants.[12] Because the Anglo-imposed segregation policy had already fixed the housing pattern, the missionaries unthinkingly fell in line and abetted the uneconomic and thoroughly un-Christian institution of racial segregation by founding two separate parishes, one for a dozen Anglos and the other to serve the several hundred Mexican families.

Father Herbert, the Roswell superior, took charge of the dozen Anglos, offering Mass in the flimsy, false-front bottling works, which looked like a stage prop for a western movie.

Father Eligius Kunkel built St. John the Baptist Church close to Chihuahuita, the Mexican quarter. Missions attaching to Roswell and Carlsbad included Hagerman, Elida, Portales, Clovis, and Melrose.

L. K. McGaffey, who owned considerable land on the South Hill, donated the lot on the southeast corner of Main and Deming streets for the location of a new church.

The Roswell, Chaves County parishes first appeared in the *Catholic Directory* the following year, 1904, listed as:

St. Peter's – Rev. Heribert Brockmann, O.F.M., Pastor.

San Juan Bautista, for Mexicans – Rev. Eligius Kunkel, in charge. (School for boys and girls in preparation).

Mission – Carlsbad, Eddy County (Tucson Diocese) S. Edward; S. José;

Stations – Hagerman, Chaves County; Portales, Roosevelt County; and other places along the P.V.N.E. railroad.

On November 14, 1903, the frame church for the Mexicans was completed[13] a few blocks east of Main Street, and in the spring of the following year the pastor opened a school for the Mexicans.

In September 1904, a small but determined congregation of St. Peter's Parish raised sufficient funds to dig and furnish a basement with a superstructure of wood; this basement served for Divine Services until a church was built.

In April 1906 Sister Mary Bonaventure came to Roswell as the first superior of the the Sisters of the Sorrowful Mother staffing the newly constructed St. Mary's Hospital.

In 1907 St. Peter's parish opened its parochial school, and a year later in 1908 the Franciscan Sisters from Lafayette, Indiana, took charge of it.

I must share with you at least a little of the interesting research of this era. It's from the reminiscences of Father Sixtus Kopp, O.F.M., and his first assignment after his ordination in 1912 was to take charge of the missions out from Roswell:

> On reaching Roswell, it did not take me long to find out that I had charge of all of the missions in Curry and Roosevelt counties and that part of Chaves county outside of the town of Roswell itself. That gave me the missions of Hagerman, Portales, Clovis, Melrose, and Elida.
>
> In those days there were no cars nor roads to get to these places and the only way it was at all possible for me to visit these missions was on the branch line of the Santa Fe railroad, with a change of trains at Clovis in order to get to the mission of Melrose. Clovis was already by far the largest and most important of all of these missions. Here I had over forty families. At Hagerman I had only about eight or ten Catholic families and at Melrose only about seven or eight families.
>
> Among my parishioners at Clovis I had six fine Catholic girls working at the Harvey House. These poor girls, some Irish and the rest Polish, came to me and told me that they had to work from six until noon every day and could not get off to Mass or the Sacraments at all on Sundays, so I arranged for them by saying Mass at five o'clock on one of the Monday mornings every month.

Both parishes were going about the task of building their present-day churches.

Bishop J. B. Pitaval, who had first come to Roswell in 1902 to investigate the need for a parish, had become Archbishop by April 27, 1913, when he dedicated the present St. John's church.[14] Four years later, on May 27, 1917, Archbishop Pitaval again came to Roswell to dedicate the present St. Peter's Church. In 1921 St. Peter's parish built a new school, and by 1922 St. John's had built their school. In May of 1925, Archbishop Daeger confirmed 320 children and adults, an indication of how much St. John's was growing. In August 1929 a building to serve both as a friary and as St. Peter's parsonage was completed. The object was to provide a suitable home for the Franciscan Fathers of the Province of St. John the Baptist of Cincinnati who, for health reasons, might be compelled to live in a high dry climate. The building, in Spanish Mission style, had twenty rooms in all.

The Sisters of Saint Casimir of Chicago, Illinois, arrived in Roswell in 1937 to take charge of the two Catholic schools.

During the 1930s St. John's began to reach out to new missions. In 1937 Father Fidelis Albrecht, O.F.M., at St. John's bought the first property on the North Hill in the hope of founding some day a new parish in the north part of Roswell. Father Lambert Brockman, O.F.M., became the pastor at St. John's in 1939. He and the people at Lake Arthur built a chapel and celebrated the first Mass there on January 20, 1945. Another chapel in the Dexter-Hagerman area, Greenfield, was completed in November 1945. Father Raynor Bartos, O.F.M., who became pastor of St. John's in July 1946, was responsible for many new developments in the parish. Building the rectory (which is today used solely for parish offices) was his first major project. He acquired barracks buildings to augment school facilities; some of these barracks buildings would later be moved to North Hill to become the St. Pius X chapel. Father Raynor instituted many innovative programs in the parish, and as far back as the 1940s – pre-pre-Vatican-II – he recruited lay volunteers and seminarians from Denver's St. Thomas Seminary to run a summer school program; he established a parish council long before parish councils were heard of in most places; and he started a Sunday parish bulletin, "La Voz de uno que clama en el desierto," for St. John the Baptist Parish. And if parish projects weren't enough, Father Raynor also saw to the enlargement of the mission chapels in Lake Arthur and Greenfield and purchased additional adjoining land on North Hill for a future church.

In 1948 a new branch was added to the Catholic family tree in the Roswell area. Mother Mary Immaculata and a small band of Poor Clare nuns from Chicago arrived to establish the new foundation of the seven-hundred-year-old Order of St. Clare.

The World War II years and the years following were a period of major growth for Roswell. The 1940 population of 13,482 mushroomed to almost 26,000 by 1950 – almost double in the ten-year period.

In 1953, Father Regis Darpel, O.F.M., began his service at St. John's. He put a great deal of emphasis on the spiritual growth and well-being of the parish. He devoted considerable energies and talents not only to the needs of the parish and the missions but also for the Poor Clares and the Sisters at St. Mary's Hospital. In 1954, with a donation from the Catholic Extension Society, he broke ground for a church in Dexter. It was completed during the following year, and on October 16, 1955, Archbishop Edwin Vincent Byrne dedicated it under the title of Our Lady of the Immaculate Conception.

One of Father Regis' greatest concerns was to develop the faith among the Catholics who lived in the northern section of Roswell. Father Fidelis and Father Raynor had as early as 1937 purchased property in this area. Father Lambert Brockman had started saying Mass in some of the homes, but this practice was dropped during the World War II years. In December 1954 Mass was started up again for the Catholics at North Hill in the homes of Frank Martínez and Ignacio Escalante. About 125 people were attending the two Masses at these homes on Sundays. In March 1955 the old St. John's barracks building that had been acquired earlier from the Prisoner of War Camp was moved to the North Hill property to serve as a church, and on April 10, 1955 the first Mass was celebrated at St. Pius X Chapel.

Father Martial Schmidts, O.F.M., was appointed administrator of St. Pius X in July 1956 and did much to improve the church and build up the faith community in the north part of Roswell.

The Franciscans from St. John's parish continued to care for St. Pius X until September 15, 1962 when a new parish was officially established in Roswell and a diocesan priest, Monsignor Bernard Burns, was put in charge. This new parish was dedicated to Our Lady of the Assumption.

At St. John's parish the baptisms, confirmations, weddings, funerals, confessions, etc. had been growing and growing. In October 1962 just as the new parish was established there were 743 Confirmations at St. Johns.

Some twenty years later, on October 18, 1982, Bishop Ricardo Ramírez was appointed the first Bishop of the new Las Cruces Diocese, which encompassed the southern area of New Mexico that had been a part of the El Paso Diocese and also included Lincoln and Chaves counties from the Santa Fe Archdiocese.

In closing, let us take a look at today's Catholic community in the Roswell and Chaves County area. What do we see?

Sadly, St. Mary's Hospital is no more. In 1989 the Sisters of the Sorrowful Mother sold the hospital to the Eastern New Mexico Medical Center for consolidation. In 1993 the Medical Center closed St. Mary's Hospital.

Our Poor Clare Monastery is celebrating its Golden Jubilee in 1998 and has three daughter houses in the United States and one in Europe. There are presently thirty-two Poor Clares at the Roswell Monastery.

We find the "newest parish on the block" – Assumption Parish – celebrating several notable anniversaries in 1997: sixty years ago (1937) the first property was purchased in anticipation of a parish in north Roswell; thirty-five years ago (1962) Assumption Parish was officially created; and ten years ago (1987) the building was completed and the present church dedicated.

Monsignor Robert Getz, the pastor and only priest at the parish, directs and ministers to a very active faith community of some 850 families. During the school year Monsignor Getz ministers also to the cadets at the New Mexico Military Institute.

At the Dexter parish, Immaculate Conception, and its missions in Lake Arthur and Hagerman, Deacon John Lucero is the officially appointed Pastoral Administrator. He capably and generously serves and ministers to a faith community with parishioners spread over a large geographic area.

A pastoral team of two Franciscans, Father Dennis Fountain, O.F.M., and Father Richard Young, O.F.M., share a joint ministry of St. Peter's and St. John's parishes.

Today St. Peter's is an active parish of some 450 families. This faith community makes a notable and very commendable contribution to the entire Roswell community by taking a leading role among the major Roswell churches in operating the Community Kitchen to feed the hungry. Another notable contribution from St. Peter's to our Roswell community is the Good Samaritan program to help the needy.

St. John's parish — San Juan Bautista, "the cradle of Catholicism in the Roswell area," the faith community where it all began over a hundred years ago — is still going strong with some twelve hundred families registered.

Notes

1. Courtesy of Freddie J. Romero, *Hispanic Settlement of Lincoln County*, October 7, 1993.
2. Billy Charles Patrick Cummings, *Frontier Parish*, p. 2.
3. Ibid., p. 4.
4. James D. Shinkle, "Missouri Plaza," p. 13.
5. Courtesy of Freddie J. Romero, *Hispanic Settlement of Lincoln County*, October 7, 1993.
6. Billy Charles Patrick Cummings, *Frontier Parish*, p. 13.
7. Courtesy of Freddie J. Romero, *Hispanic Settlement of Lincoln County*, October 7, 1993.
8. Ben R. Roche, *The Pioneer Period, Roundup on the Pecos*.
9. James D. Shinkle, *Reminiscences of Roswell Pioneers*, p. 39.
10. Ibid., p. 93.
11. Courtesy of Father Bob Wright, O.M.I., who alerted me to information in the Parish Register for 1895-1901, St. Joseph's Church, Stanton, Texas.
12. Letter of R. Hesse to A. Weber, May 25, 1903.
13. See Nancy Hanks, "Lamy's Legacy: Catholic Institutions in New Mexico," *Seeds of Struggle/Harvest of Faith*, p. 406, photo 22, Old Church of Saint John the Baptist.
14. See Hanks, *Seeds of Struggle/Harvest of Faith*, p. 406, photo 23, New Church of Saint John the Baptist.

The Priest Who Made Schools Bloom in the Desert: Peter Küppers, 1911-1957

Tomas Jaehn

On 10 March 1949 the *Santa Fe New Mexican's* front-page head-
line read: "Suit Demands Removal of Nuns From Public School
Positions." Many New Mexicans still remember the so-called
"Dixon Case,"[1] wherein a group of citizens sought to ban all Catho-
lic nuns and priests, who had taught Catholic doctrine in New
Mexico, from teaching in the public schools. The controversy, in
local and national news until the final ruling by the New Mexico
Supreme Court of 1951, signaled a new era of separation be-
tween New Mexico's religious and public education. Archbishop
Edwin V. Byrne (1943-1963) withdrew the religious teachers.
Otherwise, the Dixon case would have had, as historian Ferenc
Szasz has noted, "the potential to become a national Supreme
Court pathbreaker."[2]

Few, however, have ever heard of Peter Küppers, resident of
Dixon and parish priest of Peñasco-Dixon in Northern New
Mexico from 1921 to 1934. At the time of the lawsuit he had
already retired and was living on his fruit farm "Obscurana." During his tenure in the Peñasco-Dixon parish, he actually initiated
the climactic controversy by building the first Catholic school
and continued to play a part in the issue until 1951. Highly regarded among poor as well as politically influential Hispanics,
and friend to many well-known Anglos of the time, this obscure
immigrant from Germany wielded momentous influence over
not only the educational and spiritual well-being of New Mexicans but on their political and social lives as well. He carried so
much influence in Northern New Mexico that a differently

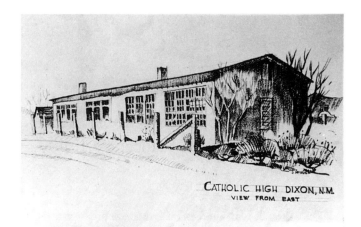

CATHOLIC HIGH DIXON, N.M.
VIEW FROM EAST

Figure 1. Illustration of Peter Küppers' Catholic High School which initiated the "Dixon Case" controversy (ca. 1934). Photograph courtesy Historic-Artistic Patrimony and Archives of the Archdiocese of Santa Fe.

minded fellow priest in the early 1930s called him the "Clerical Huey Long" and "Czar of Dixon."[3] In 1947, a reader responding to the *Time* article on the Dixon controversy, "Compromise in Santa Fe," still identified Küppers as one "who once ruled Dixon like a dictator and is still able to wield great political power behind the scenes."[4]

Küppers's significant political and social authority was fueled by his passion for the Hispanic people of Northern New Mexico and by his decidedly Catholic understanding of education. The young priest's grasp of the importance of the Church's role in education ran contrary to the opinions of many Anglo-Americans at the time. Poverty in New Mexico resulted from the fact, so their argument ran, that the Catholic Church kept the Spanish-speaking population ignorant "of reading, arithmetic, and other social and economic skills necessary for survival in the Anglo-American world."[5] In letters, in essays, and in his memoirs Küppers reiterated his convictions on Church-sponsored education. In an undated, unpublished paper "Religious Situation in New Mexico," Küppers explained, for instance, that assimilation to the Anglo-American culture required faith in the high ideals of Catholicism: "Give [the Spanish American] a good religious training and he will surpass all expectation in [Anglo-American] progressivism."[6] Considering that New Mexico's school system was still underdeveloped, Küppers may have grasped the situation like many other priests since Archbishop Lamy and tried to seize an opportunity to let the Catholic Church shape public schooling.[7] Because he passionately believed that Hispanic children, particularly in rural districts, needed a good Catholic-public education, Küppers emphasized on numerous occasions that "the highest goal of my ecclesiastical work among Spanish American children, who are often simply called Mexican, [is] to give what all children needed most: a good education."[8]

His uncompromising devotion also caused Peter Küppers to become a highly controversial figure within the Archdiocese. His methods for soliciting money and material for schools, recruiting teachers, and maintaining school buildings were often arguable, and reprimands from the Archdiocese in Santa Fe ranged from friendly criticism to outright chastisement. It depended who was in power. Archbishop Jean Baptiste Pitaval (1909-1918) had a somewhat tense relationship with Küppers, while Archbishop Albert Thomas Daeger (1919-1932), a man Küppers called " New Mexico's greatest and most humble archbishop," offered merely friendly, fatherly criticism. Daeger's successor, Rudolph Aloysius Gerken (1933-1943), kept Küppers's practices under close scrutiny. An increasing conflict between those two, combined with accusations of embezzlement and immorality against Küppers, led ultimately to Küppers's removal from his position as parish priest in Peñasco in December 1934. This chapter in the German priest's life may never be adequately resolved, remaining instead a myth of part gossip and part truth. And even an attempt to solve some of the controversy surrounding Küppers would go beyond the scope of this paper. Nevertheless, it should not detract from his service to the people in New Mexico.

Therefore, this paper will be limited to a brief sketch of Peter Küppers's life to give sufficient background to tackle his significant influence on Hispanics' education and spiritual life in Northern New Mexico. Primary sources for this paper come from the Historic-Artistic Patrimony and Archives of the Archdiocese of Santa Fe. There I found a draft of a typed autobiography, personal papers, parish files, and a few personnel files. The New Mexico

Archives and Record Center and the Museum of New Mexico also provided information about Küppers. In addition, I undertook several very rewarding field trips in San Miguel County and in the Peñasco-Dixon area where I gathered some oral history. I also located relatives of Küppers in Santa Clara, California, and in his birthplace in Germany.

Peter Küppers was born on 25 June 1885 in Kückhoven, Germany, the eldest of three children. His father was overly strict; his mother died when he was in his early teens. He did not get along with his father's second wife and soon left home for good. His autobiography indicates that his career choices were carpentry, which was his father's business, and the priesthood. Apparently, Küppers chose the latter, for he went to a seminary in Switzerland. The craftsmanship he had picked up in his father's shop, though, would come in handy once he settled in New Mexico. In 1911, the year he was ordained in the Cathedral of Cologne, Archbishop Pitaval visited Europe and recruited Peter Küppers and several other graduates from the Swiss seminary.[9]

Figure 2. Peter Küppers was devoted to children. Here he is shown entertaining young parishioners in one of the Peñasco-Dixon missions (ca. 1930). Photograph courtesy Historic-Artistic Patrimony and Archives of the Archdiocese of Santa Fe.

Küppers arrived in the United States in early 1912, and was "pretty furious that nobody in the United States spoke or understood German."[10] After a brief vacation in Pennsylvania, he undertook the long trip to New Mexico. Nothing in his memoirs or peronal letters indicates that he was prepared for this country in any way. In his memoirs he recalls that "it was difficult to get used to the thought [of living in New Mexico], and the more I studied New Mexico's geography, the more subdued I became." Like most immigrants to New Mexico since the early 1840s, he was discouraged at first by the unfamiliar sight of adobe buildings and by the poverty he encountered. He did not speak English or Spanish, nor was he familiar with New Mexican culture. Not surprisingly, comical situations arose, such as when he gave a sermon unwittingly in German for Spanish-speaking New Mexicans, or when he tried to communicate with prisoners at the penitentiary with little or no knowledge of English, or when he was tricked into eating his first bowl of chili.[11] His schooling in affluent Switzerland had not prepared him for the poverty and underdevelopment of New Mexico. What he brought with him, however, was a passion for people, a definite understanding of the value of education and distinct street smarts that would help him to succeed in his endeavors.

Once he arrived in Santa Fe, he adjusted quickly: "As Germans are used from childhood on to eat sauerkraut and to follow it with a mug of beer or a glass of buttermilk, and as the Irish eat their potatoes unpeeled, and as the French have wine with their dumplings, I had to get acquainted with new habits."[12] In the relatively comfortable environment of Santa Fe, he began to learn the languages and customs of the land. His devotion for the Spanish-American people was almost immediate and far more pronounced than that of other European newcomers. His first assignment as chaplain at the Guadalupe Church already demonstrates his activism and savvy in getting things done. When his parish priest was unfairly accused of pilfering the parish coffers, Küppers, with the help of some friends, managed to stall the proceedings and get himself elected to the church board until he could present the accurate account books to the Archbishop.[13]

When funds were lacking to complete the Guadalupe rectory, a few friends explained to him how to make money in

America. Through fund-raising efforts during the DeVargas procession and through theater performances, he collected $1000, enough to complete five rooms in the rectory and to install the first electric lighting in the church and rectory. By similar means he founded the Santa Fe chapter of the Knights of Columbus, furnished their hall with former Palace Hotel furniture, and established a library for them.[14]

He became bolder on his first mission assignment. On 23 December 1913 Archbishop Pitaval appointed Küppers parish priest of Chaperito, an isolated community east of Las Vegas with fifteen missions spread across the vast plains of Eastern San Miguel County. The parish needed many improvements, and he immediately began to fix buildings and build chapels in his missions. He worked hard to make the church in Chaperito more suitable, built chapels in La Garita and Sabinoso, and improved structures in Variadero and Los Torres. Küppers persuasively urged the local population to donate money and time to restore the early-nineteenth-century chapel in San Agustín. To improve the dismal education system, Küppers instructed his housekeeper to begin teaching school in Chaperito and Los Torres. The dedicated housekeeper sold her house in Santa Fe to support maintenance of the missions, and also supplemented mission expenses with her state income as a schoolteacher.[15]

Education has always been a point of contention between Catholics and Protestants. Both churches viewed parochial schooling as the key to the future in New Mexico, which had, prior to the early twentieth century, no school system to speak of. Each side began to set up parochial education programs, the Catholics worrying that public schools would be inevitably Protestant, and the Protestants fearing that the educational staff would be largely nuns and priests.[16]

Thus, it is not surprising that the presence of non-Catholic schools in Küppers's parish was a source of conflict for him, and his antagonism toward Protestant schools was already apparent in the 1910s in Chaperito. Although Protestant parochial schools provided their share of much-needed education, Küppers resented them as attempts to wean Catholic children and adults away from the faith.[17] So, like many of his contemporary Catholic priests, he tried to prevent Catholic children in his missions from attend-

ing the Protestant school in Trementina. With the help of influential politicians, he created new school districts and redrew the
boundaries of established ones to put the Protestant school at a
disadvantage. Once that was accomplished, he set out to improve
education and find new and acceptable school buildings for his
children.

With occasional help from villagers, he built a schoolhouse
and converted the priest's residence into a dormitory for sisters.
On 15 November 1916 the new parochial school, which was to
function as public school as well, was dedicated in Chaperito.[18]
Now all he needed were sisters to teach. Archbishop Pitaval,
though glad to see the Loretto Sisters come to Chaperito, cautioned Küppers "that it is very difficult, if not impossible, to get
[sisters], for our poor missions."[19] Küppers's efforts to find sisters
for Chaperito were indeed unsuccessful until he heard that sisters of a Spanish order were about evicted from Mexico and
needed a new home. He saw his chance and accepted their offer
to relocate without consulting with the Archdiocese in Santa
Fe. Pitaval was irritated. The sisters did not speak a word of English,
and Küppers's attempts to hide this small problem only fueled
Pitaval's anger. Furthermore, opposition began to form among
the school board and the local citizens. On 16 May 1917, less than
six months later, Küppers wrote to Pitaval that "the parochial
school at Chaperito was discontinued on account of the uncalled
for, unfriendly attitude of Your Grace against my poor refugee
sisters."[20]

That this "misunderstanding," as Küppers saw it, did not resulted in a serious reprimand was due to Pitaval's general agreement with Küppers over the importance of Catholic schools.
Pitaval strongly felt the need for Catholic schools; the lack of them
was "the weak point in the Catholic fortress," as he pointed out in
an address in 1909.[21] In Küppers's case, however, the archbishop
had to consider the larger ramifications of New Mexico's official
language of instruction, the laws for public schooling in general,
and the image of the Catholic Church, which gave him little choice
but to pressure Küppers to relieve the sisters.

Generally, the New Mexico statutes to secure public education had failed to make education truly public, and Küppers, in
particular, was not really devoted to keeping public and paro-

chial schools strictly separate.²² Yet at that time he blamed the sisters for the demise of the schools in Chaperito.²³ In his memoirs, some twenty-five years, later he apologized. Semi-ruefully, he admitted that perhaps he was most guilty because he wanted these non-English speaking sisters to teach public and parochial schools and, in turn, receive public funding.²⁴

Prior to the departure of the sisters, Küppers convinced the state school board to set up an election for bonds to build a new public school building. A savvy lobbyist, he promoted the new school building during his Sunday services and tried to counter his enemies' argument that the capital outlay and the interest on the new school bonds would run extremely high. (Incidentally, he would reverse his position in Dixon some thirty years later, when the existence of his own school was at stake.)²⁵ He also attempted to persuade the sisters to vote should that be necessary for victory. The sisters, however, refused to vote, feeling they needed special permission from their provincial. In his disappointment and anger, Küppers himself forgot to vote and the bond for the school building failed.²⁶

Figure 3. The Sabinoso chapel in the Chaperito parish is one of the many legacies of Peter Küppers' work in New Mexico (1997). Photograph by the Author.

Küppers's tenure in Chaperito narrowly focused on Catholic education. Although Küppers knew that English was supposed to be the official language of instruction in public schools, he learned quickly that the law "was operating with marginal effectiveness over most of the territory."[27] He argued in his memoirs that the nuns were good teachers with sound methodology and the fact that they spoke little or no English was irrelevant; besides, this minor point could have been easily fixed with the School Board. He felt it was no different from the fact that "today teachers, and Sisters included, don't speak Spanish but teach it in school."[28]

At Chaperito Küppers demonstrated his creative means to the perennial problem of funding Catholic schools and proved successful both in fundraising and politicking to improve schools and schooling.[29] His methods inevitably created tensions with his superiors. Pitaval reminded him more than once with "friendly advice" that he was "somewhat careless in business matters." Apparently Küppers did not heed the Archbishop's advice, and Pitaval's letters became more stern: "[F]rom now on, you will do exactly what every other priest does, that is, settle all your accounts with the Chancery, as well as with the Ordinary, on or before the 1st of February of every year."[30] In educational matters, too, Pitaval attempted to control Küppers's zealous activities: "Be it well understood, and I repeat it for the last time, that the work you intend to carry on, must be exclusively confined to your parish and missions. In abiding by this understanding, and agreement, you will save your Archbishop, the pastor of Chaperito, and the Sisters who came there upon your request, lots of trouble."[31]

Although Pitaval was concerned about some of the methods Küppers used, there is little indication of concern from Archbishop Daeger, who was appointed in 1919. A former parish mission priest in New Mexico himself, Daeger understood parish conditions and left local priests fairly free rein in handling their own affairs.[32] In addition, Küppers seems to have had a genuinely cordial relationship with his former fellow priest, now Archbishop, which benefited Küppers's almost fanatical quest to spread the Catholic faith, to provide education, and to minimize poverty among his parishioners.[33]

In 1921, against Küppers's wishes, Archbishop Daeger abruptly transferred his friend to the Peñasco mission – possibly because of an impending lawsuit over contested property between Küppers and the people of Chaperito. So Küppers exchanged the wide-open rangelands of Eastern San Miguel County for the mountainous region of Taos and Rio Arriba Counties. There he continued his quest for better schools and education using methods similar to those he used in Chaperito. The school situation in the Peñasco parish was dismal when Küppers arrived. There was no school at all in Peñasco and only Presbyterian ones in Dixon and Chamisal. In 1922 he founded the first Catholic school in Dixon (along with the church he had built in 1921, it burned down in 1928). He erected new school buildings, financed largely by himself and the Catholic Ladies of Columbus, Ohio.[34] In Peñasco, he opened a parochial and a public school with sisters in charge of both. In 1931, he opened a fully-accredited high school. While the county and state paid the sisters' salaries, the buildings and equipment belonged to the Archdiocese. State funds and donations from the East often paid for the maintenance of the schools. Daeger encouraged Küppers to make outside appeals for money and clothing, which the priest did with "tear-jerking form letters."[35] Soon, steady donations of money from the Catholic Ladies of Columbus became a reliable source of revenue. Since this northern New Mexico area was a contested battlefield between Protestant, Catholic, and other faiths and since the Catholic Church feared the competition in education from the other denominations, Küppers's activities were condoned by his supervisors and even encouraged.[36]

Within a short period of time in Peñasco, Küppers had built a political and social base among the local population and especially gained the support of the Penitentes, an Hispanic lay brotherhood of northern New Mexico; the brothers pledge themselves to Christian devotions without completely withdrawing from the daily world.[37] During Küppers's time in Peñasco, the Penitentes saw substantial changes. With the influx of many Anglo-Americans during the first decade of the twentieth century, village life grew more heterogeneous. Outsiders intruded more and more often on Penitente rituals, seeing them as tourist attractions,[38] and the same rituals caused conflicts within the church hierarchy.

Some of these customs persisted in New Mexico into the twentieth century, due in part to the extreme isolation of the people.[39]
Küppers, like Archbishop Daeger, was familiar with and sympa-
thetic toward the Penitentes, asking only that they conduct their
exercises privately.[40] Daeger even requested that Küppers write a
book on the Penitentes, and Küppers worked on a manuscript he
had entitled "Mysteries of the Mountains." At some point he stated
in a letter to Archbishop Gerken that the manuscript was ready
and that he had plans to send it to the A. A. Knopf publishing
house in New York.[41]

Küppers considered himself a confidant of the Penitentes,
for they came to him for advice and counsel and he felt he could
influence them into following church rules. He said annual
Masses and funeral Masses for them "for nothing in some instances, for three dollars in others."[42] In turn, he was a staunch
defender of their lifeways. In fact, in his memoirs, he contended
that the Catholic faith in New Mexico would be better off if more
Spanish Americans belonged to *moradas*.[43] The brothers expressed
their devotion to the Catholic faith and their opposition to sending their children to Protestant schools.[44] He defended Penitentes
against attacks from outsiders. When sensationalized publications
appeared calling them fanatics or their ceremonies horrible,
Küppers was quick to respond, defending them as law-abiding
citizens, pious, well-meaning, and without any horrors in their
ceremonies.[45] He described them as citizens of the United States
who fought for their country in World War I and as Spanish
Americans who knew their Catholic religion. He also used his
articles to plug the excellent schools in northern New Mexico
and to attack such Anglo-American deficiencies as tenement
housing in urban areas.[46]

Küppers remained loyal to the Penitentes throughout his
life, even under Archbishop Gerken, whose policy was more
diplomatic and politically driven. When Küppers asked Gerken
to authorize his forthcoming manuscript, the Archbishop replied
that

> since the book deals with the Penitentes of New
> Mexico, I will give you neither of the requested en-
> dorsements [Imprimatur or Nihil obstat], since, it
> might be detrimental. However, I will be glad to give

> my endorsement of the book, if the contents will
> not be objectionable to the Penitentes in general.
> Because, there are so many of these people in our
> Diocese, we will have to be very careful not to an-
> tagonize them unnecessarily.[47]

Küppers's successor in Peñasco apparently had his own misgiv-
ings about them, saying that "the Penitentes are the greatest drawback to the spiritual uplift of the parish. [A]ll the preaching you
do is in vain."[48]

Though the Penitentes represented a significant part of his
power structure, Küppers never understood himself as taking a
politically active role. In a letter to Governor Richard Dillon responding to accusations that he had "mixed into politics," he wrote
that a "Catholic priest should not mix into politics."[49] But contrary
to his own perception, Küppers was highly political beyond the
normal influence of a parish priest. In Chaperito he helped re-
draw school district boundaries. In Peñasco he asked for favors to
place his parishioners in better paying state jobs, he tried to intervene on their behalf with judicial authorities, and he made his
unsolicited opinions known to politicians on issues such as teachers' retirement funds and free textbooks.[50] His political influence
was most pronounced on school issues. He tangled with the school
board over parochial and state school issues, co-founded the
Peñasco Independent School District, and became its first superintendent. This gave his adversaries excellent ammunition: "If a
Priest is made Superintendent here and the schools remain independent of the County, the priest will be forced into politics at
election times in order to oppose the candidates."[51]

Küppers's social position and political strength were secure
among the Hispanic people in his parish, but his financial situation was not, despite donations and the State funds that Küppers
controlled. On at least two occasions he requested the Archbishop's
endorsement to divert public funds from the sisters' salaries directly to his schools. The Archbishop, though agreeing with the
idea in principal, refused to endorse the proposal without the
sisters' approval. Instead he counseled Küppers "to consider the
trust, that is placed in you, as an official entitled to countersign
checks, as most sacred, and that you pay the sisters according to

their contract promptly, so that we will not bring any discredit upon the Church in our Diocese and state."[52]

Ever since he accepted his first mission, Küppers controlled two nominally separate schools: a public school system and a parallel Catholic parochial system. For years the two systems overlapped in his parishes where funding was never enough for his ambitious school projects.[53] Under Daeger, Küppers's fiscal matters were rarely scrutinized, but this changed when Daeger tragically fell to his death and Rudolph Gerken was appointed the new Archbishop of Santa Fe. While Küppers's behavior and methods always rose eyebrows in Santa Fe, it is not quite clear why the rift between him and Gerken was so immediate. Gerken's administration pursued "the American way" and kept much tighter control of his diocese than did his predecessors. He was also more forceful in his attempts to bring the Penitentes, one of Küppers's main support groups, in line with church doctrine.[54] Gerken questioned Küppers's practices at every turn, and Küppers,

Figure 4. Funding shortages forced Küppers and the sisters to build and repair the parish buildings themselves. In this photograph repairs are being made to one of the many church buildings in the Peñasco-Dixon parish (ca. 1925). Photograph courtesy Historic-Artistic Patrimony and Archives of the Archdiocese of Santa Fe.

who for decades had had little outside supervision, took Gerken's concerns personally. That he may have entertained hopes of becoming Archbishop himself could have put an additional strain on his relationship with Gerken.[55]

In any event, Küppers was not willing to accept Gerken's reign nor to follow his more decisive policy to separate church and state. Küppers refused to produce fiscal statements or legal documents on demand, and he continued to amass debts to expand his programs at a time when the Depression kept monies tight in the church and in the village communities. On numerous occasions, Gerken was forced to bail him out of his obligations.[56] Furthermore, Küppers stalled in visiting Gerken despite repeated requests from the Archbishop. His refusals to visit caused Gerken, in his letters, to put the phrase "when I see you next week" into quotation marks.[57] Küppers's unwillingness to see the Archbishop, combined with accusations by fellow priests that he was embezzling money for personal gain and that he was – as the Archbishop called it – "obligated to the two women" (his two long-time housekeepers) increasingly eroded his position within the clergy. In December 1934, Küppers was forced to resign from his post as parish priest and was prohibited from saying Mass.

Küppers withdrew from church life and settled down on his orchard "Obscurana" in Dixon. He continued to shape school policy as superintendent until January 1935, when he resigned due to poor health, but thereafter he remained active in the schools as a private citizen.[58] He continued to write letters to political friends in Santa Fe on behalf of his former parishioners, to distribute clothing among the needy, and to help them fill out government forms. He also maintained contact with the Catholic Ladies back in Columbus.[59] He improved his relationship with the Archbishop to the point that they exchanged cordial letters, written in German, and in early 1936 he was reinstated as pastor of the newly created Dixon parish. Because he was still in ill health, he soon resigned this parish. Yet he remained active in the community and tended to his orchard. In 1957 he was taken to a hospital in Colorado Springs where he died on 23 March 1957, six years after the Dixon Case was decided and thirty-five years after he had built his first school in Dixon.

What was Küppers's legacy? From a young inexperienced German priest who learned the ropes in Santa Fe and Chaperito, he developed into an influential figure felt far beyond the parishes of Peñasco and Dixon. As far as the records tell, he accepted the northern New Mexican people wholeheartedly and without reservation and not as "an inferior breed of *pinto* sheep in the Lord's fold,"[60] the more common reaction Angélico Chávez ascribes to northern European clergy. Early on Küppers promoted a policy of service, accommodation to cultural traditions, and social determination that put him ahead of many of his fellow priests.[61] He built and improved chapels, churches, and school buildings. At a time when there was little education, Catholic or otherwise, and the public school issue was still a gray area, Küppers took it upon himself to provide good education. When both Chaperito and Peñasco were still far removed from the politics of Santa Fe and Albuquerque, he created the political influence

Figure 5. Küppers, now retired, stands in front of his house near Dixon with his housekeepers (1940s). Photograph courtesy Kathleen Gardiser, Mountain View, Calif.

Figure 6. A distinguished Peter Küppers poses for the camera (ca. 1955). Photograph courtesy Historic-Artistic Patrimony and Archives of the Archdiocese of Santa Fe.

necessary for his projects to succeed. Ever in need of cash for his ambitious projects, Küppers occasionally mixed state funds, Catholic funds, private donations, and personal money, and not surprisingly called in political favors. In his zeal to succeed he created a few adversaries along the way among his own clergy and among Protestants, and probably he lost a few Hispanic friends as well.

In the 1930s, Küppers did not understand the changing sentiment that promoted further separation of church and state, and he also found it difficult to conform to rapidly changing policies in the Archdiocese. In this respect he resembles Padre Antonio José Martínez, who, as one historian suggested, "had been too long accustomed to be boss in his bailiwick, and had become too deeply enmeshed in his own casuistry to listen to the voice of reason."[62] Küppers himself felt he resembled Padre Martínez. In an unpublished essay he wrote about Martínez, conflict between priest and archbishop loom prominently and the priest's devotion to the local Hispanic community is conspicuous. Overall, Küppers saw Martínez as a priest whose greatest talents went astray from the church and who should have received compassion rather than ostracism.[63]

In his eagerness to accomplish his visions, Küppers neglected to see that times had changed and that public schools were understood to be no longer the domain of a priest. The Dixon case symbolized New Mexico's "move away from a state where Roman Catholics dominated the religious and the political culture,"[64] when in 1951 the New Mexico Supreme Court upheld the ruling of the District Court and barred nuns, priests, and brothers from teaching in public schools of New Mexico. Even Peter Küppers finally had to acknowledge the change.

Notes

1.   The "Dixon case" was officially known as Zeller et al. v. Huff et al., No. 5332. *Report of Cases Determined in the Supreme Court and Court of Appeals of the State of New Mexico*, vol. 55 (St. Paul, MN: West Publishing Co., 1951), 501.

2.   Ferenc M. Szasz, "The United States and New Mexico: A Twentieth Century Comparative Religious History," in Ferenc M. Szasz

and Richard W. Etulain, eds., *Religion in Modern New Mexico* (Albuquerque: University of New Mexico Press, 1997), 187.

3.   R.H. Lewis to Archbishop Gerken, 21 November 1934, Peñasco Parish File (hereafter PPF), Folder IV, Historic-Artistic Patrimony and Archives of the Archdiocese of Santa Fe, Santa Fe, NM (hereafter HAPA).

4.   Arthur Montgomery to Editor of *Time*, 25 September 1947. Robert Jones Collection, Folder 3, "Dixon School Case, 1947-1950," State Record Center and Archives, Santa Fe, NM.

5.   Randi Jones Walker, *Protestantism in the Sangre de Cristos, 1850-1920* (Albuquerque: University of New Mexico Press, 1991), 30.

6.   Peter Küppers, "Religious Situation in New Mexico," Peter Küppers Collection (hereafter PKC), HAPA.

7.   Susan M. Yohn, *Contest of Faiths: Missionary Women and Pluralism in the American Southwest* (Ithaca: NY: Cornell University Press, 1995), 77.

8.   Peter Küppers, "Ein Deutscher Pfarrer in Neu Mexico" (A German Priest in New Mexico), Chapter "Nach Chaperito," 24. The typed manuscript is part of the PKC; it is a rough draft in German with many grammatical and syntactical errors. Translations are mine.

9.   Küppers was part of a trend of German secular clergy that began by 1880 to supplant the French clergy dominance in New Mexico. Nancy Nell Hanks, "Not of this Earth: An Historical Geography of French Secular Clergy in the Archdiocese of Santa Fe, 1850-1912" (Ph.D. diss., University of Oklahoma, 1993), 125.

10. "Deutscher Pfarrer," Chapter "Nach Neu Mexiko," 5-6.

11. "Deutscher Pfarrer," Chapter "Chapter 4," 1, 6, 7, 24.

12. "Deutscher Pfarrer," Chapter "Chapter 4," 1.

13. "Deutscher Pfarrer," Chapter "Chapter 4," 17-21; newspaper clip, n.p., n.d., PKC.

14. Angélico Chávez, Index cards to Peter Küppers' personnel file, HAPA; "Deutscher Pfarrer," Chapter "Chapter 4," 22-23.

15. In exchange, in his 1916 testament, Küppers deeded the proceeds of his life insurance policy ($3000) to his housekeeper.

16. Szasz, "Comparative Religious History," 185; Ferenc Morton Szasz, *The Protestant Clergy in the Great Plains and Mountain West, 1865-1915* (Albuquerque: University of New Mexico Press, 1988), 144.

17. Szasz, *Protestant Clergy*, 148-49.

18. Chávez, Index cards.

19. Pitaval to Küppers, 19 January 1915, PKC.

20. "Deutscher Pfarrer," Chapter "Nach Chaparito," 41.

21. Jean Baptist Pitaval, quoted in Walker, *Protestantism*, 10.

22. Janice E. Schuetz, "A Rhetorical Approach to Protestant Evangelism in Twentieth-Century New Mexico," in Szasz and Etulain, eds., *Religion in Modern New Mexico*, 135.

23. "Statement concerning the state of affairs concerning the Sisters of Chaparito," 11 May 1918, PKC.

24. "Deutscher Pfarrer," Chapter "Nach Chaparito," 41.

25. Spanish circular, 24 August 1945, Robert Jones Collection, Folder 3, "Dixon School Case, 1947-1950."

26. "Deutscher Pfarrer," Chapter "Nach Chaparito," 37-8.

27. Szasz, *Protestant Clergy*, 148.

28. "Deutscher Pfarrer," Chapter "Nach Chaparito," 40; Chávez, Index cards.

29. Hanks, "Not of this Earth," 174.

30. Pitaval to Küppers, 16 December 1914, 21 March 1917, PKC.

31. Pitaval to Küppers, 10 November 1916, PKC.

32. Marta Weigle, *Brothers of Light, Brothers of Blood: The Penitentes of the Southwest* (Albuquerque: University of New Mexico Press, 1976), 102.

33. Marta Weigle, *Brothers of Light*, 101; Robert L. Wilken, *Anselm Weber, O.F.M.: Missionary to the Navahos, 1898-1921* (Milwaukee, WI: The Bruce Publishing Company, 1955), 147.

34. Küppers's $15,000 life insurance police covered some of the construction costs.

35. Albert T. Daeger, n.d., PPF 1934, Folder III; Chávez, Index cards.

36. Hanks, "Not of this Earth," 175-7.

37. Bill Tate, *The Penitentes of the Sangre de Cristos: An American Tragedy* (Truchas, NM: Tate Gallery, 1967), 10.

38. Weigle, *Brothers of Light*, xix, 96-97. For a recent interpretation of the Penitentes, see J. Manuel Espinosa, "The Origin of the Penitentes of New Mexico: Separating Fact from Fiction," *Catholic Historical Review* 79 (July 1993), 454-77.

39. Alice Corbin Henderson, *Brothers of Light: The Penitentes of the Southwest* (New York: Harcourt, Brace, and Company, 1937), 10.

40. Weigle, *Brothers of Light*, 101.

41. Küppers to Gerken, 26 May 1934, PPF. Despite many references to the manuscript, the Peter Küppers Collection only contains fragments of a manuscript, and it appears the manuscript was never completed.

42. Lewis to Gerken, 20 March 1935, PPF.

43. Morada is the physical meeting place of the Penitentes or refers to the chapter as an organization of Brothers. See, Weigle, *Brothers of Light*, 239, ft. 17.

44. "Deutscher Pfarrer," Chapter "Soldiers of the Cross," 118.

45. Peter Küppers, Letter to the Editor, *St. Anthony Messenger,* 4 July 1938, in response to the publication by Phil Glanzer, *Religious Rites of Horror.*

46. Peter Küppers, "The Penitentes and *The Literary Digest,*" *Southwestern Catholic,* 1921. Copy of the article in Dorothy Woodward Memorial Penitente Collection, Folder 110, New Mexico Records Center & Archives, Santa Fe, NM.

47. Gerken to Küppers, 31 May 1934, PPF 1934, III. Gerken commented about Alice Henderson's book *Brother of Light* that despite inaccuracies, "it is gratifying to see that the author endeavors to be fair to the Church and to the Penitentes. At any rate it could be much worse." Gerken to Küppers, 20 June 1938, PKC.

48. R. H. Lewis to Gerken, 20 March 1935, PPF 1935.

49. Küppers to Richard C. Dillon, 28 November 1928, PKC.

50. For example, Küppers to Miguel Otero, 17 June 1936, and Küppers to Epimenio Valdez, 20 February 1939; PKC.

51. Lewis to Gerken, 5 January 1934, PPF 1934, Folder IV.

52. Küppers to Gerken, 17 October 1934; Gerken to Küppers, 19 October 1934, PPF 1934, Folder V; Gerken to Küppers, 14 December 1934, PKC.

53. Ferenc M. Szasz, "Comparative Religious History," 186-7.

54. Weigle, *Brothers of Light,* 106.

55. Küppers to Joseph Beck (in German), 13 June 1936, PKC.

56. For instance, Küppers had owed over $5000 since 1932 to John P. Daleiden Company, Distributor of Religious Articles, Chicago, and Archbishop Gerken ended up paying the debt in 1935. Daleiden to Gerken, 25 April 1935, PPF 1935.

57. Gerken to Küppers, 3 January 1934, PKC.

58. Vertical File "Dixon Case," HAPA.

59. Form letter to the Catholic Ladies of Columbus (C.L.C.), 1 November 1948, PKC.

60. Angelico Chávez, *My Penitente Land: Reflections on Spanish New Mexico* (Albuquerque: University of New Mexico Press, 1974), 257.

61. Carol Jensen, "Roman Catholicism in Modern New Mexico: A Commitment to Survive," in Szasz and Etulain, eds., *Religion in Modern New Mexico,* 3.

62. E. K. Francis, "Padre Martínez: A New Mexican Myth," *New Mexico Historical Review* 31 (October 1951): 281.

63. "Etwas über den berühmten Padre Antonio Jose Martínez," (Something about the Famous Padre Antonio Jose Martínez), no date, PKC.

64. Schuetz, "Protestant Evangelism," 138.

The Faith, Courage, and Spirit of New Mexico's Hispanic Pioneering Women: A Profile of Rural Catholicism

Pauline Chávez Bent

They were our ancient great-grandmothers, they were our ancestral aunts and cousins, some coming with their husbands and children, some coming as heads of households, yet others coming as servants. Their destination was the far reaches of la Provincia de la Nueva México. One had first crossed an ocean to the New World, but all of them walked or rode carretas across the hot Chihuahua desert from Zacatecas, Nueva España. Some gave birth along the way, others buried beloved family members during the treacherous journey. Their hardships were monumental, but their courage, their spirit, and their faith in God saw them through the long months of hardship.

These were the women that came to New Mexico between 1598 and 1693. Some came with the first colonizer of New Mexico, Don Juan de Oñate, a wealthy mine owner from Zacatecas. Others came with the equally wealthy Don Diego de Vargas to recolonize New Mexico thirteen years after the Pueblo Revolt of 1680. From the first rudimentary camp pitched at San Juan Pueblo in 1598 to the finest church in New Mexico today, the strength and tenacity of the New Mexico Hispanic woman has kept the Catholic faith alive.

Their names pop out of the documents as we try to piece together their history. Catalina López from Toledo in Spain, wife of Pedro Robledo. She buried her beloved husband on Corpus Christi Day, May 21, 1598. Pedro was one of the first colonizers to die in New Mexico. In December of that same year, Catalina would lose her son Pedro, Jr., at Ácoma as the Spaniards tried to take the Pueblo.

María de la Cruz, wife of Juan Pérez de Bustillo, came with nine children. Lucía Robledo, wife of Bartolomé Romero. Isabel Olguín, wife of Juan Vittoria Carbajal, was later accused of trafficking in magic roots. Isabel Bohórquez Baca arrived in 1600 with her family and was destined to marry Don Pedro Gómez Durán y Chávez from Llerena, Spain, thus propagating one of the largest families in America.

When the patience and stamina of the colonists began to falter and some were beginning to give up, one of the women, Doña Euphemia de Peñalosa, is quoted as saying, "Tell me, O noble soldiers, where is the courage which you professed when you enlisted in this noble cause? For shame! Such are not the actions of Spaniards. Even though everything else may be lost, there is yet land on the banks of some mighty river where we may raise a mighty city and thus immortalize our names."

Though almost a century had passed since the first colonizers arrived in the province, Don Diego de Vargas, re-colonizer of New Mexico in 1693, described the isolation as "remote beyond compare." And many of the Chávez men expressed their views that New Mexico was a "miserable kingdom."

The Pueblo Revolt of 1680 brought death and devastation throughout New Mexico to both peoples, Indians and colonizers alike, and to the churches, the homes, the fields, and the livestock. Here the bravery of one woman stands like a shining beacon. In Santa Fe, Josépha López Sambrano de Grijálva entered a burning church, bravely went through the flames up to the altar, snatched up the statue of La Conquistadora, wrapped it in her tápalo, and took it to safety. She kept the precious image in her possession until she arrived safely with the other refugees at El Paso del Norte where they were to be in exile for thirteen years.

In 1735 Josépha Baca from Pajarito courageously defied both the entrenched custom of arranged marriages and her brother Antonio as well. She conspired with a Catholic priest, Father Pedro Montaño, so that her niece Francisca could marry Manuel Armijo. Josépha, well versed in the affairs of the heart, was somewhat like the present-day Murphy Brown. When Josépha wrote her will in 1746 she acknowledged that she had been a sinner.

Though three centuries have passed since the Revolt, many women in New Mexico have been as courageous as these two Joséphas, but their deeds have been buried by the sands of time.

Figure 1. Panel on the doors of the St. Francis Cathedral in Santa Fe depicting the flight of Josépha López Sambrano de Grijálva, the 10th great-grandmother of the author, with La Conquistadora. Photograph courtesy the author.

This presentation will focus on the women of isolated New Mexico villages in general, and it will particularly profile the heartbeat of rural Catholicism as it was endured in the village of Atarque, New Mexico. Some personal vignettes will be included. This now-abandoned village is located in Cíbola County, 33 miles south of the Zuñi Pueblo.

In about 1880, during the Apache wars, Gerónimo and his followers were raiding ranches in the Mangas and El Rito Quemado area, in what is now Catron County. During one of those raids they reached as far as El Banco de La Cebolla, stealing sheep and horses and taking captives. According to an extant death record, we know that Gerónimo personally killed Lorenzo García, husband of Doña Cecilia Ortega, leaving her with young children and three grown sons.

Upon her husband's death, Doña Cecilia became head of her household, and in 1882, with the help of her sons, she made the move into uncharted territory, along with the family of Don Jesús Landavazo; they later were joined by Blas and Espiridiona Chávez. The place they settled was called Atarque de los Garcías – Garcías' Dam. The dam had been built to provide water for

Figure 2. Doña Cecilia Ortega, the founder of Atarque. Photograph courtesy Elidia Sánchez Bezzeg, Belen, NM.

their livestock as well as for household use. Later, when the post office was established, the village was simply called Atarque.

Religion was of utmost importance to these early pioneers, and immediately after their arrival they began meeting in their homes on Friday evening to pray the rosary and to celebrate the Holy Days. It would not be until about 1893 that a priest was assigned to the remote village. But the women did not despair, and in absence of a priest they kept the Catholic religion alive and well. Father Pedro Badilla, a native of South America, resided in San Juan, Arizona Territory. His home parish was in Cebolleta,

Figure 3. Doña Cecilia's funeral invitation. Courtesy Viviana Chávez, the author's aunt.

New Mexico, 160 miles to the east. From San Juan he served the Atarque people. Twice a year he would make the forty-mile trip on foot to celebrate Mass, to baptize, and to instruct. Records show that on July 20, 1893, the sacrament of baptism was administered to eleven children.

Through the oral history passed down by villagers we know who the early keepers of the faith were. More commonly they were known as *resadoras*. Their names have been verified through Territorial Census records and other civil documents. Besides Doña Cecilia, there was Gertrudes Ortega, her adopted daughter. Gertrudes came to the García family when she was nine years old as a ransomed captive from the Hopi villages of Arizona; she became the wife of Juan Chávez. Librada Ortega was listed as "India Navajosa, criada de Doña Cecilia – a Navajo Indian, servant of Doña Cecilia." Francisca Armenta, a native of Sonora, had married Patricio García, son of Doña Cecilia, during one of his trading trips into northern Mexico. The building that was to become the Atarque church was built by Don Patricio as the chapel of his personal residence. Later he sold the property to his brother David. It was Don David who donated the building to establish La Iglesia de San José. Sara Landavazo Baca was born in San Rafael and married Claudio Baca, a Civil War veteran. And Adelaida González, the wife of Guillermo Landavazo, was not only a rezadora but also a curandera. Agapita Varela later became an Aleluia when the Protestant missionaries told her that in order to enter the gates of heaven she would have to destroy all her religious statues, but on her deathbed she returned to her Catholic faith and received the sacrament of Extreme Unction before she died. And other resadoras were Elena García, Viviana Chávez, Agustina Chávez, and Gabrielita Martínez.

In the absence of priests, these women conducted the religious activities. They taught the children, and they sang Las Posadas during December, they prayed the Stations of the Cross during Lent and especially Holy Week, and they led the rosary and the Mes de María prayers during May. They also prayed over the dying and administered emergency baptism to dying infants.

Men seldom attended these religious services, and fewer attended Holy Mass when offered. Oddly enough, the seating arrangements when the men were present were similar to the Jewish Orthodox tradition, with the men on one side of the Church and the women on the other. The men did attend velorios (wakes for the dead), but after the first rosary they usually retreated to a

Figure 4. Sarah Landavazo and Claudio Baca with their son Tranquilino. Sarah was a resadora and Claudio was a Civil War veteran. Photograph courtesy the author.

room separate from where the body lay in state and where the women prayed. Since a priest was not available, the women prayed over the dying person, prepared the body for burial, conducted the services at the home of the deceased, where all the mirrors in the house were turned to the wall or draped in black. They recited many rosaries and sang many alabanzas. At midnight refreshments would be served to all, but at no time that the body was in repose would it be left alone. Early the next day the body would be taken to the camposanto in procession, the women dressed in black from head to toe, singing alabanzas. In earlier times it was customary to have music at the funeral of a child; I am fortunate to have in my possession a photograph of such a funeral taken in 1910 complete with violinist!

Infant mortality in New Mexico was very high, and it was common for a mother to give birth to a baby only to lose it a year later. Deceased infants were considered to be little angels and were dressed as such when placed in their little white coffins for burial. In 1937 my little sister Ophelia died two days after my baby brother was born. The women made an angel dress for her from my mother's wedding dress and veil and circled her precious head with the silk flowers from the bridal bouquet.

Figure 5. Adelaida and Guillermo Landavazo and children (Polo, Santanita, and Federico), ca. 1905. Adelaida was a resadora. Photograph courtesy Aniceto Landavazo, Grants, NM.

Through the writings of Helen Sánchez Ogaz we get a beautiful example a mother's love and faith as she describes an incident that took place in 1832 in Valencia, New Mexico. Her fourth great-grandmother Lorenzita's son, José María Sánchez, had been held captive by the Zuñi Indians for many years. Finally an old woman of the Pueblo decided to help him escape, telling him, "Tu madre llora por ti. Take the fast horse Capitan, and ride in the direction of the rising sun." She gave him a supply of food and

Figure 6. Blas and Agustina Chávez. Agustina was a resadora. Photograph courtesy the author.

Figure 7. Funeral of infant: back row seventh from left holding prayer book, Doña Adelaida Gonzales Landavazo; far right, José Trinidad Gonzales (violinist); front row right, Isabelita Chávez (author's mother) at age 7. Photograph courtesy the author.

Figure 8. Village of Atarque, ca. 1930s. Photograph courtesy Aniceto Landavazo, Grants, NM.

sent him on his way. When José María arrived at Valencia, the people there sent word to his family that their son was safe. Doña Lorenzita had made a vow that if her son returned, she would not look at him until she had entered the church of Saint Agustín de la Isleta to thank God. Blindfolded and with an entourage of women, she entered the church and knelt. Then on her knees she made her way up the aisle to the altar railing and thanked God, and only then did she remove the blindfold to look at her son and take him into her embrace.

When the people in Atarque finally got their church, the whole community became involved in decorating and maintaining it. An interesting twist was that the money to buy the church bell was donated to the community by a group of acrobats that had passed through. A lifesize statue of Saint Joseph was placed there by a family in 1903, and years later a matching statue of the Holy Mother was also added to the collection.

At the turn of the century Juan Bautista Pitaval, Auxiliary Bishop of the Archdiocese of Santa Fe, paid a call on the village. He celebrated High Mass and administered Confirmation to those that had not yet received that sacrament. Also, he told Don David García that as his family members passed away they might be buried in the church. Two infants of the García family are buried at that location, Hubbell in 1909 and Melquiades in 1910.

In early 1920 a priest from the Zuñi pueblo was assigned to care for the Atarque church, and so he came monthly to celebrate Mass. He would notify the mayordomos by mail, and they made sure that the church and sacristy were ready for his arrival and that a family would host the priest for supper and breakfast. He would hear confessions in the evening and lead the people in praying the rosary. The next day he would celebrate Mass and after breakfast leave for Zuñi. According to the villagers' recollections, he never preached a sermon and never socialized with the people.

Each year on October 19, Las Fiestas del Atarque were celebrated to honor Saint Joseph, patron saint of the village. The women made elaborate plans for this special time; they calcimined, they painted, they washed and ironed the altar cloths, they polished the statues, they varnished the pews, and some years they even mud-plastered the outside walls. It was a labor of love!

On the feast day the little church was resplendent in all its glory. The priest sang the High Mass, and afterward he led the people in procession through the village, with the altar boys carrying the church banner, a large cross of the crucified Christ, and four tall candles. The procession was solemn, the priest sprinkled holy water as the people followed him, and then all returned to the church for the final blessing.

One cannot complete the religious history of Atarque without mentioning El Santo Niño de Zuñi, a statue of the Holy Child that is kept in a private home in the Pueblo. It is said that the statue was brought to New Mexico from Spain in 1629 by the Franciscan priests. To many people, this statue represented the essence of their faith, and they visited the Holy Child often, many times spending the entire night praying at a velorio. Pilgrimages to visit the Santo Niño were common, not only by the women but by servicemen returning from the horrors of war.

On the evening of Good Friday in 1951, the Atarque church burned to the ground. The sacristy containing the vestments, the

Figure 9. Emma Montoya Chávez and her sons Terry Alan and Kenneth help to maintain the church at Atarque. After the 1951 fire, the church was relocated to the old high school building; note the statues that survived the fire.

sacred vessels, and the Nativity statues that the people loved so
dearly was also destroyed. The church bell survived the fire, and
it is believed that it was taken to Zuñi where it is thought to
remain to this day.

The church was relocated in the building that once had been
the Atarque High School. In 1969 another disaster struck; the
church was ransacked and the statues were stolen, including the
original statue of Saint Joseph that had been placed in the old
church in 1903 and the statute of the Blessed Mother placed
there in 1945, two statues that had survived the fire of 1951. Need-

Figure 10. Espiridiana Saavedra Chávez, great-grandmother of the author, was born in Los Padillas, NM. Photograph courtesy the author.

Figure 11. Baptism record for Candelaria Chávez, daughter of Blas Chávez and Espiridiana Saavedra. Photograph courtesy Leon García, Hacienda Heights, CA.

less to say, the Atarque people were heartbroken over the loss, especially the older folks with deep roots in the village. For in the presence of those beloved statues they had repeated their marriage vows, baptized their children, and buried their loved ones. In the presence of Saint Joseph and the Holy Mother many of us made our First Holy Communion and prayed for guidance.

Although Saint Joseph was the patron saint of Atarque, the Blessed Mother was held in equal or greater esteem by the people. To salute the women who kept the Catholic faith alive in Atarque, I would like to close my presentation with a set of verses composed by one of those remarkable rezadoras, Doña Adelaida

Figure 12. First communion at Atarque, 1941. From left: Raymundo Chávez (brother of author), Marcella Gonzáles, unknown, Libradita Chávez (sister of author), and Roberto Marez. Photograph courtesy the author.

Landavazo. She singlehandedly built a shrine to honor Mary the Mother of Jesus in a remote place known as El Cañoncito, located two miles east of the village.

Figure 13. Doña Francisca Armenta de García. Photograph courtesy Adela García Dragon, Moreno Valley, CA.

LA DESPEDIDA DE LA VIRGEN

Adios, o Virgen incomparable!
Todos los pechos latan por voz,
Adios, o Madre, la mas amable!
Una y mil veces, Adios, Adios.

Blanca paloma, casta azucena,
Mistico encanto del Salvador,
Cuanta tristesa mi pecho llena
Al darte, o Madre, mi tierno Adios.

Cuando te dejo en tu santuario,
Siento un vacio en mi corazon,
Tal me parece, que en el Calvario
Te dejaron sola, con tu dolor.

¿Como dejarte, si eres consuelo,
Como olvidarte, si eres mi amor,
Si eres la Reina de tierra y cielo
Si eres la Santa Madre de Dios?

Adios, estrella de la mañana,
Inmaculada Madre de Dios,
Flor la mas pura, la mas galana
Del paraiso, Adios, Adios!

Recibe, o Madre, la despedida
Mas cariñosa del corazon,
Quedo a tus pieses toda la vida,
Toda mi alma, todo mi amor.

Adios, o Madre, todos nos vamos
Y te dejamos el corazon,
Y en recompensa solo pidemos,
Madre amorosa, tu bendicion.

FAREWELL SONG TO THE VIRGIN

Farewell, oh incomparable Virgin!
Our hearts speak and sing of you.
Farewell, oh most kind mother,
One and a thousand times, farewell!

Oh, white dove, purist of lilies,
mystical enchantment of our Lord,
My heart is filled with sadness
to bid you Mother a tender farewell.

And as I leave you in your sanctuary,
I feel an emptiness in my heart.
It must have been so for you at Calvary
when left alone with your aching heart.

How can I leave you when you are my comfort?
Can I forget you when you are my love?
You are the queen of heaven and earth,
You are the Holy Mother of God.

Farewell, oh star of the morning,
farewell, immaculate Mother of God.
Flower most pure, and flower most gallant
of paradise, farewell, farewell!

Receive, oh Mother, this fond farewell,
from a kind and loving heart.
I'll remain at your feet forever,
with my soul and all my love.

Farewell, oh Mother, we are departing,
but to you we entrust our hearts.
And in return we ask of you only,
oh loving Mother, your blessing of love.

Souces

Baptism and death records: from my personal collection.

Bent, Pauline Chávez. *Atarque: Now All Is Silent... .* Huntington Beach: Self-published, 1993.

Bent, Pauline Chávez. "La Virgen de Filomena," *Vista Magazine,* December 3, 1994.

Chávez, Fray Angélico. *Origins of New Mexico Families in the Spanish Colonial Period.* Santa Fe: William Gannon, 1975.

Chávez, Fray Angélico. *La Conquistadora, The Autobiography of an Ancient Statue.* Patterson: Saint Anthony Guild Press, 1954.

Chávez, Fray Angélico. "A Romeo and Juliet Story in Early New Mexico," *New Mexico Quarterly* 20 # 4.

Ogaz, Helen Sánchez. *Dawn Comes to Jarales.* Mountain View, CA: Self-published, 1981.

Ogaz, Helen Sánchez. "Tu Madre Llora por Ti," *Huellas del Pasado,* Spetember 1995.

Oral history: from a lifetime of conversations with my mother, who reached her eighty-eighth birthday with complete faculties.

Pérez de Villagrá, Gaspar. *A History of New Mexico,* tr. Gilberto Espinosa. Chicago: Rio Grande Press, 1962 (orig. Alcalá, 1610).

Simmons, Marc. *The Last Conquistador, Juan de Oñate and the Settling of the Far Southwest,* Norman: University of Oklahoma Press, 1991.

Territorial census records, Valencia County, 1850-1910.

United States Federal census records, Valencia County, 1920.

The Influence of the Roman Catholic Church in New Mexico under Mexican Administration: 1821-1848

Rev. Jerome J. Martínez y Alíre, J.C.L.

The once strong status of the Roman Catholic Church in the far flung northern frontier of New Spain, now known as New Mexico, was in serious peril at the beginning of Mexican Independence in 1821. The ten-year struggle for emancipation from Spain had disrupted the entire national life of Mexico and in turn seriously affected the missions throughout the borderlands. Without the government assistance which had marked church-state relations under Spain, the church in New Mexico found itself at a crossroads. Formerly strong characteristics of its life and structure weakened and died, while new movements came to the fore. It was a time of great turmoil marked by three crucial developments: the decline of the Franciscan order and its missions, the efforts of the Diocese of Durango and its clergy to fill the subsequent void, and the emergence of lay leadership among the Catholic communities no longer able to have priestly ministrations. Just how much influence did the Roman Catholic Church have during the Mexican period?

I. The Decline of the Franciscan Order and its Missions

The Order of Friars Minor founded by St. Francis of Assisi in the thirteenth century played a pivotal role in the colonization and missionization not only of New Mexico but of the entire American Southwest. For centuries under Spanish rule its members were the sole religious leaders on the frontier. One cannot overestimate the impact of their work. They converted the Indians to Christianity and educated them in the arts of animal husbandry, agriculture, art, letters, architecture, and so forth. Their work had been primarily accomplished through the use of a mission system which gathered the Indians together in settlements around Franciscan *conventos*. The Franciscan friars were also responsible for ministering to the spiritual needs of the Spanish colonists who braved the rigors of life in New Mexico. In a word, the Franciscans held a monopoly on the spiritual leadership of the colony of New Mexico. This is not to say that the spiritual authority of the friars was not challenged or even at times compromised by the secular arm of Spanish power, as happened during the friars' seventeenth-century dispute with the royal governors over the treatment of the Indians.[1] But even after this has been said, one must admit that they wielded considerable influence over the day to day life of New Mexico's colonial inhabitants who saw the consistent cooperation of church and state as part of the divinely ordered plan for mankind.

This power began to wane in the last decades of Spanish rule, and its decline continued through the years of Mexican rule over the American Southwest.[2] The reasons for this decline are many and complex, but for the reasons of this study it is necessary to point out only two causes as primary in the demise of the Franciscan Order in New Mexico.

Secularization of the Missions

According to the charism of their founder, the Franciscans' primary apostolate was to the missions. That is, their task was to evangelize those peoples who had not heard the Gospel before, convert them to the truths of the Roman Catholic faith, and organize them into worshipping communities of faith. Ideally, once this task was completed, then they were to move on to new missionary fields, leaving the spiritual care of these new faith communities to the priests of the new local church which had sprung up. Unfortunately, this ideal was not realized very well in New Mexico during Spanish rule. After two hundred years of evangelization, the Franciscans had developed many communities of converted Christian Indians and had provided spiritual service to other communities of Spanish colonists. But they had not developed any local vocations to the priesthood in either, prefer-

ring to import Spanish-born friars. Nor did they show any incli-
nation to leave and pursue other missionary fields. Rather, their
constant excuse was that their work of converting the frontier
was not yet finished.

This excuse did not satisfy the Bishops of the Diocese of
Durango, Mexico, the nearest diocese to the New Mexican frontier. They could understand that possibly the conversion of the
Indians was not complete, but what about the Spanish colonists?
Had they not been sufficiently instructed to develop their own
leadership and not depend on missionaries? The bishops rea-
soned they had, and as a consequence, they sought to extend
their authority over New Mexico by creating parishes in the non-
Indian communities. This development gained impetus well before Mexican Independence when in 1767 the Bishop of Durango
recommended the secularization – the turning over to the secular priests of the diocese – of four of New Mexico's twenty-eight
missions: the Spanish villages of Santa Fe, Santa Cruz de la Cañada,
Albuquerque, and El Paso.[3] The Franciscans seriously questioned
the Bishop's authority to do this, but by 1820 five secular priests
served these four parishes.[4] This trend continued following Mexican Independence when Vicar Agustín Fernández de San Vicente,
representing the Bishop of Durango, ordered the secularization
of five more missions at the request of the New Mexico *diputación*.
That the Vicar paid such attention to this semi-legislative body
which assisted the New Mexican governor administrate the province is a good indication that whatever the ups and downs of
church-state relations in the Mexican period, there was still much
more collaboration between the two than not. In any case, the
Diocese of Durango was at times unable to supply the secular
priests necessary to man the former missions for reasons which
will be explored later, and Franciscans were forced to continue
providing service there.

Another impetus towards the secularization of the Franciscan
missions came from liberal elements in the Mexican government. According to the new nation's *Plan de Iguala* adopted in
1822, all classes of people were to be designated Mexican citizens and no longer divided into castes such as *españoles, mestizos,
indios,* and so forth, as they had been under Spanish law. The
missions, according to these liberals, were nothing more than

throwbacks to the condescending Spanish belief that Indians were
not people of reason who could provide and decide for themselves. Furthermore, in the view of these liberals the missions
enabled the Church to amass immense wealth through property
which in turn allowed it to wield excessive influence in secular
affairs. Consequently, in 1834, the liberal Gómez Farías administration decreed an end to all missions with the hope of curtailing
the Church's economic and political power, freeing capital for
investment, and bringing vast tracts of Church-controlled lands
back into the public domain.[5] In New Mexico, the decree had
minimal effect since these liberals were soon out of power. Nevertheless, the secularization of the missions continued to gain
momentum.

The Decline in the Number of Franciscan Missionaries

In 1760, thirty Franciscans served the missions of New
Mexico. By the dawn of Mexican independence, the number
was twenty-three. This decrease could be accounted for by the
secularization of the aforementioned missions. But in the years
following 1821, the Franciscans would drop significantly in numbers and then disappear altogether. The reasons are not hard to
understand.

As has been noted earlier, the Franciscan Order in New Spain
had depended almost entirely on Spaniards for its new recruits.
During the revolutionary war for Mexican Independence this
source of recruits dried up as many young friars preferred not to
face an uncertain future on the Mexican frontier. This fear was
well founded. The strained relations between Spain and Mexico
following independence caused the government of the new nation to order out Spanish residents of the republic in 1827 and
then again in 1829.[6] These orders applied to friars as well. As a
consequence of these orders and the earlier recruiting problem,
the Order could not replace the friars who had died, had been
recalled, or had voluntarily returned to Spain. By 1826, the number of the Franciscans in New Mexico seems to have dropped to
nine; by 1832, only five New Mexico missions had resident friars.[7] It would get worse. By 1840, the last Franciscans remaining
in the province had died, and no friars were sent to replace them
because there were none available. So sad was this situation that

even the Bishop of Durango, who had been laboring to secularize at least the non-Indian missions, sought to re-introduce the
Franciscans back into the far northern reaches of his diocese when
he sent Fray Mariano de Jesús López to New Mexico to re-establish the Order's presence. Even though Fray Mariano de Jesús
served the Indian missions of Zuni, Laguna, and Ácoma hero-
ically until his death in 1848, no other Franciscans joined him.
With his death, the Spanish Franciscans ceased being an active
influence in New Mexico affairs, spiritual or temporal.

In the short period of less than a century, the enormous influence of the Franciscan Order in New Mexico had all but been
destroyed by several factors. Efforts at secularizing the mission
system by the Bishops of Durango as well as the liberal elements
in the government of the Mexican Republic, and the declining
numbers of new Franciscans due to the aftermath of the struggle
for independence, wrote the death sentence for the Order. But if
its friars no longer held the temporal sway they once had, the
spiritual legacy of these Sons of St. Francis continued to domi-
nate the traditions and life styles of New Mexicans. The continu-
ation of the particular Franciscan piety and world view, especially evident through the lay societies founded by the friars, would
still be a factor in twentieth-century New Mexico.

II. The Diocese of Durango and its Clergy

With the disappearance of the Franciscan Order from New
Mexico, the time seemed ripe for the Diocese of Durango to fill
the vacuum in spiritual administration left by the friars. Although
the Bishop and clergy of this diocese made valiant efforts to do so,
one must conclude that they were never fully able to provide the
leadership or the resources necessary for New Mexico to develop a strong local church. Consequently, while in some ways
the New Mexican Church made substantial progress during the
Mexican period, in many others it suffered losses in its ability to
influence or improve the lot of its adherents. The reasons for this
are numerous, but almost all of them revolve around three developments.

The Loss of Financial Resources

Even before Mexican Independence was a reality, the Franciscan missions were experiencing financial troubles in the maintenance of their missions.

Government aid to the distant northern missions had all but stopped by the mid-1810s as Spanish officials diverted resources to crushing rebel forces and stopped sending the padres' annual stipends (*sínodos*) and monies for supplies. Following independence, the economic situation remained dismal. The national treasury was often empty and traditional sources of funds, such as income from estates, mortgages, and contributions from wealthy and pious individuals, had become undependable.[8]

A dismal situation became even worse when on October 27, 1833, the same liberal Gómez Farías administration which was to decree the abolition of all missions also abolished the compulsory tithe for support of the Church in 1833.[9] This meant the Church could no longer depend on the government to assist her in the collection of tithes as had been done for centuries when the Spanish state and the church cooperated.

Whatever the intention of the national congress in enacting such a law, the results, at least in New Mexico, were disastrous. The people were not accustomed to support their Church monetarily (although the contribution of in-kind services and first fruits of the harvest – *primicias* – were readily given), nor were they able to do so in such an impoverished frontier area where currency was a rarity. As a consequence, the newly arrived secular priests and the few remaining Franciscans were seriously restricted in their work and influence, and the Church's institutions stood on the verge of collapse.[10] Many church structures deteriorated through serious neglect.[11] Pastors lived in misery due to the scanty contributions and then faced old age and death as paupers.[12] This situation seriously demoralized the few clergy who sought to minister in New Mexico. Many labored in heroic dedication, some gave in to the desires for better living and started exacting fees from the people for sacramental ministration, while others gave up on their priestly life altogether. The Mexican barrister Antonio Barreiro, who in 1832 made a report on life in New Mexico, had several observations on the condition of the

New Mexican church there which have relevance to this discussion:

> The spiritual administration finds itself in a truly dismal condition. Nothing is more common than to see numberless sick folk die without confession and extreme unction, and nothing is rarer than to see the eucharist administered to them. Corpses remain unburied many days, and infants are baptized at the cost of a thousand sacrifices. There are unfortunate ones in considerable number who pass most Sundays of the year without hearing mass. The churches are almost destroyed, and most of them are surely unworthy of being called temples of God. There is an absolute deficiency of ministers, for almost all the curacies and missions are vacant... the curates and missionaries of this Territory have to subsist on a scanty competence; they find themselves separated from cultured intercourse with other people, isolated in these corners of the Republic where only disagreeable objects and oftentimes dangers are near them; they are deprived of the pleasures with which civilized places allure them; they come to live on some miserable ranch and to endure privation which weigh not a little on the spirits of men who are used to a different order of things. And if to those considerations are added the gloomy idea that they have to pass the best of their life in solitude and privation, seeing themselves in the last days of their career without any succor from their poor parishes which from the weariness of years they will now be unable to serve, and therefore reduced to subsist at the expense of charity or off the miserable revenue of some chaplaincy – on these terms, I say, what ecclesiastics will be willing to seek such unhappy lots, unless they be animated by a spirit truly apostolic?[13]

These observations would have been as relevant in 1842 as in 1832 when they were written, for the deterioration of church life begun by the exodus of Franciscans and the serious disruption of financial support due to the war for independence continued to accelerate under the secular clergy. This was due to their few numbers and the poverty they had to work under, a poverty which resulted from abolition of the tithes.

The Lack of Effective Leadership from the Bishops of Durango

Truly such a miserable situation could have been remedied by vigorous leadership on the part of the church hierarchy. A resident bishop would have been ideal, but unfortunately, New Mexico had none even though the establishment of a diocese in Santa Fe had been recommended by the Franciscans as early as 1625, then by the Spanish *Cortes* in 1818,[14] then again by the Mexican National Congress in 1823 and 1830.[15] Instead, New Mexico had to depend on the efforts of the Bishops of Durango to reverse its spiritual deterioration and provide the moral leadership to build up the local church in its direst hour.

For the most part, the Durango bishops were unable to realize this potential, mostly due to factors beyond their control. Primary among these was the disruption of the Mexican hierarchy in the aftermath of the struggle for independence from Spain. Most of the bishops serving in Mexico by 1821 were Spanish-born. Many of these decided to return to Spain in the 1820s. Those who remained died in office until mid-1829 when not a single bishop served Mexico![16]

Nor did replacements come easily. For over a decade the Vatican refused to make new appointments to fill those vacancies, in part because the papacy sought to restore Mexico to Spain and did not recognize Mexican independence until 1836. Following negotiations, however, the Vatican began to appoint new bishops in 1831, but filled those positions slowly: the Pope did not name a new archbishop for Mexico until 1838.[17]

This crisis of leadership in the Mexican Church seriously affected the spiritual life of New Mexicans. The province did not experience an episcopal visitation from 1760 to 1833! As a consequence, those sacraments and dispensations which only a bishop could administer were not received. No new priests could be ordained without someone occupying the episcopal throne. The number of clergy in Mexico dropped by half from 1810s through the 1830s. Perhaps more importantly, the total lack of bishops in a hierarchical church meant a total power vacuum. Problems could not be addressed, and discipline among laity and clergy could not be maintained. As a result, the New Mexican Church suffered from a lack of firm direction at a time when it was needed most.

This dire situation could have become worse had it not been for the appointment of José Antonio Laureano de Zubiría as Bishop of Durango in 1831 following a six-year hiatus of having no bishop there. This man was an outstanding ecclesiastic who earnestly endeavored to serve his far-flung diocese.[18] Showing special concern for New Mexico, he appointed Juan Felipe Ortiz, a native priest from an old Santa Fe family, as his vicar for the province,[19] showing his desire to develop some local leadership. Later, he made pastoral visitations to New Mexico in 1833, 1845, and 1850. Considering the distances and the danger to his person due to the possibility of attack by nomadic Indians, these visits can be called nothing less than heroic. New Mexicans responded to his solicitude with great enthusiasm, repairing roads and bridges, sweeping streets, decorating their homes, and welcoming him with as much solemnity as the poor frontier towns could muster.[20] Zubiría was very much impressed by the simple faith of these frontiers people maintained in the face of great difficulty without the certainty of priestly leadership and sacramental consolation.[21] But he was also concerned about their lack of formal education, the shortage of native vocations to the priesthood, the lack of discipline among some clergy, and the aberrations in Catholic piety being committed by a confraternity of laymen known popularly as *Penitentes*. He wrote an extensive pastoral letter to his New Mexican flock on these matters in 1833[22] and gave Vicar Ortiz more powers, including the power to confer the sacrament of confirmation.

However, without his continued presence and the assistance of more priests, the admonitions of the good bishop came to naught. When he made his follow-up visit in 1845, he found many of the same deplorable conditions of 1833 still present. He ordered his letter of that year to be read again from the pulpits and rebuked the priests for not providing a more effective leadership of their flocks. Nor did Zubiría refrain from entering the political arena when it came protecting his flock. He urged local officials to be ever on guard against the encroachments of American citizens who had begun to make their presence known in New Mexico due to the Mexican Republic's reversal of the Spanish policy of closed borders. Like most of his brother Mexican bishops, he feared the influence of American Protestantism and the Yankee belief in separation of church and state.

But all of Bishop Zubiría's influence was to have little effect on the day to life of New Mexicans, primarily because he was too far away to make any real impact. He had to depend on his local priests, and these were a mixed bunch.

The Secular Clergy Serving New Mexico

In the short period since the departure of the Franciscans, the Diocese of Durango had been unable to establish a seminary for the training of priests on the frontier. As a result, at least at the onset of Mexican independence, the Diocese of Durango had to send its own clergy north. Most were understandably reluctant to go to the hinterlands – even after a special synod of the clergy, called by the vicar-capitular (the see being vacant), was held in Durango in 1830 to discuss the need for clergy in the north.[23] However, some did go, and most encouragingly were later joined by native New Mexican priests trained in Durango. The numbers increased at a glacial pace, however. In 1821, New Mexico had five secular clergy; that number increased to eight by 1829, and then to eleven at the dawn of the American occupation in 1846.[24]

Some American authors, writing shortly after the American conquest of the Southwest, declared that all these New Mexican priests were immoral and very poor spiritual guides. While this can be said truthfully of a very few of them, the rest of the accusations can be dismissed as Protestant bias at best and racist slander at worst. Indeed, one can say that some of them were luminaries in an otherwise bleak historical period.

One example will suffice. Padre Antonio José Martínez was born in Abiquiú, New Mexico, in 1793. He was educated for the priesthood in Durango, where he was imbued with zeal for a Mexican independence founded on human rights and the radical equality of all. These ideals caused him to return to New Mexico (even though he was offered attractive parishes in Durango), where until his death in 1867 he labored for the spiritual and temporal betterment of his *paisanos*. Through his preaching he sought to challenge his fellow New Mexicans to take up their duties as citizens of the new republic rather than remain the passive subjects they had been under the Spanish crown.[25] He realized that such active participation was only possible when the populace could be educated, and so he labored to establish public schools in New Mexico, unfortunately with too little success due to the scarcity of good teachers and lack of funds. He bought the territory's first printing press and used it not only to print religious catechisms but also periodicals designed to keep New Mexicans abreast of current events. When Bishop Zubiría made his celebrated visit to New Mexico in 1833, Padre Martínez asked him to consider ordaining more New Mexicans to the priesthood. This the bishop was ready to do, but he feared they were too poorly educated and too destitute to succeed at the seminary in Durango. Padre Martínez responded that he would prepare them himself, educating them and providing for them, until they should be ready for the seminary. To this proposal the bishop acceded, and hence many of New Mexico's later priests were products of Padre Martínez's little preparatory school.[26]

Like Bishop Zubiría, Padre Martínez did not fear getting involved in politics for the sake of his people. In this, he was joined by many of the other clergy serving in New Mexico, notably the aforementioned Vicar Juan Felipe Ortiz, as well as Padres José Francisco Leyva, Francisco Ignacio de Madariaga, and José Manuel Gallegos. These men often served on the Departmental Assembly which assisted the Governor in the administration of New Mexico. In fact, Vicar Ortiz was elected by this body to represent New Mexico to the National Congress in Mexico City.[27] All this was natural since these men were not only respected by their fellow New Mexicans but often the only well educated individuals in the area. Nor were their representations only on behalf of church interests. For example, in 1843 Martínez wrote an "Exposition on Affairs in New Mexico" deploring the exploitation of the Indians by American trappers recently allowed into New Mexico, as well as the questionable policy of allowing these trappers to buy up large tracts of land at the expense of Mexican settlers.[28] So noteworthy was the report that it made its way to President Santa Ana who ordered that its recommendations be carried out by the local government. The political activities of these priests continued even after the American occupation. Martínez was elected president of the Provisional Territorial Assembly in 1848,[29] while Gallegos was elected to the U.S. Congress as New Mexico's first representative in 1853.[30]

The Diocese of Durango was unable to become a force on the New Mexican frontier due to financial restraints and the lack of effective episcopal direction due to distance and political turmoil. Positively, the Durango bishops sought to develop a native clergy. These were not many in number, and some of them proved to be less than exemplary, but among them were some outstanding leaders who exercised influence over their people in both the temporal and the ecclesiastical spheres.

III. The Emergence of Lay Leadership

The abandonment of the missions by the Franciscans and the subsequent inability of the Diocese of Durango to supply sufficient sacred ministers to serve the spiritual needs of New Mexicans left them to their own devices.[31] Though the official Church failed to provide adequate leadership for their faith communities, the New Mexicans were not about to let the faith which nurtured them throughout centuries of hard existence on the borderlands die on the vine. Instead, they turned for leadership to the emerging lay confraternities in their midst.

The Penitentes

Among these, the most influential was the *Fraternidad Piadosa de Nuestro Padre Jesús Nazareno*, popularly known as the Penitentes. This confraternity was and is a lay religious organization made up of Roman Catholics organized to foster pious observances, especially in honor of the Passion and Death of Jesus Christ, and to render mutual aid.[32] Its origin is a matter of great debate, but a majority of scholars contend that it had definite historical roots in the Third Order of St. Francis, a lay branch of the Franciscans established in every New Mexican mission during the Spanish period. After the Franciscans had withdrawn from New Mexico, the surviving Third Order members seemed to have developed a ritual, structure, and direction definitely Franciscan in spirit but increasingly independent of clerical control. This brotherhood of Penitentes grew rapidly in nineteenth century New Mexico, enlisting practically every adult male in the various villages, mostly as a result of the neglect by the institutional church.

The Penitentes provided the spiritual care the people were craving for but had been unable to get. They gathered the villagers together for the celebration of the solemn feasts of the Catholic calendar, especially Lent and Holy Week. These feasts were observed with dramatic rituals most often centered on the events surrounding the crucifixion of Jesus. A unique form of sacred song, the *alabado*, and elaborate prayer forms also formed part of their religious observances. Furthermore, the brothers of this fraternity provided cradle-to-grave care, from teaching the young basic Catholic doctrine to providing the deceased with burial services. In doing all that they did, it should be emphasized, these men neither sought to usurp the role of the ordained priesthood nor pretended to provide substitutes for the official sacraments of the Church. Rather, what they sought to do was to supplement the often non-available official ministrations of the institutional church with popular piety.[33] Their relations with the clergy were mixed. Some of the native clergy tolerated or even welcomed the assistance of this home grown lay movement,[34] while Bishop Zubiría regarded their custom of physical penance excessive.[35] Their situation vis-a-vis the institutional church would only worsen after the American occupations when French-born bishops would seek to suppress them because they did not understand their form of piety.

But they continued to flourish, and would provide political as well as spiritual leadership for their communities. They would do so by ensuring order between families, providing assistance to those in need, and exercising in their chapter meetings the only form of participatory government these people would ever see.

It would not be an exaggeration to say that these Penitentes assured the survival of the Catholic faith in New Mexico during the Mexican period and beyond. In filling the vacuum left by absent clerics, these brothers developed a lay-led folk faith — a popular Catholicism parallel to the official one. In doing so, they

enabled New Mexicans to take ownership for their church and
their destiny.

Some Conclusions

The years between 1821-1848 marked a time of great turmoil for the Roman Catholic Church in New Mexico. The hand-
in-glove cooperation between church and state so characteristic
of Spanish administration crumbled in the face of the political
turmoil in Mexico following its independence. The once strong
position of the Franciscan Order was destroyed by efforts to secularize their missions as well as by drastic decreases in their numbers. The Durango bishops and clergy were unable to fill the
resultant vacuum, even though some of these priests wielded
tremendous spiritual and political influence. The institutional
church showed serious signs of decline evident in its inability to
maintain its churches, provide the sacraments to its people, or
fund any expansion.

This otherwise black cloud had some silver lining, however.
The Spanish church leaders' greatest failure in New Mexico had
been in not developing a local leadership capable of providing
vigorous direction.[36] During the Mexican period, this was somewhat remedied by the formation of a native born clergy who
understood their people and sought to improve their lot, both
spiritual and earthly. This clerical influence was complemented
by the emergence of lay confraternities which reflected the
frontiersmen's desire to assure the preservation of their way of
life.

The Roman Catholic Church which survived this difficult
period was one whose temporal influence was somewhat weakened. Yet one must say that it survived with all its traditions,
beliefs, and preeminent place in New Mexico society basically
intact, ever ready to show its marvelous adaptability in the face
of change.

Notes

1. See Warren A. Beck, *New Mexico, A History of Four Centuries* (Norman: University of Oklahoma Press, 1962), pp. 64-73.
2. Myra Ellen Jenkins and Albert H. Schroeder, *A Brief History of New Mexico* (Albuquerque: University of New Mexico Press, 1974), p. 37.
3. David J. Weber, *The Mexican Frontier 1821-1846, the American Southwest Under Mexico* (Albuquerque: University of New Mexico Press, 1982), p. 57.
4. Weber, *The Mexican Frontier*, p. 57.
5. Weber, *The Mexican Frontier*, pp. 47ff.
6. Weber, *The Mexican Frontier*, p. 44f.
7. Paul Horgan, *Great River, the Rio Grande in North American History, Vol. II: Mexico and the United States* (New York: Holt, Rinehart and Winston, 1954), p. 547f.
8. Weber, *The Mexican Frontier*, p. 44.
9. Weber, *The Mexican Frontier*, p. 75.
10. J. B. Salpointe, *Soldiers of the Cross: Notes on the Ecclesiastical History of New Mexico, Arizona and Colorado* (Albuquerque: Calvin Horn, Publisher, Inc., 1967 reprint of 1898 original), p. 165.
11. Jenkins and Schroeder, *Brief History of New Mexico*, p. 37.
12. Horgan, *Great River*, p. 547f.
13. Antonio Barreiro's, *Ojeada Sobre Nuevo México*, translated and edited by Lansing B. Bloom, Vol. V of The Historical Society of New Mexico Publications in History (Santa Fe: El Palacio Press, 1928), pp. 40-41.
14. Barreiro, *Ojeada Sobre Nuevo Mexico*, p. 42.
15. Hubert Howe Bancroft, *History of Arizona and New Mexico, 1530-1888*, Vol. XVII of *The Works of Hubert Howe Bancroft* (San Francisco: The History Company Publishers, 1889), p. 342.
16. Weber, *The Mexican Frontier*, p. 70.
17. Weber, *The Mexican Frontier*, p. 70.
18. José R. López-Gaston, *Tradición Hispanica de Nuevo México* (México, D.F.: Editorial Progreso, S.A., 1985), 282.
19. Salpointe, *Soldiers of the Cross*, p. 165.
20. Josiah Gregg, *Commerce of the Prairies*, Max L. Moorehead, ed. (Norman: University of Oklahoma Press, 1954), p. 179.
21. López-Gaston, *Tradición Hispanica de Nuevo Mexico*, p. 282.
22. Archives of the Archdiocese of Santa Fe, Patentes XI, 1 818-1851, roll 49, frames 262 -270.
23. Lansing B. Bloom, "New Mexico Under Mexican Administration, 1821-1846," *Old Santa Fe* I (January, 1914), p. 268.

24.   Weber, *The Mexican Frontier*, p. 74.
25.   Fray Angélico Chávez, *But Time and Chance, the Story of Padre Martínez of Taos, 1793-1867* (Santa Fe: Sunstone Press, 1981, p. 51.
26.   Fray Angélico Chávez, *Très Macho – He Said: Padre Gallegos of Albuquerque, New Mexico's First Congressman* (Santa Fe: William Gannon, 1985), p. 8.
27.   Chávez, *But Time and Chance*, p. 51.
28.   Chávez, *But Time and Chance*, p. 66; also see Salpointe, *Soldiers of the Cross*, p. 169.
29.   Chávez, *But Time and Chance*, p. 86.
30.   Chávez, *Très Macho – He Said*, p. 69.
31.   Weber, *The Mexican Frontier*, p. 79.
32.   Marta Weigle, *Brothers of Light, Brothers of Blood: The Penitentes of the Southwest* (Albuquerque: University of New Mexico Press, 1976), p. xvii.
33.   See Weigle, *Brothers of Light, Brothers of Blood*, p. 182.
34.   Daniel Tyler, *Sources for New Mexican History, 1821-1848* (Santa Fe: Museum of New Mexico Press, 1984), p. 9.
35.   López-Gaston, *Tradición Hispanica de Nuevo Mexico*, p. 282.
36.   Bloom, "New Mexico under Mexican Administration," p. 268.

Begetting the Mexican American: Padre Martínez and the 1847 Rebellion

Juan Romero

The year 1998 marks the fourth centennial of the founding in northern New Mexico of the second oldest European settlement in what is now the United States. This important anniversary is bookended between two other significant events: the 150th anniversary of the 1846 United States conquest-occupation of New Mexico and the coming of the new millennium which is upon us. Padre Antonio José Martínez, Cura de Taos, is a very special person in the history of New Mexico, since he was intimately involved with events surround the American occupation of Santa Fe. He was especially involved with the 1847 Taos Rebellion which was a New Mexican manifestation of the Mexican American War. The actions of Padre Martínez at this time, and his motivations for them, reflect the momentous transitional character of the epoch. At the same time they offer important insights to Hispanics and Catholics of the Americas about becoming a new people through the pain and confusion of political and cultural transition.

Antonio José Martínez was born in Abiquiú when New Mexico was still a Spanish province. He was seventeen years old when Padre Miguel Hidalgo, in 1810, uttered his cry for independence from Spain. By the time independence was realized in 1821, Martínez had already become a young widower and was studying for the priesthood in the Durango seminary. The influence of Padre Hidalgo upon Padre Martínez was shown by a sermon the New Mexican priest preached at the main church of Santa Fe which was later to become its cathedral. He preached the sermon in 1832 on the eleventh anniversary after the shout for Mexican Independence from Spain, sixteen years before the American occupation of New Mexico.[1] Martínez praised Padre Hidalgo for his role in the independence of the Mexican people. Martínez compared Hidalgo to the Maccabees of the Old Testament who unsuccessfully fought so valiantly against their Greek conquerors in order to keep their language, religion, and cultural identity. The battle of Padre Antonio José Martínez, in the face of American occupation, was to be very similar to those of the Maccabees and Padre Miguel Hidalgo.

Martínez grew up in Taos and served as its priest for forty-two years.[2] He witnessed many changes which culminated in the transitions brought by the Mexican American War, specifically the Taos Rebellion of 1847. As mediator during the uprising, Padre Martínez begot a new people by bridging Mexican-American divergence in language, culture, religion, politics, and way of life. Although he was not one of the principal architects of the Taos Rebellion, as his enemies alleged,[3] Martínez was certainly a key actor in those events surrounding the battles. Padre Martínez was, in fact, always a peacemaker and reconciler and never a warmonger. With his priestly prestige and political savvy, he was willing and able to broker the various interests, as well as bridge the tensions and conflicts inherent in a major socio-political transformation which was to have profound cultural and economic ramifications. The life of Padre Antonio José Martínez, Cura de Taos, especially his role during the time of great upheaval and transition marked by the United States conquest of New Mexico, specifically the Taos Rebellion of 1847, is very significant. The seventy-four years of the Padre's life serve as a thread weaving together various important elements of the fabric of New Mexico's rich nineteenth-century history which witnessed the Land of Enchantment under the flags of Spain, Mexico, and the United States of America.

Padre Martínez saw the demographic shifts which were taking place in the Santa Fe and Taos area as a result of Mexican independence and the liberal border policy of the Mexican government. This was in contrast to the more strict immigration policy which the Spanish government had observed. Martínez took over as the priest of Taos in 1826, the very year that sixteen-year-old Kit Carson came to town. By 1829, Virginia-born Charles Bent made his home in Taos and became a wealthy man through fur trapping and trading of buffalo and beaver skins. He and his brothers established Bent's Fort along the northern bank of the Arkansas River, the American side of the border with Mexico, near what is today the town of La Junta in southern Colorado. Charles Bent is also a significant person in New Mexican history because he was to become the territory's first governor under United States rule and the most prestigious victim of the Taos Rebellion which took place in early 1847.

Starting in 1832, Padre Martínez complained about foreign encroachment into Mexican territory. He was of the opinion that the presence and commerce of the foreigner was often prejudicial to the wellbeing of the native American and New Mexican settler. Mexican fear of foreign immigrants coming into their northern territory was becoming severe by the spring of 1843, and in a manifesto published in November of that year, the Padre publicly criticized what he observed as unhelpful behavior of the Americanos: "Besides useful articles," they were selling alcohol to the Indians at forts, such as Bent's Fort, erected on the U.S. side of the Arkansas River. He claimed that this "forbidden article has extremely demoralized the [Indian] nations." Furthermore, the liquor contributed to their incursions and stealing horses, and "several ... among our own people ... have taken the choice of becoming horse thieves themselves ... ."[4]

Through this manifesto, Padre Martínez complained to President Santa Anna about the "lack of tact on the part of the New Mexican governors in having granted to the strangers of North America [such as Bent and others] permission to build forts along the Napeiste [Arkansas] and Chato rivers with the object of establishing in said forts commerce with the said tribes." Martínez maintained that the immigrant strangers were themselves the cause of Indian incursions because they "furnished them with arms and liquor." Martínez unfavorably compared certain policies of the Mexican government to those of the Spanish government. He complained to Santa Anna that at least under Spanish rule it was never permitted to furnish Indians with arms and liquor for fear that "los estrangeros" (American foreigners) might pervert the Indians and encourage them to revolt.[5]

As a faithful churchman as well as Mexican patriot, Padre
Martínez also advised his ecclesiastical superior Bishop José Antonio Laureano de Zubiría of Durango of his opinions in regards
to the American take-over of New Mexico which he knew was
inevitable. In a letter to Bishop Zubiría written a year before the
occupation of Santa Fe, Martínez stated that he was constantly
observing the movements of the Americans who were approaching rapidly. He saw that their principal aim was the annexation
of the country to the United States of America, and he lamented
that the Mexican authorities were very slow in taking the necessary steps to stop this. He could see that the Americans would
finally take this land which seemed left without resources to stop
the intruders. Martínez furthermore decried the abandonment of
the native New Mexican people by their own Mexican national
government, and he predicted that the consequence of such neg-
ligence on the part of his government would be the annexation
of his country to the United States of America:

> As I am observing what is going on in this part of
> the country, I will venture to predict that sooner or
> later this Department will become a portion of our
> neighbor Republic of America. There, every religion
> is tolerated according to its constitution. What in-
> clines me to believe that the time of this inevitable
> change is not far off is the clear anxiety shown by
> the Americans to effect the annexation and the dan-
> gerous negligence of our Government .... .
>
> As I have said, this time is quickly approaching, and
> our government is not taking steps to overcome this
> intrusion. I am prepared, as I always have been, to
> protest in the adoration which I owe to Our Lord
> Jesus Christ and to His Holy doctrine, to His moral
> [code] and His dogmas. I am ready with my humble
> knowledge and the confidence of my resolution, for
> which I thank God, to face and preach against the
> great diversity of sects which this government will
> introduce into this country and so to maintain my-
> self in the grace of God and obedience of His Church
> .... . It is the general talk here that the American

government will soon take control of this Department ... .[6]

Although Padre Martínez had warned Durango's Bishop Zubiría of the coming of the Americans with their Protestantizing influence, he nevertheless eventually came to favor the American occupation even before it took place.

Bent's Fort

In an 1819 treaty between Spain and the United States, two years before Mexican independence, both countries formally recognized that Spain's northernmost border extended to the Arkansas River. Under Spanish rule, the border had been virtually closed to Americans of the United States and Canada. However, for trade purposes, the Mexican government now pursued the policy of a more open border which was then at Bent's Fort along the Arkansas River in what is now southern Colorado. The Arkansas River runs southeasterly between Pike's Peak on the east and the Continental Divide on the west from its source deep within the spine of the Colorado Rockies.

It was along this Arkansas River, called Río Napeste by the Spanish, that in 1829 Charles, George, and William Bent built their fort on the ruins of a previously founded French fort. Bent's Fort marks the place where an old Navajo trail and the Santa Fe Trail both met. It is located about seven miles away from the town of La Junta, about one hundred miles west of today's Kansas-Colorado border. The Fort was a boundary point to which American soldiers used to escort goods from St. Louis and the environs, and from which Mexican soldiers would then escort and help transport these goods to Taos and Santa Fe. Bent's Fort became the focal point to which many French Canadians were drawn, and it later served as the headquarters for the very large and contentious Maxwell Land Grant. In July of 1846, Bent's Fort became the rendezvous point and headquarters for General Stephen Watts Kearny and the American Army of the West which gathered there immediately before descending upon Santa Fe to occupy New Mexico.

Bent-Martínez Antipathy

Although Padre Martínez neither instigated nor led the Taos Rebellion of 1847, he shared the perception of both Native Americans and native New Mexicans that their ancestral lands were being stolen by a coalition of new immigrants. These newcomers, mostly French-speaking Canadian fur trappers and youthful entrepreneurs from the Missouri area, entered New Mexico in large numbers during the quarter-century between Mexican Independence and the American takeover of Santa Fe. The Maxwell Land Grant was perceived as a classic instance of illicit land-grabbing. Journalist-historian William A. Keleher in 1942 wrote about the close connection between that land grant and the 1847 Taos Rebellion:

> The quarrel in 1844, under Mexican rule, between Padre Martínez, of Taos, and Carlos Beaubien and Guadalupe Miranda, over the Maxwell Land Grant and its boundaries was undoubtedly one of the most important contributing factors to the Taos Massacre of January 18, 1847 .... Subsequent to 1846 no secret was made of Bent's claim to part ownership in the Grant.[7]

Padre Martínez from the beginning was strongly opposed to the Beaubien-Miranda Land Grant, and he challenged it on legal and moral grounds. Keleher reports:

> The plan of Miranda and Beaubien to take over and occupy the land [grant] met with active resistance on the part of Rev. Antonio José Martínez, Curate of Taos, who had always opposed large grants of land to wealthy persons, claiming that the lands should be granted to poor people. Father Martínez vigorously contended ... that a part of the land granted to Miranda and Beaubien conflicted with lands claimed by Charles Bent, and that a large portion of the land involved belonged to the people of Taos, and other towns, that such lands had been long known as commons and the people had for generations grazed their live stock on them. Martínez claimed among other things that the land had been

granted to foreigners, apparently referring to
Beaubien and Charles Bent.[8]

It is clear that Charles Bent did not like the meddling priest
of Taos because Martínez challenged Bent's interests in the
Beaubien-Miranda-Maxwell Land Grant. Because of Charles Bent's
public contempt for the priest, many have assumed that the Padre may indeed have been a perpetrator of the rebellion which
made Bent its first victim. Because of the antipathy, partisans of
Governor Bent would later find it easy to ascribe his assassination to the Padre. This antipathy of Charles Bent for Padre Martínez
was reflected in his correspondence with Manuel Alvarez, whom
Bent selected as the appropriate recipient of his most strident
complaints against Padre Martínez. Alvarez functioned in Santa
Fe as U.S. ambassador to Mexico since 1839, and was also serving as American Consul in New Mexico. In an especially sarcastic letter that Charles Bent wrote to Manuel Alvarez on January
30,1841, Bent lavished vituperative epithets upon Padre Martínez.
Among his hateful and sarcastic appellations were "the Calf," "Mr.
Priest," and the "The greate literry Martianes [sic]." This last insult
is especially ironic since Bent's letter contrasts so powerfully to
Padre Martínez' true literary merits.

The Mexican-American War

In the mid-nineteenth century, it became a serious goal for
the United States to occupy and possess the land west of the
Mississippi river. With the continuing influx of Anglos into New
Mexico and the development of commerce fostered by the Santa
Fe Trail and Bent's Fort, westward expansion through military
might became, by 1845, a very powerful force in New Mexico.
The Mexican-American War of 1846-48 was a momentous event
which served as the context for the border war known as the
1847 Taos Rebellion.

The American intention to invade New Mexico, however,
was not passively accepted by the descendants of the original
Spanish settlers who, without moving anyplace, were now residing on land which was part of Mexico. For over two centuries
they had been under the Spanish flag, and after two decades
they were just beginning to become accustomed to the Mexican

flag. On July 11, 1846, New Mexican Governor Manuel Armijo asked Pascual Martínez, the brother of Padre Martínez, to invite ten principal citizens of New Mexico to meet with him in Santa Fe. The purpose of that meeting was to strategize on the best way to deal with the impending incursion of a foreign army. Four of the ten who were invited to the meeting were priests, and the first one on the list to be invited was Padre Martínez of Taos. However, the well-regarded priest chose not to come since, it seems, he no longer favored the path of resistance to American governance.

By 1846, Padre Martínez had effectively changed from being a Mexican nationalist to becoming enthusiastically pro-American. Rejecting Armijo's invitation, Padre Martínez soon thereafter accepted the personal invitation of General Kearny to come to Santa Fe and to swear allegiance to the United States of America. Padre Martínez seems to have come to the conclusion that Mexican resistance to American power was not militarily viable for the people of New Mexico. Moreover, it was now his considered opinion that the government of the United States would pay better attention to the civil needs of the people of New Mexico than had the government of Mexico.

Padre Martínez had become somewhat frustrated because his pleas for action in the face of the coming of the Americans had gone largely unheeded both by his Mexican president General Santa Anna and his ecclesiastical superior Bishop Zubiría. Consequently Martínez may have judged that the future for New Mexicans would be better served by their encroaching American neighbors rather than by the distant Mexican center of power which had historically neglected its own northern frontier and its people. In light of Padre Martínez' previous strongly expressed opinions resisting American influence, his actual favorable reactions upon the arrival of General Kearny into Santa Fe must have come as a surprise or even shock to many who knew him well. They had not kept up with the development of his political thinking.

Manuel Armijo's meeting to plan resistance against the American army took place less than a month before Kearny's entrance into Santa Fe. The majority of those who attended the meeting were influenced by Padre Martínez' noticeable absence, and the decisions were inconclusive. The clear preference of the majority was to offer no resistance to the advancing American army. This reflected the lead of Padre Martínez who had not attended the meeting called by Armijo. Martínez' absence was interpreted as a pragmatic choice not to squander New Mexican blood by attempting to resist the inevitable American occupation. It was also seen as a statement in favor of a new political order for New Mexico under the United States of America.

It is very likely that the assessment of Benjamin Read, a native New Mexican historian who had close connections to Padre Martínez, would closely parallel the Padre's thinking in regards to not resisting American military might. Read's assessment of the people of New Mexico, especially including the person of Padre Martínez, is as follows:

> The people of New Mexico in submitting to the American army deserve no censure for its apparent lack of patriotism or civic valor, but are rather worthy of admiration for having foreseen that if that war would inevitably have to result in the defeat of Mexico, and the economical material, industrial conditions of the Territory demanded, as a prudent and necessary thing, the step taken by the people in declaring in favor of the American government, insuring thus the happiness and higher civilization of the inhabitants of the Territory. The change was furthermore made necessary because of the contempt and abandonment with which the Spanish and Mexican governments had treated the inhabitants of New Mexico.[9]

In hindsight, it may have been a mistake for Padre Martínez not to have attended the meeting called by General Armijo and held in July of 1846 to plan resistance to the United States' occupation. Martínez might have suceeded in convincing the small band of Mexican nationalists of the folly of direct military resistance against the Americans. Without the sound of Martínez' more moderate voice, however, the well articulated and persuasive opinion of the minority held sway. According to them, New Mexico indeed should steadfastly resist the enemy invaders.

As soon as it was learned in Santa Fe that the American army was encamped at Bent's Fort, a private meeting was held in the City of Santa Fe, in which the principal citizens took part with the object of discussing the steps that should be taken … . The majority of the persons present preferred to surrender without resistance; the others … held that the enemy should be fought against. The latter were able to prevail. … Messers. Don Miguel Pino, Nicolás Pino, and Don Tomás Baca were entrusted to take charge, with General Armijo, of the forces which should repel the enemy.[10]

Of course, the American troops captured New Mexico in August 1846 without encountering any armed resistance. By the time of the occupation, Padre Martínez seems to have come to terms with a new political situation, not only tolerating it as inevitable but even accepting it somewhat enthusiastically. General Kearny offered Padre Martínez a personal invitation to become an American citizen. In order to extend a personal invitation, Kearny dispatched to Taos an escort of twelve soldiers ironically led by the priest's enemy Captain Charles Bent. The Padre, his two brothers, and other prominent citizens came to visit with the General in Santa Fe. During the visit, the three Martínez brothers (Padre Antonio José, José María, and Pascual) were sworn in as American citizens.

Padre Martínez offered his printing press to the General for the publication of official notices, and the press was taken from Taos to Santa Fe. The General then printed and issued the first law book of the American Southwest entitled Kearny's Code of Laws,[11] and from this time on, New Mexico was governed by the new code. General Kearny promulgated the new laws and then proceeded to enumerate to the new citizens of the United States their Declaration of Rights.

On August 30, only two weeks after the occupation, General Kearny attended High Mass in Santa Fe in order to symbolize his respect for the customs and beliefs of the New Mexican people. He promised the people that they, their lands, their customs, and their religion would remain intact despite their changed citizenship. Enthusiastic about his new American citizenship,

Padre Martínez returned to Taos determined to learn English better and to promote it among his students. In the early fall he exhorted them to be competent citizens and to study the English language.[12]

On September 22, newly promoted Brigadier General Kearny made some new political appointments. In his first official proclamation after the occupation, he expressed his joy at having taken possession of New Mexico "without firing a gun, or spilling a single drop of blood."[13] Next on the agenda was to establish a new political structure. The promise of General Kearny to protect property and lives of the *Nuevo Mexicanos* was very appealing, since the Mexican government had seemed impotent in this regard. Kearny named three new justices of the suprememe court, but the most significant appointment that General Kearny made at this time was Charles Bent as the first governor under the new American rule.

Although on the surface things seemed peaceful immediately after the American occupation, it did not take long for serious conflict to develop. Within a month after his arriving at Santa Fe, Kearny called a council of the Indian Nations in Santa Fe, but few of the chiefs came. He wanted to proclaim officially that fighting between Indians and Mexicans would no longer be tolerated, but there was little interest in hearing that message. The U.S. Army engaged in skirmishes with Indians along the Rio Grande and Chama Rivers for several months.

Indians renewed and intensified hostile activity, but General Kearny was confident that his soldiers would well enough handle the turmoil with the Indians in New Mexico. On September 25 he left for California to shore up the military operation of John C. Fremont on the California theater of the Mexican-American War. Meanwhile, from the beginning of autumn 1846 until November 25, Major William Gilpin stayed in the Abiquiú area fighting with Indians. The departure of General Kearny from New Mexico proved to be premature and disastrous for the tenuous, newly-established American government.

The Mexican nationalists and Taos Indians revived their plans for resistance and determined to put them into practice. The situation was about to heat up and explode in Taos. On December 12, 1846, the feast of Our Lady of Guadalupe, patroness of Mexican independence from Spain, Mexican patriots followed up on previous meetings, arrangements, and agreements among various Mexican citizens residing at Las Vegas, Mora and Taos. "Their plan was neither more nor less than the assassination, on the 19th of the same month [December], of all the Americans that might be found in New Mexico.[14]

At a subsequent meeting held at midnight in Santa Fe on December 16, 1846, the conspirators made a decision to postpone their deadly intent from December 19 to Christmas Eve. However, on the twenty-first, Charles Bent somehow uncovered the plot to assassinate all Americans in New Mexico. As a result, the assault was again secretly delayed this time until January 19, precisely a month after the uprising was originally scheduled to have taken place.

Bent's Assassination

What is called the Taos Rebellion of 1847 was in reality a combination of several events and battles. The first was the violent assassination of Governor Charles Bent and the killing of fifteen to seventeen other Americanos or their sympathizers in the middle of January 1847. Five Americans and two Mexican partisans died in Taos.[15] Another nine Americans were killed at Turley's Mill in Arroyo Hondo, twelve miles north of Taos, and there were one or two American casualties during the altercations at the Santa Cruz and Embudo areas.

Knowing that he was a prime target, Governor Bent nevertheless seemed unafraid. Since there was no attack by the end of December as had been anticipated, Bent was lulled into believing that no attack would occur. In spite of efforts to warn him against leaving the protection of the U.S. troops in Fort Marcy, Bent decided to leave Santa Fe on January 14 in order to have a post-Christmas visit with his family in Taos. Very early in the morning of January 19, 1847, while Bent was in his house sleeping, Taos Indians forced their way into the house and made the assault. They broke down the door, fired a rifle through it, wounding the Governor in the chest and stomach. Then they proceeded to pierce him with arrows, and scalp him.

Bent's and María Ignacia Jaramillo's daughter Teresina always vividly recalled the terrible and traumatic event of her father's
assassination, which took place before her own eyes:

> Hearing the noise, he [Gov. Bent] went to the door
> and tried to pacify the crowd yelling outside .... We
> children were trembling with fear ... . While my
> father was parleying with the mob, Mrs. Carson and
> Mrs. Boggs, aided by an Indian woman who was a
> slave (*peon*), dug a hole through the adobe wall which
> separated our house from the next. They did it with
> only a poker and an old iron spoon. I still have the
> poker that they used. We children were first pushed
> through the hole and then the women crawled
> through after us. My mother kept calling to my fa-
> ther to come also, but for quite a while he would
> not.
>
> When he did try to escape he was already wounded
> and had been scalped alive! He crawled through
> the hole, holding his hand on the top of his bleed-
> ing head. But it was too late. Some of the men came
> after him through the hole and others came over
> the roof of the house and down into the yard. They
> broke down the doors and rushed upon my father.
> He was shot many times and fell dead at our feet.[16]

The newly appointed district attorney, J.W. Leal, was also
scalped alive and then dragged through the streets. Sheriff Stephen
Lee was killed on his own housetop on the south side of the
plaza. Narciso Beaubien hid in an outhouse but was turned in by
a woman servant to the family; Narciso, whose mother was New
Mexican, was the son of Judge Carlos Beaubien. He had been
studying for five years at Cape Girardeau College, below St. Louis,
and was proficient in French and Spanish as well as English.

Pedro Sánchez' vivid description of the Taos uprising, written twenty-six years after the account by Santiago Valdez, reflects
the living memory of many people whom Sánchez knew well:

> One cold morning in January, 1847, a revolt exploded
> in Taos. Padre Martínez was awakened by a mob of
> people in his *plazuela* [courtyard] screaming, "Open

for the love of God, open! The Indians are killing
Don Carlos Bent, Don Luis Lee, and others!" The priest
in his underclothing ran and opened the door. He
bade the desperate and terrorized people to enter.
There peaceful citizens of Taos assembled. Among
them were the families of the Americans who had
perished at the hands of the insurgents as well as
the families of those who were absent from the village. All were there without distinction of race, color,
or creed, in the house of the priest whose heart was
full of compassion and the spirit of consolation and
peace .... He gave them food and provided arms for
those who could handle them. He had fortlets constructed on the roof of his house and placed sentries
on guard for the protection of the people against the
insurgents who kept up a barrage of words, yelling,
"Traitors, traitors!" Father Martínez placed himself at
the head in defense of his guests, until the arrival of
Colonel Price.[17]

Some prominent American citizens of Taos, who otherwise
certainly would have perished, were out of town during the days
of the uprising. Territorial Supreme Court Justice Charles Beaubien,
partner of Charles Bent in the Maxwell Land Grant, was away
on a shopping expedition in Santa Fe. Both Kit Carson and Colonel St. Vrain were together at Bent's Fort during those fateful days.
They all would soon return to contribute their part in the swift
and harsh retaliation against the uprising.

Padre Martínez was not a participant in the plans to over-
throw American rule in New Mexico. In fact, the Padre showed
himself very humanitarian in the heat of battle when he gave
hospitality to Elliot Lee, who ran for cover to the priest's home.[18]
With several other family members of murdered Americans, Lee
found shelter and ample protection at the Padre's house.

It is nothing but just to bear testimony to the humanitarian action of Padre Martínez, first, because a
man is worthy of praise who, in such critical moments, gives shelter to the persecuted, though in so
doing, he might have to expose his life; and in the
second place, because many writers, with an inborn

prejudice, have attempted to stain the name of Padre Martínez, charging him with being one of the movers of the vile and cowardly attack.[19]

Most accounts of the events in Taos during the year 1847 are presented from the point of view of the American victors. However, Santiago Valdez furnishes us with a unique perspective upon the Taos Rebellion in his 1877 biography of Martínez. Following are excerpts from his manuscript written ten years after the death of the Padre and thirty years after the rebellion:

While the mob was committing their treacherous work, Padre Martínez was on his way to church to say Mass, but was stopped by the howling of someone running …. He remained motionless to await and see the cause of it, and saw that it was an American named Eliah Lee who was hotly pursued by the mob. He was imploring his [Padre Martínez'] protection, and Padre Martínez immediately spoke to the crowd. Upon hearing what they had been doing in town, he reprimanded them bitterly, and denounced them as murders. Accompanied by the American whose life he had saved, he [Padre Martínez] went back from that spot to his home.

After Bent's assassination, the crowed asked their Padre's approval of their action, but he reprimanded them and directed himself especially to their leader Pablo Montoya:

"My dear Christian brothers, I am indeed very sorry to see that my parishioners and brothers in Christ have been the principal agents of this fearful crime. You have provoked the anger of this powerful government. You have made yourselves guilty of such an anti-Christian and barbarous act. There is no difficulty, my brothers, in attacking and killing defenseless individuals especially while they are asleep. However, it is very difficult to attack and kill civilized troops which are well armed."

Although the leaders of the revolution were angry and disappointed in their priest,

they knew that he had an American under his roof, and they did not dare attempt to say anything ill

about him. This is sufficient testimony that Padre
Martínez was highly respected even at the most critical moments. In spite of his reprehensions, he was
always looked upon as the most respected man of
the community.

The rebels of the Taos Pueblo were surprised by the negative
reaction of their priest to their entreaties for his support. They did
not seem to be aware that their pastor had become an American
citizen. This may explain somewhat why their priest chastised
them and gave unheeded advice to Pablo Chávez, one of the
Pueblo leaders:

"You and your followers are the reason that these
families are gathered here to escape your treacherous hands. The many privations and sufferings
which they have been undergoing is on account of
your inhuman atrocities, and for all this you have to
render a strict account before Almighty God. You
have been misled by the blindness of ignorant and
ambitious people, and you have committed an un-
pardonable blunder. You have stained your hands
and souls with the blood of your innocent victims
and thus are following not the law of God but the
law of Satan. For the law of God says: 'Every man
must obey his superiors, as his power and authority
derives from God, and he who disobeys his superiors will disobey God.' But as you take no heed of
God's commandments, you will very soon be confused, abject, and destroyed, and the day of your punishment is fast approaching. You will be sorry for all
you have done, and for the sufferings of these families."

The strong pro-American slant reflected in the account of
Santiago Valdez can be understood in light of the fact that Valdez
was well situated in the political and economic system introduced by the United States. Valdez was a successful New Mexican politician of the late nineteenth century who wrote the account of the Taos Rebellion, as part of his biography of Martínez
thirty years after the events surrounding the American conquest
of New Mexico.

Turley's Mill

At about the same time as the explosion at Taos, fireworks were also taking place at Turley's Mill in Arroyo Hondo, about twelve miles north. Besides Governor Charles Bent, another of the targets of the Taos Rebellion was Simon Turley, who was proprietor of the mill which bore his name. He was a longtime merchant in northern New Mexico and had become especially wealthy through the sale of Taos Lightning, his powerful home-brewed local whiskey which was widely used by the mountain men and also sold to Indians. Although Turley thought of himself as a good friend of the people, he nevertheless incurred the hostility of several, including the Taos Pueblo Indians, perhaps because of his trafficking in alcohol, which occasioned dependence among the Indians.

The melee at Turley's Mill in Arroyo Hondo, which lasted for a couple of days, began shortly after the murder of Governor Bent. About a dozen men were killed at Arroyo Hondo: seven whites and five Indians. Simon Turley's property – his house, mill, and still – lay at the foot of a gradual slope in the sierra, which was covered with cedar-bushes. The house was located behind the still. It had a garden enclosed by a fence and a small wicket-gate which opened from the corral. The stream of the Arroyo Hondo ran in front of the house, about twenty yards from one side of the square, and on the other side was broken ground which rose abruptly and formed the bank of the ravine.

Although Turley thought that he would not be molested, he nevertheless agreed to make preparations for defense. He closed the gate of the yard which surrounded the buildings of his mill and distillery. A few hours later, a large crowd of Mexicans and Pueblo Indians armed with guns and bows and arrows advanced with a white flag. They told Turley to surrender his house and the Americans in it and guaranteed him that his own life would be saved. At the time, eight well-armed men with plenty of ammunition were in his house. They included Americans, French Canadians, and Englishmen. When it became clear that Turley and his men would rather fight than surrender, the attackers scattered and concealed themselves under the cover of the rocks and bushes which surrounded the house. Arrows and bullets were traded in a battle which continued into the night. The Indians and New

Mexicans tried to break down the wall of the main building, used as a fort for defense, but the strength of the adobes and logs effectively resisted all their attempts.

The first assailant who tried to cross over into Turley's house was the Pueblo chief. He was shot and instantly fell dead in the center of the intervening space. Soon there would be seven dead Indians. Three more were immediately killed in their vain attempts to retrieve the body of their dead chief, and another three were killed almost immediately afterwards.

So far there were no white men killed, but "after the fall of the seven Indians ... the whole body of assailants, with a shout of rage, poured in a rattling volley, and two of the defenders of the mill fell mortally wounded."[20]

The survivors of the little garrison at the mill huddled and decided that, when night came, it would be up to each to escape as best he might. Turley himself succeeded in escaping from the mill, and seemed to be on his way to safety. However, he was shot to death, it is said, by someone whom he knew well and who had been friendly toward him. Turley's house and mill were sacked and gutted, and all the gold which had been concealed about the house was discovered and taken.

American Retaliation

Soon after the first volleys of the Taos Rebellion, Padre Martínez lent Elliot Lee his own horse to ride from Taos to Santa Fe in order to apprise Colonel Sterling Price of the situation in Taos after the murder of the governor. With 350 men of the regular army, Price marched north to Taos in late January. Thirty-six Taos Pueblo Indians, under the leadership of Pablo Montoya, were killed at Santa Cruz, while Colonel Price lost only one or two men. Jesús Tafoya, one of the New Mexicans' principal leaders, was also fatally wounded there, and within a week, Montoya was publicly hanged on a specially constructed gallows near the Taos Plaza.

Price continued upstream along the Rio Grande and came to Embudo, now called Dixon. "Embudo," meaning "funnel," well names the steep and narrow mountain pass through which both the Río Grande and a road travel along a parallel course. A second company of revolutionaries came down from Taos and en-

gaged Price's forces on January 24, 1847, but his superior fire power
easily defeated the small, ill-equipped group of warriors and
brought a quick end to this battle, for within a half hour, twenty
Indians were killed, while Price lost only one man.[21] Some of the
insurgents sought refuge in the mountains, others came back to
Taos, where they made their fortification to protect themselves as
best as they could against the American military might, and a
few went home without involving themselves further in the conflict and took advantage of the amnesty which Padre Martínez
on the very morning of the Taos Rebellion promised he would
request for the rebels who desisted from their revolutionary activity, and which Colonel Sterling Price granted.

Meanwhile, the American forces under Price continued their
northern trek toward Taos. Nearly five hundred American soldiers with their wagons and artillery of four mountain howitzers
arrived at the village of Río Chiquito, now known as Talpa, near
Ranchos de Taos where they spent the night of February 2, exactly one year before the signing of the Treaty of Guadalupe
Hidalgo which was to formally end the Mexican-American War.

Pummeling of the Taos Pueblo

Colonel Price reached Taos between ten and noon on the
morning of February 3 and presented himself to Padre Martínez
at his home, which he used as his headquarters for his Taos cam-
paign. He learned that the insurgents were entrenched in the
church of the Taos Pueblo, about three miles away. Although his
men were exhausted from the hard winter march and the fighting, Colonel Price nevertheless decided to attack immediately.
That evening he reconnoitered the pueblo-church fortification
and ordered a strategic shelling of a few rounds of artillery for
several hours. The battle was hotly contested until night when
two white flags of surrender were hoisted, only to be shot down
in disregard. At the approach of darkness, the Americans retired
to the village in a ploy to make the Indians and other rebels think
that they were leaving. The main military objective was to prevent the Indians from leaving the village during the night. It
worked, since the Indians and their companions believed that
they were victorious and flattered themselves for having defeated
the American troops. Colonel Price stayed that night at the home

of Padre Martínez, and the Indians remained enclosed as easy targets in the pueblo, and especially in the church.

> The next day [February 4] in the early morning, Colonel Price proceeded to renew the attack on the pueblo at about 9 am. There was a strong adobe wall around the village, but the Americans surrounded and attacked all around it with artillery and cavalry, while the infantry advance at the front. After a hot fight, the Americans were victorious and captured the Indian Village, and the Indians surrendered at 1:00 o'clock p.m.[22]

The Trial

The trial of the Indians and native Spanish settlers who violently opposed the American occupation took place in the spring. The far-west classic by Lewis H. Garrard, *Wah-To-Yah and the Taos Trail*, published in 1850, offers a perspective on the events that occurred in Taos during that period. It chronicles the travels of a seventeen-year-old adventurer who accompanied Ceran St. Vrain along the Santa Fe Trail from St. Louis through Bent's Fort to Taos. The timing of the journey of Garrard is serendipitous because his travels precisely coincided with climactic moments in New Mexican history.

Garrard gives a vivid description of the fate of the condemned revolutionaries to which he himself was an eyewitness:

> About nine o'clock, active preparations were made for the execution, and the soldier mustered. Reverend *padres*, on the solemn mission of administering the "blessed sacrament" and spiritual consolation, in long, black gowns and meek countenances, passed the sentinels.[23]

Garrard records the sentiments of a man hanged for "treason":

> His speech was a firm assertion of his own innocence, the unjustness of his trial, and the arbitrary conduct of his murderers. With a scowl, as the cap was pulled over his face, the last words he uttered between his gritting teeth were, *"Caraho, los Americanos!"* *The atrocity of the act of hanging that man for treason is most*

damnable [emphasis mine]; with the execution of
those for murder [according to American legal system, but pariotic defense of the homeland according
to Mexican law] no fault should be found.[24]

Garrard had moral qualms about the military and judicial retri-
bution suffered by the Pueblo Indians and New Mexican settlers. This gnawed at him because at root his sense of justice was
keen.

Court assembled at nine o'clock … . It certainly did
appear to be a great assumption on the part of the
Americans to conquer a country and then arraign
the revolting inhabitants for treason … .

After an absence of a few minutes, the jury returned
with a verdict of "guilty in the first degree" … . Treason, indeed! What did the poor devil know about
his new allegiance? …

I left the room, sick at heart. *Justice! Out upon the word,
when its distorted meaning is the warrant for murdering those
who defend to the last their country and their homes.* [Em-
phasis mine.][25]

It was clear to Garrard that the jurors, the advocates, and the
justices themselves were all people who were related to Charles
Bent by blood or business relationship; Ceran St. Vrain was the
interpreter. It was hardly an impartial jury system. Between April
5 and 24, 1847, fifteen out of seventeen men of the Taos Pueblo
were convicted of murder, one out of five of high treason, and six
out of sixteen of larceny. "The executions for murder were carried
out on an improvised gallows with borrowed lariats and tether
ropes."[26]

Conclusion

Two years after the Taos revolution and about eight months
after the Treaty of Guadalupe-Hidalgo which finally brought clo-
ture to the Mexican War, Padre Martínez again wrote some of his
reflections to Bishop Zubiría.

Some prejudiced Mexicans started a revolution here
in Taos against the Americans, similar to that of 1837
and '38, but were badly defeated by the latter in two

encounters on their way to Santa Fe. After these encounters, a conservative force was organized by the
most respectable citizens. The rebels took to the Indian Village [of Taos] and made that place their headquarters. There they were again attacked and deci-
sively defeated by the American troops, this being
the last attack. The church of the Village was completely destroyed, and the vestments, etc. pertaining
to the church were gathered by the American Com-
mander and delivered to me. The rebels after suffer-
ing a terrible loss were captured. I still keep at my
own church [Our Lady of Guadalupe in Taos Plaza]
the ecclesiastical property which was delivered to
me ... . At the early part of last year, a newspaper
undertook to attack our Religion and its ministers,
and I answered the unjust charges and defended
our cause. I will do the same, with the help of God,
at any time when circumstances may require it.[27]

Reflections

Santiago Valdez, author of Padre Martínez' biography, was a
close relative of the priest and was brought up with him in his
own household.

With historical and moral hindsight, the American retaliation to the Taos Rebellion of 1847 would very likely today be
judged immoral because of the significant disproportion in the
number of people killed. The overwhelming American military
response to a people defending the sovereignty of their own land
would today certainly be considered gravely immoral.

The Taos Rebellion was the focal point of the New Mexico
theater in the Mexican American War. The Taos Pueblo Massa-
cre was the culmination of American retaliation against the Taos
Rebellion. This conflict easily elicits a variety of serious topics
which are important to students of Latino history in the United
States. Among these are such themes as the following: the possession of land and their borders, national sovereignty, the tensions of commerce, labor, and immigration, and aspects of culture and religion which are affected by demographics and inter-

marriage. The whole gamut of economics and politics, relationship of church and state were also issues involved in the Mexican American War, specifically in the Taos Rebellion. The central figure in all of this eventful transition is Padre Martínez.

Any father wants to see unity, peace and reconciliation among his children who may be at odds with one another. The good father realizes that true reconciliation can not develop by discounting differences. They need to be dealt with justly. As a good Padre, Martínez must have been deeply disturbed by the death of hundreds of his parishioners killed at the Pueblo and the execution of several at the Taos Plaza, including the Indian Chief Tomacito Romero and Pablo Montoya. Martínez was a brilliant and compassionate man caught in between the vying factions supporting Mexican nationalism or American expansionism. He valued both, but he ultimately opted for American citizenship and the changes which the new order was bringing. He judged the change to be ultimately better for the people of New Mexico.

In the Taos Rebellion and its surrounding events, that "epoch of the most transcendental importance,"[28] Padre Antonio José Martínez did not act as a Mexican nationalist, nor as a vacillating Hamlet, nor as an opportunistic pawn of the new American forces. It is my opinion that his reactions, although perhaps surprising or disappointing to some, were principled actions born of reflection and decision. He took the unpopular stand of choosing to affirm the American occupation in spite of possible bloodshed. He had foreseen it and made every effort to avert it, but it nevertheless took place. As it was taking place, he embraced it. Had he not used his influence to broker the American presence and occupation, the bloodshed would likely have been worse.

This was a defining moment for the priest who was, as the record clearly shows, an advocate for the poor and a champion of self-determination for all of the people of New Mexico, a region which had such strong historical and cultural ties to both Spain and Mexico. The change in political leadership was a harbinger of changes in ecclesiastical leadership which were soon to follow. Padre Martínez, however, continued to be powerfully influential in the unfolding stages of American history in both the Catholic Church and the U.S. Territory of New Mexico. The tensions and conflicts of transition affecting his church in New

Mexico would prove to be more difficult for him than the political changes. Nevertheless, positive developments in the future, within both the political and the religious spheres, will have much to credit the life and work of Padre Antonio José Martínez, Cura de Taos.

Padre Martínez was proud to be an American citizen without ever losing his cultural or religious identity in the new secular and multicultural society. He also knew he had a powerful contribution to make – with the richness of his cultural and religious heritage – within both the church structure and politics of the new New Mexico. Padre Martínez can justly be called the Father of the Mexican American because he brokered the American presence in what is now called the Southwest during the events surrounding the Taos Rebellion.

Notes

1. *Reluctant Dawn*, Juan Romero with Moises Sandoval, Mexican American Cultural Center (MACC), San Antonio, 1976, pp. 25 and 51. This edition is out of print at present; a new and expanded edition is in preparation.

2. "Cura de Taos por 42 Años [1826-1867]" is engraved as part of the epitaph on the small marble headstone of the grave of Padre Martínez who is buried in the Kit Carson park and cemetery located less than a mile north of the Taos plaza. The land on which this cemetery is located used to belong to Padre Martínez, and was given over for the burial of the Americans who were killed in the 1847 Taos Rebellion which took place twenty years before the death of Padre Martínez.

3. *Life of Joseph Projectus Machebeuf, First Bishop of Denver*, W.J. Howlett, p. 227. This biased attempt to implicate Padre Martínez in the Taos Rebellion of 1847 is reflected in Twitchell, *Leading Facts of New Mexico*, and comes from Martínez' enemies who were French (Canadian) fur trappers and Missouri business partners of Charles Bent who became easy allies of the new French clergy. First among these are Bishop Jean Baptiste Lamy and his vicar-general, Father Joseph Projectus Machebeuf. Father Gabriel Ussel, one of the successors of Padre Martínez as pastor of Our Lady of Guadalupe Church in Taos, was the immediate source on Martínez for Howlett's biography of Bishop Machebeuf: "It was said that he [Padre Martínez] had much to do with the uprising of the Indians

and Mexicans at Taos when Governor Bent and about fifteen Americans and their Mexican sympathizers were massacred on January 19, 1847. He at least shared with the Indians and Mexicans in hatred for the Americans and in their ignorance of events and conditions outside of their little valley. They imagined that they were but beginning a patriotic war which would result in freeing their country from the foreigner, who was supposed to be an enemy to their race and to their religion. The suspicion is probably well founded [that Padre Martínez 'had much to do with the uprising'], although the U.S. Government did not find Father Martínez guilty of direct complicity in the unfortunate insurrection."

4.   Excerpt from "Manifesto" of Padre Martínez, quoted in Benjamin Read, *Illustrated History of New Mexico*, New Mexican Printing Company, Santa Fe, 1912, pp. 408-09. Originally printed on Martínez' press, exposing "the gloomy situation of the people of New Mexico" [B. Read] which was caused by Indian incursions and abandonment by the Mexican government. In November 1843 a copy of the Padre's Manifesto was sent to President Santa Anna, and it was acknowledged as having been read by the President.

5.   Ibid.

6.   Letter of Padre Martínez written from Taos to "His Excellency Dn. José Antonio Lauren de Zubiría, Bishop of Durango" on September 21, 1845, quoted in Santiago Valdez, "Biografía del Presbítero Antonio José Martínez, Cura de Taos, 1877," original manuscript in the Ritch Collection at the Huntington Library in San Marino, California. In 1993, translated into contemporary English by Juan Romero. Copy available at New Mexico State Records and Archives in Santa Fe, p. 99.

7.   *The Maxwell Land Grant*, William A. Keleher, University of New Mexico Press, Albuquerque, 1942, p. 125.

8.   *Ibid.,* p. 15.

9.   Read, p. 416. Benjamin Read's younger brother Larkin married Teodorita Valdez y Martínez, the daughter of Santiago Valdez. Larkin collaborated on Valdez' biography of Martínez by copying it in Spanish calligraphy, while Benjamin later translated it into nineteenth-century English. Furthermore, Benjamin Read obtained from the Martínez family many of the priest's papers and documents and used them in his *Illustrated History of New Mexico* (1912).

10.   *Ibid.,* pp. 417-18. Benjamin Read obtained this information in the year 1884 at Santa Fe from Don José Pablo Gallegos, who was present at that meeting.

370 SEEDS OF STRUGGLE/HARVEST OF FAITH

11.   It is very possible that Padre Martínez helped to formulate the
        new Kearny Code and then helped to translate it into Spanish. I
        base this inference on the following facts: Martínez was himself
        an expert in the civil law of both Mexico and Spain and was
        familiar with Anglo-Saxon law especially as enshrined in the
        great political documents of the United States. He had a reading
        knowledge of English and was most fluent in Spanish. The Kearny
        Code was based on Spanish-Mexican law as well as United States
        law. Padre Martínez willingly made available his own printing
        press so that the new code could be printed and then promul-
        gated.

12.   *Memorias Sobre La Vida del Presbítero Antonio José Martínez, Cura de Taos,*
        Pedro Sánchez, 1903; Guadalupe Baca-Vaughn, tr., ed., Rydal Press,
        1978, p. 42.

13.   "Proclamation by Stephen Watts Kearny, Brigadier-General, U.S.A.,
        upon Occupying Santa Fe, New Mexico," August 22, 1846, in *New
        Mexico Historic Documents*, Richard N. Ellis, ed., University of New
        Mexico Press, Albuquerque, 1975, p. 5.

14.   *Ibid.*, p. 445. Benjamin Read lived among many of the principals
        involved in the New Mexican dimension of the Mexican Ameri-
        can War. Over several decades, he probed their recollections and
        moreover collected many primary documents and papers which
        he used to put together his *Illustrated History* (first two editions writ-
        ten in Spanish) as well as his prior book *La Guerra Mexico Ameri-
        cana.*

15.   Besides Governor Charles Bent, the American casualties at Taos
        included Narciso Beaubien, the son of Judge Charles Beaubien,
        and Stephen Louis Lee, the Sheriff of Taos County.

16.   Account of the death of Bent by his daughter Teresina Bent, quoted
        in Michael McNierney, *Taos 1847*, p. 14.

17.   Sánchez, op. cit., pp. 43-44. Sánchez was married to Refugio
        Martínez, the Padre's favorite niece; the wedding took place at the
        Padre's private chapel (*oratorio*) in 1858, just before the final rift
        between the Padre and the new French Archbishop. Padre Martínez
        performed this marriage for his niece in his house chapel be-
        cause the new pastor of Our Lady of Guadalupe in Taos, Fr. Dámaso
        Taladrid, would not permit the venerable and sickly Padre to offi-
        ciate at the parish church. It was this event which soon after-
        wards led to the ecclesiastical sanctions Padre Martínez received
        from Bishop Lamy. Pedro Sánchez' *Memorias* of the *Cura de Taos*
        never mention the conflict with Bishop Lamy.

18.   Also referred to as Eliah or Euliah, he was nicknamed "General Lee." Elliot Lee is not to be confused with either the Confederate leader or his brother Don Luis (Stephen Louis), the acting Sheriff of Taos County, who was among the first persons killed in the Taos Rebellion. Stephen Lee's house stood on the southeast corner of the Plaza, where McCarthy Plaza was later built.

19.   Read, p. 446.

20.   George Ruxton, "Report on Battle at Turley's Mill," quoted in McNierney, op. cit., p. 19. The Americans who died at Turley's Mill were among the first to be buried at the "American Cemetery," located just north of the Taos Plaza at what is now known as Kit Carson Park and Cemetery.

21.   *Ibid.* pp. 44-45.

22.   McNierney, *passim.*

23.   *Wah-To-Yah and the Taos Trail: Scalp Dances, With a Look at Los Rancheros from Muleback,* Lewis H. Garrard, 1850, University of Oklahoma Press, Norman, 1955, pp. 187-88.

24.   *Ibid., loc. cit.*

25.   *Ibid.,* pp. 171-73. Garrard's phrase "Justice! Out upon the word" was brought to my attention by Corinna Santistevan, well respected New Mexican historian from Taos. It well reflects the keen perception of the young Anglo witness, his sense of justice, and his revulsion at the retaliatory injustice which he saw perpetrated in the courtroom.

26.   *Ibid.,* pp. 5-6.

27.   Valdez, p. 120. Padre Martínez' letter to Bishop Zubiría was written on the eve of the feast of St. Francis, 3 October 1848.

28.   Read, op. cit., p. 415. The full phrase as used by Benjamin Read in his *Illustrated History of New Mexico* is "Let us now go back to the **epoch** of the most **transcendental** importance in the historical annals of New Mexico – the American invasion and the third change of government" (boldface emphasis mine).

Lyrics of the Penitentes:
The Contributions of Los Hermanos
Penitentes to Roman Catholicism
in New Mexico[1]

Alberto López Pulido

Introduction: Contextualizing the Story

As the largest region in the state of New Mexico officially designated as Roman Catholic, the Archdiocese of Santa Fe represents a meaningful indicator as to the conditions of Roman Catholicism in contemporary New Mexico. As an Archdiocese that geographically covers some 61,142 miles, is home to over 260,000 active Roman Catholics, and is dispersed throughout 91 parishes and 216 active missions, it is accurate to conclude that Roman Catholicism is alive and well in the state of New Mexico.[2]

Yet to celebrate these impressive feats of the archdiocese solely as present-day accomplishments without a look towards the past is to present ourselves with an incomplete interpretation of New Mexican Roman Catholicism. Instead, I would argue that the contemporary story of New Mexican Roman Catholicism is intimately interwoven with the stories and expressions of people from the past, of those who have gone before us. The achievements of contemporary Roman Catholicism are molded and structured by people from the past who through their stories and expressions have created history,[3] and within this context they have created a significant and meaningful *sacred* history.

Therefore we cannot know the Roman Catholic traditions of New Mexico without having recourse to those who helped build these sacred traditions. In the case of New Mexico, we speak officially of the early missionaries, the later priests, the sisters of various congregations, and the bishops. But we must also recognize the faithful, *los viejitos* y *los ancianos* – the elders, who in the collective memory of numerous Catholic New Mexicans make up a significant part of *La Fraternidad Piadosa de Nuestro Padre Jesús,* more commonly known as *Los Hermanos Penitentes* of New Mexico. Throughout history, Penitente sacred expressions have maintained and in some cases revived the sacred traditions in New Mexican Catholicism. *Los Hermanos Penitentes* have been an integral part of the New Mexican Hispano experience for centuries.

La Hermandad is an important religious group that preserved the sacred traditions of northern New Mexico and southern Colorado as early as the eighteenth century. Whereas it remains historical fact that the relationship between the Brotherhood and the Roman Catholic hierarchy has been contentious, it is beyond the scope of this essay to document this unfortunate yet tense history of conflict. I wish only to celebrate and recognize the resilience and sacred legacy of the *Hermandad* in relation to emerging Roman Catholicism throughout New Mexican history. Therefore the main objective of this presentation is to share the *stories* and *lyrics* of *caridad, oración,* and *el buen ejemplo* that have emerged in my research as Penitente sacred categories. Charity, prayer, and good example have served and continue to serve as a guide and testament to Hispano Christianity by maintaining and supporting unified communities throughout the sacred New Mexican landscape.

Methodological Issues: Story as Method

In this presentation we examine the aforesaid sacred expressions, which are the main contributions of the Penitente Brotherhood to Roman Catholicism in New Mexico, by means of listening to and documenting their story. This approach is guided by a theoretical and methodological framework that embraces the belief that people construct and create culture through the telling of their own story. Penitente stories and narratives represent and emerge out of a people's experiences, expressions, motivations, intentions, behaviors, styles, and rhythms.[4] The significance and focus of story and story-telling lie directly in the actions of people and their roots in social and cultural life.[5] Furthermore, story provides a space through which people share in the sacred perspective or vision of a particular individual and of his or her community. Through this perspective we discover the layers of a people's history and myths by knowing their story. Therefore, a central aim of this project is to discover a community's or an individual's social, historical, economic, political, and cultural factors, for these factors shape and give meaning to a story in the context of everyday life experiences and expressions as collective groups.

In this study, a sacred story represents a *lyric* with spiritual qualities that orient us toward those things that are real and meaningful in our lives.[6] They serve as concrete and literal guides in our quest for understanding and knowing the sacred.[7] The lyrics or the stories are presented here through spoken language and narratives that serve to unlock the archaic patterns of spiritual creativity and to guide communities towards the sacred.[8] As a result, the major methodological objective of this project is through the narrative to uncover and to interpret the *lyrics of Penitente and Hispano spirituality* represented here as *caridad, oración,* and *el buen ejemplo.*

Unlike past scholarship such as the "vagabond narratives" of Charles Lummis and Carl Taylor[9] that claim to understand Penitente history, this study constructs and tells a story that takes the role of the sacred in the lives of Penitentes very seriously by listening to, recording, and retelling their story. This presentation concludes with an examination of the Penitente story in relation to the story of Roman Catholicism in New Mexico, and offers some important and significant conclusions with regards to the role of the Penitentes.

The Story of *Caridad* in Penitente History

The history of Christianity in New Mexico is predominantly the story of Roman Catholicism in the Americas as it traversed southern-to-northern geographical regions. Consequently, it is best characterized as a ubiquitous religious tradition that transcends the institutionalized parameters of American Roman Catholicism. From the first settlements until at least territorial times, the New

Mexican region had no resident bishop or major seminary, and Hispanic New Mexico suffered from a chronic shortage of priests.[10] New Mexico was perceived as isolated and dangerous with few if any rewards, and the Catholic clergy avoided it. By 1830, close to half of the 4,299 priests, the majority of whom were Spanish, had departed from the Mexican frontier.[11] As inhabitants of an historically isolated territory with little support or direction from a religious clergy, the New Mexican Catholic settlers produced a unique type of Catholicism that was self-reliant and laity-centered.[12] As a result, the sacred emerged within a unique political, economic, social, and cultural context that was intertwined with the personal everyday life experiences and expressions of a people. The evolving local faith represents a resilient people characterized as rural, communal, self-determined, and devout. From within this history and tradition emerged *Los Hermanos Penitentes.*

The Penitentes are directly credited for preserving sacred traditions in a region bereft of the official Catholic sacraments and other priestly ministrations central to the tenets of Roman Catholicism. The *Hermandad* emerged in every village as a civil and religious organization that led the community in prayer, worship, and catechism. At the same time, the Brotherhood made sure everyone had the basics for a sufficient quality of life through collective irrigation and the harvesting of the lands.[13] At the core of this belief system was charity – *caridad.*

For example, throughout various communities in New Mexico, one often hears the story about the widows or orphans who, due to the loss of family, find themselves in need of material aid and support. In the story, the plight of the widow or orphan is resolved by members of the community who respond expeditiously to the needs of the less fortunate in their community. Candy Martínez, for example, has fond memories of *"las tradiciones de antes* – past traditions" growing-up in Truchas, New Mexico. She remembers Truchas as a place where there was always community among the people: *"Siempre había comunidad* – There was always community," she recalls. "My dad owned a ranch and all of my uncles and the neighbors always came to help him. They would cut and bundle the wheat; we would make dinner, and everyone would eat and share. When the other people had work, then we in turn would go and help them."[14] She asserts, "If something ever happened, if any of the people were going through any type of *tribulación* – affliction, then the other families were ready to assist them, be it with food or with any other type of aid; but the families were always united," she concludes.[15] Candy's narrative represents part of a larger collective history that, over the centuries, has taught the values of mutuality, reciprocity, and self-determination in the New Mexican region.[16]

Layered deeply within these teachings are the sacred experiences and expressions of the Penitente Brotherhood. According to the Penitente narrative, to help a widow or orphan is to partake in *una obra de caridad* (an act of charity). We are told:

> Over the years, the Brothers *accarrearon* – gathered – these communities with much pride, but without self-aggrandizement, for it was simply a part of their teachings. They helped sustain the homes and harvest the lands of those that needed help – the widows, the orphans. They provided succor by means of prayer and spiritual exercises in the *moradas* – chapter houses. [The Brothers] could gather the community because in those days, everyone was united and knew where to go for prayer, spiritual, and personal help.[17]

An act of charity is the Hermandad's most important sacred self-expression. It is achieved through *oración* – prayer – and *el buen ejemplo* – good example. Acts of charity, prayer, and good example are at the core of the Penitente sacred experience. Through personal story and narrative, this essay explores these Penitente sacred experiences and expressions in an attempt to understand the Penitente sacred world.

Members of the Hermandad credit charitable works with having gathered and sustained New Mexican communities over the centuries. Charity has been a way to vigilantly "look out" for those in the community in need of help. The Hermandad has been known to gather communities, so the people have known where to go for spiritual help: *"Iban para las moradas porque no había clero Católico* – They would go to the moradas because there was no Catholic clergy."[18] The Brotherhood succored the community through prayer as praying was directly linked to acts of charity.

Praying and providing help or assistance to those in need are understood as synonymous sacred acts. One Penitente regards his childhood as a "complete act of charity" as he remembers his life being one of always seeking to help others in the community. "When we finished harvesting our land, it was automatic for us to go with the neighbors and help them with theirs."[19] Throughout the history of the southwest and in particular New Mexico and southern Colorado, the Hermandad continues to maintain the beliefs of charity and benevolence through their sustained actions of helping members of the community.

Doing Caridad, Oración, el Buen Ejemplo, y Penitencia[20]

The most salient characteristic that defines a Penitente is the practice of *penitencia* (penance). The attitude of penance is experienced and expressed through manifestations and demonstrations of charity (*caridad*) for the Brotherhood and for the community at large.[21] From this perspective, it is understood that charity is a penitential act and that a Penitente must strive to practice acts of charity.

Charity is described as an act of penance because "*requiere que tengo que salirme de mi camino* – it requires that I have to go out of my way" for the sake of "*haciendo oración* – doing prayer" for some individual or for the community at large.[22] An act of charity is an act one ordinarily does not have to do but which, in the doing, is transformed into an act of penance. One sacred story that defines and evokes *caridad* in the Penitente world is the story of *Valerosa Verónica*.

The *Via Crucis* devotion is a pilgrimage by which the Penitente Brotherhood accompanys Jesus in his passion on the "Way of the Cross." As a devotion that was disseminated throughout the world by the Franciscan Order, the *Via Crucis* plays a prominent role in *Semana Santa* (Holy Week) observances for Penitentes. The passion of Jesus presents a plan for living one's daily life:

The most important thing to understand regarding the passion of the Lord is that every step that He took was in order to give us an example with His life on how we are suppose to live.[23]

The Stations of the Cross are said to have originated in the twelfth and thirteenth centuries when veterans of the Crusades erected tableaux in their homes representing various places they had visited in the Holy Land. The custom was borrowed by the Franciscans, who eventually brought the practice to the Americas. Historically, the number of stations varied from as few as five to over thirty until in 1731 Pope Clement XII routinized them at fourteen.[24] It is at stations number five and six where we learn the story of *Valerosa Verónica*. The Penitente narrative of *Valerosa Verónica* is as follows:

> La historia que se ha dicho (y las tradiciones que tenemos nosotros) sucedió en la estación cinco pero la nombran número seis. Por que allí estaba una piedra que hasta el día de hoy se enseña en Jerusalén y allí se sentó el Señor mientras que hallaba quien le ayudara con la cruz. Y en eso se vino una mujer, Valerosa Verónica, y se vino por entre toda la gente sin que nadie la molestara con el valor de ir a limpiar el rostro al Señor — The story that is told and that is a part of our traditions occurred at station number five but is referred to as number six. It is said that there was a rock at this location that till this day is still shown in Jerusalem where the Lord sat while they found someone who could help him carry the cross. During this process, Courageous Veronica came forth from among the people and dared to wipe the face of our Lord, and no one bothered her.

The Penitente narrative of the passion of Jesus tells us that Jesus sat on a rock waiting while soldiers tried to locate someone who would help Him carry the cross. "No one was willing to come forward to help Him because according to the law he who carried the cross would die upon it."[25] Frustrated by their inability to locate anyone, the Penitente narrative says, the soldiers were forced to hire Simon of Cyrene to help Jesus carry the cross. This event is officially recognized as the fifth station of the cross.

During this period of waiting, the Penitente story relates, *Valerosa Verónica* came forward from among the people to wipe the face of Jesus with her veil. In response, the Lord rewarded her for her courageous act: her veil was left marked with the facial image of Jesus. Penitentes officially recognize the actions by *Valerosa Verónica* as the sixth station of the cross but are very cognizant of the fact that it may have occurred during the action of the fifth station.

In addition, a person *hace caridad* (accomplishes acts of charity) through the act of *haciendo oración* (doing prayer or praying). Charity represents the spiritual pursuit as praying represents the manner through which to realize this spiritual objective. For Penitentes, acts of charity are tantamount to prayer, and in that respect both represent acts of penance.

More importantly, prayer is talked about and understood in a very special way within the Penitente sacred tradition. To state that you are *haciendo oración* means that you are *literally* doing prayer or praying. That is, prayer is understood as an act, action, or performance by a group or individual; it is an integral part of Penitente history and traditions as described at the outset of this essay. Therefore, doing prayer or praying represents prayer in action:

> Prayer does not mean that I am going to kneel and pray. Prayer can also mean that I am going to see what the needs of those people [*aquella gente*] are and then I am going to help them.[26]

Finally, prayer as action is creatively identified as *el buen ejemplo de oración* (the good example of prayer). This means that by praying (meaning prayer that produces acts of charity) one provides a good example to the Brotherhood and the community at large. *El buen ejemplo* (good example) represents charitable acts without personal prayer, or charitable acts with personal prayer. El buen ejemplo without personal prayer represent charitable or merciful acts as good examples that are synonymous with prayer. It represents one of the most important values within the Penitente tradition:

> For my Father God prefers the good example that you do with your life rather than if you are praying. Pray all day long but don't tell no one, you understand? One goes with the other naturally.[27]

El buen ejemplo with personal prayer in performing charitable or merciful acts means that you offer personal prayer for someone in addition to assisting or helping them. Good example with personal prayer is described as

> asking my Father God through the medium of prayer that he succor a family that finds itself alone or for-

saken, and in addition, one sees if this [person] needs wood or whatever. If so, one would collect it and bring it to them.

In sum, one is told that in this life, no one *"puede ganarle a la oración y el buen ejemplo* – can do better than praying and giving good example" because it is there where one will find *caridad.*[28]

Conclusion

Through this presentation I have argued that contemporary sacred traditions of Roman Catholicism in New Mexico are molded and structured by history. With this in mind, I wish to conclude this presentation by asking, what can one learn from this historical relationship between the Penitentes and the Roman Catholic Church in New Mexico?

In response, I believe there are two important conclusions that one can take away from this. First, that as we look back towards the ecclesial development and organization of New Mexican Roman Catholicism, we find a faith community that exists directly as a result of Penitente sacred expressions and perseverance. The stories and lyrics of Penitente expressions have made significant contributions to the sacred identity, character, and survival of Roman Catholicism throughout the American Southwest, and particularly in New Mexico.

A second very important conclusion to draw from this work is to recognize the ecclesiastical importance of the laity in the Roman Catholic tradition. As Cardinal John Henry Newman has taught us that during critical moments in the history of the Church when the hierarchy failed to uphold the *traditions of the Apostles,* the laity served as a witness for maintaining orthodoxy and keeping the Christian faith alive.[29] For we must remember that as the "holy People of God" according to Vatican II, the laity shares in "Christ's Prophetic office." For they "spread abroad a living witness to Him, especially by means of a life of faith and charity and by offering to God a sacrifice of praise, the tribute of lips which give praise to His name."[30]

These I believe have been the contributions of Los Hermanos Penitentes to Roman Catholicism in New Mexico.

Notes

1. This work is part of a book manuscript entitled *The Sacred World of the Penitentes: Religious Memory and Storytelling in New Mexico* that is based on archival work, fieldwork, and oral-interview research in northern New Mexico and Albuquerque, New Mexico, beginning in 1992. The *original* and *new* research for this book comes from numerous interviews with several *Hermanos* and relatives of various Hermanos compiled over the past five years. The most important and significant contribution to this research project comes from one *Hermano Mayor* with whom I have spoken continually about Penitente sacred experiences since 1992.

   The research for this essay was funded with grants from the Cushwa Center for the Study of American Catholicism, and the Louisville Institute for the Study of American Protestantism. I thank those members of the hermandad who shared their hearts and minds with me. I also wish to thank my friend and colega David T. Abalos who helped me in conceptualizing and developing the arguments presented in this essay.

2. These represent 1997 figures from the Office of the Archbishop, Archdiocese of Santa Fe, New Mexico.

3. See Alberto L. Pulido, "Mexican American Catholicism in the Southwest: The Transformation of a Popular Religion," *Perspective in Mexican American Studies* 4 (1993): 93-4.

4. Charles H. Long, *Significations: Signs, Symbols, and Images in the Interpretation of Religion* (Philadelphia: Fortress, 1986), p. 7.

5. This is drawn directly from the work of Richard Bauman, who refers to storytelling as "oral literature" and asserts that it has its primary existence in the action of people and their roots in social and cultural life. Richard Bauman, *Story, Performance, and Event: Contextual Studies of Oral Narrative* (New York: Cambridge, 1993), pp. 1-2.

6. This interpretation of the sacred draws from the works of Mircea Eliade and Charles Long. See Mircea Eliade, *Ordeal by Labyrinth* (Chicago: University of Chicago, 1982); Charles H. Long, *Significations: Signs, Symbols, and Images in the Interpretation of Religion* (Philadelphia: Fortress, 1986).

7. See Wendy Doniger O'Flaherty, *Other People's Myths: The Cave of Echoes* (Chicago: University of Chicago, 1988).

8. David Carrasco, "A Perspective for a Study of Religious Dimensions in Chicano Experience, *Bless Me, Ultima* as a Religious Text," *Aztlán* 13 (1982), 206-7. Additional lyrics identified in Carrasco's "lyrics of Chicano spirituality" are art and political performances.

9. Charles F. Lummis, *The Land of Poco Tiempo* (Albuquerque: University of New Mexico, 1952). Carl N. Taylor, "Agony in New Mexico," *Today*, February 15, 1936, p. 3.

10. Robert Sprott, O.F.M., "Making Up What Is Lacking: Towards an Interpretation of the Penitentes," (Southwest Hispanic Research Center, University of New Mexico, Fall 1984, Working Paper # 110), p. 3.

11. Alberto L. Pulido, "The Religious Dimension of Mexican Americans," in *The History of the Mexican American People*, ed. Julian Samora (Notre Dame: Notre Dame Press, 1993), p. 225.

12. Moises Sandoval, *On the Move: A History of the Hispanic Church in the United States* (New York: Orbis, 1990), pp. 21-2.

13. Alberto L. Pulido, "Mexican American Catholicism in the Southwest: The Transformation of a Popular Religion," *Perspectives in Mexican American Studies* 4 (1993): 93-108.

14. Candy Martínez, Personal Interview, 19 July 1994.

15. Candy Martínez, Personal Interview, 19 July 1994.

16. In one of his many collections of stories of the Río Puerco Valley by Nasario García, we are introduced to the stories of Teodorita García-Ruelas and Adelita Gonzales. Both of these stories speak to the mutual and reciprocal relations established among neighbors in New Mexican communities. See Teodorita García-Ruelas, "Baile y baile y sin harina!" and Adelita Gonzales, "Dios nos tenía bendecidos con la comida que teníanos," *Abuelitos: Stories of the Río Puerco Valley*, ed. Nasario García (Albuquerque: University of New Mexico Press, 1992), pp. 99, 125.

17. Penitente Brother, Personal Interview, 12 August 1993.

18. Penitente Brother, Personal Interview, 12 August 1993.

19. Penitente Brother, Telephone Interview, 23 February 1997.

20. The noun *"doing"* is translated literally from the Spanish *haciendo*. *Haciendo* comes from the verb *hacer* which means "to do" or "to make." "Doing" is used in this essay to describe an act, action, or performance by a group or individual. Therefore, *haciendo oración* means literally *"doing prayer,"* or simply "praying." In this study, prayer in the penitente sacred world represents an act or action.

21. The perspective taken in this essay represents a major and significant departure from past Penitente studies that focus obsessively on alleged flagellant practices of the Brotherhood and ignore the fact that the sacred is at the core of Penitente identity, experience, and expression.

22. Penitente Brother, Personal Interview, 12 August 1993.

23. Penitente Brother, Telephone Interview, 17 April 1997.

24.   Marta Weigle, *Brothers of Light, Brothers of Blood: The Penitentes of the Southwest* (Santa Fe: Ancient City, 1976), pp. 162-66.
25.   Penitente Brother, Telephone Interview, 17 April 1997.
26.   Penitente Brother, Personal Interview, 12 August 1993.
27.   Penitente Brother, Personal Interview, 12 August 1993.
28.   Penitente Brother, Personal Interview, 12 August 1993.
29.   John Henry Newman, "On Consulting the Faithful in Matters of Doctrine," *Newman the Theologian: A Reader*, Ian Ker, ed. (Notre Dame: University of Notre Dame Press, 1990).
30.   Vatican II, "Lumen Gentium," article 12.

Lamy's Legacy: Catholic Institutions of New Mexico Territory

Nancy Hanks

With the 1848 treaty of Guadalupe Hidalgo, the United States annexed New Mexico, and ecclesiastical control of the region passed from the diocese of Durango, within the Mexican Catholic church, to Baltimore, Maryland, within the United States Catholic Church. In 1850, French-born Jean Baptiste Lamy (Figure 1) was appointed to administer the Vicariate Apostolic of New Mexico, an enormous area that included all of the present-day states of New Mexico and Arizona (except the Gadsden Purchase area) and parts of Colorado and Nevada (Map 1).[1] Lamy, who had served for eleven years in Ohio and Kentucky when he was named Vicar Apostolic of New Mexico, arrived in Santa Fe in the fall of 1851.

New Mexico Territory's population increased rapidly with the United States' occupation, and Lamy's vicariate was elevated to the Diocese of Santa Fe in 1853 and to the Archdiocese of Santa Fe in 1875. With each administrative change, diocesan boundaries also changed; Arizona and Colorado eventually broke off to become dioceses of their own, although they were still under the eye of the Archdiocese of Santa Fe. As Lamy's title changed through the years – from vicar apostolic to bishop to archbishop – he always looked to his former seminary in Clermont-Ferrand, France, to recruit his parish priests for New Mexico. As a result, French secular clergy dominated the Catholic parishes of New Mexico Territory.[2] The impact of the French Catholic presence can be seen most prominently in the capital of New Mexico Territory, Santa Fe.

Santa Fe Institutions

The French secular clergy viewed their mission as nothing less than introducing culture and civilization to the people of New Mexico Territory. Upon arrival in Santa Fe, the Frenchmen were dismayed by the adobe churches, the "poverty-stricken and

Figure 1: Jean Baptiste Lamy, ca. 1860s. Photograph courtesy of the Museum of New Mexico, Santa Fe, Neg. no. 35878.

shabby-looking houses of public worship."[3] Unaccustomed to seeing mud used as a building material, the French and other Anglos
viewed local adobe architecture with disdain.

Lamy's first project in Santa Fe was to repair *La Castrense*, also
known as Our Lady of Light Chapel, which had been built as a
military chapel in 1760 and 1761 on the south side of the plaza.
The chapel, fallen into disrepair during the first half of the 1800s,
had been used as storage space for munitions by the occupying
American military from 1846 until August 1851, when Lamy
repossessed it for the Catholic Church.[4] Lamy repaired *La Castrense*
and used it as his parish church instead of the old Spanish *parroquia*
of Saint Francis, which was occupied by Vicar Juan Felipe Ortiz.[5]
Ortiz left for Durango, Mexico, in late 1852 or early 1853, and
Lamy moved into Saint Francis, closing *La Castrense* two years
later.[6]

Lamy was determined to remodel Saint Francis, and major
restoration of Saint Francis began in 1859, when Lamy had Father Jean Baptiste Salpointe move the great stone *reredos* used
behind the altar at *La Castrense* into the *parroquia's* old sanctuary.[7]
By 1869, however, Lamy decided to build a completely new

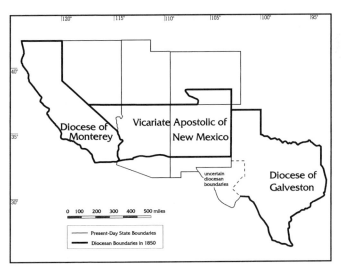

Map 1: Catholic Diocesan Boundaries in the American Southwest, 1850.

church that would look more like a cathedral than the *parroquia*, and he began a program to construct the present Saint Francis Cathedral. Lamy's method was unique: erect the new building around the old *parroquia* and continue to use it for services while construction was underway, thus enclosing the old building "like a huge stone vault" (Figure 2).[8] He was wise to leave some place of worship – construction of Saint Francis lasted until well after Lamy's death in 1888. Although the actual blessing of the cathedral took place on March 7, 1886, its consecration on October 18, 1895, was the work of Father Fourchegú, who assumed the entire cathedral debt so that it could be ready for Archbishop Chapelle's reception of the pallium (Figure 3).[9]

Further construction in Santa Fe occurred after 1852, when Lamy recruited ten Sisters of Loretto from Bardstown, Kentucky, to educate the young women of the Territory.[10] In 1853, the Sisters of Loretto opened the Academy of Our Lady of Light in an adobe residence that Father Charles Brun built for Lamy.[11] Three more sisters arrived in 1855, and a novitiate, the Convent of Our Lady of Light, was established by the Sisters of Loretto at Santa Fe, at "the best looking house in town," *La Casa Americana*, so called because it had a shingle roof, "all the other roofs in town being flat and covered with earth."[12] In 1873, construction began on the Chapel of Our Lady of Light (now known simply as Loretto Chapel) ending in 1878; Loretto Academy was built in 1880 (Figure 4). The chapel was supposedly adapted from Sainte-Chapelle in Paris and was the only stone building completed by the time the railroad arrived in Santa Fe in 1880.[13] Loretto Chapel, in true Gothic Revival style, features a pointed arch, pinnacles used to weight the buttresses, and window tracery at the top of the pointed-arch windows.[14] At the top of the steeple is a cast iron statue from France of Our Lady of Lourdes, placed on Loretto Chapel in 1888 (Figure 5). This is a twin to the one imported by Father Camile Seux for San Juan Pueblo, which soon became a pilgrimage shrine (Figure 6). Both statues were bought in Paris and probably brought back to Santa Fe by Father Eguillon, but at the expense of Father Seux.[15]

Lamy acquired San Miguel Chapel, south of the Santa Fe River, in 1859 for the Christian Brothers, an order of educators imported by Lamy to New Mexico from France.[16] Lamy also acquired the property next to the old San Miguel Church for the Christian Brothers' Catholic school for boys. In the late 1860s, this became Saint Michael's College; a new building was completed by 1887, which later became Saint Michael's High School.[17] During this time, the Christian Brothers tried to improve the dilapidated chapel (Figure 7), but the triple-tiered tower of San Miguel collapsed in the 1870s. It was replaced in 1887 with a square tower and shuttered louvers (since removed) (Figure 8).[18]

In 1865, Lamy brought four Sisters of Charity to New Mexico from Cincinnati, Ohio. They were housed in the old Episcopal "palace," where they established Saint Vincent's Hospital and an orphanage (Figure 9).[19] In 1880, the Sisters of Charity opened an "industrial school" for orphan girls in Santa Fe, and in 1882, another building (later known as Seton Hall) was constructed nearby and used for ambulatory tuberculosis patients and for aged and infirm clergy.[20] At that time, the only hospital, the only orphanage, and all the schools in New Mexico were Catholic institutions. In 1887, the Sisters of Charity opened a new Saint Vincent's Hospital in Santa Fe (Figure 10), and they began to build its replacement in 1907.

Another Santa Fe chapel south of the river is the Santuario de Guadalupe, built in the early 1800s as a shrine to the Virgin of Guadalupe. Like the other churches in Santa Fe when the American Catholics arrived, the Santuario was initially found to be in poor shape. In 1881, Lamy assigned the French priest James Defouri to establish a new parish in Santa Fe at Guadalupe Chapel (Figure 11). Defouri promptly covered the dirt floor with wood, cut tall Gothic windows in the nave, and added a pitched roof, designed to protect the adobe walls and giving the structure a "Queen Anne Victorian facade with a central pointed tower and a clock in the window above the front door" (Figure 12).[22]

Institutions Outside of Santa Fe in New Mexico Territory

Upon Lamy's arrival in New Mexico in 1851, seven-eighths of the population was considered illiterate.[23] The only schools in the region had been a "college" briefly operating in Santa Fe in the late 1820s and Padre Martínez's academy in Taos.[24]

Lamy felt it was urgent to establish an educational system, but there was no public funding to do so—the citizens of New Mexico had never had any such direct tax, and they were too poor to pay such a tax anyway. In 1855, the issue of a public school system supported by a general tax was placed before the voters, with 37 votes in favor and 5,016 opposed.[25] The early schools of New Mexico, therefore, were supported by private donations, fees, and the Catholic Church, and this led to Lamy's placement, with the Governor and the Secretary of the Territory, on a committee created to manage the educational system in New Mexico Territory in 1863 when the first Territorial School Law was passed.[26] Lamy's efforts to promote education involved two distinct groups of religious workers—those who were secular

Figure 2: Saint Francis Cathedral Under Construction Around the *Parroquia*, Santa Fe, ca. 1883. Photograph by B. H. Gurnsey, courtesy of the Museum of New Mexico, Santa Fe, Neg. no. 131794.

clergy and generally served as parish priests, and those in religious orders, which generally ran the hospitals and boarding schools.

In 1851, there were about twenty secular clergy working in New Mexico, and they all had been born there.[27] By the end of 1852, that number had dwindled to fourteen native-born priests and six priests brought in by Lamy, three of whom were French. By the end of 1857, there were twenty-nine secular clergy in New Mexico, only twelve of whom were native New Mexicans.[28] The rest were all from Europe, most of them Frenchmen from Lamy's home diocese, Clermont-Ferrand. Throughout the rest of the Territorial Period, there was a steady decline in native New Mexican clergy and an increase in French clergy, to the extent that the Frenchmen comprised the majority of secular clergy serving in New Mexico during its 62-year territorial period.

As the French clergy started new parishes away from Santa Fe, they were followed by techniques and materials used by the

Figure 3: Visit of Cardinal Gibbons and Archbishop Kain of Saint Louis at the Installation of Archbishop Chapelle, Santa Fe, New Mexico, October 1895. Photograph courtesy of the Museum of New Mexico, Santa Fe, Neg. no. 65110.

French and Italian architects, stone masons, and carpenters who built Saint Francis Cathedral and Loretto Chapel in Santa Fe (Map 2). In Las Vegas, New Mexico, the church of Our Lady of Sorrows (Nuestra Señora de los Dolores) shows touches of both Gothic and Romanesque Revival, with its pointed archway resembling the Loretto Chapel's and its gabled roof and towers resembling those of Saint Francis Cathedral (Figure 13).[29]

In other parishes, church exteriors and interiors were remodeled in an effort to disguise the "Old Adobe" religious structures. The churches remodeled by the Catholic clergy showed a "Folk Gothic" or "Gothick" style, probably due to the fact that the purer "Gothic" Revival of Santa Fe lost something in its translation to the hinterlands when given to local carpenters for execution.[30] Nuestra Señora del Socorro Church (Figure 14) in Socorro illustrates the "Gothick" style, with its wooden steeples, spires, and pitched roof. Saint Augustine Church at Isleta Pueblo looked like a Spanish mission in 1867 just after Father Augustin Brun arrived (Figure 15), but had changed considerably by 1931 (Figure 16), under the leadership of Frenchman Father Antoine Docher. Saint Francis of Assisi Church in Ranchos de Taos received "Gothick" front doors and arched windows, and French Father Joseph Giraud placed wooden belfries atop its flat roof.

Figure 4: Loretto Academy (on left) and Loretto Chapel (on right), Santa Fe, ca. 1889-1902. Photograph courtesy of the Museum of New Mexico, Santa Fe, Neg. no. 72294.

While the number of French secular clergy was increasing in the parish churches of New Mexico Territory, the number of religious orders was also growing. Lamy had already imported Sisters of Loretto, Christian Brothers, and Sisters of Charity to work in Santa Fe. Subsequently, these groups became the first religious orders to work outside of Santa Fe as well.

Figure 5: Statue of Our Lady of Lourdes atop the Loretto Chapel, Santa Fe. Photograph courtesy of author.

After establishing themselves in Santa Fe, the Sisters of Loretto expanded north to open the Academy of Our Lady of Guadalupe school for girls in Taos (in 1863) and then the Academy of the Annunciation in Mora (in 1864).[31] The Sisters of Loretto expanded south from Santa Fe to Albuquerque, at the request of Father Truchard, and started Our Lady of Guadalupe School in 1866. That school closed in 1869 and the Sisters of Loretto opened Immaculate Conception School in Las Vegas, New Mexico, that same year (Figure 17).[32] In Bernalillo, with the financial backing of Don José Leandro Perea, the Sisters of Loretto opened the Sacred Heart Academy around 1875.[33] This operated as a Catholic school until

Figure 6: Statue of Our Lady of Lourdes, San Juan Pueblo, ca. 1899. Photograph by Huish and Hinshaw, courtesy of the Museum of New Mexico, Santa Fe, Neg. no. 56417.

1885, when the Sisters of Loretto turned it into the Bernalillo Contract School for girls, which continued until 1937.[34] Further south, in Las Cruces, the Sisters of Loretto established the Visitation Academy in 1870 and the Loretto Academy in 1899.[35] In nearby Mesilla the Sisters of Loretto opened a school in 1892. In Socorro, Father Bernard asked for Sisters of Loretto to open a school in his parish, and the Convent of Our Lady of Mount Carmel was established there in 1879.[36] In 1912, the Sisters of Loretto took over the Immaculate Conception School in East Las Vegas.[37]

The Christian Brothers, like the Sisters of Loretto, expanded north from Santa Fe to Taos to establish Saint Joseph's school for

Figure 7: San Miguel Chapel, Santa Fe, ca. 1871. Photograph by Timothy H. O'Sullivan, courtesy of the Museum of New Mexico, Santa Fe, Neg. no. 10110.

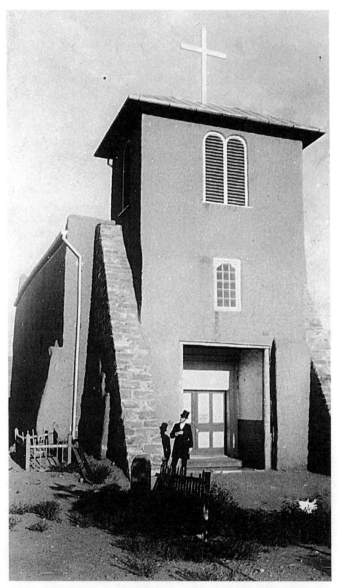

Figure 8: San Miguel Chapel restored, Santa Fe, 1887. Photograph by Dana B. Chase, courtesy of the Museum of New Mexico, Santa Fe, Neg. no. 56977.

boys around 1863 and to Mora to establish Saint Mary's College in 1867.[38] In 1872 four Christian Brothers opened a school for boys in Bernalillo, and in 1888 the Christian Brothers opened another boys' school in Las Vegas called the LaSalle Institute.[39]

The Sisters of Charity, after establishing Saint Vincent's Hospital in Santa Fe, were invited to take over an existing school in Old Albuquerque's San Felipe Neri parish in 1881 or 1882. It was theoretically divided into two schools: the Old Town Public School until the county ran out of money every year in about February and Our Lady of the Angels Private School thereafter.[40] The Sisters of Charity purchased land in New Albuquerque for Saint Vincent's Academy for girls, which opened in 1883. Evidently around this same time the Sisters of Charity established the Sacred Heart Academy in San Miguel with the help of Father Fayet.[41] Later, the Sisters of Charity opened Saint Mary's parochial school in Albuquerque and then expanded to El Paso in 1892.[42]

A different order of the Sisters of Charity – these from Leavenworth, Kansas – were invited by Archbishop Chapelle in 1887 to establish a hospital in Las Vegas to fight "the Great White Plague," as tuberculosis was called, and Saint Anthony's Sanitarium was dedicated on January 26, 1897 (Figure 18).[43] Saint Anthony's Sanitorium grew into an up-to-the-minute three-story stone structure of semi-colonial design. The Sisters of Charity established Saint Joseph's Sanitarium in 1902, the first of its kind in Albuquerque (Figure 19).[44]

In 1867, the Society of Jesus arrived in New Mexico Territory, and the five Jesuits – all Italians – took over Bernalillo, considered at that time to be one of the best parishes in the diocese, and moved the next year to Albuquerque.[45] By 1873, Jesuit Superior Donato Gasparri established the printing press *Imprenta del Rio Grande*, but when the Rio Grande flooded the next year, he "ordered that the press be dismantled and stated that never again would it be erected in Albuquerque until such time as it would be perfectly secure from flood waters."[46] Father Gasparri moved to the safer ground of Las Vegas and began publishing the *Revista Católica* in 1875. By 1874, the Jesuits had opened a school for boys in Albuquerque, and another, *La Casa Redonda* (Figure 20), in Las Vegas in the Romero house on South Pacific Street. This led to the founding of Las Vegas College in 1877 (Figure 21), which was

Figure 9: Daughters of Charity, Santa Fe[21]. Photograph courtesy of the Museum of New Mexico, Santa Fe, Neg. no. 1412.

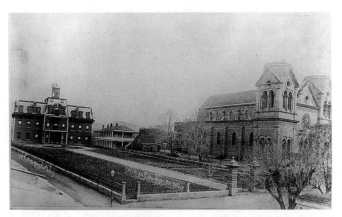

Figure 10: Saint Vincent's Sanitarium (left) and Saint Francis Cathedral (right), Santa Fe, ca. 1888. Photograph courtesy of the Museum of New Mexico, Santa Fe, Neg. no. 105949.

transferred to Denver in 1888 and later became Regis College and later yet Regis University.

The Sisters of Mercy, like the Jesuits, bypassed Santa Fe altogether and went to Silver City, New Mexico, to establish Saint Vincent's Academy in 1870. They opened Sacred Heart Academy in Mesilla around 1880 and opened a boarding and day school in the Sapelló parish between 1881 and 1883.[47] In 1887 they founded Mercy Hospital in Silver City, where the Sisters of Saint Joseph had opened a school in 1879.[48]

In 1899, the Franciscan Fathers returned to New Mexico at Archbishop Bourgade's request, and they based their community in Peña Blanca. They branched out to Jémez in 1902 and Clovis and Roswell in 1903.[49] In 1904, Sisters of Saint Francis came to Peña Blanca to teach, and they opened another school in Jémez in 1905 or 1906.[50] Franciscans opened Saint John the Baptist

Figure 11: Our Lady of Guadalupe Chapel, Santa Fe, 1881. Photograph William H. Jackson, courtesy of the Museum of New Mexico, Santa Fe, Neg. no. 132561.

Figure 12: Our Lady of Guadalupe Chapel, Santa Fe, 1912. Photograph courtesy of the Museum of New Mexico, Santa Fe, Neg. no. 10036.

Figure 13: Our Lady of Sorrows Church, Las Vegas, ca. 1907. Photograph by Jesse L. Nusbaum, courtesy of the Museum of New Mexico, Santa Fe, Neg. no. 61252.

Church for Mexicans in Roswell in 1903 (Figures 22 and 23), and Saint Peter's Catholic School in Roswell in 1905.[51] Some of the teachers at Saint Peter's were Sisters of Saint Casimir from Chicago, but lay teachers were also used. Also in Roswell, the Sisters of the Sorrowful Mother came from Chicago to establish Saint Mary's Hospital in Roswell in 1906, and by 1909, the Sisters of the Blessed Mother had built a hospital in Roswell, at the south end of Main Street.[52]

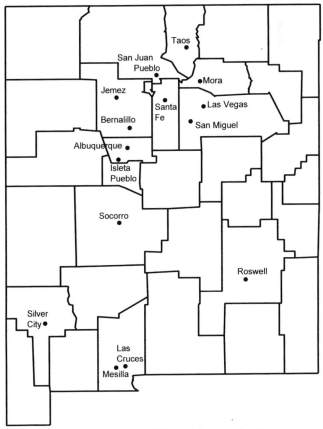

Map 2: Cities and Towns in New Mexico Mentioned in Text.

Figure 14: Nuestra Señora del Socorro Church, Socorro, ca. 1886. Photograph by J. R. Riddle, courtesy of the Museum of New Mexico, Santa Fe, Neg. no. 76076.

Figure 15: Saint Augustine Church, Isleta Pueblo, ca. 1867. Photograph by Dr. William Bell, courtesy of the Museum of New Mexico, Santa Fe, Neg. no. 12321.

Figure 16: Saint Augustine Church, Isleta Pueblo, 1931. Photograph courtesy of the Museum of New Mexico, Santa Fe, Neg. no. 2669.

Figure 17: Loretto Academy, South Gonzales St, looking Southeast, Las Vegas, 1885, Photograph by F. E. Evans, courtesy of the Museum of New Mexico, Santa Fe, Neg. no. 14710.

Figure 18: Saint Anthony's Sanitarium, Las Vegas. Photograph courtesy of the Museum of New Mexico, Santa Fe, Neg. no. 70705.

Figure 19: Saint Joseph's Sanitarium, Albuquerque, ca 1900. Photograph by Lewis H. O'Rear, courtesy of the Museum of New Mexico, Santa Fe, Neg. no. 139767.

Figure 20: Parochial School, Las Vegas, ca 1885. Photograph by F. E. Evans, courtesy of the Museum of New Mexico, Santa Fe, Neg. no. 72308.

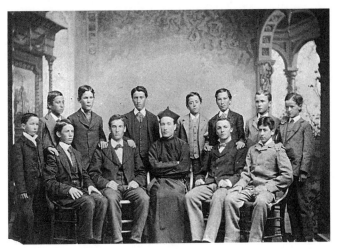

Figure 21: Classical Dept., Las Vegas College, 1881. Photograph by James N. Furlong, courtesy of the Museum of New Mexico, Santa Fe, Neg. no. 56290.

Figure 22: Old Church of Saint John the Baptist, Roswell. Loyola University Chicago Archives: Catholic Church Extension Society Photo Collection, 14-R-13.

Figure 23: New Church of Saint John the Baptist, Roswell. Loyola University Chicago Archives: Catholic Church Extension Society Photo Collection, 14-R-12.

Lamy's Legacy

Lamy was relentless in his efforts to bring in workers to establish the Catholic institutions of the Territorial Period—whether secular clergymen, craftsmen to build new churches, or religious orders to operate and build schools, newspapers, hospitals, and orphanages. Lamy was succeeded by four French archbishops (Table 1), who carried the archdiocese through the end of the Territorial period. Lamy's legacy and the legacy of the religious men and women who followed him to New Mexico Territory is best remembered by the Catholic institutions that they built.

ARCHBISHOP	BIRTHPLACE IN FRANCE	YEARS AS ARCHBISHOP
Jean Baptiste Lamy	Auvergne	1850-1885
Jean Baptiste Salpointe	Auvergne	1885-1894
Placide Louis Chapelle	Lozère	1895-1897
Pierre Bourgade	Auvergne	1899-1908
Jean Baptiste Pitaval	Loire	1909-1918

Table 1: Archbishops of the Archdiocese of Santa Fe, New Mexico Territory.

Notes

1.   Edwin A. Ryan, "Ecclesiastical Jurisdiction in the Spanish Colo-
     nies," *The Catholic Historical Review* 5 (1919), 5. For details on Lamy's
     appointment, see Finbar Kenneally, ed., *United States Documents in
     the Propaganda Fide Archives: A Calendar*, First Series, vol. 6 (Washing-
     ton: Academy of American Franciscan History, 1976), 46, nos.
     271-273.

2.   Fray Angélico Chávez, *My Penitente Land: Reflections on Spanish New
     Mexico* (Albuquerque: University of New Mexico Press, 1974), 208,
     writes that secular priests are the "ordinary and most numerous
     clergymen of the Church. Unlike 'religious' priests like the
     Franciscans, they take no vows in community. As independent
     individuals they are subject to their respective bishops in minis-
     terial matters only."

3.   Josiah Gregg, *Commerce of the Prairies*, Max L. Moorhead, ed. (Norman:
     University of Oklahoma Press, 1954), 144.

4.   John L. Kessell, *The Missions of New Mexico Since 1776* (Albuquerque:
     University of New Mexico Press, 1980), 46. Kessell describes the
     brief struggle over ownership of *La Castrense* between Lamy and
     an American judge, Grafton Baker. Underestimating the strength
     of the Catholic church in Santa Fe, Baker declared he would have
     Lamy and Machebeuf hanged from the same gallows before he
     would give up the chapel space. For more on Baker's *faux pas*, see
     also Paul Horgan, *Lamy of Santa Fe: His Life and Times* (New York:
     Noonday Press, 1988), 115; W.J. Howlett, *Life of Bishop Machebeuf*,
     eds. Thomas J. Steele, S.J. and Ronald S. Brockway (Denver: Regis
     College, 1987), 176-77, 430-31.

5.   Kessell, *The Missions of New Mexico Since 1776*, 39; Bruce Ellis, *Bishop
     Lamy's Santa Fe Cathedral* (Albuquerque: University of New Mexico
     Press, 1985), 129; and Horgan, *Lamy of Santa Fe*, 174.

6.   Bruce T. Ellis, ed., "New Notes on Bishop Lamy's First Years in
     New Mexico (concluded)," *El Palacio* 65 (April 1958), 74, quotes
     Don Demetrio Pérez: "Señor Lamy therefore determined to close
     the church after his return from one of his trips to Europe (I think
     it was in 1856)." It was Machebeuf who went to Europe in 1856;
     Lamy was in Europe for almost all of 1854, so it is more likely that
     it was after Lamy returned from that trip in mid-November 1854
     that he closed *La Castrense*. Lamy sold part of the land on the east
     side of *La Castrense* to the Spiegelberg Brothers in 1858, and the
     next year he sold the building and the rest of the land to a parish-
     ioner, Simon Delgado; David Snow, Cross-Cultural Research Sys-
     tems, *Santa Fe Historic Plaza Study II: Plaza Excavation Final Report* (Santa
     Fe: City of Santa Fe, 1990), 49. Both sets of buyers eventually set

up businesses on the property; the high level of noise and activity on the plaza was one reason Lamy did not want to keep the church.

7. Ellis, *Bishop Lamy's Santa Fe Cathedral*, 129; and Kessell, *The Missions of New Mexico Since 1776*, 48-49. The *reredos* is now in the Church of Cristo Rey in Santa Fe.

8. Ellis, *Bishop Lamy's Santa Fe Cathedral*, 14. Ellis draws a parallel between Lamy's substitution of his new cathedral for the old *parroquia* and the building of Franciscan missions on old kiva sites of New Mexico's Indian pueblos (p. 10). Ellis also mentions (p. 2) that Lamy was not alone in his desire to build a new church—the *Santa Fe Weekly Gazette* was also "stridently anti-Old Adobe."

9. Fray Angélico Chávez, *The Santa Fe Cathedral of St. Francis of Assisi* (Santa Fe: Schifani Bros. Printing Co., 1947, reprinted 1987), 25 and 31-36. The finished cathedral is best classified as Romanesque Revival, a round-arched medieval style that became popular in churches and public buildings in the United States in the 1850s; Marcus Whiffen, *American Architecture Since 1780: A Guide to the Styles*, rev. ed. (Cambridge, MA: MIT Press, 1992), 61-63. This may have been preferred by Lamy because it was similar to the church where he frequently stayed in Clermont-Ferrand, the little Notre Dame du Port. Also, Lamy may have realized that the type of stone building material on hand in New Mexico would not physically support the grand scale of a true Gothic cathedral, nor would the finances of New Mexico's Catholics.

10. Jean Baptiste Lamy, Annual Report to the Société de la Propagation de la Foi, August 31, 1851, Record no. 6920, Jammes Project. The full name of the order is the Sisters of Loretto at the Foot of the Cross, although its members are sometimes simply called "Lorettines," and it was the first female religious order founded in America (1826) without foreign affiliation or connection; Elinor Tong Dehey, *Religious Orders of Women in the United States*, rev. ed. (Hammond, IN: W. B. Conkey, 1930), 101-8.

11. Louis Avant, *The History of Catholic Education in New Mexico Since the American Occupation* (Master's thesis, University of New Mexico, 1940), 13; and Mary Lilliana Owens, "Our Lady of Light Academy, Santa Fe," *New Mexico Historical Review* 13 (1938), 136. It was later given to the Sisters of Charity for the first hospital in Santa Fe; Clark Kimball and Marcus J. Smith, *The Hospital at the End of the Santa Fe Trail* (Santa Fe: Rydal Press, 1977), 37.

12. James H. Defouri, *Historical Sketch of the Catholic Church in New Mexico* (San Francisco: McCormick Bros., 1887), 42.

13. Sheila Morand, *Santa Fe, Then and Now* (Santa Fe: Sunstone Press, 1984), 48; George Kubler, *The Religious Architecture of New Mexico in the Colonial Period and Since the American Occupation,* 5th ed. (Albuquerque: University of New Mexico Press, 1990), 141.

14. Whiffen, *American Architecture Since 1780,* 53; Mary J. Straw, *Loretto: The Sisters and their Santa Fe Chapel* (Santa Fe: Loretto Chapel, 1983), 69.

15. Straw, *Loretto,* 58, writes that the Loretto statue was purchased in 1887 from the firm of J. Daniel in Paris. Correspondence of Father Eguillon shows a letter dated June 1, 1887 from J. Daniel, Editeur and Fabricant, Au Saint-Coeur de Marie, 76, Rue Bonaparte (Place St. Sulpice), Paris. Father Eguillon was in Paris during September 1887 and could have bought the statues at that time. Father Seux did not go to France during this time.

16. The first group was comprised of five Christian Brothers from the Institute of the Brothers of the Christian Schools in Clermont-Ferrand; by 1864, there were six Christian Brothers working at Saint Michael's College in Santa Fe and more elsewhere in New Mexico. Although the first Christian Brothers in New Mexico came from the same area of France as did Lamy and Machebeuf (recruited in Clermont-Ferrand by Father Eguillon), later Christian Brothers came from French Canada, and by 1870 they were being recruited primarily from the U.S. According to Brother Leo, *Seventy-Five Years of Service, 1859-1934, An Historical Sketch of St. Michael's College* (Santa Fe: St. Michael's College, 1934), 59, "In 1880 the New Mexico schools were incorporated in the St. Louis province and from then on the personnel came almost exclusively from the midwest."

17. Writers' Program, *New Mexico: A Guide to the Colorful State,* compiled by Workers of the Writers' Program of the Work Projects Administration in the State of New Mexico, American Guide Series (New York: Hastings House, 1940), 203. Lamy got the parcel of land and the buildings adjoining the San Miguel Chapel in 1859, when he sold *La Castrense* to Delgado.

18. Historic Santa Fe Foundation, *Old Santa Fe Today,* 3rd ed. (Santa Fe: Historic Santa Fe Foundation, 1982), 47.

19. Also in 1865, Lamy recruited four Sisters of Charity from Cincinnati; Horgan, *Lamy of Santa Fe,* 321; and Sytha Motto, "The Sisters of Charity and St. Vincent's Hospital: An Amplification of Sister Mallon's Journal," *New Mexico Historical Review* 52 (1977), 229-30. The Sisters of Charity of Cincinnati, Ohio, were founded by Mother Seton in either 1809 (Dehey, *Religious Orders of Women,* 85) or 1812

(Motto, "Sister Mallon's Journal," 229). The "old Episcopate" was the old Bishop's residence; he was having a new one built when they arrived.

20. Motto, "Sister Mallon's Journal," 232. The ubiquitous Sister Blandina Segale claims to be the builder of the industrial school. She arrived from Trinidad, Colorado, in 1876, and returned in 1889.

21. Dehey, *Religious Orders of Women in the United States*, 78-9, writes that the Daughters of Charity were separate from the Sisters of Charity until 1850, when "the long desired affiliation with the French Community took place" in Paris. After that, in the United States, the Central House and Novitiate of St. Joseph's, at Emmitsburg, Maryland, became the site of the Province of the Daughters of Charity until 1910, when the Western Province Motherhouse was moved to Normandy, Missouri.

22. Victor Johnson, "Northern New Mexico's Historic Churches," *Mass*, Vol. 3 (Fall 1985), 19. In the 1920s, a fire destroyed much of this remodelling, and the next phase for Guadalupe was the popular California mission style.

23. Mary Lilliana Owens, "Historical Sketch of the Bernalillo Public High School, 1891-1945," *Journal of the American Catholic Historical Society* (1946), 74.

24. Fray Angélico Chávez, *Old Faith and Old Glory, 1846-1946* (Santa Fe: Santa Fe Press, 1946), 9. It is unclear what level of training these schools provided, although Pedro Sánchez, *Memories of Antonio José Martínez*, with translation, notes, and profiles by Guadalupe Baca-Vaughn (n. p.: Rydal Press, 1978), 22, states that the school had courses in "Latin grammar, rhetoric, and theology, in order to meet the needs of the young men who aspired to become priests."

25. Owens, "Bernalillo Public High School," 74, citing L. Bradford Prince.

26. Chávez, *Old Faith and Old Glory*, 11.

27. Jean Baptiste Salpointe, *Soldiers of the Cross: Notes on the Ecclesiastical History of New Mexico, Arizona and Colorado* (Albuquerque: Calvin Horn, [1898] 1967), 282, lists ten priests in the Territory when Lamy arrived in 1851: José Manuel Gailegos [Gallegos], José de Jesús Leiva [Leyva], [Mariano] Lucero, José de Jesús Lujan, Antonio [José] de Jesús Martínez, Vincente Montaño, Fernando Ortiz, Juan Felipe Ortiz, Ramón Salazar, and Juan Trujillo. Richard L. Nostrand, *The Hispano Homeland* (Norman: University of Oklahoma Press, 1992), 109, working from 1850 census rolls, counts fifteen priests and one vicar, all Hispano. Jean Baptiste Lamy, Annual Report to the Société de la Propagation de la Foi, August 31, 1851, Record no. 6920, Jammes Project, lists eighteen missionaries, twelve

of which had been "born in the country" (it is probably that "born in the country" is the same as "born in New Mexico"). Signatures on parish records (birth, confirmation, marriage, and death) for 1850 *and* 1851 show twenty different names of priests working in New Mexico, when Lamy arrived. Besides the ten priests listed by Salpointe (above), the following are listed: José Abeyta, José de Baca, Rafael Chávez, Rafael Ortiz, José Antonio Otero, José Antonio Salazar, José María Salazar, Eulogio Valdez, Nicolás Valencia, and José de la Cruz Vigil. All had been born in New Mexico. No religious orders were working in New Mexico when Lamy arrived (the last Franciscan died shortly after Anglo occupation).

28. Five of them were part of the original group that had been serving in New Mexico in 1851: Fathers Abeyta, Martínez, Ramón Salazar, Trujillo, and Valencia. One of the native clergymen was Abiquiú-born Father Antonio José Martínez, who was ordained in Durango, Mexico, in 1822, and took over the Taos parish and opened a school there in 1826. In 1833, Bishop Zubiría of Durango granted Martínez permission to open a preparatory or minor seminary in Taos to train young men for the diocesan or major seminary in Durango; eventually, eighteen of Martínez's students were ordained in Durango and most returned to serve in New Mexico. Four native New Mexico clergy who began their training in Martínez's school in Taos were ordained by Lamy in Santa Fe. They were Father Ramón Medina (ordained in 1856), and Fathers Manuel Felipe Chávez, José Tafoya, and José Miguel Vigil (ordained in 1859).

29. The Las Vegas church was actually completed before the Santa Fe structures; it was begun in 1862 and finished in 1869. Christopher M. Wilson, "Out on the Santa Fe Trail/Railroad," in *The Architecture and Cultural Landscape of North Central New Mexico*, 106, describes Our Lady of Sorrows as a "provincial Gothic Revival design," but Ellis, *Bishop Lamy's Santa Fe Cathedral*, 1-2, comments on its "simplified Romanesque design, its façade, towers, arched fenestration, and gabled roof strikingly foreshadowing Santa Fe's much larger and more ornate cathedral." The Las Vegas church also predates access to modern building materials via the railroad, and it is made of Anton Chico sandstone.

30. Father Salpointe contended that, because of the parishioners' "limited knowledge of proportions, and less taste in their work," it fell upon the local priest "to make his plans and superintend the work from beginning to end, as much as possible, in order to prevent the mistakes of his mechanics"; Salpointe, *Soldiers of the Cross*, 236.

Examples of this "Gothick" style were abundant during the Territorial Period, although almost non-existent today due to re-remodeling in the popular mission or pueblo style.

31. Chávez, *Old Faith and Old Glory*, 8, writes that the Annunciation Academy became a public school in 1881 and burned down in 1888.

32. The Albuquerque school closed in 1869 when there was a change of ecclesiastical administration in the parish; Avant, *Catholic Education in New Mexico*, 18; Minogue, *Annals of the Century*, 155. Later, contributions financed the construction of a large, two-story frame building near the Las Vegas Plaza, and in 1876, while it was being constructed, the original quarters burned down, so the new building was put to use later in that year before it was quite ready; Lynn Perrigo, *Gateway to Glorieta* (Boulder: Pruett Publishing, 1982), 133.

33. Owens, "Bernalillo Public High School," 75; Avant, *Catholic Education in New Mexico*, 21.

34. Owens, "Bernalillo Public High School," 77; Minogue, *Annals of the Century*, 159.

35. Hugh G. Quinn, ed., *The Anniversary of the Foundation of the Diocese of El Paso* (El Paso, TX: Diocese of El Paso, 1965), 55.

36. Edward Mary Zerwekh, "John Baptiste Salpointe, 1825-1894," *New Mexico Historical Review* 37 (1962), 138-39; and Avant, *Catholic Education in New Mexico*, 25. "Sister Euphrosyne offered painting, drawing, piano, guitar, and organ classes at Socorro's Mount Carmel Convent, located adjacent to the town's Catholic Church. By 1891 the school had expanded, admitting male students after starting as a 'girls only' operation. Sixty girls and ninety boys were taught a full schedule of classes by five teachers," Bruce Ashcroft, "The Territorial History of Socorro, New Mexico" (Southwestern Studies Series No. 85, El Paso: Texas Western Press, 1988), 35, citing the *Daily Sun*, 6 September 1883, for the Mount Carmel classes; New Mexico Superintendent of Public Instruction, *Report for 1891*, 22, for the enrollment.

37. Owens, "Trans-Mississippi West," 325-26.

38. Defouri, *Historical Sketch*, 42, incorrectly writes that "in 1853 the Convent of St. Joseph was established in Taos under the care of the Rev. Gabriel Ussel, the parish priest of Taos [my emphasis]." Ussel did not arrive in New Mexico until 1856, and was not parish priest of Taos until approximately 1859. Also, there is no mention of a school or convent in Taos until 1866, though some of this delay may be due to the problems of communication caused

by the Civil War. Defouri also states that the Mora convent was
founded in 1854 under Father Salpointe, but since Salpointe did
not arrive in New Mexico until 1859, this must be another error
on Defouri's part. See New Mexico (Territory) Bureau of Immigration, *The Resources of New Mexico* (Santa Fe: New Mexican Press Co.
[1881], 1973), 27, for information about St. Mary's Academy in
Mora.

39. Perrigo, *Gateway to Glorieta*, 136.
40. Marc Simmons, *Albuquerque* (Albuquerque: University of New
Mexico Press, 1982), 307.
41. Defouri, *Historical Sketch*, 104. Chávez, *Old Faith and Old Glory*, 8,
gives an earlier year, but the 1887 *Catholic Directory* is the first to
mention of the school. Chávez states that the school was discontinued in 1905.
42. Quinn, *Diocese of El Paso*, 56.
43. The earlier Sisters of Charity had been from Ohio. According to
Sister Julia Gilmore, *We Came North* (Kansas City, KS: Sisters of
Charity of Leavenworth, Inc., 1958), 19, years earlier, while pastor
of Assumption parish in Topeka, Father James Defouri had asked
for Sisters to "continue the teaching of his 'select school' and to
care for his seminary." When the Sisters of Charity established St.
Anthony's in Las Vegas, it was with the help of Father T. O'Keefe,
once a resident of Leavenworth where the Sisters of Charity were
based and later pastor of East Las Vegas, New Mexico.
44. Simmons, *Albuquerque*, 346.
45. Thomas J. Steele, *Works and Days: A History of San Felipe Neri Church,
1867-1895* (Albuquerque: The Albuquerque Museum, 1983), 24.
Early in 1872, the territorial legislature offered $600 to the Jesuits
to start a public school in Albuquerque, the Holy Family Select
School for Boys; Simmons, *Albuquerque*, 306.
46. Owens, *Jesuit Beginnings*, 68.
47. The school in Sapelló is listed as being in "Los Alamos" in the
annual Catholic directories. The Sisters of Mercy were founded in
Ireland in 1831; Dehey, *Religious Orders of Women*, 373.
48. Chávez, *Old Faith and Old Glory*, 11.
49. Chávez, *Old Faith and Old Glory*, 17.
50. Avant, *Catholic Education in New Mexico*, 72. The full name of their
order was the Poor Sisters of St. Francis Seraph of the Perpetual
Adoration, established in Germany in 1860 and in the United
States in 1875; Dehey, *Religious Orders of Women*, 463.
51. Turibius Christmann, "The Parishes of Roswell, New Mexico," *The
Franciscan Missions of the Southwest*, No. 2, 1914, p. 13.
52. Clarence S. Adams, *Little Town West of the Pecos–1909* (Roswell: Pioneer Printing, 1983), 2 and 29.

No Strangers to Adversity: The Jesuits of the New Mexico-Colorado Mission

Lt. Col. Edmund Verdieck, USAF,
and Thomas J. Steele, S.J.

Shortly after the first Jesuits arrived in New Mexico, Father Donato Maria Gasparri, S.J., became superior of the New Mexico Mission of the Society. In 1871, when these Neapolitan Jesuits finally achieved enough financial stability as a group to think of opening a novitiate, he asked the leading citizens of Albuquerque to help found a college – what we would describe as a junior high, a high school, and a junior college. Bishop Lamy had attended one as a lad and wanted one in New Mexico as soon as possible.[1]

That plan of Gasparri's failed, but another of his projects, begun at the same time, greatly furthered the work of the Jesuit Mission in New Mexico. He set about raising money to buy a printing press as an apostolic instrument, intending to supply the diocese with newspapers and books. By February 1873 it was in operation, printing elementary textbooks for public and parochial schools and religious pamphlets for Spanish Catholics throughout the Rocky Mountain area. He also planned to start a weekly Spanish newspaper. However, the severe Rio Grande flood that crested at Albuquerque during the last week in May convinced Gasparri that he ought to dismantle his press and move it elsewhere.[2]

Gasparri had preached a parish mission – the Catholic equivalent of a revival – in Las Vegas during Lent of 1874, and he so impressed the population that they set up a select committee, petitioned the Jesuits to bring their printing press to the banks of the well-behaved Gallinas River, and promised to establish a college in town. Gasparri and several of the Fathers moved to Las Vegas on 1 September 1874 along with the printing press, and they resumed publishing books and pamphlets and published the first issue of the twelve-page weekly newspaper *Revista Católica* on 2 January 1875. Then, finally, the college came into being. One resident offered his own Las Vegas home until such time as the Jesuits should be able to erect a suitable college building of their own; and from this point forward Las Vegas, now the political and intellectual headquarters of the New Mexico-Colorado mission, became such a center of activity that the Methodist minister, Thomas Harwood, made this observation:

> The Country has been stirred from center to circumference by the recruits to the priesthood of banished Jesuits from other countries. They come in flocks like blackbirds to a corn field, twenty-five or more can be seen in a single village.[3]

The publication of the first issues of *Revista Católica* coincided with the opening of a dispute over New Mexican public schools. It wasn't really a question of separation of church and state, it was instead a question of which religion was to control the tax-supported system. Back East, the public schools were non-sectarian only in the sense that no single Protestant church controlled them; rather, they were "generic Protestant" in being steadily tilted against "Romanism." Many ministers of the time eked out their scant clerical pay by teaching in public schools. Father Gasparri promptly took the lead in lobbying for the Catholic Church's majority-rule position, involving himself and by association the Jesuit order rather deeply in politics for the next few years.[4]

In December 1875, Father Gasparri copied out an act to incorporate the Jesuit Fathers as a tax-exempt educational body and got a friendly legislator to introduce it into the Territorial Legislature. Without its passage the Society would indeed be hard pressed to pay taxes, and the college would be unable to confer high school diplomas or college degrees. Since the proposed bill was an exact copy of earlier ones which the Sisters of Loretto and the Christian Brothers had presented successfully to the Legislature, Father Gasparri expected favorable action. But he had reckoned neither with the bitter animosity of Territorial Secretary William G. Ritch nor with that of Territorial Governor Samuel B.

Axtell.[5] Gasparri first came to Axtell's attention when the incorporation bill passed the lower house but was defeated in the Legislative Council because the chair of the Standing Committee on Education, William Breeden, declared that it violated a federal law saying that territories could not grant "private charters or specified privileges," though they could charter colleges.[6]

During the next two years Gasparri worked hard to secure the bill's passage in the next meeting of the Territorial Legislature, and the Governor developed a distinct dislike for him to the point where his hatred exceeded even that of Secretary Ritch. The Territorial Legislature passed the Jesuit Act in January 1878, indeed, whereupon Axtell returned the measure with a veto message "which, regardless of the merits of the controversy, will go down as one of the most stinging and fearless rebukes that has emanated from the pen of a New Mexico chief executive." The tone of the veto message clearly indicated how Axtell's feelings for Gasparri had become something of an obsession, for he declared that "it is difficult to decide whether the man who seeks to establish the Society or the Society which he seeks to establish is the worse. Both are so bad you cannot decide between them. This Neopolitan [sic] adventurer, Gasparri, … urges you to violate your oaths and pass the bill." And Axtell quoted an opinion drafted by the same William Breeden mentioned above, whom he had since named Attorney General. Secretary Ritch commented at the time that "Gasparri cracks his whip and the Sublime bigotry called the Legislative Assembly of New Mexico comes tumbling down as direct as a shot."

The governor had underestimated the strength of the supporters of the Jesuits' measure, for the bill was promptly passed over Axtell's veto by a vote of eleven to two in the Legislative Council and eighteen to four in the House. Jesuit historian Edward Vollmar concluded that "Gasparri's activity in support of this bill of incorporation is the principal foundation for the accusation that the members of the New Mexico-Colorado Mission tried to control the politics of New Mexico." The Jesuits no doubt felt they had no choice but to enter the political arena for their self-preservation and the perpetuation of their centuries-old, very successful educational program.[7]

With the passage of the Act to Incorporate the Society of the Jesuit Fathers on 23 January 1878, the institution at Las Vegas could now grant diplomas and degrees and be exempt from taxation. Father Gasparri had shown his strength in New Mexico; but unlike Ritch and Axtell, he had no political clout in Washington. Working through Trinidad Romero, the New Mexican delegate to Congress, Axtell and Ritch obtained the annulment of the Jesuit Act on 3 February 1879 (one of the few times Congress and the President annulled territorial legislation). Squarely supporting the governor's legal objections to the measure, the act of Congress cited statutes that had been in effect when the Sisters of Loretto and the Christian Brothers had gotten themselves incorporated and declared the Jesuits' incorporation "disapproved and declared null and void."[8] Ironically, because of Governor Axtell's complicity in the Santa Fe Ring, the Lincoln County War, and the Colfax County chaos, Carl Schurz removed him from office before Congress and the president had reached their decision on the Jesuit Act. Again ironically, Axtell bounced back to become Chief Justice of New Mexico a few years later, and – astonishingly – a good one.

In spite of the legal setback that denied it tax exemption, the College of Las Vegas progressed rapidly and smoothly, with enrollment increasing even before the new quarters were officially opened. In time, granted, the practice of the parents paying tuition in kind created certain financial difficulties, and "there is no evidence that any degrees were awarded in the eleven-year history of Las Vegas College." But hundreds of students did complete the required courses to serve their communities as better-informed and more competent citizens.[9]

Gasparri moved to Albuquerque in 1880 to oversee the building of a convent for the Sisters of Charity, only to die two years later, on 18 December 1882, of an apoplectic stroke at the age of forty-eight. Founder and superior of the New Mexico mission during its infant years, an eloquent speaker, superb administrator, and zealous pastor, he had fulfilled Bishop Lamy's hopes for a Jesuit-run college in New Mexico.

When the Jesuits lost their conflict with Axtell, they began to look for greener pastures. Since they had preferred Bishop Joseph Machebeuf to Bishop and Archbishop Jean Baptiste Lamy, they had steadily moved northward into Machebeuf's Vicariate-Apostolic of Colorado, taking over established parishes or founding new ones in Conejos, Pueblo, Trinidad, and Denver. They approached Machebeuf and received a positive response, so Father Domenico Pantanella, the president of the College of Las Vegas since 1882, traveled to Italy and persuaded the General of the Society to approve a new school in the Denver area, where they could expect to secure a college charter from the State of Colorado. Machebeuf bought a failing resort hotel in the foothills town of Morrison, sixteen miles southwest of Denver, and in the fall of 1884 Father Pantanella, vice-rector of the College of Sacred Heart, opened the hotel doors to the first students of a Colorado Jesuit college.[10]

In 1879, when the College of Las Vegas was two years old, the Atchison, Topeka, and Santa Fe Railway had approached Las Vegas. Instead of going to the Old Plaza, it created a "New Town" about a mile away. By 1883, with Archbishop Lamy's permission, the Jesuit Fathers had organized a Catholic chapel in a rented storefront there, and the next year the Archbishop elevated it to the status of a parish and named it Immaculate Conception.

This division of the parish did not sit well with Father Joseph-Marie Coudert, the pastor of Nuestra Señora de los Dolores on the Old Plaza, particularly when many of his own parishioners abandoned him and attended services in the college chapel and the new parish. Father Coudert and the new Archbishop, Lamy's successor Jean Baptiste Salpointe, charged that there were often day-students among the First-Communicants in the Jesuits' college chapel.[11] This may not sound all that pernicious to us, but Archbishop Salpointe maintained that it was the strict right of the pastor to admit worthy children to the sacrament, a right that was spelled out in certain synods of the Council of France and had become an established custom in New Mexico during the years since Bishop Lamy's arrival in 1851. And as the weeks and months of controversy went by, the Archbishop also accused the Jesuits of giving First Communion to some youngsters who the pastor discovered were not properly prepared; of forbidding the day-students from confessing to their pastor, Father Coudert;

of raising money in ways contrary to Church law by staging fairs, dances, and plays; and finally of assuming powers that they altogether lacked – and the litany of accusations continued. One Jesuit document lists seventeen separate charges against the Fathers and then wearily concludes with "Etc. etc. etc."[12]

But every time the Archbishop slid another accusation onto the table, the Jesuits justified themselves with arguments based upon good reasons, or at least with the high-class rationalizations that Jesuits are so famous for. National councils, they insisted, could not pass a law for the universal church. Moreover, it was impossible for First Communion to be a parochial right by *custom* in the Archdiocese because until the previous ten years – too short a time to establish a custom – New Mexico had had no chapels that pertained to exempt religious orders. Pupils throughout the world were admitted to First Communion in Jesuit chapels, a practice which the Society would not allow if parish rights were being violated. Neither Canon Law nor any of its interpreters considered the First Communion of young people among parochial rights. Furthermore, youngsters could maintain their recollection in the college chapel more successfully than if they were distracted amid men and women and young members of the opposite sex. And finally, the ceremony, which in parishes is sometimes drawn out until midday, would proceed more smoothly and quickly in the school chapel.[13] Having thus justified themselves, the Jesuits continued doing things their way.

This tedious recital of ecclesiastical accusations and excuses serves merely as a sample of the kind of non-communication that results when a central motive is never mentioned – probably, I would guess, because neither party to the dispute consciously recognized that it existed. This concealed fact only came to the surface on 3 April 1890, twenty months after the controversy boiled over, at a time when Roman authorities were pretty far along in solving the problem: the trouble was money. "Cherchez l'argent – follow the money!" and the money had gone a mile east. During the time that the Panic of 1873 had stalled the Santa Fe railhead in southeastern Colorado, almost all the freight traveled by wagon to Las Vegas, was warehoused, and was then sorted out for shipment to Taos, Santa Fe, or the Rio Abajo. With the return of national economic health, the railroad passed through

Las Vegas and on to Albuquerque, Belén, and El Paso and the West Coast, and it took the best of the Vegas economic prosperity with it. Las Vegas had been the most affluent boom town of the whole Front Range from the Mexican border to the Canadian during the credit squeeze, but as the 1880s went on, all the surviving affluence centered in East Las Vegas around the railroad station, impoverishing West Las Vegas and its Old Plaza and leaving poor Father Coudert with the smallest slice of a diminishing pie.[14]

The omission of the main motive left the Archbishop and his Jesuit interlocutor – one of a series of college rectors and mission superiors – engaging in a non-conversation that Eugene Ionesco or Samuel Beckett would have been proud to have written. In those days, verbal battle proceeded by quoting authorities; canon law was such an authority, and papal canon-law documents were always trumps. When the Archbishop didn't like the conclusion the Jesuit-du-jour reached, he simply denied that whichever authoritative author the Jesuit relied on *was* an authority, or that he was relevant, or whatever. And the Jesuits never figured out until the game was long over what the rules of the game were, what the point of the game was, or even where the playing field was really located: in the collection basket. In retrospect, we believe, Archbishop Salpointe should have given Father Coudert a nice parish elsewhere and stuck the Jesuits with the whole town of Las Vegas to do with what they pleased. They would have learned pretty soon what the problem was.

Meanwhile back in reality, the Archbishop, doubtless hoping to dismiss the subject, rattled the archiepiscopal saber in its canon-law scabbard:

> Unless the Jesuit Fathers cease to disturb matters of the Parish of Las Vegas by opposing the things which I justly think about the case, and which I have ordered to be observed, we will submit the matter to the authority of the Holy See so as not to waste time in useless correspondence.[15]

The Archbishop accused the Jesuits of claiming infallibility in the case as if they possessed divine power: "Touch the mountains and they will smoke," then he finished by saying that the Jesuits who published *Revista Católica* could remain at Las Vegas providing that they stayed within the bounds of action which he would specify, thereby removing all occasions of dissension in the future. Father Joseph Marra replied that the mission had violated neither the rights of anyone in the local parish nor any of the laws of the church. Since nonetheless they saw that these things were being turned into a charge against them, they could perhaps be excused if they believed that the Archbishop was hostile to them: "If the rights of religious orders must be considered as violations of ecclesiastical laws, it is not in our power to live peacefully in Las Vegas because it would be a crime to renounce these rights."[16]

As 1887 had moved toward its close, the Jesuits' plan leaked out: their two colleges, Las Vegas and Morrison, would both disappear at the end of the school year and reappear as one college in northwest Denver. In 1888, the men of Las Vegas tried to become involved, but neither the Jesuits nor the Archbishop consented to let them become players. The citizens held monster rallies anyhow and drafted impressive petitions, but the Jesuits just touched the mountains and blew smoke at their fellow-townsmen, and Salpointe dismissed a handcarried petition backed by 3900 signatures with four words, "Esto no vale nada – This is worth nothing." One of the members of the handpicked committee that traveled to Santa Fe to deliver the petition, Benigno Romero, turned a little surly, and several weeks later the Archbishop told Father Marra,

> "They have picked out the most insolent of the whole [Romero] bunch, Benigno, and have sent him here to lay down the law to me. I won't stand for it, and as long as I am bishop you won't have any jurisdiction in Las Vegas."

> "Illustrious Lordship," Marra replied, "do you mean that in order to give the Romeros a lesson you're going to punish *us?*"

> "I'm not punishing you," retorted the Archbishop.

> "If this is not a punishment," Marra replied, "it is only because we have not deserved it."

If the citizens wouldn't have enjoyed being involved in a poisonous verbal battle like that one, maybe they were better off being ignored.[17]

And so letter followed letter, interview followed interview. The Archbishop eventually demanded that all Jesuits remaining in Las Vegas after the College closed must "spontaneously renounce the office of preaching. The sermons they give tend to the ruin of the Christian people, since indeed because of them they are withdrawn from the parish priest." Father Marra, doubtless finding it difficult to remain calm, replied that the Society could not perform its rightful function, upheld by the popes down through the centuries, if it was barred from the pulpit. At this point the meeting ended with Salpointe asking Marra to provide him with a document listing the privileges of the Society. When he reviewed Marra's enumeration a few days later, the Archbishop stated that none of them had any bearing on the case, and then he asked for another conference in Santa Fe, which predictably led to no progress at all. By springtime, the Archbishop had begun to insist that if the college closed, on that very day "the Fathers who were living in Las Vegas would be deprived of every jurisdiction" – that is to say, they would be suspended from acting in public as priests.[18] Talks and letters continued, but realistic hope had died.

On 28 July 1888, Father Marra sent Father General Anderledy a telegram at his Italian headquarters notifying him that the Archbishop had suspended the Jesuit Fathers in Las Vegas; that is, he had officially forbidden them to say Mass or preach in public or to hear confessions. Anderledy urged the Vatican to take charge of the case, particularly after Marra's letter of 2 August expressed his anguish over the Jesuits' leaving Las Vegas in disgrace. On 25 August the General replied:

> I allowed no time to elapse before I prodded [the Roman curia] into dealing strongly and thoroughly with the matter. ... The Archbishop, admonished by Cardinal Simeoni, replied by telegram in these words: "What is to be done? The jurisdiction of the fathers ceased on the first of this month." [The Cardinal] ordered in these words the restoration of their

faculties: "Give the fathers back their faculties; the question is being looked into"; [and the Archbishop] replied on the eleventh, "I returned the faculties to the fathers." Since this is so, I trust that you have already received some solace, after you had been tried and tested.[19]

In early 1889, the Holy See decided that the Jesuits could continue operating *Revista Católica* and its press at Las Vegas and could resume their ministrations to the local populace, and told them to compose their differences with the Archbishop. Firmly convinced that a return to the status quo would not work and so upset by the Jesuits' victory that he told a friend that he planned to resign, Archbishop Salpointe undertook the long journey to Rome to discuss the matter with Anderledy in the presence of Pope Leo XIII himself.[20] Anderledy recounted later that he had been summoned to the Vatican, where the Pope told him in Salpointe's presence that peace and tranquility could never come about among the Jesuits, the pastor, the other diocesan clergy, and the parishioners unless the Jesuits gave up their Las Vegas ministry:

> Since he said these things in such a way as to let me know that they had been thought out and decided upon beforehand, ... nothing seemed to remain for me than to agree instantly to obey all the wishes of His Holiness. ... Therefore, since we are the sons of obedience, we must deal with the Supreme Pontiff with a suitably open heart. ... Your reverence should keep me informed of all that is done to bring about compliance with the wishes of the Supreme Pontiff and myself.[21]

But Marra did not remain silent for long, for he went to Rome in 1891, reopened the question, and managed to obtain an annulment of the agreement that Salpointe and Anderledy had reached the previous year.[22] The Archbishop received instructions in the summer of 1892 to permit the Jesuits to continue their work at Las Vegas; in four words, the Jesuits had won. Four events enabled the town to regain heavenly harmony: Coudert moved to

Bernalillo; Marra moved to Colorado; the diocese took over the East Las Vegas parish; and the Pope assigned Placide Chapelle to be coadjutor Archbishop of Santa Fe with right of succession, a move that led smoothly to Salpointe's resignation and retirement.

The decision reached as the 1880s wore on that the College should move from Vegas to Denver had been a wise one for three reasons: the unlikelihood of getting chartered so long as New Mexico continued as a territory, the difficult personalities of the local pastor and the Archbishop, and the dormant economy of the Old Las Vegas Plaza. By contrast, up in Denver Father Pantanella begged ninety acres of land in northwest Denver with two hundred miles of the Front Range of the Rockies to look at, and while the original building was still under construction the Legislature of the State of Colorado passed and the governor signed an act that incorporated the College, empowered it to confer diplomas and degrees, and exempted it from taxes. Pantanella got Old Main Hall ready for use as school, dormitory, and Jesuit residence, and classes began in northwest Denver on 5 September 1888. A hundred and ten years later, classes continue still.

Notes

1.   Paul Horgan, *Lamy of Santa Fe* (New York: Farrar, Straus, and Giroux, 1975), p. 15.
2.   Sister Lilliana Owens, S.L., *Jesuit Beginnings in New Mexico* (El Paso: Revista Católica Press, 1950), pp. 64-65; Albuquerque *Republican Review*, "The Flood" (30 May 1874), p. 1; Thomas J. Steele, S.J., *Works and Days: A History of San Felipe Neri Church, 1867-1895* (Albuquerque: Albuquerque Museum, 1983), pp. 63-64, 129.
3.   Gabino Rendon remarked about hearing the 1874 parish mission in Las Vegas that Gasparri "was the most eloquent preacher that I had ever heard. Even my father had never heard such preaching"; *Hand on My Shoulder* (New York: Board of National Missions, Presbyterian Church, 1953), p. 31. For the 1874 mission that Gasparri preached see Steele, p. 63.
     For *Revista Católica*, see Edward R. Vollmar, S.J., "La Revista Católica," *Mid-America* (58 (1976), 85-96; for the College of Las Vegas, see Harold L. Stansell, S.J., *Regis: On the Crest of the West* (Denver: Regis Educational Corporation, 1977), pp. 8-13.

Report of Rev. Thomas Harwood written from Elizabeth City ("E-town"), New Mexico, 2 January 1874, quoted in Frederick G. Bohme, *A History of the Italians in New Mexico* (New York: Arno Press, 1975 [orig. 1958]), p. 56, from Harwood's *History of New Mexico Spanish and English Missions of the Methodist Episcopal Church from 1850 to 1910*, 2 vols. (Albuquerque: El Abogado Press, 1908, 1910), 1:205. Harwood must have been in Las Vegas and seen a general gathering of all the Catholic clergy in the whole of New Mexico, since there were only about a dozen Jesuit priests in New Mexico and Colorado at that time.

4.   Gasparri served, at the request of the public officials of Bernalillo County, as Superintendent of Public Schools since 1872. Elsewhere in the territory, public schools tended to come more and more under the direct or indirect control of the Catholic Church, often by default. Moreover, the textbooks in a majority of the schools were those published by the Revista staff, and the material in them was taught, in many cases, by members of the clergy in the absence of qualified lay teachers. In ten instances ward officials contracted with parochial schools to teach public-school children. Even though the majority of schools by 1875 were taught by laymen, as reported by the Commissioner of Education for the Territory, non-Catholics understandably resented the growing involvement of the Catholic clergy in public education.

One of the bills introduced in the Assembly that year was written by the Secretary of the Territory, William G. Ritch, a vigorous Protestant with an abiding distrust of the Catholic religion. Ritch was "obsessed with the idea that free schools were the key to modernizing, secularizing, and Americanizing New Mexico.... . Ritch's bill would have prohibited New Mexico from diverting any public monies into parochial institutions and would have forbidden clerics to teach in public schools." At this point Father Gasparri's *Revista Católica* began to take an active part in the school controversy. Secretary Ritch considered this weekly newspaper "an insignificant and comparatively harmless creeping worm ... transformed into the winged insect of destruction ... forced upon the people by means only possible among a bigoted laity under an aggressive and exacting priesthood." Angered by such antiCatholic and anticlerical bias, Gasparri referred to Ritch's bill as a "cancer which corrodes and consumes the societies of the United States"; Bohme, pp. 67-69; Howard R. Lamar, *The Far Southwest* (New York: W.W. Norton, 1970), pp. 167-68.

5.   Samuel Beach Axtell was born in Columbus, Ohio, in 1819, gradu-
      ated from Western Reserve College and Law School, and was
      admitted to the bar in 1842. He moved to California where he
      was elected to Congress in 1866. Late in 1874, President Ulysses
      S. Grant appointed Axtell Governor of Utah Territory; he discred-
      ited himself in the eyes of Utah's anti-Mormon element and re-
      quested his reassignment to New Mexico as the Territorial Gov-
      ernor, but after three years he was removed in disgrace, only to
      return several years later as Chief Justice and perform very cred-
      itably. He died in 1891.

6.   For the defeat of the 1875-76 bill in the Legislative Council after
      House of Representatives had passed it, see the Council Journal
      for Tuesday 30 December 1875, pp. 43, 64-65, 69-70, Territorial
      Archives of New Mexico microfilms 5:254, 265, 267-68; Lamar, p.
      168.
      It was standard procedure for the chairman of each body of the
      legislature "to invite such persons of distinction that may visit
      [us] to take a seat within the bar"; see p. 13 of the Council journal,
      TANM 5:239.

7.   Poldervaart, p. 122; *Diario del Consejo, 1878*, p. 50 (attack on Society
      of Jesus and on Gasparri, quoted in Bohme, p. 79); pp. 51-52
      (Breeden's letter); p. 53 (11 to 2 vote to override the veto); *Diario de
      la Camara, 1878*, pp. 54-55 (18 to 4 vote to override the veto); Ed-
      ward R. Vollmar, S.J., "History of the Jesuit Colleges of New Mexico
      and Colorado, 1867-1919," Master's Thesis, St. Louis University,
      1938, p. 17.

8.   The Proceedings of the Forty-fifth Congress, session 3, chapter 41
      (3 February 1979), p. 280; Giuseppe M. Sorrentino, S.J., *Dalle
      Montagne Rocciose al Rio Bravo* (Naples: Editrice Federico ed Ardia,
      1948), p. 77.
      Sections 1,889 of the Uniform Code was passed in 1862 and re-
      vised in 1872, and Section 1,890 was passed in 1867, so both laws
      were in force when the Christian Brothers and the Loretto Sisters
      were incorporated in 1874.

9.   Stansell, p. 18.

10.   Stansell, pp. 25-26.

11.   At the time, Catholics did not usually receive Communion before
      the age of twelve, so many if not most of the students in the
      College of Las Vegas needed to make First Communion.
      Archbishop Lamy hoped for the appointment of Vicar-Apostolic
      of Arizona Territory Jean Baptiste Salpointe as his coadjutor with
      right of succession. When Salpointe told Lamy that he would

rather remain where he was, Lamy drafted a *terna* (list of three candidates) with Jesuit Giuseppe Marra as the first choice, Pierre Bourgade, later Archbishop of Santa Fe, as the second, and William Howlett, Bishop Joseph Machebeuf's biographer, as the third. Rome chose Salpointe anyhow; Marra soon rose to Mission Superior.

Salpointe was born in Clermont February in 1825, ordained in 1851, and crossed the Santa Fe Trail to New Mexico in 1859; he went to Arizona in 1866, was appointed Vicar-Apostolic of Arizona in 1868, and was consecrated bishop in France the next year. He was named coadjutor with right of succession to Lamy in 1884, took office as archbishop the next year, and added Chapelle as his coadjutor with right of succession in 1891. He resigned in 1894 and died and was buried in Tucson in 1898.

12.   Letter of 13 April and 19 April 1886, Archbishop J.B. Salpointe to Father Luigi Gentile (superior of the Mission); "De Controversia," undated document, probably early 1889, pp. 18-19.

On the other hand, some laymen who met with Archbishop Salpointe on 6 March 1888 complained of Father Coudert's leaving the Church and the cemetery in a mess, being an hour or more late for Mass much of the time, not bothering to preach, and being unpleasant to confess to; account of 6 March 1888 meeting, pp. 3-5.

13.   Letter of Gentile to Salpointe, 4 March 1887; the Christian Brothers and the two groups of sisters were technically congregations under the local bishop's jurisdiction in most matters rather than orders exempt from his control.
Revista Católica 12 # 17 (25 April 1886), 193.

In 1896 Giuseppe Marra was named Provincial of the Naples Province, but after his stint as superior in Europe he returned as superior at Las Vegas in 1904. He was recalled to Naples again in 1907 and returned to Las Vegas as mission superior once again. In 1914 he returned to Naples in failing health, was elected to a General Congregation of the Society, and received a significant number of votes as General, but he lost to Wladimir Ledochowski largely because he was not in good health. Marra died in Naples in 1915. For his success in controversial writing he was not so affectionately called "The Scalper." Sorrentino, pp. 265-67; Sister Blandina Segale, S.C., *At the End of the Santa Fe Trail* (Milwaukee: Bruce, 1948), p. 178; Vollmar, "La Revista," pp. 89-92.

14.   "Let me add something privately," Father General Anton M. Anderledy wrote to Marra, "that the nub of the whole matter comes to this: the subsidies the faithful give [Coudert's] parish are said to

have diminished so much that it cannot stay open"; letter of Anderledy to Marra, 3 May 1890. I am grateful to Stanley Hordes for his help with Las Vegas economics.

15. Letter from Salpointe to Persone, 12 March 1887.

16. Letter of Salpointe to Marra, 16 December 1887; in the quotation from Psalm 144:5, the Psalmist addresses God, "Tange montes et fumigabunt – Touch the mountains and they will smoke" – a borrowing from Psalm 104:32. Letter of Marra (quite likely composed by Father Estéban Antícoli) to Salpointe, 31 December 1887.

17. Minutes of meeting, Salpointe and Committee, 6 March 1888, p. 6; minutes of meeting, Salpointe and Marra, 20 May 1888, p. 2.

18. "De Controversia," pp. 12-14; the Santa Fe interview which is summarized in the document probably took place in January 1888; letter of Salpointe to Marra, 13 May 1888.

19. Letter of Father General Anderledy to Marra, 25 August 1888; the final phrase echoes Wisdom 11:10-11.

20. Father Joseph A. Stephan, Director of the Bureau of Catholic Indian Missions, letter of 22 February 1889 to Mother Catherine Drexel, Archives of the Sisters of the Blessed Sacrament for Indians and Colored People, Cornwell Heights, PA, quoted in Zerwekh, p. 218.

21. Letter of Anderledy to Marra, 4 February 1890. The meeting occurred on 27 January 1890; the decree was dated 14 February 1890. Anderledy provided Marra and ourselves some insight into what transpired by writing two letters to Father Marra on this day, the first formally and officially telling him to pull the Jesuits out of Las Vegas and the second (addressed to him confidentially) to explain the manner in which this decision had been made and to extend his sympathies.

22. Roman Congregation for the Propagation of the Faith, final decision on the controversy, 1 August 1892. The Pope and the cardinals followed Marra's suggestion exactly.

Contributors

Félix D. Almaráz, Jr., Professor of History at the University of Texas at San Antonio, received degrees from St. Mary's University (B.A. and M.A.) and the University of New Mexico (Ph.D.). He has served as president of the Texas Catholic Historical Society and the Texas State Historical Association. He belongs to the Equestrian Order of the Holy Sepulchre of Jerusalem. In 1988, he lectured in Argentina as a Senior Fulbright Scholar, he portrays Senator Sam Houston and broadcaster Edward R. Murrow under the Chautauqua tents, and he is presently revising book manuscripts on the San Antonio Missions and on Carlos Eduardo Castañeda, eminent Catholic historian.

José Antonio Esquibel is a genealogical researcher and author of articles related to Spanish Colonial genealogy and history with particular regard to New Mexico. He has served as a research consultant for El Camino Real Project and is co-author with Christine Preston and Douglas Preston of *The Royal Road: El Camino Real from Mexico City to Santa Fe*, forthcoming from the University of New Mexico Press, 1998.

James Ivey is an architectural historian with the National Park Service in Santa Fe. Specializing in the cultural and structural history of the Spanish Southwest, he has investigated Spanish missions, presidios, ranches, and settlements from Texas to California. He has written the structural histories of the four San Antonio Missions and the four Salinas Pueblo Missions and is presently researching the missions at Pecos and Tumacácori.

Dr. Joseph P. Sánchez is Director of the Spanish Colonial Research Center, a partnership between the National Park Service and the University of New Mexico. He is the author of numerous studies dealing with Spanish Colonial history, including *The Río Abajo Frontier: A History of Early Colonial New Mexico 1540-1692* (1987); *Spanish Bluecoats: The Catalonian Volunteers in Northwestern New Spain, 1767-1815* (1990); and *Explorers, Traders and Slavers: Forging the Old Spanish Trail, 1678-1815* (1997). He is also founder and editor of the *Colonial Latin American Historical Review* (*CLAHR*).

Paul Kraemer is an independent historian, a member of the Friends of the Palace of the Governors, editor of the Los Compadres Newsletter for the Palace, and an officer of the Board of the Historical Society of New Mexico. He is a cell biologist by profession, holds doctoral degrees from the University of Pennsylvania (Ph.D.) and Tulane University (Dr.P.H.), and has published more than ninety papers. His historical interests emphasize the Spanish Colonial period in New Mexico.

David H. Snow is a consulting historical anthropologist with Cross-Cultural Research Systems in Santa Fe; his forty years of professional interests, documentary and archaeological research, and publications have focused on colonial New Mexico and the greater Southwest. Currently, Snow is part-time Curator of Historical Collections with the Museum of New Mexico in Santa Fe, and he is writing a book about Santa Fe's colonial past.

Rick Hendricks is an editor of the Vargas Project at the University of New Mexico. His has co-edited several books and written a number of articles on the history of the church in colonial New Mexico. He is also involved in editing the guide to the microfilm collection of the Archivos Históricos del Arzobispado de Durango at the Rio Grande Historical Collections, New Mexico State University Library.

Lois Stanford completed her Ph.D. in anthropology at the University of Florida in 1989 and is an associate professor of anthropology at New Mexico State University. She has published on cofradías, Holy Week observances, and devotions to saints in El Paso's Lower Valley. She is preparing a book manuscript on the history of popular Catholicism in these communities from the 1890s to the 1960s, examining the persistence and change in religious faith and practices through oral histories and documentary research.

A native of Ysleta, Texas, *Eduardo Fernández* is a Jesuit priest presently teaching at the Jesuit School of Theology in Berkeley, California. His education includes an M.A. in Latin American Studies at the University of Texas at Austin in '87. In 1995 he completed doctoral studies at the Pontifical Gregorian University in Rome. He has worked both in parochial and university settings and is the author of several articles and a forthcoming book on U.S. Hispanic theology.

John Taylor has a masters degree in nuclear engineering from Stanford. He currently manages the Nonproliferation Programs Department at Sandia National Laboratories. He has authored or coauthored forty-seven technical papers and three books. UNM Press published his *Bloody Valverde: A Civil War Battle on the Rio Grande*, and he and Thomas S. Edrington have coauthored *The Battle of Glorieta Pass: A Gettysburg in the West*.

Patricia (Patty) Burke Guggino received her undergraduate degree in Latin American Affairs and Spanish from the University of New Mexico and returned there to earn a masters in the History of the U.S. West. She currently teaches for the University of New Mexico's Elderhostel program and is a history instructor for TVI. She is also President of the Valencia County Historical Society and a historical consultant to the Village of Los Lunas, where she and her family reside.

Margaret Espinosa McDonald has a Ph.D. in American Studies with an emphasis in Southwest Studies from the University of New Mexico. She lives in Belén, NM, where she teaches New Mexico history at Belén Middle School. McDonald is past President of the Valencia County Historical Society and Second Vice-President of the Historical Society of New Mexico.

Marc Simmons is a free-lance author and historian who resides in Cerrillos, NM. His research, writings, and lectures focus on the Hispanic heritage and culture of the Southwest. He has published thirty-five books and numerous articles in scholarly and popular journals. In 1993 the King of Spain awarded him membership in the royal Order of Isabela la Católica for his contributions to Spanish Colonial history.

Robert Wright is a member of the Missionary Oblates of Mary Immaculate, a worldwide missionary congregation. Raised in Texas, he gained an appreciation for New Mexico and southern Colorado from his parents and grandparents. Ordained a priest in 1974, he has served in parish and formation ministries in South Texas. Since 1983 he has taught about the history and culture of the Church in the Southwest at Oblate School of Theology in San Antonio.

Pedro Ribera-Ortega, Santa Fean, Cathedral of St. Francis parishioner, Mayordomo and Officer of La Cofradía de la Conquistadora (Our Lady of Conquering Love of All Peoples, Our Lady of Peace) for over forty years; retired from teaching in the Santa Fe Public Schools for thirty years and former Bilingual Director; former Caballeros De Vargas Presidente-General, former Santa Fe Fiesta Council officer, Director of the Truchas-Ortega Research Center for graduate students, teachers, and scholars, and recipient of Governor's Award for Excellence in Literature, 1997, Mayor's Award for Excellence, 1997, and the Hispanic Cultural Center Award for Lifetime Achievement, 1998.

Josephine Gutiérrez lives in Roswell, retired from the oil and gas industry. She holds a BA in Inter-American Affairs from the University of New Mexico, where she studied under George P. Hammond, Dorothy Woodward, and Joaquín Ortega. She is an avid genealogist, and in searching through New Mexican documents covering four hundred years she has found family roots leading back to eighteen of the Oñate colonists – and suspects that there are more.

Tomas Jaehn holds a Ph.D. in Western American History from the University of New Mexico and has published several essays in New Mexican and Western history. He is the Curator for American and British History at the Stanford University Libraries.

Pauline Chávez Bent was born in Atarque, New Mexico. She has traced her roots to Mexico, Spain, Portugal, the Canary Islands, Greece, and Belgium as far back as the mid-sixteenth century. In 1993 she self-published *Atarque: Now All Is Silent*, and she contributes to *La Herencia* del Norte, *Vista Magazine*, and *Nuestras Raices* (a genealogical journal) and lectures extensively on New Mexican genealogy. She is a founding member and current president of the Genealogical Society of Hispanic America, Southern California. She and her husband Jerry live in Huntington Beach.

Father Jerome J. Martínez y Alíre was born to an Hispanic family whose roots in New Mexico extend back for ten generations. Catholic grade school, high school, college, seminary, and university provided him with specializations in Southwestern and Church history, liturgy, and canon law, and his many pastoral and administrative responsibilities in the Archdiocese of Santa Fe have led to involvements in historic preservation and the chairmanship of the Catholic Cuatrocentennial Commission which sponsored the 8-9 September 1997 "Conference on the History of the Catholic Church in New Mexico" which occasioned these papers and this book.

Father Juan Romero, a native of Taos, is a priest of the Archdiocese of Los Angeles and has worked on the national level relating to Hispanic ministry. From 1972 to 1976, he worked out of San Antonio as the Executive Director of PADRES, a national Hispanic priests' organization. In 1984, he worked in Washington as coordinator for the American bishops' *Tercer Encuentro Nacional*. For over twenty years he has written about Padre Antonio José Martínez, Cura de Taos.

Alberto López Pulido is a recognized scholar in the study of religion in the Chicano/Latino community. He has published extensively in the emerging field of Chicano religions in both domestic and international journals and is currently completing *The Sacred World of the Penitentes: Religious Memory and Storytelling in New Mexico*. An assistant professor in the Department of American Studies at Arizona State University West, López Pulido is also a research associate with the Hispanic Research Center at the Tempe campus.

Nancy Hanks received her Ph.D. in historical geography from the University of Oklahoma. She has been honored by the City of Santa Fe for the first city-wide comprehensive archaeological research database and map, she was the 1995 recipient of the Gilberto Espinosa Prize for the best article appearing in Volume 70 of the *New Mexico Historical Review*, and she has authored *An Annotated Bibliography of New Mexico Acequias* for the New Mexico Acequia Commission.

Lieutenant-Colonel Edmund Verdieck, USAF Retired, was a graduate of Regis Jesuit High School (where his priest brother Arthur taught for many years) and of Regis College. He earned a master's in economics at the University of Denver and a master's in history at the University of Colorado in Colorado Springs. After a full career in the Air Force, he taught history at the University of Colorado in Colorado Springs. While working toward a doctorate, he wrote the first versions of this paper using manuscript materials from the Regis Jesuit History Library. He died in November 1996.

Jesuit *Father Tom Steele,* a student of New Mexican religious culture and a former English teacher at Regis University, shortened, focused, and revised his friend's paper for presentation and publication. Steele, the curator of the Regis University (Denver) Collection of New Mexican Santos, also served as primary editor for all the symposium papers. He is the author of *The Regis Santos: Thirty Years of Collecting, Santos & Saints,* and many other books and articles on New Mexican art, culture, and history.

Barbe Awalt and *Paul Rhetts,* the publishers of *Tradición Revista* – a quarterly magazine on the art and culture of the Hispanic Southwest, also served as editors for this project. They are also the authors of *Charlie Carrillo: Tradition & Soul* and *Our Saints Among Us: 400 Years of New Mexican Devotional Art.* They have curated a traveling exhibit by the same name.

The Most Reverend Archbishop Michael J. Sheehan has served as the 11th Archbishop of the Archdiocese of Santa Fe since August 1993. Born in Wichita, Kansas, he grew up in Texarkana, Texas. He graduated from the North American College in Rome. He is a contributor to two recent books – *By the Grace of Light* and *400 Years of Faith.*